Fratricide in the Holy Land

Fratricide in the Holy Land

A Psychoanalytic View of the Arab-Israeli Conflict

Avner Falk

THE UNIVERSITY OF WISCONSIN PRESS
TERRACE BOOKS

The University of Wisconsin Press
1930 Monroe Street
Madison, Wisconsin 53711

www.wisc.edu/wisconsinpress/

3 Henrietta Street
London WC2E 8LU, England

5   4   3   2   1

Printed in the United States of America

Library of Congress Cataloging-in-Publication Data
Falk, Avner.
    Fratricide in the Holy Land: a psychoanalytic view of
    the Arab-Israeli conflict / Avner Falk.
       p.   cm.
    Includes bibliographical references and index.
    ISBN 0-299-20250-X (cloth: alk. paper)
      1. Arab-Israeli conflict—Psychological aspects.   2. Psychoanalysis—
Social aspects—Palestine.   3. Psychoanalysis—Political aspects—
Palestine.   4. Palestine—Ethnic relations—Psychological aspects.
I. Title.
    DS119.7.F318   2004
    956.05'3'019—dc22   2004005378

Terrace Books, a division of the University of Wisconsin Press, takes its
name from the Memorial Union Terrace, located at the University of
Wisconsin–Madison. Since its inception in 1907, the Wisconsin Union
has provided a venue for students, faculty, staff, and alumni to debate
art, music, politics, and the issues of the day. It is a place where theater,
music, drama, dance, outdoor activities, and major speakers are made
available to the campus and the community. To learn more about the
Union, visit www.union.wisc.edu.

Contents

Acknowledgments

I wish to thank Steve Salemson, my editor at the University of Wisconsin Press, for his unfailing support and assistance throughout the writing of this book, and his colleagues at the Press for their tireless efforts in making this book a reality. I also am grateful to my mentor, friend, and colleague Vamık Volkan for encouraging me to expand what was initially meant to be a long journal article into a full-fledged book, to Norman Itzkowitz for his helpful corrections and suggestions, to Howard Stein and David Rothstein for reviewing the manuscript for the Press, and to all my colleagues, friends, and family members who supported me during this time. Without them, this book might never have been published.

Fratricide in the Holy Land

Introduction
A Duel in Quicksand

In most books and articles about the intractable Arab-Israeli conflict, it is conceived of as an essentially rational matter: two ethnic groups fighting over a single territory which both of them consider to be theirs by historical right. However, a close psychohistorical examination shows that the two parties to this tragic conflict have missed innumerable opportunities for a rational partition of the territory between them and for a permanent state of peace and prosperity, rather than perennial bloodshed and misery. I present one of Goya's Black Paintings, *Duel with Cudgels*, as a paradigm of this tragic conflict.

The irrational aspects of the conflict become more obvious when one looks at absurd examples of prolonged conflict such as the one square mile of territory in the Egyptian Sinai village of Taba which was irrationally disputed by Israel for many years—even after Israel had ceded to Egypt the entire Sinai peninsula, a territory three times the size of Israel itself. One of the ways to understand and explain irrational matters is to examine their unconscious aspects: group narcissism—the psychological underpinning of nationalism, the unconscious attachment to the motherland as an early-mother figure, the unconscious need for enemies as repositories of unconscious splitting, projection and externalization, the inability to mourn, denial, and splitting. In an earlier study I attempted to do this with the Arab-Israeli conflict (Falk 1992). This book is an expansion and updating of that study.

In 1773, at the age of 27, the Spanish painter Francisco José de Goya y Lucientes (1746–1828), considered by some to be the father of modern art, married Josefa Bayeu, a younger sister of his teacher, colleague, and friend Francisco Bayeu y Subias. The fertile Josefa bore her husband many children—scholars have stated their number as being anywhere from five to twenty. A modern Spanish scholar has found that from 1774 to 1784 the loving Josefa bore Francisco eight children. Infant mortality, however, was very high, and Goya's first seven children died at birth or in infancy, with only the eighth, Francisco Javier de Goya y Bayeu, surviving into adulthood (Canellas López 1981, 1991).

Unable to mourn his losses and deal with his trauma, the unhappy Goya eventually fell ill with an inner-ear infection and became partly or totally deaf in 1792. Two years later, in 1794, Francisco began a love affair with Maria del Pilar Teresa Cayetana de Silva y Alvarez de Toledo de Alba (1762–1802), wife of the Duke of Alba. The Duchess of Alba was one of the most controversial and influential figures in Goya's life. Their intense, passionate, stormy, and neurotic relationship reflected the characters of both, particularly of Cayetana. In 1796, after the death of the Duke of Alba, Goya moved in with the widowed Cayetana on her country estate, where they lived together for 11 months.

The beautiful and fiery Duchess of Alba had a tragic rivalry with Queen Maria Luisa de Parma, wife of King Carlos IV of Spain. Cayetana de Alba died in 1802, at the age of 40, and legend has it that she was poisoned by her many enemies, led by the queen. Whether or not that was true, her death was yet another blow to Goya, a man beset by constant losses. A year later, in 1803, Goya's boyhood friend Martin Zapater died, inflicting yet another devastating abandonment and loss on the painter. Five years later Goya saw his country's tragic occupation by Napoleon's imperial French army (1808–1814), a terribly bloody conflict later glorified by the Spaniards as their war of independence. During that horrific war, in 1812, Goya's wife of 39 years, Josefa, died, yet another blow to the deaf and aging painter. Unable to adequately mourn the losses of his lover, his best friend, and his wife, Goya became a bitter man, beset by inner demons which expressed themselves in a series of paintings he was to execute, which came to be known as the Black Paintings.

In 1819 Goya was 73, in the last decade of his creative but troubled life. With his married 30-year-old companion, housekeeper, and mistress, Leocadia Zorilla de Weiss, who loved the old painter deeply, Goya moved into *La Quinta del sordo* (the Deaf Man's Villa), a two-story house outside Madrid so named after a previous owner who had also been deaf.

Between 1820 and 1824, an old and deaf Goya, often in a black mood, created a series of somber paintings on the walls of the dining room on the ground floor of his *Quinta del sordo,* which art historians have called the Black Paintings, and this nightmarish dining-room art has been the subject of psychoanalytic studies (Wolfenstein 1966, Morgan 2000). Goya himself did not title his Black Paintings, which were given their titles posthumously by his son. Francisco Javier de Goya titled one of the most famous of his father's Black Paintings *Duelo a garrotazos, o La riña* (Duel with cudgels; or, the fight). It shows two men furiously swinging their cudgels at one another while sinking knee-deep in wet soil, quicksand, or mud (see the cover illustration).

Impressed with Goya's striking painting, two of my Israeli colleagues thought that his *Duel with Cudgels* "might as well have been painted to capture the craziness of the situation in the Middle East today" (Kutz & Kutz 2002). Goya's *Duel with Cudgels* may indeed epitomize the tragic conflict between the Israeli Jews and Palestinian Arabs—two traumatized groups of people on a tiny piece of real estate that keep on traumatizing one another and themselves. These two groups, or nations, which had shared a small sliver of land along the eastern Mediterranean coast known as the Holy Land, became locked in a tragic and endless war that neither can win and which causes further deaths, trauma, and misery to both (Morris 1999). In the rest of this book I shall attempt to explain why this tragic duel—irrational by any measure—has been going on for over a century at such terrible cost to the two antagonists.

The title of this book, *Fratricide in the Holy Land,* begs the question of whether the Arabs and Israelis in general, or the Palestinian Arabs and the Israeli Jews in particular, are in fact brothers. My reply is psychological rather than biological: both the Jews and the Arabs believe that they are descended from two biblical half-brothers, Isaac and Ishmael. While the biblical Ishmael had nothing to do with the biblical Arabs, the myth of Ishmael as the forefather of the Arabs developed among the Jews during the early Middle Ages and was adopted by the Muslim Arabs as part of their Koran. Moreover, from the psychological viewpoint, the Israeli Jews and the Palestinian Arabs think, feel and act like rival brothers who are involved in a fratricidal struggle. The object of this struggle may be the motherland—like two brothers fighting over their mother—but it also has less tangible though no less crucial objects such as self-esteem. Israelis and Arabs jokingly refer to one another as "our cousins." This book explores the hidden, unconscious aspects of this tragic struggle.

In order to simplify the reader's task and organize the complex material into easy-to-follow parts, this book is divided into fourteen sections: this introduction, twelve chapters, and the conclusion.

Chapter 1 reviews the scholarly literature on the Arab-Israeli conflict, both the general and the psychoanalytic, whose paucity is noted, and looks at its contributions and deficiencies. Chapter 2 examines the relativity of perceived reality: one man's terrorist is another's martyr, one nation's achievement is another's disaster. In all the realms of human endeavor and discourse—religion, politics, history—there is no absolute truth, nor absolute reality. As William Shakespeare put it, "there is nothing either good or bad, but thinking makes it so" (*Hamlet,* act II, scene 2). Psychological reality is as important as objective reality— which, in any case, may not exist. In the Arab-Israeli conflict, the two parties' psychological realities—and worldviews—are indeed very different. One might even say that the Israeli Jews and the Palestinian Arabs are living in two different worlds. Chapter 3 is a psychobiographical study of the life and personality of the current Israeli prime minister, Ariel Sharon, who displays the character of a destructive charismatic and narcissistic leader. Chapter 4 is a similar study of the Palestinian leader Yassir Arafat.

Chapter 5 examines nationalism as a form of collective narcissism, and the key issue of the self—self-esteem, self-love, self-hate, self-image—as a central psychological factor in the Arab-Israeli conflict. Chapter 6 looks at the role of psychogeography—the unconscious emotional meaning of countries, cities, mountains, lakes, borders, and other geographical entities, which is always connected to personal objects. Chapter 7 deals with the pervasive—and pernicious—unconscious defensive process of denial in this conflict, in which each side denies not only the history, the feelings, and the political rights of the other, but also the very existence and the very humanity of the enemy—and its own misdeeds, defects and failures as well. Chapter 8 analyses the unconscious processes of splitting, projection, projective identification, and the unconscious need for enemies, both on the individual and on the collective level. Chapter 9 deals with the psychoanalytic theory of war as an expression of the large human group's collective unconscious inability to mourn its losses, or what one psychoanalyst has called "the paranoid elaboration of mourning" (Fornari 1974).

Chapter 10 surveys the many studies of the Arab mind, character, and personality conducted by Arab and non-Arab scholars and examines critically their contribution to our understanding of the Arab-Israeli conflict. Chapter 11 attempts to understand and explain the psychology of suicidal terrorists and its intimate connection to fantasies of death, rebirth, and fusion with the early mother. Chapter 12 examines the Israeli mind, the special traits and characteristics of the members of a nation of Israeli Jews who hail from many diverse places, cultures, and languages, with a minority of about one million Israeli Arabs, many of whom call themselves Palestinians—a nation that has felt itself under siege and has been almost constantly at war throughout its existence.

Finally, the concluding section seeks to integrate and review what had been achieved in the first 12 chapters, and also analyzes the conscious and unconscious motives of scholars who reject the psychological method in the study of the Arab-Israeli conflict. An extensive bibliography, for those who might wish to do additional reading on any of the issues addressed in this book, is provided at the end.

1

A Review of the Literature

In this chapter I summarize and discuss a large body of scholarly literature on the Arab-Israeli conflict, which is listed in the bibliography. Various theoretical models of the conflict as proposed by these scholars are reviewed. The reader can see that most if not all of that literature implies an assumption of rationality of the parties' actions in this conflict—a not entirely correct assumption, to say the least. In this psychoanalytic study of the Arab-Israeli conflict, I will explore the irrational aspects of the parties' actions and their possible unconscious emotional motives.

The scholarly literature on the Arab-Israeli conflict is extensive: Hadawi 1967; Safran 1968; Laqueur 1969; Kurzman 1970; Kurland 1973; Gilbert 1974; Caplan 1983–1997; Saunders 1985; Bickerton & Pearson 1986; Smith 1988; Lukacs & Battah 1988; Friedman 1989; Beinin 1990; Bleaney & Lawless 1990; Deegan 1991; Stebbing 1993; Tessler 1994; Fraser 1995; Ross 1996; Eisenberg & Caplan 1998; Toufée 1998; Pappé 1992; Morris 1999; Thomas 1999; Shlaim 1999; Bard 2001; and Minnis 2003. However, its psychological aspect has been largely neglected. Most experts agree that the Arab-Israeli conflict is the most intractable conflict in our world, yet very few scholars have produced any psychological explanation—let alone a satisfactory one—of this conflict's intractability (Nisan 1977; Heradstveit 1979; W. Reich 1984, 1991; Grosbard 2003; Sibony 2003).

Unfortunately, the only serious book-length psychoanalytic study of the Arab-Israeli conflict so far has been largely unsatisfactory. The Moroccan-born French scholar Daniel Sibony—a Jewish mathematician, philosopher, and psychoanalyst—held that emphasizing the religious component of this conflict, which assumes an original or inherent conflict between Islam and Judaism, is not only imprecise but also risks obfuscating the roots of the conflict under an incorrect label. To him, the problem has to do with "fundamental narcissistic fantasies" that each people had about itself, its origins and its history (Sibony 2003, p. 9).

Sibony thought that the key aspect of the Arab-Israeli conflict was not the apparent one of territory but the symbolic one. To explain it, he put forward two supposedly new concepts—the haunted or possessed land (Sibony 2003, pp. 13–17), and the dispute over texts (Sibony 2003, pp. 44–48). The Palestinian Arab drama, wrote Sibony, is neither facing the strong military state of Israel, nor to have been sacrificed by the Arab world, which has used them to express its rejection of Israel. The Palestinian Arab drama is not knowing that the land which they claim as their own by virtue of being born there is possessed by great symbolic power. This land, Sibony thought, is haunted by an unconscious force that persists through the centuries, and which has injected itself into the Arab text. This notion, Sibony claimed, calls into question the very roots of Jewish and Arab identities, which play themselves out in an incredible struggle between the Bible and the Koran.

Sibony sought to analyze the psychopathology of each of the three primary actors in this drama: (a) the Arab world and its sacrificial spearhead, the Palestinians, who must express the Arabs' original rejection of Israel and are bending under the weight of this burden; (b) the Judeo-Israeli drama, in which the Jewish people idealize Israel, and are at times disappointed with it, while Israel for its part wishes to detach itself from the millennial Jewish drama of exile and diaspora; and (c) Western witnesses, European and American, who are deeply divided, as we have seen with the war in Iraq. America tries to brutally force the Arab Muslim world into its "democratic" worldview, even if it means destroying its fantasy of unity, while Europe struggles with its own legalistic and leadership fantasies.

In this complex game, as Sibony called it, he sought to clarify the role played by unconscious fantasy in the Middle East tragedy (Sibony 2003, p. 7). Anthropomorphizing history as "the real analyst of events," Sibony wrote that it has set itself the strange task of resolving in the Middle East that which it has not resolved anywhere else: the division of being and existence, which he also called "the opening of the symbolic" (Sibony 2003, pp. 8–9). To explain these notions, Sibony put forward "a new interpretation of the narcissistic dynamics" in this conflict and stipulated a "return of the repressed"—an early concept of Sigmund Freud (1856–1939), the father of psychoanalysis—that "crosses the religious" and accompanies these dynamics (Sibony 2003, pp. 71–73).

One of the problems with Sibony's psychoanalytic study of the Near East conflict is his nonchalant anthropomorphizing of books, history, texts, and lands. Another flaw is his sweeping attribution of individual psychological processes to large groups. Yet another difficulty is that his book ignored most of the central unconscious issues of this tragedy: the problem of empathy, the inability to mourn, large-group psychodynamics, the psychology of suicidal terrorism, issues of psychogeography, the unconscious processes of denial, externalization, projection and splitting, the need for enemies, and other aspects of this conflict. Moreover, Sibony used the linguistic notions of the French psychoanalyst Jacques Lacan (1901–1981), which seem as strange and foreign to non-French psychoanalysts as the Middle East conflict appears strange and foreign to Sibony. The following quotation from the current electronic version of the *Encyclopedia Britannica* (Pappas et al. 2004) presents Lacan in a charitable light:

> Lacan emphasized the primacy of language as the mirror of the unconscious mind, and he tried to introduce the study of language (as practiced in modern linguistics, philosophy, and poetics) into psychoanalytic theory. His major achievement was his reinterpretation of Freud's work in terms of the structural linguistics developed by French writers in the second half of the twentieth century. The influence he gained extended well beyond the field of psychoanalysis to make him one of the dominant figures in French cultural life during the 1970s. In his own psychoanalytic practice, Lacan was known for his unorthodox, and even eccentric, therapeutic methods.

The word *psychology* is not often used in the scholarly literature on the Arab-Israeli conflict; in vain will you search for it in the indices of most books on the conflict. There are several well-known books about widely held popular myths about the Arab-Israeli conflict (Davis 1981; Flapan 1987; Taylor 1993; Ben-Yehuda 1995; Harsgor & Stroun 1996; Sternhell 1997; Shalit 1999; Bard 2001; Rogers 2002), yet none of them analyzes the psychological motives that created the myths in the first place. In an earlier publication, I attempted an analysis of the unconscious motives underlying the conflict (Falk 1992). However, my only Israeli colleague who has analyzed the conflict did so without any review of the literature, without any footnotes, and without any references—as if he were the first and only person ever to attempt such an analysis (Grosbard 2003).

The total ignorance or avoidance of psychological considerations by most scholars of the Arab-Israeli conflict is striking. One might expect some of the more open-minded New Israeli Historians, such as Benny Morris, Avi Shlaim, or Ilan Pappé, to throw a new *psychological* light on this difficult subject by using the insights of psychoanalysis. Instead, they have put their impressive scholarly energies into proving Israel's responsibility for the Arab refugee problem or for Israel missing opportunities to make peace with the Arab states around it (Morris 1987, 1990, 1993, 1999, 2004; Shlaim 1988, 1999; Rogan & Shlaim 2001; Pappé 1988, 1992, 1999, 2004). A prominent New Israeli Historian has called Zionism "a colonizing and expansionist ideology and movement" (Morris 1999, p. 652), a statement that has enraged many Israeli Jews.

Some Israeli Jews consider those New Historians post-Zionist while others have attacked them as anti-Zionist (Karsh 1997). Karsh's attack on the New Israeli Historians has given rise to a highly emotional scholarly controversy. One of the American reviewers accused Karsh of numerous contradictions and distortions (Lustick 1997), while an Israeli reviewer was equally hostile (Bartov 1997). A later reviewer, however, more sympathetic to Karsh, thought that Karsh had "delivered a crushing blow" to the New Israeli Historians (Maccoby 1998, p. 40) and complained in a scathing footnote that Lustick had given "no instances [of Karsh's contradictions], except by citing the page numbers, 84, 93, 118, 132n., 133 and 137. I have checked all these pages, and found no contradictions in them. Lustick himself is so out of touch with the material that he confuses Ernest Bevin with Aneurin Bevan, in the composite personality Prime Minister Aneurin Bevin. Actually, as Karsh points out clearly, Aneurin Bevan was pro-Zionist. Neither he nor Ernest Bevin was Prime Minister" (Maccoby 1998, p. 41, note 2). Bartov's review was followed by a heated exchange in the *Times Literary Supplement* involving Benny Morris and Efraim Karsh himself.

The violence and persistence of the Arab-Israeli conflict have defied rational analysis. Despite the relatively fragile Israeli-Egyptian and Israeli-Jordanian peace treaties, Syria, Lebanon and Palestine are still at war with Israel. A fragile and uneven peace process has limped along ever since the Madrid Middle-East Peace Conference of 1991. The Washington peace talks that followed, the Oslo Peace Accords of 1993, and the Camp David meetings of 2000 between the top Israeli and Palestinian leaders all have failed to bring peace to the Middle East. The irrational obstacles, resistance, and fears on both sides are so deep that peace negotiations are expected to break down at any time. Iranian Shiite leaders and Arab Islamic extremists have held war conferences calling for *jihad* (holy war) against Israel.

Rational and Irrational Aspects of the Conflict

From a social science viewpoint, there are at least two different ways of looking at the Arab-Israeli conflict: the rationalistic and the psychoanalytic. Rationalistic views of the conflict, which are common among Israeli scholars, focus on the conscious aspects of competing ethnic identities, territorial claims, and nationalisms. Writing during the terrible persecution of the German Jews under Hitler, when masses of European Jews were seeking refuge in Palestine, George Antonius (1891–1941), a prominent Lebanese Christian politician who had settled in Palestine, concluded the history of what he called the Arab Awakening with what he saw as "the inexorable logic of facts," stating that "no room can be made in Palestine for a second nation [the Jews] except by dislodging or exterminating the nation in possession [the Arabs]" (Antonius 1965, p. 412). By that "inexorable logic," the conflict between the two groups over the same territory and the wars that followed were ineluctable.

The psychoanalytic view, by contrast, focuses on the irrational aspects of the conflict—the unconscious role of the nation as mother, defensive group narcissism, historical hurts, narcissistic injury, denial, projection, splitting, externalization, and lack of empathy. It is no accident that the Latin word *natio* means "birth" as well as "nation." Just as our mother holds us in her arms when we are babies, our motherland or nation holds us and protects us when we are grownups. Many people have died for their motherland, which they loved above all things. While these unconscious processes and symbolisms play a vital role in the conflict, I believe that a still more powerful role is played by *a society's inability to mourn its losses,* a major problem on both sides of the conflict (Falk 1996). In this book I review the psychohistorical and psychopolitical literature on the conflict and attempt to support my thesis with evidence from Jewish and Arab historiography.

It should be pointed out that rationalistic Israeli political scientists, historians, international-relations scholars, and Arabists often vehemently object to the application of psychoanalysis to their disciplines: they see it as an invasion of their territory. On closer inspection, their attitude is ambivalent. They display both an attraction to and a fear of psychoanalysis. This combination of resistance and ambivalence has many grounds, conscious and unconscious, which will be discussed at the end of the book.

An Inherent Clash?

Faced by a tragic, intractable, and incomprehensible conflict between two seemingly implacable foes, social scientists have made great efforts to comprehend the causes of this tragedy. Many questions remain unanswered. For example, is religion a cause of the problem or a potential solution for it (Carroll 2001)? There have been countless religious wars in human history in which each side was convinced that it had God's holy faith and truth. While many scholars of Islamic culture have pointed out the incompatibility of religious beliefs between Judaism and Islam and the problematic foundational narratives of the latter, an American Jewish political scientist and an Israeli American psychiatrist thought that "there is nothing inherent in either Judaism or Islam that inspires the conflict" (Zonis & Offer 1985, p. 268).

This overly rosy view of the relationship between Judaism and Islam may have drawn on the work of the French Arabist Louis Massignon (1883–1962), who coined the term "Abrahamic faiths" for the three monotheistic religions of Judaism, Christianity and Islam (Massignon 1997). Massignon had an extraordinary religious experience at the age of 25 following a painful personal crisis in Egypt during which he had a tormented homosexual involvement with a young Spaniard named Luis de Cuadra, and was accused of espionage. He experienced the revelation of the Isalmic mystic El Hallaj, which he called "the Visitation of a Stranger," returned to France, and took the vows of "fraternal substitution for the Muslims." Thereafter he devoted his life to the study of Islam while remaining a loyal son of the Catholic Church (Basetti-Sani 1974; Massignon 1982; Destremau & Moncelon 1994; Gude 1996).

While some scholars—especially religious ones—strive to find common ground between the "Abrahamic" faiths of Judaism and Islam (Gopin 2002), others consider Jewish culture part of Western civilization and believe that there is an inherent clash between it and Islamic culture; this clash often leads to collective violence and war (Kimche & Kimche 1960; Lewis 1990, 2002; Huntington 1993, 1996; Rashid 1997; Labib & Salem 1997–1999; Ali 2002). An American Jewish psychiatrist has pointed out that one can find anything one wants in both religions: "Messages of universal love or division and exclusion, of lasting peace or holy war can all be found in the Bible and in the Koran. It is a matter of interpretation. Religion and religious institutions can serve to polarize and stimulate violence, or to unite and transcend it" (Mack 2002, p. 178).

Anti-Jewish feeling has permeated Islam ever since Muhammad fought a series of battles with the Jewish Arabian tribes from 624 C.E. to 628 C.E. Muhammad had 11 wives. Muslims believe that his fifth wife, Zainab bint al-Harith, a Jewish widow whom Muhammad acquired through his military victory, poisoned their prophet in revenge for the death of her husband, father, and brother, and that he had her executed before he died (Falk 1996, p. 374). There are several different versions of this story in Islamic tradition. By one of them, the Prophet had three concubines, two Jewish and one Christian. Muhammad became ill "from poison," but he lived three years after this. As he lay dying, he accused one of the two Jewesses of having poisoned him. These are foundational Islamic narratives that orthodox Muslims venerate (Guillaume 1924, 1954; Wensinck 1975; Barakat 1979; Andrae 2000).

The hatred of Israel as a symbol of Jewry is a major element in modern Muslim Arab culture. During the years of Israel's existence there has been a deluge of anti-Jewish writing and cartoons in the Arab mass media. One of Islam's basic tenets is the notion of *dhimmi,* the protected but subjugated class of the "peoples of the book," the Christians and the Jews. The word *dhimmi* comes from the Arabic root meaning "to blame." Following the African leader Léopold Sédar Senghor's notion of *négritude* (Senghor 1967), a French-speaking, Egyptian-born Jewish scholar coined the term *dhimmitude* to refer to the humiliated and submissive state of Jews and Christians under Islamic rule (Bat Ye'or 1985, 1996, 2002). Since the Muslim notion of *jihad* calls for the killing of the infidel, however, Muslims think that the *dhimmi* owe them a debt of gratitude for sparing them and protecting them. *Dhimmitude* is endorsed throughout the Muslim world. One of the basic Muslim *fitras* or beliefs is that each human being is born a Muslim, and that it is only because the parents of non-Muslims did not raise them properly that they still need to see the light and revert to Islam. The entire world is to become Muslim (Maqsood 2001, p. 51). However, many Muslims would dispute their characterization by Bat Ye'or as seeking to convert the whole world to Islam or to make all non-Muslims *dhimmis.*

Three Theoretical Models of the Arab-Israeli Conflict

Religious beliefs, however, at best explain only part of the problem. The quest for a satisfactory explanation or understanding of this troublesome conflict, which would give us a feeling of mastery over a great tragedy, has caused political psychologists to devise schemes, theories, frameworks, and models for explaining it. Zonis and Offer (1985, pp. 268–287) outline three different theoretical models—or conceptual frameworks—for understanding the Arab-Israeli conflict: the national-character model, the psychopathology model, and the self-system model. They found the first two models unsatisfactory, while the third, based on the self-psychology of the psychoanalyst Heinz Kohut, had much more explanatory power for them. Let us take a brief critical look at each model.

The national-character model includes the various studies of Arab, Muslim, Jewish, and Israeli character that look for a typical or modal Arab or Israeli personality (Feldman 1958; Hamady 1960; Glidden 1972; Patai 1973, 1977; Laffin 1974). It has been pointed out that national-character studies of any kind are inherently problematic, and those of Middle East societies more so (Duijker & Frijda 1960; Beit-Hallahmi 1972, 1976; Inkeles 1990–1991). Zonis and Offer (1985, pp. 269–270) also criticized this model saying that the national-character studies of Arabs and Israelis cited did not examine specific individuals over extended periods of time, ignored other effects on behavior, lacked a systematic examination of the correspondence between personality and other behavioral characteristics, did not test the distribution of character traits among individuals, and ignored the unconscious dynamics of character structure. These scholars believed that the national-character model is inappropriate for understanding the Arab-Israeli conflict and that the relationship between national character and leadership in the Arab world and in Israel has not yet been studied properly. The leader-follower relationship is highly complex and involves deep, unconscious aspects beyond any national character (Schiffer 1973).

The psychopathology model discussed by these two scholars focuses primarily on the psychological pathology of political leaders. We have known for many years about the intimate relationship between political leadership and emotional disorders (Lasswell 1930; Robins 1977; Robins & Post 1997). One of the psychological hallmarks of political activity in general and of political leaders in particular is unconscious projection. Politicians tend to have paranoid personalities: they unconsciously project and externalize all that they hate about themselves upon their rivals and enemies. In a recent study, two American scholars outlined the seven elements of political paranoia: suspicion, centrality, grandiosity, hostility, fear of loss of autonomy, projection, and delusional thinking (Robins & Post 1997, pp. 8–13). This does not mean, of course, that every political leader is a paranoid schizophrenic, but that paranoid personality and ideation do characterize many political leaders.

Zonis and Offer believed that many Middle Eastern leaders actually suffered from mental disorders. The right-wing Israeli Prime Minister Menachem Begin (1913–1992), for example, used to talk about the Arab attitude to Israel in terms borrowed from the *Shoah*, or Holocaust. Begin thought of Yassir Arafat in his Beirut bunker as of Hitler in his Berlin bunker. After meeting an American diplomat, Begin hummed a Yiddish song which had been sung by Jewish prisoners in Auschwitz, according to the former Israeli interior minister Avraham Burg (Zonis & Offer 1985, pp. 272–273). Begin was living in the past. In the last years of his life Begin suffered from a severe clinical depression following the death of his wife, to whom he had been fusionally attached (Silver 1984; Sofer 1988).

One of the problems with scholars making pronouncements of psychopathology about political leaders, however, is that it these scholars can be blamed for wielding the disciplines of political psychology, psychiatry, and psychoanalysis as political weapons rather than as illuminating theories. Besides, psychopathology is not the exclusive province of political leaders: their followers, too, have their own pathology, although these two scholars thought this occurred "less frequently" (Zonis & Offer 1985, p. 274).

Zonis and Offer thought that there were severe emotional problems on the Palestinian Arab side as well as on the Israeli Jewish one. The conflict has much to do with how each side feels about itself. Self-hate may drive one to desperate self-destructive acts. Ever since their expulsion from Spain and the loss of what they saw as their great empire in the late fifteenth century, Arab Muslims have suffered from European colonialism. The British and other Europeans often treated their Arab colonies contemptuously, and Arabs, on a group level, may have internalized this treatment as a self-image.

Zonis and Offer (1985) thought that the Palestinian terrorists unconsciously sought to change their self-image. The Palestinians see themselves as the most humiliated and neglected of Arabs. Whether intentionally or unconsciously, Yassir Arafat, with his unshaven face, his paunch, his slovenly garb and his shabby appearance, symbolizes this bad Palestinian self-image. Has Arafat's dress or personal appearance changed since Palestinian independence was declared? Will it change after Arafat declares Palestinian statehood? The Palestinian Arab terrorists may wish to present the Palestinians as strong and heroic because deep down they feel themselves to be weak, oppressed, poor, and downtrodden. Zonis and Offer cited the case of Fawaz Turki, a Palestinian Arab refugee-turned-terrorist who hated himself and the entire world and went out to destroy Israelis (Turki 1972, 1975, 1988, 1994).

The problem of the self—both individual and collective—is indeed a key issue in the Arab-Israeli conflict (Group for the Advancement of Psychiatry 1978, 1987; Moses 1980, 1982; Gilman 1986, 1996). The quest for a less painful self-image, for less shame and humiliation, for more self-esteem and self-worth, underlies much of this tragic conflict. Self-love and self-hate are not immediately visible but very powerful factors in both camps. The crucial issues of nationalism, narcissism, and the problem of the self will be discussed in Chapter 5.

2

Reality Is in the Eye of the Beholder

The idea may discomfit some readers, but, like any human truth, historical truth is relative rather than absolute, and psychological reality is more powerful than objective reality. One man's terrorist is another's freedom fighter. Israel's "glorious" 1948 war is regarded by many Palestinians as the *naqba* (disaster). The Israeli Jews regard the Palestinian-Arab suicide bomber as a murderer, while the Palestinian Arabs call him a *shaheed* (holy martyr). While not entirely new, the idea that there is no single absolute truth was expressed dramatically in 1915 by the Japanese writer Ryunosuke Akutagawa (1892–1927) in his novella *Rashomon*, which was made into a film in 1950 by the renowned Japanese director Akira Kurosawa (1910–1998). In this chapter, the history of the Arab-Israeli conflict, which began in the late nineteenth century with the rise of political Zionism, is recounted—from both sides. The reader can sense the dramatic differences between the two parties' views of the conflict. It seems at times as though the two parties are living in two distinct psychological realities.

In addition to discovering the all-important role of the unconscious mind, Sigmund Freud, the father of psychoanalysis, made another major discovery: passively suffered trauma unconsciously tends to be repeated or relived actively by traumatized people, to their own detriment and self-destruction. This astonishing but universal human phenomenon, commonly known as the *repetition compulsion*, has been widely discussed in the psychoanalytic literature (Lazar & Erlich 1996). The English poet W. H. Auden (1907–1973) wrote these oft-quoted lines in his poem "September 1, 1939"—the date of Hitler's invasion of Poland, which launched the Second World War:

> I and the public know
> What all schoolchildren learn,
> Those to whom evil is done
> Do evil in return.

The phenomenon of self-destructive and traumatic reliving of painful pasts is experienced by both Israeli Jews and Palestinian Arabs. The former are haunted by the trauma of the *Shoah*, in which six million Jews were murdered by Hitler's Nazis and their collaborators between 1941 and 1945. We Israelis, who call the war of 1948 our war of "liberation, independence and uprightness," have vowed never to let another *Shoah* happen to us again; yet in 1948, we unwittingly inflicted a catastrophe on the Palestinian Arabs, and we continue to inflict humiliations and even death on some innocent Palestinian civilians, believing that we are merely fighting terrorism.

While many of us Israeli Jews are survivors or children of survivors of the Nazi concentration camps, incredibly to us our Arab enemies often compare us to the very people who murdered us—the German Nazis. The Arabs do so savagely—in vicious cartoons, articles, and television series. At the same time, the Israeli political right wing often compares the Palestinian Arabs to the Nazis. When the first Palestinian Arab *intifada*—an Arabic word used to describe an angry horse shaking off its rider—began in 1987, the right-wing Israeli writer Moshe Shamir (1921–2004) compared the Palestinian *shabiba* youth movement to the *Hitlerjugend* and Yassir Arafat to Adolf Hitler himself. Shamir was living in the past. All the horrors of *Hamas, Islamic Jihad, Fatah,* and Arab terrorists cannot compare either in scale, in method, or in enormity with what the Nazis did to the Jews. Those Arabs who compare the Israeli Jews to the Nazis are not living in reality either—at least not in our reality. We come up against the question of reality: Whose reality?

The Palestinian Arabs, for their part, are haunted by their defeat, shame, and humiliation in the catastrophic war of 1948 in which hundreds of thousands of Palestinian Arabs lost their homes in Palestine and were displaced by Israeli Jews in what they call *an-naqba* or the catastrophe. The war of 1948 actually lasted through early 1949 (Shlaim 2000, p. 34). Each year on May 15th, the date of the beginning of the war of 1948, the Palestinians mourn their *naqba* and march through their cities in commemoration of their national disaster. Interestingly enough, they refer to that date as that of the proclamation of the State of Israel, which actually occurred the day before, May 14th (Morris 1999, p. 215).

Moreover, the *naqba* of 1948 is not the first catastrophe of Palestinian Arab history. Before 1948, the *naqba* was that of the year 1920. Here, at the San Remo peace conference following World War I, lands formerly under the control of the Ottoman Turks were divided among the victorious Allies, with control of Palestine going to Great Britain. The Arabs saw it as "their betrayal by the Powers of the West" (Antonius 1965, pp. 305-306). To the Palestinian Arabs, the *naqba* of 1948, like that of 1920, is the source of an unbearable feeling of loss of *sharaf* (honor), shame, humiliation, and the need for vengeance. They must restore their lost *sharaf* and repair the damage to their self-esteem by whatever means necessary. As we shall see below, these are among the key aspects of modern Arab culture.

Psychologically, the Israeli Jews and the Palestinian Arabs live in two different and separate worlds. Both the Israeli Jews and the Palestinian Arabs unconsciously inflict upon the other group the very horrors that they consciously wish to avoid. Israeli soldiers and border guards—some of them Israeli Arabs of the Druze faith, which is an offshoot of Islam—stop Palestinian Arabs at roadblocks and checkpoints and humiliate them. Young Palestinian Arab suicide bombers, incited and brainwashed by their "teachers," filled with blind hatred for the Israeli Jews and with righteous rage at their oppressors—and imagining 72 *houris* or virgin angels awaiting them in Heaven—murder dozens of innocent Israeli civilians while killing themselves and unconsciously fusing with their victims in an orgy of death and destruction (Volkan 2001a, pp. 209-211).

The Israeli Jews and Palestinian Arabs think of one another at the same time as cousins and enemies. Unconsciously projecting their own unacceptable wishes upon the other group, they harbor fantastic images and stereotypes of one another. David Shipler, a perceptive American journalist, thought that most Israeli Jews see the Palestinian Arabs as "violent, craven, primitive, and exotic" (Shipler 1986, pp. 181, 222), while most Arabs see the Jews as "violent, craven, alien, and superior" (Shipler 1986, pp. 199, 250). This journalist thought that "of all the anti-Jewish themes in Arab textbooks, newspapers, and literature, none has more prominence than the portrait of the aggressive, brutal Jew who embraces violence without remorse. Here the Arab and Jewish stereotypes of each other attain remarkable symmetry, even down to the counter image of Jews as cowards, which mirrors the Jewish notion of the Arabs' lack of courage" (Shipler 1986, p. 199).

> For many Israeli Jews, the Arab dwells at the heart of darkness, deep in the recesses of fear and fantasy. He appears almost as another species, marching to the beat of some primordial drum whose resonance stirs an ancient dread and fascination. He is backward, uncivilized, a man of animal vengeance and crude desires, of violent creed and wily action. He is also the noble savage, the tribal chieftain, the prince of the desert dispensing a cruel justice enviable in its biblical simplicity. Somewhere in the core of Israeli anxiety, he seems more authentic, more intrinsic to the brutal, circuitous ways of the Middle East, where the Jew yearns to belong. (Shipler 1986, p. 222)

The prevailing group's image of itself as *the* human species and of other groups as inhuman species had been noted by the psychoanalyst Erik Homburger Erikson (1902–1994) in his notions of *pseudospecies* and *pseudospeciation*, which will be discussed in Chapter 5.

Word choices for the same event between the Hebrew of the Israeli Jews and the Arabic of the Palestinian Arabs—two closely related Semitic languages—are striking and significant. While the Israeli Jews call a suicide bomber *mekhabel mitabed* (suicide saboteur), the Palestinian Arabs call him a *shaheed* (martyr)—as they call all their brethren who have died fighting against the Israeli Jews. Every day, Israeli troops make the lives of many ordinary Palestinian Arabs miserable and hopeless. The Israelis call their helicopter-launched missile attacks on cars bearing the planners and organizers of suicide bombings, such as the ones that killed the *Hamas* leaders Sheikh Ahmed Yassin and Dr. Abdelaziz Rantissi in 2004, *sikulim memukadim* (focused foiling), while the Palestinian Arabs call them "criminal executions." Tragically, such attacks often kill innocent civilians while targeting the elusive terrorist masterminds, who take cover amid these innocent civilians. Why can these two groups, with close ties of language and culture, not end their tragic duel in which neither can win by military force and both only sink deeper into the mire?

Whose Reality? Which Truth?

It seems indeed that the Israeli Jews and the Palestinian Arabs are living in two different psychological realities, worlds, or worldviews (Mack

2002, p. 176). Neither side truly understands the reality of the other. Without a proper understanding of the emotional roots of the conflict within ourselves—our own unconscious conflicts with ourselves; our struggle with our self-image and with our group and national self, the problem of our grandiose self; our collective inability to mourn our losses and give them up; the unconscious us-and-them splitting process that separates us from our enemies, making us all good and them all bad; projection of the bad aspects of our self upon the enemy; and similar processes within the Arabs—we cannot hope to begin to resolve this conflict. On the other hand, the ineluctable need to live together in the tiny sliver of land called the Holy Land, or Israel and Palestine, may yet lead us to mature, to give up infantile psychological defenses, and to finally make peace in this long-suffering region.

This situation is strongly reminiscent of Ryunosuke Akutagawa's *Rashomon*. In 1915, the 23-year-old Akutagawa published his arresting psychological novella, which was to gain international recognition and eventually become a very successful and even classic film. The plot involves a young samurai who travels through a forest with his newlywed wife. As a passing woodcutter watches through the brush, a violent brigand rapes the young woman and murders her husband. The story is then retold four times during the trial, with each witness—the brigand, the wife, the woodcutter, and the dead husband (who speaks through a medium)—telling a very different story

Rashomon's startling point was that the truth cannot be known, that there is no such thing as absolute truth, that truth is in the eye of the beholder. While some considered Akutagawa a genius, he himself was never happy with his own work: his narcissistic perfectionism demanded ever more success, and he constantly saw himself as a failure. After a period of unbearable severe depression, the increasingly unstable Akutagawa took his own life with an overdose of sleeping pills at the age of 35. His gripping *Rashomon* became world-famous in 1950, when the Japanese film director Akira Kurosawa made it into a classic film that faced us with the uncomfortable relativity of human truth. The Arab-Israeli conflict can be seen as another *Rashomon* story.

Israel and the Mass Media

Some scholars are reluctant to quote the work of journalists, which ignores the rigorous rules of scientific investigation. However, I find it worthwhile to cite the views of the award-winning American Jewish

New York Times reporter Thomas L. Friedman (born 1953), who has been covering the Arab-Israeli conflict for over two decades. Friedman has observed that Western mass media—by which he means the non-Arab and non-Muslim media in Christian Europe, America, and Oceania—"clearly have a fascination with the story of Israel that is out of all proportion to the country's physical dimensions," or, for that matter, to its tiny population (Friedman 1989, p. 427). Friedman thinks that the irrational and vastly exaggerated preoccupation with Israel in the Western media is due to the fact that the Western world identifies the Israeli Jews with the ancient Biblical Israelites, whose stories are an essential part of their Christian culture (Friedman 1989, p. 428).

At the same time, Friedman noted, the Western Christian world seeks to find fault with the Israeli Jews. The Western media report with glee any incident of humiliation or brutalization of Palestinian Arabs by Israelis. On February 18, 1988, the *Boston Globe* published an editorial about an incident in which four Palestinian youths were buried alive under piles of sand by several Israeli reservists. The four Palestinians had been dug out quickly by their friends and had suffered no serious physical injuries, although they may have been traumatized. In prophetic Biblical tones, the *Globe* declared that these four Palestinian victims would be identified with their entire people, and compared the "supremely brutal" act of the Israeli soldiers to the Czarist pogroms in which Jews were massacred, to centuries of persecution of the Jews in Europe, to the Babi Yar massacre, and to the Nazi death camps. Friedman could not help expressing his utter amazement: "To be sure, Israel's handling of the Palestinian uprising was at times both brutal and stupid. But to compare it to the genocide at Babi Yar, where 33,000 Jews were massacred solely for being Jews? To the mass graves of six million Jews systematically liquidated by the Nazis?" (Friedman 1989, p. 432).

On March 22, 1988, the *International Herald Tribune* carried a photograph on the top of its front page showing an Israeli soldier *grabbing* a Palestinian youth. Friedman expressed his amazement at this lack of proportion by his colleagues at the *International Herald Tribune:*

> The actual story was so insignificant that it merited only a two-paragraph brief inside the paper. Yet the lead picture in the *Herald Tribune* that day, at the very top of its front page, was of an Israeli soldier not beating, not killing, but grabbing a Palestinian. I couldn't help but say to myself, "Let's see, there are 155 countries in the world today. Say five people grabbed other people in each country; that makes 775 similar incidents

worldwide. Why was it that this grab was the only one to be
photographed and treated as front-page news?" (Friedman
1989, pp. 431–432)

Why indeed this intense preoccupation with Israel and its exaggerated condemnation in the Western media? Friedman believed that we
Israeli Jews play a twofold psychological role in Western Christian
consciousness—the yardstick of morality and the symbol of hope, or to
use Freudian terms, the superego and the ego ideal:

> First, the Jews historically were the ones to introduce the
> concept of divine universal moral code of justice through the
> Ten Commandments. These divine laws, delivered at Mount
> Sinai, formed the very basis of what became known as Judeo-
> Christian morality and ethics. Modern Israel, therefore, is ex-
> pected to reflect a certain level of justice and morality in its ac-
> tions. But the Jews also played another role, which modern
> Israel is expected to live up to: as a symbol of optimism and
> hope. It was the Jews who proclaimed that history is not, as the
> Greeks taught, a cyclical process in which men get no better
> and no worse. No, said the Jews, history is a linear process of
> moral advancement, in which men can, if they follow the di-
> vine laws, steadily improve themselves in this world and one
> day bring about a messianic reign of absolute peace and har-
> mony. . . . Because Israel has inherited these two roles of the
> Jew in Western eyes . . . the way Israel behaves has an impact
> on how men see themselves. (Friedman 1989, pp. 432–433)

Friedman quoted the American Israeli scholar David Hartman (born
1931) as saying that the Western media are eager to catch Israel mis-
behaving, because it alleviates their feelings of guilt and allows them to
act normally without having to look up to the morally superior Jews.
Friedman thought that while very few reporters or editors were overtly
conscious of these feelings, they were nevertheless very real (Friedman
1989, pp. 433–444).

It is a heavy emotional burden on us Israeli Jews to have to live up
to the highest moral standards of the Western world. Tragically, however, it was our own Biblical ancestors who promulgated these high
standards to begin with, and who thought of our people as "a light
to the nations" (Isaiah 42:6, Revised Standard Version). Unfortunately,
we Israeli Jews still think of ourselves in such terms, an aspect of our
defensive group narcissism, which will be discussed in Chapter 5.

Needless to say, despite the great strides made since 1948, Israel still has much to improve in every aspect of its national life: its quality of life, its moral standards, its treatment of its minorities, its social justice, and economic health. In 2003 an Israeli political leader, Avraham Burg (born 1955), became a latter-day Isaiah when he castigated his country-men about the end of Zionism (Burg 2003, 2003a).

Psychohistorical Origins of the Conflict

Scholars have spent a great deal of time and energy on fixing the point in time in which the Arab-Israeli conflict supposedly began. Some thought that the Arab-Israeli conflict was rooted in the years preceding World War I—at the end of the Ottoman period—and that Arab anti-Zionism was born some time between the rise to power of the Young Turks in 1908 and the beginning of World War I in 1914 (Mandel 1976). In fact, the Arab-Israeli conflict is a very complex and drawn-out process whose beginning cannot be fixed to any single point in time.

One major turning point in Arab-Jewish relations in Palestine came in late 1917, when the British commander of the Egyptian Expedition-ary Force, General Edmund Henry Hynman Allenby (1861–1936), in-vaded Ottoman Palestine from Egypt with his army and pushed the Ottomans from Gaza and Beer-Sheba northward toward Jerusalem. Allenby's men took Jerusalem as well, after a terrible battle with many thousands killed on both sides. After two years of British military government in Palestine between 1918 and 1920, the League of Nations granted Great Britain an indefinite mandate over Palestine, which lasted from 1920 to 1948, being extended in 1945 by the League's suc-cessor, the United Nations. During those years, as more Jewish refugees came to Palestine, a violent and bloody conflict erupted between the Palestinian Jews and the Palestinian Arabs, whose anti-Zionism became increasingly fiercer. Some historians think that the bitterness of the Arab *fellaheen* (peasants) toward the Jews sprang from their being forced to sell their lands to the Jews and from the Jews refusing to share their grazing fields with the Arabs, as had been the custom earlier. When an Arab sold his lands to another Arab, he could still have his cattle graze on his former land, which the Jews refused to let him do. The Jews dis-played an amazing lack of empathy for Arab feelings—and vice versa (Laqueur 1972, p. 214).

There were two major psychological problems on the Jewish side of the conflict from the outset of political Zionism: (a) the Zionists'

denial of the existence of the Arabs in Palestine and of the Arab hostility
to Zionism, and (b) the Jewish lack of empathy for Arab feelings, the
Zionists' inability to comprehend the feelings of the Arabs and to adapt
themselves to Arab ways. The Zionist denial of reality followed centuries of denial by the Jews of their own unhappy history. The Jews had
denied their painful history from the first century, following the destruction of the Second Temple, all the way to the sixteenth century, following their expulsion from the Iberian peninsula. During those 15 centuries there was no real Jewish chronological historiography. For over
14 centuries, from the destruction of the First Temple by the Romans in
the year 70 C.E. to the expulsion of the Jews from Spain in 1492 C.E. all
Jewish and Hebrew literature, religious and secular, was ahistoric and
anachronistic (Yerushalmi 1982; Falk 1996). I advance a psychoanalytic
interpretation of this astounding fact in the next chapter.

Like the Jewish messianism that preceded it, Zionism was a yearning to turn back the wheel of time, to reverse the clock of history, to
restore to the Jews their great historical losses, to undo their terrible
catastrophes—and to be reborn in a new motherland of Palestine which
the Zionists called "The Land of Israel" (Gonen 1975; Falk 1996, p. 698).
Consciously or not, the Zionists wished to restore those historical losses,
to be reborn in the ancient motherland or fatherland. They wished to
revolutionize Jewish life and to make sure that the Jewish future was
not one of persecution and humiliation like the past; yet they longed for
past glories at the same time. To them, the alternative to Jewish rebirth
in Palestine was the extinction of the Jewish people or the continued existence of the Jews in a state of insecurity, vulnerability, and indignity.
Yet the obvious, real and attractive alternative to Palestine was America, where some 2.5 million Jews had migrated from Russia and elsewhere between 1880 and 1914. Fewer than 1 in 60 of those Jews had
come to Palestine during that period, and among these 40,000 immigrants there was a very high turnover.

The Israeli War of Uprightness and the Palestinian *Naqba*

After many British and international commissions of inquiry over
nearly thirty years, Palestine was formally partitioned by a vote of the
United Nations General Assembly on November 29, 1947. During the
ensuing Arab-Israeli war of 1947 to 1949, the tiny Israeli Jewish community of 600,000 souls lost 6,000 men (1% of its population), while hundreds of thousands of Palestinian Arabs lost their homes and became

refugees in the surrounding Arab countries—Jordan, Syria, Lebanon and Egypt—where they were kept in abominable refugee camps. On May 14, 1948, the State of Israel was officially proclaimed by its 62-year-old leader David Ben-Gurion (1886–1973), and was soon recognized by the United States, by the Soviet Union, and by most of the members of the United Nations, of which it too became a member. The Palestinian Arabs, however, experienced their defeat by Israel as a *naqba*, an expulsion from an imaginary heaven. The Arab writer Arif al-Arif called Palestine the "Paradise Lost." For many years the Arabs have denied the reality of Israel and of its capital, Jerusalem. They have called Israel "occupied Palestine," "the Zionist entity," or "the illegal Zionist government of Tel-Aviv." These psychogeographical fantasies became a psychological reality that helped make the conflict intractable.

The Biblical place name Sepharad appears only once in the entire Bible. It is mentioned in a prophecy about the return of the exiled Israelites to their homeland: "And the captivity of the host of the children of Israel shall possess that of the Canaanites, even unto Zarepath; and the captivity of Jerusalem, which is in Sepharad, shall possess the cities of the south" (Obadiah, 1:20). Zarepath was the name of a northern Canaanite city, now in Lebanon, while Sepharad was probably the Hebrew name for the ancient Greek kingdom of Sardis in Asia Minor. In a striking psychogeographical fantasy, however, the early medieval Jews in Europe applied the name Zarepath to the Roman province of Francia (now France) and the name Sepharad to the Roman province of Hispania (now Spain), in which some of them lived after being exiled by the Romans in 70 C.E. The secret hope behind this fantastical naming was to return one day to their ancestral land. To this day, Spain is called Sepharad in modern Israeli Hebrew and the Jews originating in Spain are called Sephardic Jews. Similarly, the medieval Jews applied the Biblical Hebrew name of Ashkenaz, a mythical great-grandson of Noah (Genesis 10:3), to the Roman land of Germania. In modern Israeli Hebrew, Ashkenazi is any Jew originating from Europe or the other Western countries. This Jewish living-in-fantasy had its own psychological dangers.

The lack of empathy is not limited to one side in this tragic conflict. Whereas the old Jewish community of Ottoman Palestine was mostly Sephardic and non-European, spoke Ladino (Jewish-Spanish), Turkish, and Arabic—and got on rather well with the Arabs under Ottoman rule—the Ashkenazi Zionist immigrants of the first and second *aliyah* (this Hebrew word for immigration to the Land of Israel literally means "ascent") displayed an amazing insensitivity to the emotional

makeup of the Arabs they met in Palestine. The Zionist Jews in Palestine could not and would not comprehend Arab customs. They were
self-centered, displaying profound individual and group narcissism.
Given the great traumata of Jewish history, some Jewish group narcissism could well be expected, but the lack of empathy led to many a violent quarrel. This conflict, in increasingly more violent and dangerous
form, has continued and escalated to this very day, when suicide bombings and the murder of innocent civilians are commonplace.

Jewish Religious Nationalism

Geography is often in the mind of the beholder (Stein & Niederland
1989). To some of its residents, and to many believers outside it, Israel is
the Biblical Holy Land, the center of the world. Yet Israel is in reality a
tiny land surrounded by vast Arab territories. During its first five years,
between 1948 and 1953, the new Jewish state absorbed large numbers
of mostly poor and uneducated Jewish immigrants from the Islamic
countries of the Middle East and North Africa, vastly changing the country's formerly European demography and culture. From 1948 to 2004
Israel has been at war with its Arab enemies, both within and without.
During those 56 years the Israeli Jews and Palestinian Arabs denied
each other's political and national reality (Falk 1992; Oz 1993).

The great stress of the Arab-Israeli wars has generated fantasies,
which are lived out as realities. Religion and nationality became con-
fused with each other. One example is the Israeli Druze community.
The Arab Druze are an important offshoot sect of Islam found mainly in
Syria, Lebanon, and Israel. Between 1947 and 1948 many Palestinian
Druze initially fought with their fellow Arabs against Israel. After Israel's victory in 1949 the Israeli Druze leaders chose to side with the Israeli Jews against their fellow Arabs. Curiously, in Bosnia and Israel, religion and nationality were given new Orwellian meanings. Although
the only thing that separated them from the Serbs and Croats was their
religion, the Bosnian Muslims, mostly Islamized Slavs and Turks, are
defined as an *ethnic* rather than a religious group. Flying in the face of
reality, the Israelis similarly defined the Druze as a *nationality*, rather
than as a religion. The Israeli Druze Arabs seemingly accepted this fiction for decades, denying their Arab ethnicity. While Israeli Muslim and
Christian Arabs are *not* drafted into the Israeli army and police, the Israeli Druze Arabs are. It was only after the first Palestinian-Arab *intifada*
began in late 1987, and especially after the Israeli-Palestinian accords of

September 1993, that some Israeli Druze Arabs began to identify themselves again as Arabs, and some Israeli Arabs as Palestinians. After the second *intifada* of 2000, many Israeli Druze Arabs as well as Israeli Beduin Arabs began to openly identify with the Palestinian Arab enemy.

It was not only the Israeli Druze Arabs who denied their ethnic identity. The Israeli Jews themselves had a serious problem with their own ethnic and religious identity. Was being a Jew a matter of religion or nationality? The creation of a Jewish state named Israel was an outcome of a Zionist ideology that saw all the world's Jews as having been exiled from their land of Israel and living in a Jewish diaspora. Consequently every Jew in the world could now return to Israel and receive its citizenship. The political system adopted by the new state, most of whose founders had come from Europe, was that of a European parliamentary democracy. The 120-member parliament was named the Knesset. The name harked back to Persian rule in Judaea in the fifth and fourth centuries B.C.E. when the Great Knesset had been the supreme legislature of the Jews. In 1950 the Knesset enacted the Israeli Law of Return which granted Jews automatic residence and citizenship rights in Israel. This naturally raised the legal question of who was a Jew.

The answer to this question was settled by the paradoxical realities of Israeli politics. Although most Israelis were secular, there was a large orthodox Jewish minority. Because of the fractiousness of Israeli politics, no single Israeli political party was large enough to form a government. The party that won the plurality of votes was forced to form a coalition with the religious parties, which exacted a religious definition. A Jew was defined as a person who was born of a Jewish mother or had converted to Judaism in accordance with the *Halachah* (Orthodox Jewish law). Not only were the strict Jewish dietary laws enforced countrywide, so that only kosher food could be imported and sold, but all matters of birth, death, marriage, divorce, personal status, religion, and nationality were placed under the jurisdiction of the Orthodox-controlled Interior Ministry and the Orthodox rabbinical courts. Conservative and Reform Judaism have no official status in modern Israel, although this may change as the result of an Israeli Supreme Court ruling in 2004 giving the liberal Israeli interior minister discretion in this matter.

The new Jewish state kept many of the trappings of British colonial rule in Palestine: military government over the Israeli Arabs, the supremacy of the national government over local government, emergency regulations restricting citizens' movements, foreign currency controls,

and other abridgements of civil rights. Over the next 56 years some of
these were eased, but many remain. Compulsory military service was
universal for men and women from age 18 to 21, as well as endless
years of reserve duty. Every Israeli citizen and resident had to carry an
identity card, on which his nationality and religion were inscribed. The
Jews were defined as a nationality, rather than a religion, and so were
the Druze, even though they were clearly a religious group. The adoption of the Orthodox definition of Judaism in Israeli law excluded immigrants to Israel who had been born of Jewish fathers and non-Jewish
mothers, who had Jewish mothers but had converted to Christianity, or
who had been converted to Judaism by Conservative or Reform rabbis.
Some of these had been victims of Nazi persecution, some had saved
Jews during the Holocaust, and some had served in the Israeli army.
These people were denied Israeli citizenship and even residence by the
then-Orthodox interior minister. They were denied registration as Jews
in the Ministry's rolls. Many appealed to the Israeli Supreme Court.

East and West are *psychogeographic* terms. Australia, lying southeast
of the Asian Far East, is considered a Western country. Throughout its
existence as a state, Israel, *a West Asian country*, has lived in a fantasy
of belonging to Europe. Israel has been an affiliate member of the European Economic Community and of the European Union, has traded
with Europe more than with any other continent, has been a member of
the European Broadcasting Union, of the various European sports asso-
ciations, has taken part in the annual European soccer and basketball
tournaments and EuroVision song contests, has received the European
editions of major international newspapers and magazines, and in
other ways has pretended that it was in Europe.

While in the West the term Oriental often means Far Eastern, in Israel
it means Arab or Middle Eastern. One of the most painful Israeli social
and political issues has been the relations between Jewish immigrants
from Western countries and those from Arab, Muslim, and other Oriental lands. The issue became acute after millions of mostly poor and uneducated Jews from the Arab and Muslim world migrated to the newly
created Jewish state of Israel in the late 1940s and early 1950s. Most of
the wealthy and educated Jews from these Muslim countries migrated
to France, Britain, the United States, Canada, and other Western countries. The "Asiatic" immigrants, as the European-born Israeli community called them, aroused deep anxieties which produced hostility, lack
of empathy, discrimination, and lack of understanding. Tragically, the
immigrants' patriarchal family structure often crumbled in Israel's

relatively free society. Sons rebelled against their fathers, who reacted to their loss of authority and status by drinking, violence, or both. Crime, drugs, and prostitution became endemic in these communities. A large percentage of Israel's prison population comes from these families.

The self-image of the Israeli Jews who came from Arab and Muslim countries was badly damaged. Israel was at war with the Arab world, the Arabs were generally denigrated and despised, and being labeled Arabs was unbearable to these Jews. While Israeli Jews from Germany simply call themselves German Jews, and Israeli Jews from Turkey call themselves Turkish Jews, Israeli Jews from Arab countries do not call themselves Arab Jews but Oriental or Sephardic Jews. Their mother tongue may be Arabic, their food basically Arabic, and their favorite music Arabic, yet they refuse to call themselves Arabs. The Iraqi Jews in Israel call themselves the Babylonian community, and the Moroccan Jews call themselves the *Mughrabi* or Western community, because they come from the *Maghreb* (West) in North Africa. Yet, by Israelis, they are considered Oriental Jews—which proves, as we shall see, that geography, too, is in the eye of the beholder.

To make matters even more absurd, Western Israeli Jews are collectively called Ashkenazi, the medieval Hebrew term for German, whose Biblical origin had nothing to do with Germany, while Oriental Jews are identified as Sephardic, the medieval Hebrew term for Spanish, whose Biblical origin had nothing to do with Spain. Most of the so-called Ashkenazi Jews did not come from Germany, and most of the so-called Sephardic Jews did not come from Spain. An Israeli Jew from Morocco, in northwest Africa, is considered Oriental. Jewish-owned restaurants serving Arabic food in Israel are always called Oriental restaurants, never Arab restaurants. Arab-hatred among Oriental Jews is significantly more extreme than among Ashkenazi Jews. This can be understood as an unconscious externalization of the bad self-image upon the Arabs.

From 1948 onward, the highly heterogeneous Israeli Jewish society made great military, economic, social, cultural and political progress. Even today, it integrates millions of immigrants from widely differing cultures. Some Israeli scientists and scholars won international renown. Israel moved from a third-world country to one of the world's most progressive. But Israeli Jews still refused to face reality. They insisted that all the world's Jews not only belonged in Israel but would eventually settle there. They kept thinking of themselves and their country as the center of the world. They lived in a garrison state and believed that the Arab hostility to them would go away when the Arabs saw reality. Instead, several bloody wars were fought between the Arabs and the Israelis, in particular in 1956, 1967, 1973, and 1982.

Each Arab-Israeli war gave rise to striking Israeli fantasies. The *names* we Israelis gave to our wars with the Arabs betray our fantasies. When Israel seized the Sinai peninsula from Egypt during the Suez War of October and November 1956, we were ecstatic. We believed we had returned to Mount Sinai, where our Jewish Torah had been given to Moses 3,300 years earlier. Prime Minister David Ben-Gurion ecstatically proclaimed the Third Kingdom of Israel. Songs were written about the miraculous return, victory albums were published, memorials were erected. Reality hit Israel in the face when international pressure forced it to withdraw from the Sinai shortly thereafter. During the Six-Day War of 1967 Israel not only recaptured the Sinai but also the Gaza Strip from Egypt, the West Bank from Jordan, and the Golan Heights from Syria. We Israelis now believed in our omnipotence. The West Bank, populated by over a million Palestinian Arabs, was called Yehudah and Shomron, the Hebrew names for the ancient Biblical lands that were populated by Jews (Judaea and Samaria are the Latin names for the same places).

It took the Yom Kippur War of 1973 to shake us Israelis out of our complacency. When the Israeli troops repelled the Egyptians at one point on the Suez Canal, crossed the canal and established a foothold on its west bank, the Israelis called that part of Egypt "Africa" and the Land of Goshen. The Biblical land of Goshen, in which the Jews had lived, was on the Nile River, not on the Suez Canal, which of course had not existed. Nonetheless the Israelis insisted on calling that small area of Africa the Land of Goshen. They had returned to their ancestral land. At first the conflict was called the War of the Day of Judgment, implying that God would pass judgment on our enemies, but that name fell by the wayside. The name Yom Kippur War (War of the Day of Atonement) not only referred to the day on which the war broke out, but also, unconsciously, to our need to atone for our sins of complacent narcissistic grandiosity. The Lebanon War of 1982 was given the Orwellian name of the War of the Peace of the Galilee because its stated aim was to give the Galilee respite from murderous Arab attacks. Only years later was the name changed to the War of Lebanon.

The unconscious obstacles to an Arab-Israeli reconciliation were very deep (Falk 1992). After five bloody Arab-Israeli wars from 1948 to 1982 and six years of bloody Palestinian-Arab *intifada* against Israeli rule from 1987 to 1993, and after several months of secret negotiations in Norway, Israeli Prime Minister Yitzhak Rabin (1922–1995) and Palestinian leader Yassir Arafat (born 1929) agreed to recognize each other and create a Palestinian political entity in the Gaza Strip and Jericho, leading to Palestinian autonomy and eventually to a Palestinian state in the West Bank and Gaza.

What were the psychological changes that made such an agreement possible? I believe it was *the process of mourning* that enabled Rabin and Arafat, and more generally the Israeli Jews and Palestinian Arabs, to come to terms—however fragile their agreement later turned out to be. It was only through the gradual acceptance of and reconciliation to their losses that both sides could recognize each other. Each group had to accept the painful losses of territory, sovereignty, and control that went with mutual recognition. The breakup of the Soviet Union and the Gulf War of 1991 helped this process along. So no doubt did U.S. pressure and promises of financial support. But the most important change was the acceptance of painful reality after going through the mourning process.

A Jewish Suicide Murderer

On February 25, 1994, which happened to be the Jewish holiday of *Purim,* an emotionally disturbed American Jewish immigrant physician full of murderous rage named Baruch Goldstein (1955–1994)—after tenderly kissing his four children good-bye—tragically massacred 29 Palestinian Muslim Arabs and was killed by the survivors of the attack. This occurred in Hebron's Al-Ibrahimi Mosque (Mosque of Abraham), which the Israeli Jews call *Me'arat HaMachpelah* or the Cave of the Patriarchs. Goldstein was a member of the outlawed far-right Israeli Jewish political group *Kach,* founded by the fanatical Arab-hater Rabbi Meir Kahane (1932–1990), an American Jewish immigrant to Israel. In 1968 Kahane had founded the Jewish Defense League in the United States, a tiny "self-defense" group listed as a terrorist group by the FBI because it kept physically attacking Arabs in the United States. In 1990 Kahane was assassinated in New York by El-Sayid Nosair, a member of the *Al-Qaeda* terrorist group (Shahak & Mezvinsky 1999).

In 1968, for his Bar-Mitzvah in Brooklyn, Goldstein had written a pacifist essay saying that God's greatest commandment was Thou Shall Not Kill. Nonetheless when he grew up, he joined the Jewish Defense League and wanted to kill Arabs, which he later did. Israelis argued whether this disaster would destroy the chances for peace between them and the Arabs or enhance them, while the rest of the world's Jews were assimilating into their non-Jewish environments. Some Israelis complain that American Jews have a superficial knowledge of their Judaism; but these Israelis do not think that the Judaism of American Jews is nearly as important to them as being Jewish is to the Israelis, or that their own national Jewish pride may be defensive. *Modern Israel was a fantasy that became a reality.* The price for living a fantasy was very high. Perhaps, if peace with the Arabs ever becomes a reality, we Israelis will begin to live normally and let the rest of the world's Jews take care of their own Judaism and be whatever kinds of Jews they wish.

"Oriental" Jews, Arab Jews, and Jewish Arabs

As we have seen, it is customary in Israel to distinguish between Western or Ashkenazi Jews, whose families came from European countries, and Oriental or Sephardic Jews, who came from Muslim countries or from Spain, whence they were expelled in 1492 and found refuge in North Africa and in the Ottoman empire. In Israel, the term Oriental Jew is a code word for Arab Jew. The latter term is never used, even though most of the Oriental Jews come from Arab countries and their mother tongue is Arabic, which by the accepted definition makes them Arabs. The word "Arab" however is emotionally charged in Israel. We look upon the Arabs as our mortal enemies, and ascribe to the Arabs lower social status than Jews. Therefore, being called Oriental makes these non-European Israeli Jews non-Arab—and not the hated enemy. On a deeper level, Oriental Jews being so similar to the Arabs, they may fear their own unconscious wish to merge with the hated enemy, and have to set themselves apart by calling themselves Oriental rather than Arab. Perhaps if we could recognize and accept that being an Arab does not make a person any less human than ourselves, then our Oriental Jews could begin to call themselves Arab Jews—and we could make some headway toward achieving peace with the Palestinian Arabs.

Israeli public opinion polls have found that Israelis from Muslim countries hate the Arabs more and adopt more hawkish right-wing nationalist political stands than Israelis from Western countries. It may be that the painful inferior social status of the Oriental Jews in Israel made them try to distance themselves from the Arabs and to feel superior to the latter. It may also be that the Oriental Jews collectively suffer from a negative self-image, which makes them externalize unacceptable aspects of their selves onto the Arabs. Most of the Oriental Jews in Israel came from Islamic countries; given their Arabic acculturation, they are naturally more like the Arabs in their looks, character, food, habits, and customs than they are like Western Jews. But the Arabs are the epitome of the hated out-group, the murderous enemy, the negative self-image in Israel. The Western Israeli Jews, who had been the dominant majority for over half a century, used to look down upon both Arabs and Oriental Jews.

In a multicultural, multiethnic society like Israel, there are naturally many racist jokes, which betray the fear and hostility that the members of each group feel for the other. One such joke says that Khayim Nakhman Bialik (1873–1934), the Zionist Hebrew poet who immigrated to Palestine in 1924 and died in Vienna ten years later, hated the Arabs because they resembled the Oriental Jews. It may well be for this reason that the Oriental Jews have a strong unconscious need to ascribe their own negative self-image, which at least partly results from their discriminatory treatment by the Ashkenazi Israelis, to the Arabs. The need to attribute to others the unpleasant aspects of our self, in order not to be aware of them inside us, creates an emotional and physical distance between us and the others, the erection of psychological walls—and recently a physical one—between Israelis and Palestinians, between Us and Them. This makes it possible to keep projecting and externalizing. Those who believe that massive denial and projection occur among the Palestinian Arabs cannot escape the fact that they occur among the Israeli Jews as well. We are all human, and we cannot help our unconscious mind defending itself against "the heartache and the thousand natural shocks that flesh is heir to" (Shakespeare, *Hamlet*, Act III, scene i, line 68).

3

Destructive Charismatic Leadership I
The Case of Ariel Sharon

This chapter offers a brief psychoanalytic biography of the Israeli leader Ariel Sharon (born 1928), who for most of his life has been personally involved in the Arab-Israeli conflict both as a military commander and as a political leader. The thrust of this analysis is to uncover the hidden links, which feed the intergroup conflict and hinder its resolution, between emotional trauma, narcissistic personality structure, and destructive action. It studies Ariel Sharon's own memoirs and other sources to uncover how his very painful early-life feelings of shame, humiliation, rage, guilt, and emptiness played a major role in his choice of a military (and later a political) career—and in the conflicts and wars that he has provoked and pursued. It studies the tragic personal losses and traumas of his life as an additional clue to his complex personality. The key discipline to be used here is psychoanalysis, and this study uses the methods and insights of psychobiography and psychohistory.

The aggressive, intransigent, destructive, often irrational and at times tragic actions of Ariel Sharon have defied rational analysis. Long before Sigmund Freud, poets had understood the crucial emotional importance of childhood in the shaping of adult personality. In 1671, the blind English poet John Milton wrote in his *Paradise Regain'd* that "The childhood shows the man, as morning shows the day." In 1802, the English poet William Wordsworth wrote a poem entitled "My Heart Leaps Up When I Behold," in which he coined the phrase "The Child is father of the Man." Struck by Wordsworth's memorable phrase, his obsessively alliterative successor, Gerald Manley Hopkins, wrote a poem entitled "The Child is Father to the Man, " in which he observed that Wordsworth's "words are wild." Can an exploration of Sharon's childhood help us grasp the psychological make-up of this Jekyll-and-Hyde freedom fighter, terrorist, dictator, warrior, and peacemaker?

In the first chapter of his autobiography, Ariel Sharon recalled the personal suffering that the bitter conflicts between his parents and their neighbors had brought him as a child. The family lived in a small cooperative Palestinian Jewish village, 15 miles from Tel-Aviv. The parents' difficult characters caused chronic tensions with their neighbors, which in turn brought about the boy's social ostracism and his humiliation by his friends. Sharon later described his painful feelings in an especially poignant passage:

> All of this had its effect on me as I was growing up. The social tensions did not limit themselves to the adults. In a village of so few families there was no way that the children would not feel them too. I suffered from it, feeling that the friction between my parents and many of their neighbors put a heavy burden on me, that their relationships affected my relationships. I don't know if my friends felt it as strongly as I did, but the effects were obvious. The games we played in the fields and orchards stopped at the doors of their houses. *I felt isolated, lonely.* I wondered what their homes were like inside. *The slights hurt deeply and filled me at times with rushes of turbulent emotion* [italics added]. (Sharon 2001, pp. 16–17)

Sharon did not say what his "turbulent emotion" was. We have known for a long time that painful early emotions have a profound effect on one's personality development, choice of career, and often tragic actions (Lasswell 1930), and that was certainly true with Sharon.

Ariel Sharon is commonly known by his nickname of Arik. The objects of Arik's "turbulent emotions" were not only his friends but also—and primarily—his parents, Samuil and Vera Scheinerman. By his own testimony, the boy Arik suffered these painful feelings of rejection and humiliation because of his parents. More than likely, he was enraged at them for causing him to be rejected and humiliated by his friends. In a moving paragraph at the beginning of his autobiography, Sharon described how during the exhausting battles of 1948 and 1973 his affectionate subordinates tenderly covered him with a blanket and helped him get some sleep. He felt warm, secure, and protected by "a family"—which he had never felt as a child:

> Perhaps these emotions had seemed especially sharp because I
> had not often experienced the same kind of outward affection
> from my own family. My father Samuil, and my mother, Vera,
> were a different sort of people, not given to displaying their
> feelings, no matter how strong these might have been. Though
> they loved my sister, Dita, and me deeply, it was not their way
> to show it, certainly not through demonstrations of physical
> affection. They did not wear their hearts on their sleeves.
> What my parents did exude was strength, determination, and
> stubbornness. In Kfar Malal, the *moshav* [co-operative village]
> where they worked their farm and where in 1928 I was born,
> these were qualities they were famous for. Even among the
> stiff-necked pioneers who had dragged Kfar Malal's farmland
> from the barren soil, their own stubbornness set them apart,
> often far apart. (Sharon 2001, p. 10)

If the grownup Arik believes that his parents loved him deeply, the boy
Arik did not necessarily feel that way. Both of his parents were very difficult people. His father Samuil, born in the late 1890s, was a proud and
stubborn man in chronic conflict with his neighbors. As Arik himself
put it, "The man was by nature unable to compromise . . . nor was he
the kind to keep his mouth shut and nurse secret resentments . . . if he
was convinced of his position, he would not give in, not if a majority
was against him and not if everyone was against him" (Sharon 2001,
p. 15). The narcissistic father, who had studied agriculture, haughtily
insisted that every other farmer in the *moshav* address him as Agronom
Scheinerman. The bitter conflict and hatred between Samuil Scheinerman and the other farmers in the village had a direct effect on his son,
who was ostracized, rejected and humiliated.

   In addition to those difficult character traits, Arik's father was very
hard on his son, demanding the perfect achievements and fighting spirit
that the maintenance of his grandiose self required. In fact, Samuil
Scheinerman abused his son. The father's painful feelings of helpless
rage when his son did not do his bidding or misbehaved exploded in un-
controlled violence, and he often beat up his son—which, in turn, provoked feelings of patricidal rage in the latter: "Samuel [sic] Scheinerman
was a strict father who demanded absolute obedience. The young Arik
received an almost tyrannical education at home: one of prohibitions,
orders and corporal punishment, but it taught him to honor and obey
the will of his father" (Benziman 1985, p. 17). In fact, Arik could only

survive such a difficult father by unconsciously denying his terrible feelings of shame, humiliation, and rage at him, identifying with this aggressor and becoming a tyrant like his father.

It is no accident that Arik Sharon became a warrior, and that he chose that word as the title of his autobiography. Ever since Arik could remember, he was engaged in violent war. War—both within his family and outside it—permeated his early life. His family was at war with its village, he was at war with his parents, every member of his family was at war with himself or herself, and the entire Palestinian Jewish community with its Arab neighbors. Violence was palpable not only in his family but also in the surrounding society. In addition to its often violent internal struggles, the small community of Palestinian Jews was struggling for its survival against a much larger Arab community. Killings and reprisals were common.

Arik's village had been destroyed by Arabs in 1921, the year before his parents settled there, and nobody felt safe. His parents packed handguns. The violence could not help affecting the young boy. Arik's latest biographers thought that it is "probably not possible to exaggerate the traumatic effect of this violence and social ferment on the young Sharon's consciousness" (Miller, Miller, & Zetouni 2002, p. 3). In 1933, when Arik was five, a Zionist labor leader, Khayim Arlozorov, was assassinated. The Jewish left-wing political parties accused the right-wing nationalists of his murder, and violent feelings of political and personal hatred swept the Palestinian Jewish community. The Scheinermans were ostracized, expelled from the local clinic and synagogue. When the teenage Arik attended school in Tel-Aviv, he went to the beach "to watch the violence of the sky and breakers pounding the shore" (Sharon 2001, p. 28), which echoed his own feelings.

Arik's mother, Vera Schneorov Scheinerman, was a difficult person as well, aggressive, suspicious, and rigid. Arik himself, when discussing his parents' initial attraction to one another, wrote, "Perhaps my father recognized in Vera a streak of rock-hard willpower and determination and understood that she would make a good companion in the pioneer's life he was planning." In fact, unlike her husband, Arik's mother was not a Zionist. She had not planned a pioneer's life and did not wish to go to Palestine. Coming from the only Jewish family in a small Byelorussian village, she had gone to the university of Tbilisi, Georgia, in 1917 to study medicine. In 1921 Vera was two years away from graduation, but her marriage to Samuil Scheinerman and the

Russian Revolution cut short her ambitions. The Russian Bolsheviks and their Red Army, who hated all non-Russian nationalisms, advanced on Georgia, arresting the Zionists and exiling them to Siberia.

In February 1922, after Communist activists raided the Tbilisi Zionist Club, Samuil and Vera Scheinerman fled to the Georgian port city of Batum on the Black Sea, where they got married and boarded a ship for British-administered Palestine (which Sharon consistently referred to as "Israel" in his autobiography). Vera felt that her husband had "converted her to Zionism by force" and resented it (Benziman 1985, p. 12). She and Samuil settled in the Palestinian Jewish village of Ein Hai, outside Petakh Tikvah, 15 miles northeast of Tel-Aviv. This village had become a cooperative *moshav* the year before as part of the new *moshavim* movement, and was later renamed Kfar Malal after the Hebrew acronym of Moshe-Leib Lilienblum (1843–1910), an early secular Zionist leader.

In 1926, two years before Arik's birth, the Scheinermans, in chronic and bitter conflict with their neighbors due to their difficult personalities, had their first child, a baby girl. They named her Yehudit (Judith), but their pet name for her was Dita. The young mother Vera invested all her emotional energies in her baby girl. Seeing her own grandiose self in her daughter, she gave her the self-mirroring "love" that a narcissistic mother is capable of, dressed her up in the finest clothes she could afford and gave her all her attention. Her second child, a boy, was born on February 27, 1928. They named him Ariel—a Hebrew name meaning "El is a lion," or "Lion of God"—but called him Arik. The little baby lived in the shadow of his elder sister, who was jealous of the new arrival. Dita eventually escaped her family and her country by marrying an American physician and emigrating to the U.S.

Like many narcissistic people, Arik's mother Vera could not mourn her losses. She remained fixated in the past, clinging to her memories of what could no longer be recovered. Many years after she was forced to drop out of medical school and leave Russia for Palestine, she lived as if she were a physician still living in Russia:

> As I grew older, I became aware that though my mother had transformed herself into a veteran farmer, she had never really integrated herself into the world of the *moshav*. In a special place on the shelf she kept her old surgical scalpel and her student anatomy books, which from time to time she took down and looked through. It seemed to me that she kept inside

> herself somewhere a different life, separate from the farm—a
> life where *she loved other things and other people* [italics added].
> She took out her loneliness and her longing by writing letters—
> to her parents and friends in Baku and Tiflis, her older sister in
> Tashkent, her brothers in Paris and Istanbul. On occasion she
> would even take an entire day off, closing herself in her room
> and not coming out until dinner. My father called those her
> "letter days." That meant, "Today you better watch out."
> (Sharon 2001, p. 15)

In other words, Vera was either a volcano of rage or cold, remote, and
wrapped up in her past. She could not give Arik the love he needed.
The boy Arik painfully felt that his mother did not love him and that
she was living in another world. His hurt and his rage were deep.

When he was born, on February 27, 1928, a date that he curiously and
perhaps significantly omitted in his autobiography, Arik's last name
was Scheinerman. He changed it to the Biblical Hebrew name of Sharon,
that of the region of his birth, when he was a young officer in the Israeli
army, in 1953, under pressure from the Israeli prime minister, David
Ben-Gurion. Consciously, Arik's name change was due to the prevailing nationalist Israeli custom of Hebraizing non-Jewish names. Unconsciously, it was Ariel's declaration of independence from his tyrannical
father and his embracing of a new, idealized father, Ben-Gurion (cf.
Falk 1975–1976).

Rites of Initiation

The teenage Arik went through two initiation rituals. In 1941, at the age
of 13, he had his Bar-Mitzvah, the traditional Jewish rite of initiation
into adulthood. On that occasion his father gave him an engraved Cau-
casian dagger, a symbol of violence and male sexuality (Sharon 2001,
p. 23). At the same time Arik began to attend high school in Tel-Aviv,
which enabled him to escape from his painful family life during the entire day. "For me," he later wrote, "Tel-Aviv was a godsend" (Sharon
2001, p. 27). At night, armed with a club, Arik sat in the dark "helping to
guard the fields" of his village against armed attack by hostile Arabs.
"Spending the nights alone like that," he later recalled, "added to the
sense of self-sufficiency that I was already acquiring" (Sharon 2001,
p. 23). This sense of self-sufficiency was to become part of his narcissistic personality. The following year, the 14-year-old Arik was initiated

into the illegal *Haganah,* or Jewish Defense Force. Standing in front of a Bible and a pistol, he swore allegiance to his new mother—the *Haganah.* He was soon selected to join "an elite platoon" called the Signalers (Sharon 2001, p. 30).

Arik began his military career three years later, in June 1945, at the age of 17, as a *Haganah* Youth Corps fighter. The British government of Palestine made the *Haganah* illegal and kept trying to capture its leaders and its arms. In 1947 the 19-year-old *Haganah* fighter met his future wife, the 16-year-old Margalit Zimmermann, whose nickname was Gali. She had been born in 1931 to Hungarian-speaking Jewish parents in Transylvania, Romania. Gali had survived the Second World War and the Holocaust as a child with her parents, then immigrated to Palestine illegally in 1946 with her elder sister to join her two brothers who had already moved there, leaving her parents and two younger sisters behind. In a powerful unconscious transference reaction, Arik fell in love with the teenage Gali, whom he greatly idealized: "It seemed to me I had never in my life seen anyone so beautiful. . . . Being with her was intoxicating . . . what I felt now seemed completely different from what I had felt before . . . her eyes . . . were hazel and seemed speckled with gold" (Sharon 2001, pp. 37–38). The two were married a few years later, and their marriage was to end with Gali's tragic death in a road accident.

The State of Israel came into being in 1948 amid a bitter all-out war between the Israeli Jews and their Arab neighbors. That tragic war had begun after the United Nations General Assembly passed its Palestine Partition Resolution on November 29, 1947. Ariel Scheinerman was a 20-year-old platoon commander, later a company commander, in a battalion that was repeatedly beaten in the tragic battle with the Jordanian Arab Legion at Latrun, on the Tel-Aviv-Jerusalem road, and with the Egyptian army at Faluja in southern Israel, where the Egyptians had seized a pocket of land but were surrounded by Israeli troops. The young soldier was seriously wounded in his leg and abdomen, and he felt damaged and injured. He was "eaten up by despair and the shame of defeat" (Miller, Miller, & Zetouni 2002, p. 16). He unconsciously sought ways to repair the injury, the damage to his self-esteem, which, as we shall see, had been injured and shaky from early childhood.

The cease-fire signed between Israel and its neighbors Lebanon, Syria, Jordan, and Egypt on the Greek island of Rhodes in 1949 did not dispel the painful Palestinian Arab feeling of defeat, shame, humiliation and disaster, a major blow to their self-esteem. From 1951 to 1956, there was a series of murderous attacks by Palestinian Arab terrorists called *fedayeen* or *fedayoun* on Israeli Jews, including innocent civilians. While in Arabic the term *fedayeen* means "men of sacrifice," the Hebrew-speaking Israeli Jews called these men *mistanenim* (infiltrators), *rotskhim* (murderers), and *mekhablim* (saboteurs).

In the fall of 1952, Ariel Scheinerman received a leave of absence and enrolled as a student at the Hebrew University of Jerusalem. At the end of that year, General Mordechai Makleff became Chief of the General Staff of the Israeli army and General Moshe Dayan (1915–1981) was named Chief of the Operations Department. Dayan was to have an initially friendly but later ambivalent and even hostile relationship with the young officer who became Ariel Sharon.

On March 29, 1953, after several years of courtship, the 25-year-old college student Ariel Scheinerman married his 20-year-old girlfriend, the nursing student Margalit Zimmermann. At first, Arik was happy: "The first half of 1953 was a wonderful time. Not only had we finally gotten married, but I was also deeply involved in my studies and absolutely luxuriating in the experience of being a student" (Sharon 2001, p. 77). The marital happiness did not last long, however.

Faced with a seemingly endless series of murderous attacks, in mid-1953 the General Staff of the Israeli army decided to set up a special commando force that would carry out daring retaliatory raids on Palestinian Arab terrorist bases in Jordan, Syria, Lebanon, and Egypt. (The present West Bank was then part of Jordan.) Arik's brigade commander, Colonel Mishael Shakham, thought that only an elite commando force could carry out such raids successfully. Shakham wanted Arik Scheinerman to command this new unit. General Dayan at first opposed setting up this unit, which was proposed in May 1953. He later said that his priority had been to improve the Israeli army's fighting capacities, "not what to do to the Arab terrorists in reprisal" (Dayan 1976, p. 173). Dayan, however, soon became enthusiastic about the young officer who was proposed to command the new unit, Major Ariel Scheinerman, at that time a reserve battalion commander in the Jerusalem brigade. Since the previous fall, Major Scheinerman had been focusing on history and Arab studies at the Hebrew University of Jerusalem, but now he was eager to quit his academic career and return to military service.

In mid-July 1953 Major Arik Scheinerman was summoned by his brigade commander, Colonel Shakham, who told him about the mounting wave of Arab terrorist attacks on innocent Israeli civilians, and asked him to lead a daring military raid against one of their leaders, Mustafa al-Samuili of Nebi Samuil (the Prophet Samuel), an Arab village north of Jerusalem. Arik accepted eagerly. Was he conscious of the fact that the name of the terrorist that he sought to kill and of the village that harbored him were those of his own father, Samuil?

Major Scheinerman's raid on Nebi Samuil ended in failure (Sharon 2001, pp. 78–81). Did his feelings of shame and humiliation at his botched operation echo in his unconscious mind with the same feelings that he had suffered at the hands of his tyrannical and violent father as a child? Arik himself blamed the failure of his raid not on himself but on his men's lack of professional training: "In the full report I wrote for Mishael Shacham I concluded that this type of action should only be carried out by professionals" (Sharon 2001, p. 81).

Despite the failure of his subordinate's raid, Arik's commander, Colonel Shakham, agreed with his report and wanted him to command the new commando unit. Shakham sent a report to Prime Minister Ben-Gurion and to CGS Makleff recommending the creation of a new commando unit with Major Ariel Scheinerman at its head. The General Staff approved the recommendation in the absence of Operations Chief General Moshe Dayan, who was on vacation at that time. Later, however, General Dayan met Major Scheinerman and was impressed with the self-confidence and fighting spirit of the unconventional young officer. He decided to let Scheinerman collect unconventional fighters from various units, soldiers who could not adapt to the rigid military structure and had come into conflict with their own units. It was Dayan who reportedly called the special new force Unit 101. Was it unconsciously named after the famous torture chamber in George Orwell's *1984*?

At the end of July 1953, Major Arik Scheinerman was summoned to the office of the Israeli army's Chief of the General Staff, General Makleff. The CGS made him a formal proposal to lead a new commando unit:

> Makleff told me that he was going to establish the commando unit Mishael Shacham had recommended and asked if I would be willing to lead it. After a moment I told Makleff that of course I would do it. But I also hoped that at some point I would be able to finish my studies. His response had an edge to it. "I can't make any commitments like that," he said. On my way home I thought about Makleff's attitude. I was enjoying my student's life so much, and now I was going to be ripped away before I even had a chance to really get used to it. For Gali it would mean facing all over again those worries she had had when we were friends during the War of Independence.

> When I talked to my parents about it later, I could see that they
> too were worried, though they only expressed support. They
> knew, as did I and everyone in those days, that worries and
> private lives were one thing, security matters were something
> else. Certain things you simply accepted. (Sharon 2001, p. 83)

Unconsciously, however, Arik wanted to undo his feelings of failure,
shame, and humiliation over his botched raid on Nebi Samuil. His heart
was in the army, not in college. After eight months of studying at the
Hebrew University, Arik quit college and returned to the army to lead
the new commando unit, headquartered at Sataf Camp, outside Jerusalem. His wife, Gali, continued studying nursing and later became a psychiatric nurse.

The elite nature of Unit 101 reinforced the young major's narcissistic
sense of importance and uniqueness. The few dozen fighters that he
collected around him were not normal people. Most of them harbored
pent-up rage and were seeking objects for their violent aggression. The
Israeli need to retaliate against the *fedayeen* and to do justice to their victims gave these young fighters a rational justification for their personal
feelings of revenge. One of them, Meir Har-Tsiyon, personally slit the
throats of several Jordanian Beduin Arabs in revenge for his sister's
murder. Dayan made the young fighter an officer without making him
go through the mandatory officers' training course.

Sharon's Unit 101 became notorious for its controversial raid on the
Palestinian Arab village of Kibieh (also spelled Kibbiya or Kibiah), on
the road to Ramallah in the Jordanian West Bank, where dozens of civilians were tragically killed. This raid followed the murder of an innocent
Israeli woman and her two little children, which had brought to 124 the
total number of Israelis killed by the Arab *fedayeen.* Major Sharon commanded 103 fighters—about twenty men of his own Unit 101 and a
company from the Paratroop Battalion 890. On the night of October 14,
1953, 69 Arab civilians, half of them women and children, were killed inside their own homes, which were blown up by Sharon's Israeli troops.
Covering up the illegal actions of Major Ariel Scheinerman, Prime Minister Ben-Gurion lied to the Knesset, to his own people, and to the whole
world by declaring publicly that no Israeli military unit had left its base
that night. Along with the Deir Yassin massacre of 1948 and the Kafr
Kassem massacre of 1956, the Kibieh massacre became one of the best-
known and most notorious tragedies of the Arab-Israeli conflict.

Sharon himself later claimed that when he went to bed on the night of the raid he had only known of 10 to 12 Arab casualties that his force had inflicted, and that his men had even saved the lives of some Arab children. He was deeply shocked the next morning by the news of the 69 Jordanian civilian deaths; he had believed that the people of the village had fled their homes. Sharon boasted that his raid had surpassed all previous Israeli ones: "For years Israeli reprisal raids had never succeeded in doing more than blowing up a few outlying buildings, if that. Expecting the same, some Arab families must have stayed in their houses rather than running away" (Sharon 2001, pp. 89–90). Sharon, however, had taken no steps to verify that the homes he was about to blow up were empty. Did he unconsciously wish for those very deaths that so shocked him consciously?

The Kibieh raid (which became a massacre), brought the 25-year-old commander his first summons to see the legendary Israeli prime minister, David Ben-Gurion, whom he had admired from afar. "It was an exciting moment for me," Sharon wrote later, "the first time I had met him." While Ben-Gurion himself did not mention this meeting in his diary, Sharon later claimed that the prime minister was happy with his performance: "It doesn't make any real difference about what will be said about Kibbiya around the world," the old man said. "The important thing is how it will be looked at here in this region. This is going to give us the possibility of living here." Sharon added, "I knew that Ben-Gurion was talking about the years in which we had had no answer to give to terrorism, when people in other nations just shook their heads and clucked in sympathy. But now we had an answer, a unit that would force those who wanted us dead to take notice and think again about what they were doing. I couldn't have agreed with him more" (Sharon 2001, p. 91).

The brash young officer had unconsciously found a new father in the older leader, who, in turn, found a new son in the dashing young warrior. Ben-Gurion made Major Scheinerman his favorite officer, ignored his generals when Arik was around (which provoked much jealousy and hostility on their part), and idealized the young officer, who in turn saw his own narcissistic grandiosity reflected in the great leader. As he did with all his subordinates, officers, and diplomats, Ben-Gurion made Arik change his last name from the Yiddish-sounding Scheinerman to the Hebrew Sharon (Benziman 1985, p. 58), the Biblical name of the coastal area of Canaan north of Jaffa. Arik said nothing about this in his autobiography, but the name change was very significant: he had abandoned his father's name and taken the name given to him by his new and idealized father figure.

Commando Unit 101 existed for less than a year. In late 1953 General Dayan replaced General Makleff as Chief of the General Staff of the Israeli army, and in early 1954 he merged Unit 101 with Battalion 890, the paratroop battalion, replacing its commander with none other than Lieutenant Colonel Ariel Sharon. While some company commanders and other officers resented this bitterly, Dayan later justified the appointment. He claimed in his autobiography that Unit 101 had carried out its assignments very well and had raised the fighting capacity of the Israeli army. He said that it was an elite unit which set an example for the other units of the Israeli army. Dayan made no mention whatsoever of the tragic Kibieh massacre (Dayan 1976, p. 173–174).

Among his military peers and superiors, the young paratroop commander Arik Sharon gained a reputation for ruthlessness. He was eager to carry out bloody assignments that other officers considered dangerous, unwise, irrational, irresponsible, and even impossible. Sharon repeatedly killed the enemy, making no distinction between soldiers and civilians, apparently without feeling any pangs of conscience, compunctions, guilt, or regrets. Sharon truly believed that he was doing the right thing, and that the enemy needed to be killed in order to prevent him from killing Israeli Jews. He had a take-no-prisoners policy. In his autobiography he said that he did not kill prisoners, but that he also made no special efforts to take them.

In early March 1955, after a series of murderous *fedayeen* attacks on Israeli civilians, Sharon sent 149 of his paratroopers to raid the Egyptian forces in the Gaza Strip, then administered by Egypt. Thirty-seven Egyptian soldiers and eight Israeli men were killed, including the company commander. There were numerous Israeli soldiers wounded. After meeting Major Sharon in the hospital where the wounded were treated, Prime Minister Ben-Gurion wrote in his diary, "In my opinion this was the pinnacle of human heroism" (Ben-Gurion 1949–1973, entry of March 3, 1955, author's translation from the Hebrew). The old man had taken to the young officer, whom he seems to have idealized as an extension of his own grandiose self (Falk 1987).

The men around Sharon often noted his emotional instability and his Jekyll-and-Hyde personality. While he could be nice, smiling, funny, and generous, he also had uncontrollable outbursts of rage. His instability was a hallmark of what psychiatrists call "the borderline personality." Despite Sharon's unpredictability—his overeating and obesity (discussed in detail further on), his profanities and verbal abuse against the leaders of the Israeli army and government, his impulsive firing of subordinates who dared to disagree with him, and his paranoid attitude toward his superiors—Dayan promoted and advanced him. While Sharon kept his rank of lieutenant-colonel, he was given command of a brigade, normally a colonel's or brigadier-general's job. This was the newly formed 202nd Brigade or Paratrooper Brigade.

On October 10, 1956, after two Israelis had been brutally murdered by Arab *fedayeen*, Lieutenant-Colonel Sharon led his Paratrooper Brigade in a retaliatory raid on the Jordanian police station at Kalkilyeh, a Palestinian Arab town north of Ramallah. General Dayan had authorized Sharon to carry out a limited operation, capturing and destroying the police station only. The ambitious Sharon, however, wanted to capture positions of the Jordanian Arab Legion east and north of the town. In a classic case of military incompetence (Dixon 1976), Sharon unnecessarily sent his men into a tight spot, where one company was surrounded by enemy troops. The daring rescue operation and the ensuing battle cost the Paratroop Brigade 18 dead and over 50 injured. Sharon's botched operation also damaged Israel's relations with Great Britain, which had a defense treaty with Jordan. Chief of Staff Dayan became very upset with Sharon, yet he did not remove him from his command, nor did he mention Sharon by name when discussing this tragic operation in his autobiography (Dayan 1976, pp. 208–210).

Dayan had convinced his reluctant prime minister, David Ben-Gurion, to join the British-French war on Egypt. In the last week of October 1956, during the Suez War, known in Israel as the Sinai Campaign, after having killed numerous Egyptian soldiers Sharon's Paratrooper Brigade captured key Egyptian positions in the Sinai peninsula. On October 31st Sharon advanced his brigade south and west to the Mitla Pass, just east of the southern end of the Suez Canal, and asked Dayan for permission to take the Pass. Wary of yet another botched operation, General Dayan dispatched his chief of staff, Lieutenant-Colonel Rehav'am Ze'evi (1926–2001) by light plane to Sharon with orders denying him this permission. After a heated argument, Ze'evi authorized Sharon to carry out a "limited patrol action." Without mentioning Sharon by name, Dayan claimed that "the brigade commander" had been given specific permission to send out a reconnaissance patrol on condition that it avoid combat. Sharon himself recalled Ze'evi telling him, "You can go as deep as possible, just don't get involved in a battle" (Dayan 1976, p. 241; Sharon 2001, p. 147).[1]

In retrospect, it was impossible to obey such contradictory orders. If the paratroopers entered the Pass, they would have no way of avoiding battle with the Egyptian troops guarding it. Those impossible orders were the result of Sharon's relentless pressuring of his superiors. Sharon felt that he knew better than anyone else what needed to be done, and disregarded his superior's orders. Staying behind, Sharon sent forward a large force consisting of two half-track companies, a tank platoon, a truck-mounted reconnaissance unit, and a mortar battery into the Mitla Pass, ordering them to advance to the western end of the Pass and take it from the enemy. In case of strong enemy resistance, they were to fire mortars at the enemy and break his power. The tragic outcome of this irresponsible action was that Sharon's paratroopers were caught in an ambush set by the Egyptian soldiers, who fired at them from all directions. The bloody battle lasted seven hours and cost Israel 148 casualties—38 killed and 110 wounded. A furious General Dayan ordered a military commission of inquiry into Lieutenant Colonel Sharon's behavior. Twenty years later, without mentioning Sharon by name, Dayan wrote several pages in his autobiography rationalizing his lack of disciplinary action against the brigade commander (Dayan 1976, pp. 241–244).

Why did Sharon order his men into the Mitla Pass death trap in defiance of his orders? Sharon himself later had this to say about the tragic battle:

> After the [Sinai] campaign an inquiry was opened to determine if I had acted according to the orders I received or if I had overstepped the bounds. I believed that no excuses were necessary for what I had done. I had not gone personally to oversee the battle, because my judgment was that the most serious peril to our forces at that time was from the Egyptian armor to

---

1. The combative, extreme-right-wing, ultra-nationalist Ze'evi—ironically known in Israel by his nickname of "Gandhi"—later became a general in the Israeli army and graduated from the U.S. Army Command and General Staff College. After his discharge from the army, he became active in Israeli politics and founded a political party named *Moledet* (Motherland) whose chief plank was the forced transfer of the entire Palestinian Arab population from the West Bank across the Jordan River into the Kingdom of Jordan. In 2001, after Ze'evi became a minister in Sharon's cabinet, he was assassinated by Palestinian Arab gunmen who then fled to Yassir Arafat's offices in Ramallah, where Sharon's troops surrounded them and sought to capture them. They were later apprehended.

> the north. In addition, my second in command (Yitzhak Hoffi) and two battalion commanders (Motta and Raful) [the future Chiefs of the General Staff Mordechai Gur and Rafael Eytan] were already inside the pass. Consequently the greatest need for me was to get the brigade organized into defensive positions. It was for the same reason that I had sent a substantial unit into the pass—not to get involved in a battle but to penetrate to the far end and secure it so that we could deploy deep inside and defend ourselves in what I saw as the coming action. (Sharon 2001, p. 151)

In fact, with his grandiose sense of self, Sharon had overestimated his own power and underestimated that of his enemy. Unconsciously, he thought himself superior, omnipotent, and omniscient. This self-image is typical of high-level narcissistic personalities. Dayan himself had such a personality, but his narcissism was less malignant than Sharon's (Falk 1983, 1984, 1985). Sharon acted as if the world were his apple, as if he were more powerful than anyone else and always deserved to win. He denied the reality of the enemy's power and the mortal danger to his men. Yet another part of him knew that he was mortal, for he stayed behind and survived. In an army whose officers' motto was "Follow me!," this act was severely censured by his peers.

Chief of Staff Dayan was furious with Sharon. Dayan appointed his close aide, General Khayim Laskov (1919–1983), to investigate the Mitla Pass debacle. Sharon claimed that unforeseen developments had forced him to act as he did. For deep emotional reasons of his own, not the least of which was his unconscious identification with Sharon, Dayan could not relieve Sharon of his command (Falk 1983, 1984, 1985). Rather than dismiss Sharon from his post, Dayan dragged him to a meeting with Prime Minister Ben-Gurion, who refused to decide between the military opinions presented to him. Despite the bitter criticism of his subordinates, peers and superiors, Sharon remained in the Israeli army, being promoted and advanced further.

The Birth of the Son and Death of the Father

For three years after their wedding in March 1953, Gali did not become pregnant. Arik was disappointed, sad, angry, and unhappy. He wanted a child. In 1954 the young couple received bad news from their doctors: "Both of us had wanted many children, but . . . we had been told we would be unable to conceive. The news had put a cloud over our lives"

(Sharon 2001, p. 156). Then, in March 1956, Gali finally conceived. This was a turning point in their marriage, which temporarily improved. "When she finally did get pregnant, our joy and expectation were heightened by the sadness that had preceded it" (Sharon 2001, p. 156).

On December 27, 1956, Ariel and Margalit Sharon, after almost four years of childless marriage, finally had a son. Three days later Arik's father, Samuil Scheinerman, died in his sixties after a two-month hospitalization. Even on his deathbed, the proud father tried to show his son who was the stronger of the two. Arik recalled that during his last visit with his dying father he picked up his "weak and light" father in his strong arms, at which point the dying man said softly to his son, "It's a pity I'm going to die. You still need my help in so many ways." Arik was stunned by his father's words:

> It had sounded so incongruous. There I was, twenty-eight years old, young and strong, as determined and self-confident as anybody could be. I was the paratroop brigade commander and had been through all these battles. I was at the stage of life where young men think they can do anything, when they are sure that they are immortal and can conquer the world. And here was my father on the edge of death whispering, "You still need my help." When he said it, the words struck me as such a contradiction. But over the years I remembered, and eventually it came to seem that he had been right. (Sharon 2001, p. 156)

Arik had had an ambivalent and complicated relationship with his proud and tyrannical father, but he had denied his painful feelings of murderous rage at him. While his father's death was the fulfillment of Arik's unconscious boyhood wish, he also felt it as a loss and an abandonment. Like other narcissistic people, Arik could not mourn his losses. On January 4, 1957, Arik and Gali Sharon had their newborn son circumcised, at which point, following Jewish tradition, they named him Gur Shmuel, the second name being the Hebrew version of the English "Samuel" and the Russian "Samuil." The son was a "linking object" to the dead father, and bore his name. This boy, whom Arik called "my beautiful, unexpected son" (Sharon 2001, p. 157), would die tragically ten years later, when another boy accidentally and fatally shot him while playing with Ariel Sharon's own antique shotgun.

Unable to mourn his losses properly, Sharon did not give himself the time to feel the sorrows of his personal life, but plunged back into his stormy military career. Sharon had made many enemies in the Israeli army, among his superiors, his peers, and his subordinates. His rapid advancement was halted for seven years. In the fall of 1957, at CGS Dayan's request, Sharon quit his job as commander of the Paratrooper Brigade and left for Camberley in Surrey, England, to attend the British Army's staff college. Lieutenant-Colonel Ariel Sharon spent one year at Camberley, although little is known about his record there. His wife Gali and his baby son Gur stayed in a London apartment. Arik enjoyed the civilized service and elegant manners of the British. "I felt strongly that here was a break with the past, that I was beginning a new stage in my life" (Sharon 2001, p. 158).

On October 25, 1957, with Arik in England, Prime Minister Ben-Gurion met with CGS General Dayan to discuss the question of Dayan's successor, as Dayan himself planned to leave office the following year. Ben-Gurion asked Dayan whether Arik Sharon might be a future CGS. Dayan replied that while Sharon might be considered for the job militarily, his ambition and arrogance made him hated by his close aides in the Paratrooper Brigade such as Motta Gur. Ben-Gurion, who admired Arik's "heroism," wrote optimistically that "this error may be corrected" (Ben-Gurion 1949–1973, entry of October 25, 1957, author's translation from the Hebrew).

In 1958 General Moshe Dayan was replaced as Chief of the General Staff by General Khayim Laskov, who had investigated Sharon's debacle in the 1956 war. Both Laskov and his successor, General Tsvi Tsur, refused to appoint Sharon to senior positions in the Israeli army, although they could not stop him from moving up the ranks. Thus, when Sharon returned from England to Israel in 1958, he was promoted to Colonel, but was given command of the army's infantry school, a relatively minor position which he had to occupy for four years. In his autobiography, Sharon made no mention of this painful humiliation. The ambitious Colonel Sharon commanded the Israeli army's Infantry College from 1958 to 1962, biding his time and awaiting his chance for promotion and a better job. He called these years "exile in the wilderness, years of frustration which despite (or perhaps because of) my desire to command an active unit threatened to draw out indefinitely" (Sharon 2001, p. 161).

In early May 1962 Arik suffered a great personal tragedy. His 29-year-old wife Gali, a supervising psychiatric nurse in the Israeli public mental health system, was killed in a road accident outside Jerusalem, near the Arab village of Abu Ghosh. Driving under pressure, in a hurry, Gali had tried to pass a slow car in front of her, and had rammed her small Austin into an oncoming truck. She was dead on arrival at the hospital in Jerusalem. Arik learned the terrible news that evening from his friend and neighbor Colonel Mordechai Hod, a future commander of the Israeli air force.

Gali's Austin had a British right-hand steering system, made for driving on the left-hand side of the road in England, whereas in Israel people drive on the right. This had made it very hard for Gali to see on-coming traffic. Officially, the accident was blamed on her right-hand steering system, but obvious questions remained: Why had the Sharons kept the Austin that they had bought in England? Did they not know that driving a right-hand-drive car in Israel could lead to catastrophe? Did Gali's independent character upset the domineering Arik? Did Arik let his wife drive this fatally dangerous car out of an unconscious death wish for her?

Arik himself described Gali's strong character when he discussed their wedding: "At the age of twenty, Gali had lost the shy demeanor of the girl I had first seen working in the agricultural school's vegetable field and had emerged as an adult with a strong personality and a cool, analytic way of thinking. . . . Gali kept a gentle but firm authority" (Sharon 2001, p. 77). Arik and Gali's marriage had been on the rocks. Gali had suspected—perhaps rightly—that Arik was two-timing her with her younger sister Lily—who later became Arik's second wife. Gali was upset and preoccupied with her husband's betrayal, as well as with her 5-year-old son, who was unwell. She was hurt and angry, and may have felt that Arik wanted her dead. Was the accident an unconscious suicide?

Arik cried bitterly when he heard the news, but later pulled himself together. The following day, at his wife's funeral, the widower displayed no emotion. "He approached the newly-excavated grave and removed a piece of paper from his pocket, tearing it into scraps—a note or a poem he had written for her" (Benziman 1985, p. 91). In his autobiography, Arik said not a word about his grief or any other feelings, only about those of his little son, who became deeply depressed and anorectic:

> I was left alone with Gur, who was now five years old. How do you tell a five-year-old child such a thing? He was so tied to her. He trusted her and relied on her so. When I finally brought myself to say it, Gur told me, "No, I don't believe you, Mommy wouldn't leave me." And how do you organize your life? How do you save yourself and your child too? He became so quiet, so withdrawn. I read to him hour after hour, taking

> the intervals in the stories to explain, to talk about what had
> happened and what it meant. It was so hard to be alone with
> him there, waiting for him to come back from wherever it was
> his mother's death had taken him. (Sharon 2001, p. 163)

As we have seen, Ariel Sharon was unable to mourn his personal losses.
An Italian psychoanalyst believed that war was "the paranoid elaboration of mourning" (Fornari 1974). When a preliterate tribe loses a member, it often believes that a neighboring tribe has killed him by witch-
craft and makes war on it. In our Western society, those who cannot
mourn their losses unconsciously externalize their rage and project
their guilt feelings, making war on those they think hurt them. This
may have been true of the wars that Arik's parents had waged with
their neighbors when he was a boy, as well as of the Arab-Israeli wars
(Falk 1992). Certain it is that Sharon has spent his entire life making
war—whether on the military, political, or personal battlefield.

Arik's sister-in-law, Lily Zimmermann, moved in with Arik and Gur.
"Lily came to stay with him, Gali's younger sister whom Gur had always loved. She nursed him and mothered him. It was just what he
needed. Eventually he even started putting back some of the weight he
has lost, and the fragile, hollow look that made me so anxious gradually faded from his eyes. He began to seem more like the boy he had
been before" (Sharon 2001, p. 163). Arik did not say what he himself
needed, but soon a close, sexual liaison was established between the
young widower and his sister-in-law. In August 1963 Ariel Sharon married Lily. She too was to die tragically, of breast cancer, many years later.
There was much strife between the second wife and her mother-in-law,
Arik's widowed mother Vera, who blamed her son's new wife for the
death of Gali. It never occurred to the mother that her son himself may
have unconsciously contributed to his first wife's death, and that she,
Vera, might have been the origin of his trouble.

In early 1964, the 42-year-old general and future prime minister Yitzhak Rabin succeeded General Tsvi Tsur as Chief of the General Staff of
the Israeli army. His Chief of Operations was General Khayim Bar-Lev,
another future CGS. Rabin's appointment opened up Ariel Sharon's
stalled career, which had been blocked for seven years. Rabin named
Sharon Chief of Staff of the Northern Command, under General Avraham Yoffe, whose job was to hold back the Syrian forces on the Golan
Heights and in Lebanon. Once again, Sharon's subordinates noted his
Jekyll-and-Hyde personality:

> Among the officers of the northern command, Arik Sharon
> was known to be thoroughly unpredictable, given to sharply
> changing moods. One day he could be friendly and the next,
> for no apparent reason, he would turn hostile and malicious.
> When his superiors agreed with him he would be loyal; how-
> ever, when differences of opinion arose, he would undermine
> their authority by demeaning them at every opportunity in
> front of his officers. The members of his staff came to learn that
> when his mood turned ugly, it was better to keep your dis-
> tance. His audacity and perspicacity in planning missions
> against the enemy were recognized by everyone, but many
> also saw in these plans an undiscriminating and often impoli-
> tic courting of war with the Syrians. In only one instance did
> this opposition come to the surface, because, for the most part,
> Sharon's intimidation assured that this defiance would remain
> subdued. (Benziman 1985, p. 97)

While General Yoffe did not let Sharon fire his subordinates at will, the
new Chief of Staff was a tough taskmaster. He was eager for battle, and
did whatever he could to provoke the Syrians into fighting. Sharon's
trigger-happiness brought him into conflict with his fellow Northern
Command officers as well as with General Staff officers like Colonel
Mordechai Gur, who took a more cautious approach.

Sharon could be bold and resolute, but also foolhardy, irresponsible,
and dangerous, and his character provoked unnecessary border inci-
dents between Syria and Israel, which cost many lives on both sides. He
was a narcissistic charismatic leader who could inspire his followers
with confidence but could also let them down at critical junctures.
Whenever his tactics failed, he blamed other people for the debacle
(Benziman 1985, pp. 97–99).

In August 1964 Ariel Sharon had his first son by his second wife, Lily.
He named him Omri. Did Arik, who had studied the Hebrew Bible at
school for many years, remember that Omri was the name of a Biblical
king who "wrought evil in the eyes of the Lord, and did worse than all
that were before him" (I Kings 16:25)? He later recalled that he was
happy with this "alert, robust baby who immediately smiled his way
into our hearts" and that Lily wanted at least seven children. In the
meantime, the seven-year-old Gur had become the apple of his father's
eye. He rode horses, had "leadership qualities," was popular with all
his friends, and had his own mare, which his proud father gave him
(Sharon 2001, p. 168).

In late 1964 General David Elazar (1925–1976), another future CGS, replaced General Avraham Yoffe as chief of the Israeli army's Northern Command. Arik did not like Elazar, whom he considered "insecure"—and who had forced him out of office. Sharon later recalled that his commander, General Yoffe, had been "an ultimately secure man, capable and strong, the son of a farming family in Yavniel whose three boys were each as large and stout as tree trunks. He was not a person concerned in any way with jealousy or intrigues. But with the advent of Elazar the atmosphere changed: restrictions, tricks, suspicions—it all came back with a vengeance" (Sharon 2001, p. 169). Sharon took a five-week leave of absence and traveled to Africa with his former boss, General Yoffe.

When Colonel Ariel Sharon returned to the Israeli army's Northern Command, he found that his new boss, General Elazar, had appointed another chief of staff in his absence. "I had not been relieved; they [*sic*] had just appointed someone else to share the duty" (Sharon 2001, p. 179). A furious but cautious Sharon "stepped as lightly as I could through a mine field of bickering and intrigue" (Sharon 2001, p. 179). In October 1965, when he came up for promotion, Sharon took an indefinite leave of absence from the army. In early 1966—after keeping him jobless for three months and giving him a blunt speech on his character flaws—and despite Sharon's many enemies and critics, CGS Yitzhak Rabin nevertheless promoted Sharon to the rank of general and made him Chief of the Training Division in the General Staff. "I was as happy as I was surprised. Lily prepared a small party, and many of our friends from the *moshav* came to help celebrate. Our apartment in the farmhouse was crowded with people and flowers, a wonderfully warm occasion." In the summer of 1966 Arik and Lily had another son, whom they named Gilad Yehuda. Although this was his second son by his second wife, he called him "our third son" (Sharon 2001, p. 180).

In his capacity as Chief of the Training Division, General Ariel Sharon became a member of the Israeli army's General Staff and a regular attendant of its meetings. Sharon worked closely with CGS Rabin. Some of his colleagues thought him a daring and original commander, but his detractors considered him self-centered, paranoid, hypersensitive to personal criticism, dishonest, restless, obsessive, and very difficult to deal with. Sharon was a high-level but destructive narcissistic personality. Some of his subordinates realized that Sharon was ruthless in his aggression, criticism, complaints, threats, and verbal violence. People became afraid to cross him, and even to be near him. One of the few senior officers who stood up to Sharon publicly was Colonel Meir Pa'il, commander of the Officers Training School. Sharon took any professional criticism of his military performance as a personal attack on him and reacted with unbridled rage and chronic vengefulness (Benziman 1985, pp. 100–101).

During the tense three-week waiting period that preceded the Six-Day War of 1967, General Sharon was named to command one of the three Israeli army divisions in the southern Negev desert, on the Egyptian border. The other two divisional task forces were commanded by General Avraham Yoffe, Sharon's former superior, and General Yisrael Tal, an armored-corps hero and the future designer of the Israeli army's vaunted *Merkavah* tank. The commander of the entire Southern Command was General Yeshayahu Gavish (Dayan 1976, p. 361). In the presence of General Sharon and his fellow division commanders, CGS General Rabin presented Prime Minister Levi Eshkol with a cautious plan to attack the Egyptian forces in the Sinai and take over the coastal areas of Rafah and El-Arish, south and west of the Gaza Strip. Some senior officers thought that Rabin's plan was not bold enough, and that its author lacked courage and resolution. General Sharon urged Eshkol to approve a much larger and bolder plan, capturing the entire Sinai and destroying all the Egyptian forces in that peninsula.

On June 1, 1967, under intense pressure by the fearful Israeli public, a national unity government was formed, and General Moshe Dayan, the former CGS and hero of the 1956 Sinai Campaign, was named Israel's Security Minister. The Six-Day War broke out on Monday morning, June 5th. The Israeli air force destroyed most of Egypt's air force on the ground. General Arik Sharon's division carried out what Dayan called the "breakthrough" in the Sinai, moving south and west and capturing the Egyptian positions all the way to the Suez Canal and the Gulf of Suez (Dayan 1976, pp. 361–364). Sharon's colleagues praised his resourcefulness. Those near the division commander, however, noted his imperious behavior and his gluttonous appetite. Sharon had made no fewer than 16 different battle plans, replaced three operations officers during the three weeks before the war, had terrible outbursts of rage at subordinates he did not like, and drove those near him almost crazy. Many staff officers feared and hated him (Benziman 1985, pp. 105–106).

In his memoirs, Security Minister Dayan praised Sharon's conduct during the Six-Day War (Dayan 1976, pp. 361). In fact, Sharon's primary concern had been his own reputation. He had surrounded himself with journalists who would later crown him with laurels. In his report to the General Staff on his division's actions during the war, Sharon claimed to have ordered one of his brigade commanders, Colonel Mordechai Tsippori, to block an Egyptian escape route in the Sinai, but the colonel later claimed never to have received any such orders (Benziman 1985, pp. 106–107).

Security Minister Dayan, however, tended to idealize dashing young commanders, in whom he saw his own ideal self as in a mirror. During the Six-Day War, Dayan was "vastly impressed" with the commander of the Seventh Armored Brigade, Colonel Shmuel Gonen, known by his nickname of "Gorodish." Dayan was struck by the young commander's self-confidence and fighting spirit (Dayan 1976, p. 323). Gonen's armored brigade spearheaded General Tal's divisional task force, which "routed an Egyptian division" in the Sinai (Dayan 1976, pp. 361). In 1973, however, during the Yom Kippur War, General Gonen headed the Israeli army's Southern Command, on the Egyptian front. He committed serious blunders, caused numerous casualties, and proved incompetent. An enraged Dayan replaced him with General Khayim Bar-Lev, a former CGS and a calm, competent commander (Dayan 1976, pp. 497–499). The very same thing had happened to Dayan a few years earlier with Major Ariel Scheinerman, who later became General Arik Sharon. Dayan gradually found out that the young officer who had so impressed him committed blunders, acted irresponsibly, stayed behind while his men went forward to die, and caused his own army and country serious damage.

Ego Strength and Ego Weakness

In his classic study on the psychology of military incompetence, Norman Dixon described the "neurotic paradox" of conservative military leaders with a character not unlike that of Ariel Sharon:

> To understand the psychology of these reactionary elements in the military establishment, of men who choose to make the Army their career, painstakingly work their way up the hierarchy to the highest positions, but then behave in such a manner as to ensure that if they are remembered at all it will be only for their conservatism, we needs must have recourse to ego-psychology. Thus it seems that, in the present instance, military leaders like Deverell, Montgomery-Massingberd, Milne, Ironside, and Gort displayed behaviour symptomatic of extremely weak egos. In this light, their behaviour typifies the neurotic paradox in which the individual's need to be loved

> breeds, on the one hand, an insatiable desire for admiration
> with avoidance of criticism, and, on the other, an equally de-
> vouring urge for power and positions of dominance. The par-
> adox is that these needs inevitably result in behaviour so unre-
> alistic as to earn for the victim the very criticism which he has
> been striving so hard to avoid. (Dixon 1976, p. 115)

Ariel Sharon has repeatedly claimed that—and acted as though—he does not care whether people like him or not: he cares only about doing the right thing by the State of Israel (a feminine word in Hebrew), and saving her from destruction by her enemies. Yet Sharon is a vengeful man who tirelessly and ruthlessly persecutes his enemies while forever trying to clear himself of guilt or repair his self-image.

During the 1980s and 1990s he pursued lengthy, costly, and exhausting libel suits against the respected U.S. news magazine *Time* and the equally respected Israeli newspaper *Haaretz* and one of its top political commentators, Uzi Benziman. *Time* had blamed Sharon for the Sabra and Shatila massacres of 1982; the *Haaretz* story, published in 1992 after Prime Minister Begin's death, said that Begin "had known full well that Sharon had deceived him" during the invasion of Lebanon that year. The official Israeli commission of inquiry had found that Sharon "did not do enough to prevent the killings that were carried out in the camps by the Christian militiamen" and forced Sharon to resign his post of security minister. In his lawsuit against *Time*, Sharon won an out-of-court settlement that his court journalist, Uri Dan, trumpeted as a great victory (Dan 1987). Sharon lost his suit against *Haaretz* and Benziman, and his appeal to the Israeli supreme court was dismissed. During the *Al-Aqsa Intifada*, Sharon has repeatedly humiliated Palestinian leader Yassir Arafat in his Ramallah compound by destroying almost everything around him and leaving him in a desolate shambles. Sharon's profound need for absolute power—an antidote to the feelings of helplessness that he had suffered in his early life—along with his rigidity and cruelty, his avoidance of responsibility, his lies, and his sadomasochistic character have cause as many people to hate him as his charisma has caused others to admire him.

Yet, despite his obvious emotional conflicts and character defects, Ariel Sharon seems—and feels—like a strong person. In line with Friedrich Nietzsche's saying, "Whatever does not kill me makes me stronger," Sharon's personal failures and the blows he has suffered have made him tougher, thanks to his ego strength as well as to the rigidity of his unconscious defenses—projection, denial, and externalization. He has repeatedly provoked crises in his own life which he had to struggle very hard to overcome.

From 1967 to 1973 the young general suffered a series of personal blows that could have felled a lesser man. For example, on October 4, 1967, on the eve of the Jewish new year, *Rosh HaShanah*, Arik's son by his deceased first wife, Gur Shmuel Sharon, not yet 11 years old, was accidentally killed by a friend who had pulled the trigger on an antique shotgun that had hung on the wall within easy reach. Arik himself said that one of his friends had given this shotgun to Gur as a present; Benziman said it was Arik's "old hunting rifle" that he had left hanging on the wall of his house (Benziman 1985, p. 108; Sharon 2001, p. 214).

Arik had been talking on the telephone to friends who had called to wish him and his family a happy new year. He heard the shot ring out, rushed outside, and saw his beloved son "with a terrible wound in his eye, his face covered with blood" (Sharon 2001, p. 214). Gur died in the hospital. Although he had loved his firstborn son deeply, and his grief and rage were enormous, Arik denied his feelings: "I was in shock, hardly thinking or feeling anything" (Sharon 1989. second edition 2001, p. 215). In fact, the deeply traumatized Arik blamed himself bitterly for the death of his son:

> Standing in front of the grave, I remembered five and a half years ago when we had buried [my first wife and Gur's mother] Gali. I had given a brief talk then and it came back to me that I had said, "The only thing I can promise you is that I will take care of Gur." Now I could not shake the thought that *I had not kept my promise.* At such times one doesn't really think, but this kept coming back to me again and again. *I didn't take care of him. I just didn't take care of him* [italics added]. After the funeral Lily and I went home. For the first time in my life I felt that I was facing something I could not overcome, that I could not live through. *I was obsessed by all the things I might have done if only I had not stayed on the phone, if only I had watched more carefully, if only I had told him more forcefully about guns* [italics added]. A thousand ifs. The hardest times were at night, when sleep was impossible and the scene played and replayed itself in my head. Awake during the nights, Lily and I cried together. During the day there was work, then at home if we did not talk about it we could hold the pain inside. But once we would start to talk, it was impossible to put a barrier to the tears. Neither of us could find any comfort or relief from the terrible

grief. There seemed to be no single moment when it was not
present. Nothing could soothe it, nothing could lay it to rest.
(Sharon 2001, pp. 215–216)

Arik's grief was endless, because he could not mourn his loss. Unconsciously projecting his guilt feelings for having left the gun accessible to
his child, Arik was murderously enraged with the boy who had killed
his son. He stalked the young boy, yelled "murderer" at him, threatened him and his family with legal action, finally forcing the distraught
family to leave the neighborhood (Benziman 1985, p. 109).

In January 1968 General Khayim Bar-Lev became Chief of the General Staff of the Israeli army. Sharon, the Chief of the army's Training Department, attempted to make friends with his new boss, but Bar-Lev remained cold to him. Bar-Lev, who created the Israeli line of fortifications
along the east bank of the Suez Canal, did not like General Sharon. Like
many other senior officers, Bar-Lev found Sharon a very difficult man.
Sharon did not get along with his colleagues in the General Staff, unilat-
erally moved training bases into the occupied Palestinian Arab West
Bank and constantly disputed the decisions of the CGS. The only other
member of the General Staff who disagreed with his chief was Armored
Corps General Yisrael Tal, who was something of a maverick himself.
Sharon used his contacts in the press to publicize his views and to attack
his colleagues. His arrogance, self-centeredness, and manipulations further alienated his colleagues. Bar-Lev deliberately kept Sharon away
from key positions in the Israeli army, such as the Central Command
chief and the commander of the Armored Corps, to which he named
generals Rehav'am Ze'evi and Avraham Adan. Sharon felt unjustly discriminated against and humiliated. It was a further narcissistic injury.

In late 1969 General Bar-Lev called a meeting of all his generals.
General Moshe Dayan, the security minister, was also invited. This
meeting was ostensibly called to discuss the deteriorating security in
the south and the escalation of the Egyptian war of attrition against Israel. Its real agenda, however, was to let the generals blow off steam
against their colleague Ariel Sharon. General David Elazar, the commander of the Israeli army's Northern Command, facing Syria and
Lebanon, got up and said angrily that he had had enough of Arik's verbal attacks on the high command—and on himself, for not seizing a
larger chunk of the Golan Heights in 1967 and for not expelling more
Syrian Arabs from it. Other generals stood up and attacked Sharon for

his disloyalty, his lack of camaraderie, the bad atmosphere prevailing wherever he commanded, his manipulation of the communications media to change the CGS decisions, and his personal attacks on his colleagues. They said that he was a dishonest, violent, threatening intriguer and that they could not work with him.

CGS General Bar-Lev listened calmly to the generals' verbal attacks on Sharon. He had obviously been in on their plan. Sharon himself rose and left the room, saying that he had not come to attend a "This Is Your Life" session (Benziman 1985, p. 112). Air Force Chief General Mordechai Hod said that he could not agree to the use of a General Staff meeting for a personal attack on one its members. CGS Bar-Lev removed General Sharon from his job as chief of the army's Training Department, forcing Sharon to take another indefinite leave of absence from the army. Bar-Lev later exploited Arik's accidental failure to file a standard form applying for the extension of his military service in order to try to force Sharon to quit the army altogether. Sharon tried to get Prime Minister Golda Meir to intervene, but she insisted that the matter was up to Security Minister Moshe Dayan. Obviously, Golda was not the good mother that Arik had been seeking.

In 1970, a frustrated and furious General Sharon threatened to quit the army and establish a right-wing political bloc. One of the leaders of the left-wing Labor Party, Pinhas Sapir (1909–1975), and the leader of the right-wing Herut Party, Menachem Begin, pressured CGS Bar-Lev into naming General Sharon to head the Southern Command of the Israeli army. This was the second time Sharon's dismissal from the army was foiled by politicians: in 1958 Prime Minister David Ben-Gurion had talked General Joseph Geva out of firing Sharon from the army for lying.

From 1970 to 1972, General Sharon carried out an iron-fist strategy against the Palestinian-Arab gunmen in the Gaza Strip. Hundreds of Arab terrorists—who called themselves freedom fighters—were killed, dozens of homes bulldozed, and not a few innocent civilians lost their lives and property. No prisoners were taken—captured gunmen were killed. Masses of desert Beduin were driven out of the Rafah area of northeastern Sinai into the southern areas. The Israeli regional commander in Gaza, Lieutenant General Yitzhak Pundak, who sought to improve the lives of the people of the Gaza Strip, came into direct conflict with General Sharon (Benziman 1985, p. 117).

In early 1972, a new CGS replaced Bar-Lev. He was David "Dado" Elazar, an armored corps general who did not like Sharon and had been the first to confront him at the famous General Staff meeting in late 1969. Elazar appointed General Aharon Yariv, the chief of military intelligence, to look into the legality of Sharon's actions. Yariv found that Sharon had exceeded his authority, but, once again, surprisingly, the CGS did not take any serious action against his subordinate: Elazar settled for a verbal reprimand of Sharon. Security Minister Moshe Dayan reportedly asked General Yariv why the CGS was so passive against Sharon, but Yariv referred Dayan to CGS Elazar. The result was that no serious action was taken against Sharon for exceeding his authority.

What was it about Sharon that repeatedly stopped his military and political superiors from taking any serious action against him for his lack of discipline, his illegal actions, his defiance of their orders, and his other transgressions? The narcissistic charisma of such Jekyll-and-Hyde people casts a spell not only on their subordinates but also on their superiors. These narcissistic people inspire admiration, fear, awe, even love, among their followers—and grudging respect among their superiors. Sharon's obsessional and narcissistic perfectionism, his demands for perfect execution of his orders as well as his impossible demands on himself, made him look the epitome of thoroughgoing planning (Rothstein 1980). His paranoid traits were overlooked. Charisma, after all, is in the eye of the beholder. It is the product of the beholder's needs and fears (Schiffer 1973).

On July 15, 1973, the 45-year-old Ariel Sharon was finally discharged from active duty in the Israeli army, after 28 years of military service. He had begun his career in 1945 as a Youth Corps fighter in the illegal Palestinian Jewish *Haganah* defense force. With his wife Lily and their sons, Omri and Gilad, Sharon withdrew to his large Sycamore Ranch in the Negev desert, which he had purchased with loans from two American millionaires, one of them a former Israeli. While the heavy Omri Sharon became involved in his father's political affairs, the wiry Gilad preferred to take care of the ranch.

By the end of July 1973 Ariel Sharon had joined the Israeli Liberal Party—a center-right group—and during that summer he manipulated the Israeli right-wing parties into uniting and forming a new right-wing bloc, the *Likkud*, a Hebrew word meaning union or consolidation. The new political grouping included the nationalist *Herut* party, heir to the Palestinian Jewish freedom fighters of the *Etzel* and *Lehi* (the British had called them the terrorists of the *Irgun* and Stern Gang), who had fought the British and the Arabs to win a Jewish state in Palestine, and

the Liberal Party, heir to the Progressives and General Zionists. Menachem Begin became the leader of *Likkud*, and Sharon himself its elec-
toral campaign chief.

During the Yom Kippur War of late 1973, General Ariel Sharon commanded a division as a reservist, crossed the Suez Canal with his
troops, and successfully set up a bridgehead in Egypt while, yet again,
defying his superiors' orders. In 1974, Sharon's former boss Yitzhak
Rabin replaced Golda Meir as prime minister of Israel, but in 1977 the
Likkud won the elections and Menachem Begin became prime minister.
Begin joked that Sharon, if given the job of security minister, would sur-
round his office with tanks and stage a *coup d'état* against him. Nonetheless, he named Sharon to this post.

In 1982, following a series of terrorist attacks on Israel by Yassir
Arafat's Palestine Liberation Organization, Security Minister Ariel
Sharon plunged Israel into a tragic war in Lebanon that caused the
deaths of hundreds of Israeli soldiers. Sharon had promised Prime Minister Begin to go no more than 40 kilometers into Lebanon, in order to
drive out the terrorists who had been launching attacks from there, but
actually drove his army all the way to Beirut, where he laid siege to Yassir Arafat and his PLO fighters. That war saw the horrible massacre of
the Sabra and Shatila refugee camps. On September 16, 1982, following
a meeting between Sharon and Bashir Gemayel, head of the Lebanese
Christian Phalange Party, some 150 Christian Lebanese Arab Phalangist
gunmen entered the Sabra and Shatila refugee camps, where they killed,
raped, mutilated or injured anywhere from 700 to 3,500 Muslim Palestinian Arab refugees, including women and children. The ensuing up-
roar around the world and in Israel itself forced the Israeli government
to name an official commission of inquiry, chaired by the Supreme
Court president, Justice Yitzhak Kahan, to investigate the massacres.
The other two members of the commission were Supreme Court Justice
Aharon Barak, later Kahan's successor, and Yonah Efrat, a retired Israeli
army general.

Sharon later claimed that he had instructed his subordinates to
cooperate fully with the Kahan commission and to submit all available
documents to it. He had nothing to hide. However, "as the commission
started its work I had very bad feelings about the outcome. The public
atmosphere was murderous; a cry for blood was in the air . . . blood
was needed from the political echelon, someone to bear the blame for
what had happened" (Sharon 2001, p. 509). The somewhat paranoid
Sharon even believed that the two judges on the commission pursued

him in black attire wherever he went "staring at me with the blackest of looks . . . like two black ravens" (Sharon 2001, p. 510).

In late 1982 the Kahan Commission sent formal letters of warning to Ariel Sharon and other ministers and officers that it was investigating, warning them that they might face criminal charges in connection with the events in Lebanon. Sharon was informed by the legal counsel to the Israeli government (a kind of attorney general) that he could no longer use the services of his Security Ministry's legal counsel. Looking for a private attorney to represent him in this difficult situation, he contacted Shmuel Tamir, a former justice minister and a colorful maverick politician. Tamir asked to think it over. Two days later, when Sharon came over to see him at his home, Tamir told him that he would not be able to take him on as a client because he was considering going back into politics, and the association with Sharon could hurt his chances. Rather than express his natural shock, disappointment, or anger at this news, Sharon denied his feelings: "I didn't answer a word when I heard this; I just said thank you, goodbye. Then I left. After this I lost interest in looking around for anyone else" (Sharon 2001, p. 515). This was an exact repetition of what had happened to Arik when he was a child, with Tamir playing the role of his self-centered and rejecting father or mother. When the child was rejected by his parents, he "lost interest in looking around for anyone else."

On February 8, 1983, the Kahan Commission issued its formal report. It found that the massacre at Sabra and Shatila had been carried out by a Lebanese Phalangist unit acting on its own, but that its entry into the camps had been known to Israel. The commission found that "no intention [had] existed on the part of any Israeli element to harm the non-combatant population in the camps," and that no Israeli soldier or civilian bore direct responsibility for the tragic events in the camps. However, the commission assigned "indirect responsibility" for the massacre to Israel, as the Israeli army held the area (Kahan 1983; Sharon 2001, p. 518). Prime Minister Menachem Begin was found responsible "to a certain degree" for not having exercised greater involvement and awareness in the matter of introducing the Phalangists into the camps and for having left matters in the hands of his security minister.

In his autobiography, Sharon claimed that "according to the Kahan Commission," he personally bore an "indirect responsibility" for the Sabra and Shatila massacres (Sharon 2001, p. 519). In fact, the commission had unequivocally assigned him a clear personal responsibility for the massacre:

> We have found, as has been detailed in this report, that the
> Minister of Defense bears *personal responsibility*. In our opin-
> ion, it is fitting that the Minister of Defense draw the appropri-
> ate personal conclusions arising out of the defects revealed
> with regard to the manner in which he discharged the duties
> of his office—and if necessary [that is, if Sharon does not re-
> sign his post], that the Prime Minister consider whether he
> should exercise his authority under Section 21A (a) of the Basic
> Law: the Government, according to which "the Prime Minister
> may, after informing the Cabinet of his intention to do so, re-
> move a minister from office." (Kahan 1983)

The dry legal language of the commission's report could not conceal
the deadly seriousness with which it viewed Sharon's conduct in the
Sabra and Shatila massacre.

Sharon, who had earned a law degree in 1966, was incensed by the
commission's "imputation" of "indirect responsibility" to him: "The
concept had no basis in Israeli law. But far more importantly, in my
heart I knew that I had never anticipated what had occurred, despite all
my familiarity with Lebanese affairs" (Sharon 2001, p. 519). Sharon
claimed that no one had foreseen the tragic turn of events in the Palestinian camps. He saw himself as a sacrificial lamb. "Or was it perhaps
that the judges had made a decision that in such a national trauma
someone had to be found to bear the blame. Whichever, it was a stigma-
tization I rejected utterly" (Sharon 2001, p. 519).

The Kahan Commission had found Sharon "indirectly but personally responsible" for ignoring the danger of bloodshed and revenge
when he approved the entry of the Phalangists into the camps as well
as not taking appropriate measures to prevent bloodshed. The commission also found that Foreign Minister Yitzhak Shamir had erred by not
taking action after being alerted by Communications Minister Mordechai Tsippori, and that Chief of Staff Rafael Eytan had not given the
appropriate orders to prevent the massacre. The commission recommended that the security minister resign, that the director of military
intelligence not continue in his post, and that other senior officers be removed (Kahan 1983). In yet another instance of pulling punches, the
Kahan Commission allowed Sharon to remain in the cabinet as a minister without portfolio.

Under Israeli law, a state commission of inquiry submits its report to
the cabinet, which must decide whether to accept the report in whole or
in part and whether to implement its recommendations. Rejecting the

report in whole entails the cabinet's resignation and new elections. On February 10, 1983, the Israeli cabinet under Menachem Begin held a fateful meeting to discuss the Kahan Commission's report. After driving through hostile demonstrators outside his farm and in Jerusalem, whose "mad rage" (Sharon 2001, p. 519) reflected his own, an agitated and indignant Sharon made it to the meeting. He angrily told his colleagues that if they accepted the Kahan Commission's report they would be branding the mark of Cain not only on his own forehead but also on that of the Jewish people and of the State of Israel. The cabinet nevertheless voted 16 to 1 against Sharon.

Arik was overwhelmed with narcissistic rage. "I regarded what had happened as a betrayal, a real betrayal by people who didn't have the strength to stand up for the things they had been discussing for years" (Sharon 2001, p. 523). It never occurred to him that his colleagues could have agreed with the Kahan Commission's view that he bore personal responsibility for the tragic massacres in Lebanon. On February 14, 1983, Ariel Sharon resigned his post as minister of security. The furious Sharon also contemplated resigning from the cabinet altogether, but his journalist friend and alter ego Uri Dan talked him out of it, telling him that Israel needed him (Sharon 2001, p. 524).

On Saturday night, November 4, 1995, the 73-year-old Israeli Prime Minister, Yitzhak Rabin, was assassinated by a young Jewish religious fanatic with a narcissistic-borderline personality disorder (Falk 2001). Rabin was succeeded by his lifelong rival and fellow winner of the 1993 Nobel Peace Prize, Shimon Peres, who soon lost his job to the right-wing leader Benjamin Netanyahu, who was in turn displaced in May 1999 by the labor leader and military hero General Ehud Barak, who then was succeeded by Ariel Sharon in 2001. In the fall of 2000 Sharon had helped set off the second Palestinian Arab uprising, the *Al-Aqsa Intifada,* with a provocative visit to the Muslim shrines on Jerusalem's Temple Mount. In early 2001 Sharon defeated the incumbent Barak and became Israel's prime minister. Under him, the Israeli-Palestinian conflict worsened, Palestinian Arab suicide bombers blew themselves up among innocent Israelis, the Israeli army re-occupied Palestinian Arab towns, and many more people on both sides became victims of the tragic cycle of violence.

In 2004, however, Ariel Sharon initiated an Israeli pullout from the Gaza Strip, to be completed by the end of 2005. His initiative aroused violent opposition from extreme right-wing Israeli political groups, and Sharon lost a referendum on this issue in his own party. This initiative led to the resignations of some far-right members of his cabinet, which in turn almost brought down his government. Sharon's motives for this seeming about-face were hotly disputed in Israel: many thought he was trying to avoid having criminal charges brought against him by the Legal Counsel to the Government for his illicit financial activities, whereas others saw it as an attempt to curry favor with U.S. president George W. Bush.

Emptiness, Guilt, and Shame: The Personal Roots of Sharon's Wars

What early life events or relationships had formed Ariel Sharon's Jekyll-and-Hyde personality—his sensitivity, kindness, and humor on the one hand, and his ruthless ambition, unquenchable thirst for power, cruelty, and vengefulness on the other? His military genius on the one hand and his military incompetence on the other? His gentleness on the one hand and his outbursts of violent rage on the other, his courage and his cowardice? How did this man become one of the most admired Israeli military and political leaders on the one hand yet one of the most hated and reviled on the other?

Back in 1930, the American political scientist Harold Dwight Lasswell (1902–1978) found that a politician's craving for power had its roots in early feelings of helplessness and rejection (Lasswell 1930, 1977). The British psychologist Norman Dixon ascribed the battlefield incompetence of power-hungry senior military commanders to similar causes (Dixon 1976). Ariel Sharon's obsessive rigidity, his narcissistic pursuit of perfection, his inability to admit responsibility, his lying, his sadomasochistic cruelty, and his shaky self-esteem were a classic case of the personality of "military incompetence." Such people unconsciously deny the feelings of rejection, inferiority, shame, humiliation, and helplessness that they harbor from their early life; yet it is precisely these feelings that drive them to seek power and to make major blunders at the same time (Steinberg 1996).

One of the telltale signs of Ariel Sharon's deeply painful unconscious feelings is his lifelong overeating, which seems to worsen as he grows older. His obesity has been the butt of many Israeli jokes. In fact, it is a tragic aspect of his life and personality. Obesity has many different emotional causes (Stunkard 1967, p. 1060), but most frequently overeating is an unconscious defense against the painful feelings of anxiety, emptiness, and the lack of a clear sense of self. Most psychoanalysts think that obesity conceals "the unconscious wish for reincorporation

of the object or part object (e.g., breast or penis) for the purpose of se-
curing a symbiotic fusion between the ego and the object" and that it
may also represent "the gratification of delusional fantasies involving
grandiosity and omnipotence" (Eidelberg 1968, p. 277). Several psychoanalysts have noted the relationship of bulimia and obesity to serious
emotional trouble beginning in one's early life: feelings of emptiness,
lack of a coherent self, infantile fusion with an overwhelming mother
and the failure to separate and individuate from her. People who cannot express their emotional pain in words and do not go into psychotherapy may eat to relieve pain and fill up the emptiness within them
(cf. Schick 1947; Bychowski 1950; Friedman 1972; Rand & Stunkard
1977; Glucksman & Rand 1978; Slochower 1987; Resier 1988; Glucksman 1989; Farrell 1995).

As we saw at the beginning of this chapter, by his own testimony,
when Ariel Sharon was a child his friends would not let him into their
homes, and this rejection aroused "rushes of turbulent emotion" within
him (Sharon 2001, p. 17). There is clear evidence in our subject's autobiography that these feelings were shame, humiliation, and rage. His
unconscious defense against these painful feelings was to deny his
"turbulent emotions," turn them into their opposite—pride—and escape them by engaging in interminable fighting activity, or as he called
it, "work," which has occupied him to this day. One should read the following quotation carefully:

> At some point in my youth I began to understand in an indis-
> tinct way what was happening with my parents. It was not
> that they were rejected by their peers, it was just that they were
> different. And the differences were nothing to feel ashamed of
> or resentful about. I could even be proud of them. Not that this
> slowly dawning realization made my own burdens any easier.
> But there were compensations—the music, the stories, the
> unusual personalities who came to visit. There was also the
> work. Whatever went on in school or with my friends, work
> was such a constant that everything else seemed unimportant.
> You could lose yourself in it. (Sharon 2001, p. 19)

Feelings of shame and humiliation in one's early life, especially when
the child's emotional support within the family is shaky, are deeply
traumatic. Like a traumatized battered child who grows up to become a
battering husband and father, the humiliated person tends to humiliate
others in order to feel better about himself (Steinberg 1996). This is what
Sharon has done all his life. Unconsciously telling himself that he was

not ashamed, humiliated, or enraged at his parents, but rather proud of being different, the narcissistic Sharon channeled all his rage into mostly tragic and destructive wars, both military and political, in which his chief aim has been to defeat and humiliate his enemies and thereby to shore up his own self-esteem.

Like other narcissistic people, Ariel Sharon denies that he needs anyone else, but in fact needs constant attention, love, and adulation. He received this adulation after doing well in the Six Day War of 1967 and in the Yom Kippur War of 1973, as a member of the Israeli cabinet and the "father" of the Israeli settlers in the occupied territories, after he captured Beirut in 1982 and forced Arafat and his PLO gunmen to leave Lebanon. Then he was in top spirits, generous, happy, witty, and charming. After being officially censured by the Kahan Commission for the Sabra and Shatila massacres and removed from his post of security minister, he became sour, enraged, and very hard to be with.

One of the prominent traits of Sharon's character is what political psychologists call authoritarianism. The authoritarian person cherishes discipline, orderliness, and obedience. He wants his subordinates to agree with him on everything and to obey him unquestioningly, and usually becomes enraged when they do not. He has fired numerous subordinates for the slightest disagreement. While this concept has been debated in the political psychological research for half a decade, Norman Dixon, author of the celebrated study on the psychology of military incompetence, summarized the problem as follows:

> At first sight the traits of orderliness, tough-mindedness, obedience to authority, punitiveness and the rest may well have seemed the very embodiment of hard-hitting masculinity— ideally suited to the job of being a soldier. Unfortunately, as represented in the authoritarian personality they are only skin deep—a brittle crust of defenses against feelings of weakness and inadequacy. The authoritarian keeps up his spirits by whistling in the dark. He is the frightened child who wears the armour of a giant. His mind is a door locked and bolted against that which he fears most: himself. (Dixon 1976, p. 280)

While some military leaders outwardly appear confident, strong, commanding, and masculine, they are not always so inwardly. The British general Sir Redvers Henry Buller (1839–1908), who seemed strong but was irresolute, passive, and dependent, lacked self-confidence and caused the unnecessary death of innumerable British soldiers in the Second Boer War (1899–1900). His men called him Reverse Buller. The

British psychologist said, "Never has a nation been more wrong-headed in its selection of its generals. Never has a general been more disastrous in the execution of his duties" (Dixon 1976, p. 56). Similarly, the distant, stern, and unapproachable British field marshal Lord Douglas Haig (1861–1928), while seemingly self-confident, caused half a million British casualties at the Battle of the Somme in 1916 through his incompetence. Dixon believed that such incompetent generals had pushy or overprotective mothers, who shaped their personalities and careers:

> If this maternal pressure is towards achieving status, authoritarianism would seem the likely outcome, but if primarily protective then the traits of field-dependency might be more in evidence. That the two outcomes are not mutually exclusive but could reflect a shift in emphasis can be illustrated by considering again the characters of Haig and Buller. Both were strongly influenced by their mothers—Haig's the more pushing, Buller's the more protective. Both developed authoritarian traits and those administrative abilities which follow from the need to preserve orderliness. And both were ambitious to the point of being touchy about their status. But, following on these speculations, there their paths divide. The mother inside Haig drove him to command one of the largest armies the world has ever seen, and to do so with remarkable self confidence. But the mother inside Buller, the mother to whom he had been devoted, whose photograph he always carried, kept her boy passive and dependent. It is significant that when Buller married he took a mature and motherly woman for his wife. It is significant that when stressed by being placed in top command, with no parental figure to whom he could appeal, he himself took on the traits of his internalized mother, becoming over-protective towards his men. And it is significant that when stressed his mind turned to food and drink. He became obese. (Dixon 1976, p. 283)

Ariel Sharon, too, took a big maternal woman for his second wife—Lily, the sister of his deceased first wife. Lily, who died of cancer in 2001, blindly admired her husband. She said that she lived only for him and that he was her whole life. Their relationship was fusional. But this was not the first relationship of its kind in Sharon's life. When he was a child, even a baby, he had had a similar symbiotic relationship with his mother, Vera, from whom he never separated and individuated inwardly. It was his relationship with her—no fault of either, but a tragic situation nonetheless—that shaped his perfectionistic, sadomasochistic, narcissistic character and caused the other tragedies of his life: the tragic death (or unconscious suicide) of his first wife, the seemingly accidental death of his firstborn son, the numerous useless deaths of both Israelis and Arabs that he unintentionally caused, the interminable tragic wars, the inability to make peace. While this unhealthy relationship with his mother, and a grudging identification with his tyrannical father, gave Ariel Sharon his inner strength, the ability to face a hostile world and persevere, it also made him a lifelong combatant who is never able to stop fighting and make peace.

4

Destructive Charismatic Leadership II
The Case of Yassir Arafat

In this chapter I attempt a psychological sketch of the Palestinian leader Yassir Arafat (born 1929), the Arab leader with the greatest influence on the Arab-Israeli conflict and on the fate of millions of people in Israel and Palestine. Amazingly, even though Arafat seemingly has a vastly different biography from Sharon's, the two leaders share many personality traits and psychological patterns. Both are perfectionistic, narcissistic, sadomasochistic, charismatic, and destructive in the way they have comported themselves and led their people. By exploring Arafat's early biography, I attempt to shed light on his irrational behavior, and to understand his tragic decisions. The process of unconscious displacement of violent feelings from private and personal to public and political objects is explored.

Arafat, whose given name was Muhammad Abdel-Rauf ibn Abdel-Rauf Arafat al-Qudwa al-Husseini, and who is also known as Abu Amar, began his professional career as an engineering student in Egypt, but moved on to become a Palestinian freedom fighter—or terrorist, as the Israelis saw it—and the eventual leader of the Palestine Liberation Organization (PLO), which later became the Palestinian Authority. Arafat's full name includes his given names, the name of his father, and the name of his mother's clan. The Arabic name Yassir, which means "easy" or "easygoing," was given to him by friends during his youth and hardly applies to his difficult personality. The last name Arafat was that of his mother: his maternal grandmother, Amira Musa Arafat, was born in Gaza, Palestine, and married into the Abu Saud clan of Jerusalem. Her daughter, Zahwa Arafat Abu Saud al-Husseini, was Arafat's mother (Gowers & Walker 1990, p. 9).

Born in Cairo, Egypt, Arafat has been fighting the Palestinian Jews—who later became the Israelis—ever since he was a teenager in the mid-1940s. He reportedly took part in the Arab-Israeli war of 1948 as a 19-year-old Egyptian student-soldier fighting the Israelis in his father's birthplace of Gaza, which at the end of the war in 1949 came under Egyptian rule. Arafat's father died in 1952. In 1958 Arafat founded *Al-Fatah*, the key Palestinian-Arab terrorist organization—or freedom-fighting group, depending on one's point of view. In 1964, he founded the Palestine Liberation Organization, later to become the chief Palestinian political group, which was taken over by *Al-Fatah* in 1969. By 1964 the young Arafat was organizing terrorist raids into Israel, in which scores of innocent civilians were killed. In September 1970 Arafat's military actions in Jordan caused its king, Hussein ibn Talal (1935–1999), to mount a bloody raid on *Al-Fatah* and the PLO. Many Palestinian fighters were killed, and the survivors were driven into Lebanon. They founded a new group called Black September.

Arafat's hatred of Israel was violent and all-consuming, and his men staged bloody raids on Israeli civilian targets. In late 1971 the Black September terrorists assassinated Wasfi al-Tell, the 52-year-old Jordanian prime minister who had sent his troops to kill their brethren the year before. Al-Tell was murdered while attending an Arab League summit meeting in Egypt. In 1972, the Black September *mujahideen* assassinated 11 Israeli athletes at the Olympic Games in Munich, Germany. The Palestinian acts of terror and assassination against Israel continued throughout the 1970s. In addition to Arafat's PLO there were several other Palestinian terrorist—or freedom-fighting—groups, some of them Marxist-Leninist, such as the Popular Front for the Liberation of Palestine (PFLP) led by George Habash (born 1925 or 1926), and the Democratic Front for the Liberation of Palestine (DFLP) led by Nayef Hawatmeh (born 1937), as well as many other splinter groups. In 1974 the DFLP staged an especially bloody attack on a northern Israeli high school in which 21 teenage schoolchildren were murdered. In 1975 members of Arafat's PLO attacked a Tel-Aviv hotel, blowing themselves up and killing eight hostages when they were cornered by Israeli commandos. In 1978 eleven *Fatah* gunmen hijacked a bus on Israel's coastal highway, shooting at civilians along the way. In the shootout that resulted,

35 innocent people were killed. In 1982, after a decade of bloodletting, an Israeli invasion of Lebanon initiated by Defense Minister Ariel Sharon drove Arafat and his men to Tunisia. Never giving up, and surviving numerous attempts on his life, Arafat continued to fight Israel, the hated occupier and oppressor of his people.

In 1988, however, Arafat seemed to have radically changed his Israel policy. On November 14th, in Algiers, the Palestine National Council voted to reject terrorism, declare an independent Palestinian state, and, for the first time, recognize Israel's right to exist. On December 13th, in a speech at a special United Nations General Assembly session in Geneva, Switzerland—held there because the United States would not let him enter the country to attend a session in New York—Arafat declared that the PLO had renounced terrorism and supported "the right of all parties concerned in the Middle East conflict to live in peace and security, including the state of Palestine, Israel and other neighbors."

Arafat's feelings about this issue, however, were deeply ambivalent. The day after his address to the UN General Assembly, Arafat issued a statement at a news conference in Geneva which—by a pre-arranged deal—the U.S. Administration immediately and formally construed as signifying PLO acceptance of UN Security Council Resolutions 242 and 338, recognition of Israel's right to exist, and renunciation of terrorism. Since those had long been the U.S. conditions for a dialogue with the PLO, U.S. President Ronald Reagan authorized the State Department to enter into such dialogue forthwith. However, on January 13, 1989, the PNC speaker declared that "if you read the [PNC's] political statement carefully, you will find that what some [people] term recognition of the Security Council's resolutions and consequently recognition of the Zionist entity is untrue."

Arafat himself continued to pursue every possible political and military means to achieve his goal of pushing Israel out of "occupied Palestine" and, if possible, obliterating the Jewish state altogether. He repeatedly said one thing to the world in English and another to his own people in Arabic. In 1993, after protracted secret negotiations in Oslo, Arafat signed the historic Oslo Accords with the Israeli leaders Yitzhak Rabin and Shimon Peres in Washington, D.C., an act that earned the three men the Nobel Peace Prize in 1994. Yet Arafat covertly continued to support the violent *intifada* and terrorist acts against Israel. He also covertly—and at times openly—supported the *Al-Aqsa Intifada*, which began in 2000, and the terrible Palestinian suicide-bombing attacks on Israeli civilians. As he aged, Arafat became increasingly dictatorial, causing vast pain and suffering to his own people (Aburish 1998).

The witty Israeli Jewish statesman Abba Eban (1915–2002) said that Arafat "never missed an opportunity to miss an opportunity" to make peace with Israel. Arafat's most controversial decision—some say his most tragic ever—came during the second Camp David peace talks with Israeli Prime Minister Ehud Barak in July 2000, where U.S. President Bill Clinton was the host and mediator. During these talks a fascinating dance on the doorstep took place, in which Arafat and Barak each jokingly tried to usher the other into the house before him. Arafat vigorously wagged his finger at Barak, moved behind him and tried to push him forward, as if to say, "No way, you don't push me. You go first." This little power struggle was psychologically revealing: Arafat felt that Barak was patronizing him. As we shall see below, Arafat had been bossed and humiliated by his father when he was a child. He would never let another "father" push him around or humiliate him. Tragically, or fortunately, depending on your viewpoint, Arafat rejected the most generous concessions ever made by an Israeli government to the Palestinians.

From his own viewpoint, Barak had made unprecedented concessions to Arafat. He had agreed to divide Jerusalem by transferring sovereignty in some Arab neighborhoods in Jerusalem to the Palestinian Authority. Barak had also offered to transfer sovereignty in the Muslim and Christian quarters of the Old City of Jerusalem to the Palestinians, while maintaining Israeli sovereignty on the *Haram ash-Sharif* (the Noble Enclosure, known to the Western world as the Temple Mount), and to assign the Palestinians the custodianship of the Holy Places on the Temple Mount, while allotting a small site of the Temple Mount for Jewish prayers. He also offered to transfer some pre-1967 Israeli territories to Palestinian Authority control in exchange for settlements in the territories to be annexed by Israel. Barak accepted the humanitarian principle of family reunions, offering to allow some Palestinian-Arab refugees to return to Israel as well as to the Palestinian state. Barak offered to withdraw Israeli troops from parts of the Jordan valley.

Tragically—or courageously, as his admirers saw it—Arafat rejected Barak's generous offer and presented his own nonnegotiable demands: the full and unconditional implementation of two key United Nations resolutions concerning the Arab-Israeli conflict. One was UN Security Council Resolution 242 regarding Jerusalem, namely, Palestinian sovereignty not only in Arab neighborhoods of Jerusalem but also in the Old City, including all of the Temple Mount and Western Wall. The other resolution was UN General Assembly Resolution 194, stating Israel's responsibility for the Palestinian refugee problem and the right of all Palestinian refugees to return to Israel if they wish. According to the former Palestinian prime minister, Mahmud Abbas (Abu Mazen), a rival of Arafat, the Palestinians opposed any limitation on the number of refugees allowed to return to Israel "even if they [the Israelis] offered us the return of three million refugees." Abu Mazen stated that billions of dollars were offered to the Palestinians (presumably by the United States), but "we rejected these [offers] and said that our rights are not for sale" (Abbas 2000).

Both Barak and Arafat emphasized at Camp David that on the refugee issue and on the issue of Jerusalem the two sides had reached an impasse. Barak himself noted that the Palestinians did not yield on the Palestinian right-of-return issue, which might prevent the sides from reaching an agreement to end the conflict. In a Ramallah speech, on his return from the summit, an intransigent and defiant Arafat emphasized that "the return of the refugees is sacred, and its sanctity is not less than that [assigned to] the holy places [in Jerusalem]." The Camp David peace talks collapsed, and the following years saw a very bloody *intifada* with countless suicide bombings and hundreds of innocent civilians killed on both sides, and with thousands of bereaved families, traumatized survivors, physically and mentally devastated people, both Israelis and Palestinians.

As in *Rashomon*, there is no single way to look at Arafat's fateful decision of July 2000. His supporters said that he was right to reject a proposal that did not include full Palestinian sovereignty over all of East Jerusalem, including the *Haram ash-Sharif*, the right of return to Israel for all Palestinian Arab refugees of the 1948 war, and the complete dismantlement of all the Israeli Jewish settlements in Palestinian Arab territory. Arafat's detractors, on the other hand, believed that he was personally responsible for the terrible bloodshed and unimaginable suffering of both his own people and the Israelis in the years that followed, and that having accepted Barak's offer would have brought his own people that coveted peace and prosperity which had eluded them for so long.

How can we solve the psychological riddle of Arafat's combativeness, intransigence, and destructiveness—and of his extraordinary hold on his people? How did this narcissistic and seemingly abnormal man become the single most charismatic Arab leader with so much personal power and influence on the fate of millions of people in the Holy Land? The key would seem to lie in Arafat's early life, so it would make sense to explore the key events of Arafat's childhood in the hope of understanding his adult personality.

It may not be accidental, however, that the facts of Arafat's life—especially those of his early life—cannot be established with certainty. His biography is riddled with contradictions, exaggeration, and obfuscation. This extraordinary leader, terrorist, and statesman has confounded, fascinated, and puzzled many biographers, psychologists, and other scholars (Black 1975; Kiernan 1976; Hart 1984; Capanna 1989; Favret 1990; Saint Prot 1990; Gowers & Walker 1990; Wallach & Wallach 1990; Reische 1991; Polito 1992; Vanaert 1992; Koskas 1994; Colbin 1994; Rubinstein 1995; Boltansky & El-Tahri 1997; Aburish 1998; Baumgarten 2002; Van Assche 2002; Downing 2002; Karsh 2003; Kimhi & Even 2003; Rubin & Rubin 2003; Brexel 2003; Headlam 2004).

One major issue in Arafat's biography is the seemingly obvious one of where he was born. While Arafat has repeatedly claimed to have been born in Jerusalem, Palestine, his biographers found that he was born in Cairo, Egypt, in 1929, and spent only the years between 1933 and 1937 in Jerusalem (Boltanski & El-Tahri 1997). These researchers went to the University of Cairo and "innocently" asked the clerk for the registration documents of one Muhammad Abdel-Rauf Arafat al-Qudwa al-Husseini at the School of Civil Engineering in 1956. Arafat's birth name apparently meant nothing to the Egyptian university clerk, who, as the biographers relate in their book, sat down behind a rickety wooden table, almost completely hidden by the pile of dusty files bound in black leather, blew off a layer of grime in a most professional way, and finally handed over the records. In blue ink faded by time, the researchers found that their man had been living at 24A Baron Empain Street in the Cairo suburb of Heliopolis. With this information in hand, they went to the Egyptian State Registry office and found Arafat's birth certificate, which gave the birth date as August 24, 1929. Arafat himself has claimed to have been born in Jerusalem 20 days earlier.

The Orphan Boy

Arafat's father and his family seem to have emigrated from Jerusalem, Palestine, to Cairo, Egypt, in 1927, two years before Arafat's birth. Why did the father leave Palestine for Egypt? Arafat's followers like to think that their leader's father "was one of hundreds of Palestinians with strong nationalist feelings who were quietly exiled [from

Palestine] by the British" (Hart 1994, p. 68). The facts, however, are less heroic. Yassir's father, Abdel-Rauf Arafat al-Qudwa al-Husseini, was born around 1900 in the Ottoman Palestinian city of Gaza to an Egyptian mother of the Al-Radwan clan. He married Zahwa Abu Saud of Jerusalem around 1920. The couple had five children by 1927, when they moved to Cairo to pursue a legal claim to a large parcel of land called *Hadikat al-Izbakia,* which had been the property of the Al-Radwan clan, located east of the city, in an area now occupied by Ain-Shams University (Gowers & Walker 1990, p. 8; Rubinstein 1995, p. 13). Apparently, after many years of ardent litigation, Arafat's father failed to get his hands on this property.

In Cairo, between 1927 and 1932, Arafat's mother had two more children—Yassir and his kid brother Fatkhi. The little boy Yassir was the sixth of seven siblings, and not the one most wanted by his parents. In 1933, after his mother Zahwa died of kidney failure, his father could not take care of the youngest children, or perhaps he did not want to keep them. The four-year-old orphan boy and his 18-month-old baby brother Fatkhi were sent away to his maternal uncle, Selim Abu Saud, in Jerusalem. The uncle's house in which the little boy Arafat spent four years, from 1933 to 1937, was in an old complex of fine sixteenth-century Mameluke buildings in *az-Zawiya al-Fakhriya,* a Sufi Muslim complex in the Arab part of the Old City of Jerusalem. The main part of the *Fakhriya* is inside the *Haram ash-Sharif,* while its other part extended west into the *Harat al-Maghariba* (the Moroccan or *Maghrebi* Quarter), immediately adjacent to the south part of the Western Wall of the *Haram ash-Sharif,* better known as the Wailing Wall.

By the time he was four years old, then, the little boy Arafat had already suffered several serious emotional blows: the first blow came when he was two and a half years old, when his brother Fatkhi was born and their mother nursed her new baby, emotionally abandoning her sixth child. This aroused deep feelings of rage at the mother and jealousy of the younger brother. Eighteen months later, the four-year-old boy's mother died, abandoning him for good. This was a tremendous loss and trauma for the little boy, one that marked him for life. He was enraged at being abandoned by his mother, as well as hurt, sad, and depressed. He felt both helpless and worthless. Shortly thereafter, the orphan boy suffered yet another blow: his father sent him away from home to live with his maternal uncle and his family.

The four-year-old orphan boy felt rejected and abandoned not only by his mother but also by his father. One would imagine that his painful feelings of hurt and helpless rage were boundless. However, Arafat unconsciously denied his unbearable feelings of sorrow and rage at the death of his mother, and this defensive denial—which became a life-long character armor—enabled him to cope with the loss of the most significant figure in his life at so young an age.

This denial came at a high price, however, for it had a significant and unhealthy effect on his personality. Using the psychological method of behavior analysis—mainly a content analysis of Israeli newspaper stories about Arafat—two Israeli Jewish scholars found that Arafat had many unhealthy personality traits—considerable emotional instability, a compulsive need for independence at all costs, a need to show his superiority at all times, a limited ability to establish intimate relations with others, a tendency for double-talk, a restricted emotional world, an intense isolation of feeling stemming from a lack of emotional need for intimacy (therefore, this isolation is not oppressive), an obsessive need for control, an extreme need for respect and honor from others, and a difficulty in understanding and empathizing with others. At the same time, however, Arafat became the very symbol of the Palestinian revolution, to which he was wedded. Palestine had replaced his idealized lost mother in his feelings (Kimhi & Even 2003, pp. 365–367).

Denial, however, is an infantile unconscious defense, and one pays a high price for it. We shall deal with the massive collective denial of reality by both the Israeli Jews and the Palestinian Arabs in Chapter 7. On the individual level, too, denial is a maladaptive process. Arafat's violent unconscious feelings of helplessness, rejection, abandonment, sorrow, rage, and vengeance continued to simmer inside him. From the age of four he had two paramount unconscious emotional quests: finding a better mother and father to make up for those who had rejected and abandoned him, and seeking revenge on unconscious representations of the Bad Mother and Bad Father. Jerusalem and Palestine became the idealized Good Mother, with whom he totally identified, and Israel—as well as the Arab states that "betrayed the Palestinians"—took the role of the hated bad parents who had "brought a catastrophe upon the Arabs" (Hart 1994, p. 77).

The Personal and the Political

As we have seen, in 1930, when Arafat was a year-old baby in Cairo, an American political scientist in Chicago named Harold Dwight Lasswell discovered a key psychological fact: the private feelings of the political man are unconsciously displaced onto political objects and then

rationalized in terms of the public good (Lasswell 1977, p. 75). The little
boy Arafat was at war with himself, unable to reconcile his violent and
contradictory feelings of love and hate for his parents—and his own
contradictory feelings of worthlessness and grandiosity. In 1936, when
the orphan Arafat was seven years old, a violent Arab uprising against
the British erupted, with bloody Arab attacks on Jews throughout Palestine lasting until 1939. His biographers thought that the little boy
"saw trouble between Muslims and Jews in the narrow streets of Old
Jerusalem . . . [and] he observed the detention of relatives by the British
authorities, whose rule was becoming steadily more oppressive; and
he was present during anguished family debates about the future of
Palestine" (Gowers & Walker 1990, p. 9). As the violence outside unconsciously echoed his own violent feelings, Arafat unconsciously displaced his painful private feelings to political objects—primarily Palestine, Jerusalem, and the Palestinian Arabs.

The sense of betrayal and victimization became one of Arafat's pre-
dominant feelings. Just as he personally identified himself with poor
and unhappy Palestine—an identification evident in his unshaven and
slovenly appearance, and his *kuffiyeh* or headgear in the shape of the
map of Palestine—his early sense of betrayal by his mother, who had
abandoned him by dying, and of his victimization by his father, who
sent him away from home soon thereafter, merged in his unconscious
mind with the collective Palestinian Arab feeling of betrayal by their
Arab brethren and by the West. Arafat's sensitivity to betrayal could be
one of the explanations of his reluctance to come to a confrontation
with his Palestinian opposition, such as *Hamas* and *Islamic Jihad*. He was
very sensitive to accusations of betrayal, and would do anything to
come to terms with the opposition and to reach a compromise with it, if
only to avoid having to fight it and to be accused by some of his people
as having betrayed them. He would tolerate the opposition so long as
it did not directly threaten his rule or the realization of his strategic ob-
jectives. As part of his political perception of the betrayal of the Palestinians, Arafat also expressed a strong sense of their being the victims.
Arafat has a fundamental sense of himself as a victim, which is insepa-
rable from his perception of the Palestinian people as victims.

What kind of personality did the little orphan boy Yassir Arafat develop after the loss of his mother and his expulsion from his father's
home at the tender age of four? What were the four years of his life like
from age four to age eight in his uncle's home in Jerusalem? It is likely
that being sent away from home was a two-edged sword: it forced him

to be self-sufficient, but it also made him more narcissistic and emotionally deficient. Some sources have described Arafat as a domineering boy. One of his female cousins, who played with Arafat when they were children in Jerusalem, recalled that "he always wanted to be the boss" and that "he exhibited an early gift for showmanship" (Gowers & Walker 1990, p. 9). By trying to dominate his environment and to attract its attention, Arafat was unconsciously defending himself against unbearable feelings of abandonment, rejection, and helplessness.

Arafat himself has repeatedly said that one of his earliest memories from Jerusalem is of British soldiers breaking into his house after midnight and beating up his family. He did not say whether the family included his father. If this actually happened, it must have happened during the years 1933 to 1937, when he was living with his uncle in Jerusalem. Early memories, whether screen memories or actual ones, are psychologically important. In this memory, the sense of helpless victimization is paramount, and it is a key feeling in Arafat's mind. It is not impossible that, in a classic case of repetition compulsion, he has unconsciously kept himself in the role of a helpless victim throughout his political career by rejecting Israel's peace overtures.

"I was born in Jerusalem"

Strikingly, even though the Egyptian documents clearly show that he was born in Cairo, Arafat stubbornly imagined that he was born in Jerusalem. He has often and repeatedly said that he was born in his mother's birthplace, and even in the same house as his mother—actually his maternal uncle's house. He fondly recalled his birthplace in a stone house abutting the Western Wall of the *Haram ash-Sharif* and how he lived with his Uncle Saud in Jerusalem. Arafat's emotional attachment to Jerusalem is so powerful that, during the Israeli siege of his Ramallah headquarters in 2001, he told a British interviewer that he hoped the next time they met would be in his mother's house in Jerusalem. "It was next to the Wailing Wall," he explained, "and it had only been partially destroyed when the Israelis demolished the ancient Mograbi quarter, immediately after their conquest of East Jerusalem in 1967" (Hirst 2001). Arafat added, "I will return. I have my ways, you know. I always used to come here secretly. This is my land. Here I shall die" (Hirst 2001). Arafat longed to return to his mother's house—even though his mother had left that house years before his birth to marry his father, his parents had left Jerusalem and Palestine two years before his birth, and the house itself had been razed by the Israelis in 1967 to clear the way to the Wailing Wall after they had captured the Old City from the Jordanians.

Arafat also had a wishful fantasy of dying a *shaheed* in Jerusalem. As he grew older, this fantasy became more powerful. In 2003, at the age of 74, he was reportedly searching for a burial plot on the *Haram ash-Sharif*—not only the third holiest place in Islam, but also the area in which his mother's family's house had stood until 1967. While the Arabic term *shaheed* is usually rendered in English either as "martyr" or as "suicide bomber," the Muslim idea of *shuhada* is not quite the same as the Christian concept of martyrdom. The term *shaheed* is applied to those who sacrifice their lives for Allah's cause. A *shaheed* supposedly has no fear of death: he fears only Allah and wants to obey and serve Him. The *shaheed* believes that his life is a gift from Allah, his Creator, and that he should not be selfish about it. The *shaheed* obeys Allah and strives to implement what he believes Allah has commanded—the pursuit of truth, justice, and liberty, which includes killing the evil infidel and losing his own life while doing so. The love of Allah motivates the *shaheed* to sacrifice the precious gift of life. The *shaheed* is assured of a great reward in the end for his unselfish act. His focus is on the next life and on pleasing Allah; in his next life in Paradise he believes he will enjoy the sexual favors of 72 *houris* (angelic virgins).

It is by no means certain, however, that sexual satisfaction is the key element in Arafat's wish for martyrdom. In reality, Arafat's sexual life and his emotional relationship to women, including his wife Suha, were less than heavenly. In fact, because of his traumatic early relationship with his mother, his rage at her, and his profound fear of abandonment, they were tormented. Some who knew him reported that Arafat was homosexual (Pacepa 1987), while others have said that he had several love affairs (Kiernan 1976; Rubinstein 1995). Arafat first married at the age of 61, in 1990. His wife Suha was 34 years younger than he, and he hardly invested his deepest feelings in her. Arafat's way of life did not change after his marriage. He continued to conduct a lifestyle and a daily agenda that were filled to the point of exhaustion, and hardly devoted any time to his wife and to his daughter. Suha Arafat spent much more time in Paris, where she had spent her youth, than in Ramallah with her husband.

Among the fascinating psychological questions about Arafat, then, are, why did he imagine that he was born in Jerusalem, why did he so ardently wish to die a martyr in his mother's house, and why did he avoid women most of his life? It is not hard to detect behind the born-in-Jerusalem fantasy the overwhelming longing of the little boy Muhammad for reunion with Zahwa, the mother who had abandoned him by dying when he was four years old. This deeply traumatic event was clearly the most formative one of his life, and he never adequately mourned his loss. Instead, his entire life was unconsciously spent trying to recover what he had lost—in symbolic form. It is safe to assume that when Arafat was a little orphan boy in his uncle's house, Jerusalem, and Palestine as a whole, had already taken his mother's place in his deepest emotions. In an unconscious process of splitting, Jerusalem, whose Arabic name of *Al Quds* means "the holy one," became the idealized Good Mother, while Israel, which had thrown out the Palestinians, became the denigrated Bad Mother. It is his tie to Jerusalem that may have caused Arafat to reject Barak's offer at Camp David, as it did not give him sovereignty over all of his beloved Mother Jerusalem.

Arafat's highly idealized yet tortured emotional attachment to Jerusalem and Palestine is not unique to him. The unconscious emotional meaning in our minds of cities, countries, rivers, seas, islands, and other aspects of our geographic world is known as psychogeography (Stein 1987; Stein & Niederland 1989). In a previous study I have shown that, more often than not, Jerusalem has an unconscious maternal meaning (Falk 1987). The fiery Palestinian Arab leader suffered traumatic maternal loss at a tender age. The feeling of loss had permeated his family of birth, which had left its hometown of Jerusalem and country of Palestine and migrated to Egypt. Whether or not the family could adequately mourn its losses is uncertain, but it seems quite certain that Arafat had great trouble mourning his.

As we have seen, in addition to the feeling of betrayal, another key feeling in Arafat's mind is that of victimization. Even though his father left Palestine for Egypt in 1927 to pursue a land claim, and even though he himself was born in Egypt in 1929, Arafat sees himself as a victim of Zionism, someone who lost his Palestinian home, his worldly belongings, and his place in the world due to Israel's coming into existence in 1948. The same feeling of victimization was shared by Arafat's most prominent Palestinian American compatriot, Edward William Said (1935–2003), even though the facts may not have been exactly as Said remembered them (Said 1999; Weiner 1999).

In fact, Arafat's first victimization was by his parents: not only may he have been an unwanted child, but his mother had abandoned him by dying, and his father had sent him away from his home. This double blow left him with a lifelong feeling of injustice and victimization, and with a longing to avenge that victimization. He could not, however, avenge it on his mother, who was dead. His revenge on his father, who died in 1952, when Arafat was 23, was to not attend his funeral. Arafat's feelings of murderous rage and vengeance were unconsciously displaced to Israel, which, the way he saw it, had victimized the Palestinian Arabs in 1948 and ever since. He was unconsciously the poor Palestinian Arab, and Israel was the Bad Mother and Bad Father rolled into one.

In addition to the trauma of immigration in 1927, Arafat's family of origin had serious emotional problems. The ambitious upwardly mobile lower-middle-class father from Gaza had married an upper-middle-class woman from Jerusalem. The young *paterfamilias* had begun his career as an Ottoman policeman, prior to the First World War, after which he became a moderately successful trader and cheese maker. The father was stubborn, excitable, domineering, and violent. At the age of eight the young boy suffered another trauma: his widowed father had remarried in Egypt, and the boy was sent back to live with his father and his new stepmother. Arafat's elder sister, who took care of her younger brother after he returned to Egypt in 1937, described their father as a man with great physical strength and an iron will and as an excitable and passionate man who was always shouting.

The Arafat household was full of tension, shouting, and family rows which hurt and scarred Yassir emotionally. His elder sister complained that she and her siblings saw little of their father's wealth, because he gave it all to poor people who asked him for help. He was a devout Muslim, and, as was customary in Egypt, named his son Muhammad after Allah's Prophet. The little boy Yassir did not love his father, and admitted to a biographer that his childhood was unhappy (Hart 1994, p. 69). Arafat rarely mentioned his father either in public or in private and did not attend his funeral. In fact, he hated his father, especially after the latter sent him away to Jerusalem after his mother's death, and perhaps even more so after he returned to Cairo in 1937 to find that his father had brought home a new wife who hated her stepson and was cruel to him and his siblings (Hart 1994, p. 69). Arafat's hatred for his father, who had kicked him out of his home at the age of four, was unconsciously displaced to the "cruel Israelis" who had kicked the poor Palestinian Arabs out of their homes.

As William Wordsworth put it in 1802, "the Child is father of the Man." The anxiously bossy boy Muhammad turned into the ever-controlling leader Yassir Arafat. Keeping constantly busy allays Arafat's anxiety, while having nothing to do makes him anxious, depressed, volatile, and even suicidal. He is deeply suspicious, even paranoid at times, and, like Sharon, has a Jekyll-and-Hyde personality. Ever since his youth, Arafat has been suspicious of enemies and allies alike. He did not trust anyone, and his suspicions were accompanied by extreme sensitivity to any criticism from his own people. He was personally hurt when people in his own camp expressed criticism—even constructive criticism—regarding his political courses of action. He also could not adapt to his new circumstances. "He continues to conduct a lifestyle and a daily agenda that are much more appropriate for an underground revolutionary, or a leader of a secret organization, than for a leader of a country" (Kimhi & Even 2003, p. 368).

The two Israeli Jewish scholars thought that Arafat perceived himself as a leader of extraordinary historic stature. His interpersonal relationships were very difficult, stemming from his need to manipulate people, bringing them closer or distancing them as needed. He has neither intimate relationships nor any close friends, and apparently feels no need for them (Kimhi & Even 2003, p. 366). Incredibly, these two "psychological" scholars never mentioned the fact that their description of Arafat's personality closely matched that of the American Psychiatric Association's description of the narcissistic and borderline personality disorders (American Psychiatric Association 1994; Kupfer et al. 2002). As with Sharon, unconscious sadomasochism is a cornerstone of Arafat's narcissism (see Gear et al. 1981). It requires him to constantly act out his inner conflicts in a manner that is destructive both to his foes and to himself, both to the Israelis and to the Palestinians.

5

Nationalism, Group Narcissism, and the Problem of the Self

Nationalism has been a major aspect of—and a major contributor to—interethnic conflict. There is a vicious circle between nationalism and organized warfare, each feeding on and augmenting the other. Each nation has it flag, its anthem, its military and police uniforms, and other distinct political and psychological symbols. Citizens of each nation are raised from early childhood on their nation's cultural heritage, including its heroic historical myths and legends, and grow up feeling that their nation is special, unique, and superior to all others. With organized human warfare dating back some 13,000 years (Mansfield 1982), one nation's victory is its neighbor's defeat, one nation's pride its neighbor's shame. The twentieth-century institutions of the League of Nations and the United Nations were created after two horrific world wars in which tens of millions of people were killed and hundreds of millions traumatized. The conflicting nationalisms of the Israeli Jews and of the Palestinian Arabs play a key role in the Arab-Israeli conflict. Understanding the psychology of nationalism is therefore a prerequisite for understanding this tragic conflict.

The Territorial Imperative or the Human Imperative?

Nationalism and organized warfare are human phenomena. Other mammal species may form small groups that stake out and defend a common territory, and may be in conflict with one another, but they do not have the tools, weapons, language, consciousness, and large-group structure of the human species that make organized warfare possible. In the mid-1960s several studies were published which purported to explain why human beings form nations that keep waging war. In *The Territorial Imperative*, an expatriate American writer, with the help of his wife's pretty drawings, explained that the possession of a defined territory is a basic need of all territorial species, including most mammals and, of course, humans (Ardrey 1966). *The Territorial Imperative* became popular with young people who thought that it explained much of what troubled them about their world.

Ardrey's revolutionary "discovery" was a popularization of the scientific work of two prominent biologists—the Austrian ethologists Konrad Zacharias Lorenz (1903–1989) and his Dutch colleague Nikolaas Tinbergen (1907–1988). Lorenz, who had sympathized with the Nazis, called aggression "the so-called evil" (Lorenz 1963, 1966). Tinbergen was an anti-Nazi, but had worked in close association with Lorenz. Studying animal behavior, Lorenz and Tinbergen had shown that intraspecies aggression was common and natural in many species, and Ardrey capitalized on their work. A few years later, an American anthropologist countered Ardrey's "territorial imperative" with a book entitled *The Human Imperative*, in which he argued that the most basic human needs were not aggression and the possession of territory but self-actualization, forming emotional and social bonds, helping others and receiving their help, giving and taking (Alland 1972).

At the same time that Ardrey popularized the ethologists' discoveries in his *Territorial Imperative*, a psychoanalyst from Central Europe made an important contribution to the study of human behavior in general and of human aggression in particular. This was the German-born Erik Homburger Erikson (1902–1994), the father of identity theory. Erikson, who became a Christian in his later years, had a Danish Jewish mother but never knew his biological father. In 1966 Erikson addressed the Royal Society of London about the pseudospecies mentality that characterized large human groups (Erikson 1966). At Konrad Lorenz's suggestion, Erikson coined the term *pseudospeciation* for the process through which large groups that are part of the human species develop a sense of themselves as being a species unto themselves—the human species—and of other groups as subhuman or inhuman. Erikson defined *pseudospeciation* as follows:

> The term denotes the fact that while man is obviously one species, he appears and continues on the scene split up into groups (from tribes to nations, from castes to classes, from religions to ideologies) which provide their members with a firm sense of distinct and superior identity—and immortality. This demands, however, that each group must invent for itself a place and a moment in the very center of the universe where and when an especially provident deity caused it to be created superior to all others, the mere mortals. (Erikson 1968; 1969, p. 431)

Erikson, then, thought of large human groups as pseudospecies that behave toward one another as if they were different species. Such groups do indeed act like separate biological species. During their formation, over many millennia, most human groups—clans, tribes, and nations, or what we now call the peoples of the earth—developed "myths of election" by which the group in question believes itself to be special, unique, or elected by God as His chosen people (Falk 1996, pp. 311–312). Other groups are considered inferior and even inhuman. A British Jewish historian has described how, for each of us, "the values of *my* group—for the nationalist, of *my* nation; these thoughts, feelings, this course of action, are good or right, and I shall achieve fulfillment or happiness by identifying myself with them" (Berlin 1979, p. 346).

A religious group typically considers its god or gods to be the only true deities. The German word *deutsch* (German) comes from the archaic *teutsch* meaning "the people," and the name of the ancient Celtic god Teutates means "the god of the people." The Germans have thought of themselves as the world's *Herrenvolk* (master people), the Japanese have considered themselves more intelligent and of a higher culture than any other nation, the Apache have called themselves *indeh* (persons) and other people *indah* (enemies). This group narcissism, which is a major cause of interethnic conflict, and which afflicts Jews and Arabs in no small measure, is explained as an unconscious defense against the emotional hurts, losses, injuries, and blows that each group has suffered over its collective history, as well as a means to preserve a vital sense of separateness.

An American Jewish psychiatrist has pointed out that nationalism and religion powerfully augment the human tendency toward dualistic thinking, which, as we shall see, is the result of the unconscious defensive process of *splitting* (Mack 2002, p. 177). This process does not

operate alone: it is accompanied by unconscious projection and externalization, the hallmark of the paranoid attitude. An Israeli Jewish psychologist thought that we Israelis are a paranoid nation because we see
ourselves as the victims of this world, with the whole world as our enemies. We live in constant fear of annihilation and as a group have no
empathy for the suffering of our antagonists. Even our national anthem
is paranoid (Grosbard 2003, pp. 61–64). This psychologist, however, er-
roneously applied individual psychological processes to large groups
without justifying this methodologically.

The issue of *empathy* and the lack of it are closely related to that of
group narcissism, splitting, projection and externalization. On the individual level the narcissistic or paranoid person indeed has little empathy for the feelings of others. On the collective level, a large group that
is collectively fixated on its own specialness or greatness has little collective empathy for the sufferings of other groups, especially that of its
neighbors and enemies. In this chapter, the key role of empathy in the
resolution of interethnic conflict (and the lack of empathy in interethnic
wars) is analyzed.

The chief psychological problem in the Israeli-Palestinian conflict is
not necessarily its objective reality but our emotional perception and
distortion of that reality. Both Israeli Jews and Palestinian Arabs suffer
from deep narcissistic injuries. Both we and they have historical reasons for feeling an ownership of Israel or Palestine, as well as deep hurts,
discrimination, and wrongs. The *Shoah,* or Holocaust, of the European
Jews, the vast majority of whom were murdered by the Nazis and their
collaborators between 1941 and 1945, left an indelible traumatic mark
on us Israeli Jews, who have lived in fear of annihilation ever since
(Shalit 1994). This fear is also a legacy of many centuries of persecutions, pogroms, and massacres. Our powerful tendency to identify the
Arabs with the Nazis and Arafat with Hitler, as our prime minister
Menachem Begin did in 1982, is unrealistic and irrational. It is motivated by our deepest fears, projections, and living in the past.

Many Israeli Jews and Palestinian Arabs are traumatized survivors
and refugees. It is very hard for traumatized people in their emotional
pain to be aware of the pain of others and to empathize with them. It is
even harder for people engaged in violent conflict with one another to
empathize with their enemies. Nevertheless, empathy is the only way
to head off more violent conflict. As one Israeli psychologist put it,
"Surely, you cannot ask someone whose existence is being threatened
to be empathic to the party that wants to destroy him, although, in our

case, that could have spared us from the Yom Kippur war" (Grosbard 2003, p. 53). The lack of empathy and what is perceived as arrogance by the other side are surefire prescriptions for prolonged violence.

The Grandiose Group Self

Zonis and Offer (1985) felt that the self-system model, based on the self-psychology theories of the psychoanalyst Heinz Kohut (1913–1981), was the most useful one for understanding the Arab-Israeli conflict. The concept of the self is central to Kohut's "new psychoanalysis," which gained prominence in the 1970s and 1980s. Kohut's "self" is similar to Erik Erikson's concept of ego identity yet different from it. Kohut refrained from defining the self, but his concept includes all our feelings about ourselves and our internalized self-image. Our self is formed during the first and second years of our life, when we separate and individuate from our mother and begin to sense ourselves as an entity distinct from her. Narcissism is an emotional state of great investment of feeling in the self. Narcissistic injury is a psychological blow to the self, to our self-image, self-esteem, self-love, and pride. Kohut published many books and articles on the narcissistic and borderline disturbances of the self and on their psychoanalytic treatment (Kohut 1971, 1972, 1976, 1978).

Kohut, in his classic essay on narcissistic rage, coined the term "group self" (Kohut 1972). To some psychoanalysts, this term was too similar to Carl Gustav Jung's "collective unconscious" and to other controversial ideas of the group mind which were rejected or disputed by colleagues. Kohut returned to this subject in his later work (Kohut 1976). The group self is a key concept to the psychoanalytic view of the Arab-Israeli conflict, embodying as it does our feelings about ourselves as an ethnic, national, and religious group. Our Jewish myth of election, the belief that the Jews throughout the world are one people, God's Chosen People, the People of Israel, is part of our group self (Falk 1996). The name Israel itself was originally an attribute of the Canaanite father-god El, meaning "El shall reign" (Cross 1973).

Two Israeli psychoanalysts and their American colleague discussed the vast operation of the process of denial on both sides in the Arab-Israeli conflict (Winnik, Moses, and Ostow 1973). Despite the obvious aggressive feelings mobilized in soldiers by the fighting and killing, another Israeli psychoanalyst pointed out in the same book that when Israeli soldiers discussed their feelings during the Six-Day War of 1967

(Shapira 1970) they avoided the word aggression. This book at the same time ignored the crucial issue of the self. We now recognize that the issue of the group self is central to our conflict (Falk 1992, pp. 221–225).

Psychoanalysts have argued about the issue of the grandiose self, which may simply be called an inflated self-image. In extreme, pathological cases it becomes paranoia and megalomania. While Kernberg (1980) believed that the grandiose self is a pathological development of the self—caused by serious difficulties in the psychic development of the infant and child—Kohut (1978) regarded the grandiose self as a normal structure in the psychic development of the self, a stage of the development that we must pass through and emerge from. The grandiose self is much more remarkable and dramatic when it occurs in groups. Each human group we belong to, beginning with our family of origin and ending with our nation, plays an important emotional role for us. It not only holds us, giving us a feeling of security, but also helps us define our identity and the boundaries of our self, who we are and what we are. In this sense, each group unconsciously replaces our early mother, and our feelings about it are largely determined by our relationship with our mother during the early phases of symbiosis, separation, individuation, and differentiation, when our self is formed.

Each human group we belong to has its psychological boundaries that determine who belongs to it and who does not. The Israeli Law of Return of 1950 defines the limits of the imaginary group we Israelis alternately call the Jewish People and the People of Israel and imagine to be based in Israel. We maintain and defend the boundaries of our group very jealously. The less our internal and personal boundaries are clear and secure, the more we need a clear demarcation of the secure boundaries of our group. The geopolitical boundaries of our country unconsciously represent our own internal and interpersonal boundaries (Falk 1974, 1983). The Israeli police's Border Guard, whose members wear olive-green uniforms looking much more military than police, is not just a police force: it also expresses a deep emotional need—the need to protect oneself against the feared emotional fusion with the Arab enemy. Some of the Israeli Border Guard's members are Arabic-speaking Druze Arabs, yet they prefer to identify themselves as Druze rather than Arabs, while other Israeli Arabs call themselves "Palestinian Arabs who are citizens of Israel."

The national group's language, religion, culture, history, and mythology help transmit from one generation to the next the sense of belonging to the in-group and of being different from all out-groups. The unacceptable aspects of the group are externalized, or projected, upon neighboring out-groups. An Israeli-American scholar thought that after our victory in the Six-Day War of 1967, we Israelis saw ourselves as much bigger and stronger than we were in reality, and that it was this dangerous and tragic illusion that brought us our disastrous Yom Kippur War of 1973 (Gonen 1978). This scholar is deeply pessimistic about "the impossible Palestinians and Israelis" (Gonen 2002). In psychoanalytic terms this illusion is called the grandiose group self. The exaggerated, grandiose self-image of a large ethnic or religious group can be fatal, as was the case of the catastrophic Jewish Bar-Kochba revolt against the Romans between 132 and 135 C.E. The grandiose self is caused by an unconscious mental process designed to protect us from painful feelings of inferiority, worthlessness, helplessness, and nonexistence. The grandiose group self begins in our infantile attitude to our "unique" family, and is then displaced to our nursery school, kindergarten, grade school, class, youth movement, adolescent group, military unit, employer, university or hospital department, and any other reference group.

The narcissistic rivalry between Sydney and Melbourne, New York and Washington, Zurich and Basel, and so on is well known. The residents of each city believe their city to be ever so much better than its rival. The residents of Jerusalem believe that their city is more beautiful, better, nicer, and bigger than Tel-Aviv, while those of Tel-Aviv believe there is no city like theirs in Israel, perhaps not in the entire world. Some of the professors at the Hebrew University of Jerusalem seriously believe themselves to be several notches above those of all the other Israeli universities. Many Israelis imagine their remote little country as the best, most beautiful, strongest, most important, and most sacred in the entire world, as the Holy Land, the Land of Milk and Honey, the center of the world. Jerusalem has been idealized as perhaps no other city in the entire world has (Falk 1987).

While a child needs to idealize, an adult person is able to see reality for what it is. Although Israel is a country of significant military power, allied with the United States and with strong ties to world Jewry, it is still a tiny land in the Middle East, its military power is limited, it is economically weak relative to other First World countries, it lives beyond its means, and it depends on the United States and world Jewry for its economic and military survival. Israel has grave social, economic, political, and security problems, with a long and interesting but far from glorious past. Israel may be a special place, but we

Israelis are neither the Chosen People nor a Light unto the Nations, as many Israelis—especially the nationalistic, religious, and right-wing parties—believe.

In ancient times, the Israelites and Jews had lost several kingdoms. The First Kingdom of Israel was destroyed by the Assyrians between 722 and 721 B.C.E., the Kingdom of Judah was overrun by the Babylonians in 586 B.C.E. and the Hasmonean or Maccabean Second Kingdom of Israel was conquered by the Romans in 70 C.E. The more nationalist Zionists wished to restore those ancient losses. In the 20th century, during the Suez War, on November 7, 1956, after the Israeli army had captured the Sinai peninsula from Egypt, the 70-year-old Israeli prime minister, David Ben-Gurion, ecstatically proclaimed the establishment of the Third Kingdom of Israel. Ben-Gurion was unconsciously expressing his grandiose personal self, which he had fused with the grandiose group self, the group narcissism of the Israelis. The following day, however, Ben-Gurion had to sober up from his narcissistic inebriation when U.S. President Dwight Eisenhower and other angry world leaders threatened to cut off all aid to Israel and intervene militarily. After a severe personal crisis, Ben-Gurion announced with deep pain, grief, and disappointment that the Israeli army would withdraw from the Sinai. Israeli group narcissism was reinforced by the spectacular Israeli victory in 1967 in the Six-Day War, only to suffer another sobering blow six years later in the Yom Kippur War (Falk 1987a, 1987b).

Indeed, the disastrous Yom Kippur War of 1973 sent emotional shock waves throughout Israeli society. We Israelis were forced to give up our illusions of omnipotence (Gonen 1978). It was precisely such illusions that led to the failure of the Israeli intelligence services to foresee the coming Arab attack in October 1973. The 1977 visit of Egyptian president Muhammad Anwar as-Sadat (1918–1981), the Camp David peace process that followed, and the ensuing Egyptian-Israeli peace treaty of 1979 reduced our tendency to project all evil on our enemies. It is no accident that this sobering-up process was followed by scholarly reassessments of Israeli Jewish national heroes such as Bar-Kochba, the second-century leader of the Jewish uprising against Rome, that showed them to be the worst military catastrophes in our history (Harkabi 1983). The disillusionment with our great might and the scholarly attack on old Israeli national myths may have been interconnected.

Our harsh military, economic, and political reality had forced us Israelis to modify our grandiose group self and to see ourselves life-size as a tiny country in a remote place in the Middle East without any great significance in world affairs. The grandiose self, ethnocentrism, and ethnic group narcissism, whether personal or national, often develop as defenses against deep, painful feelings of helplessness and worthlessness. On the surface, it may seem absurd to attribute to the proud and often cocksure Israelis feelings of inferiority, helplessness, or worthlessness. Pride, however, and especially arrogance, masks precisely such unconscious feelings. The Jews, who lost their motherland and suffered from terrible catastrophes—persecutions, massacres, and humiliations over many centuries, culminating in the *Shoah*—and the Arabs, who lost their glorious Caliphate in the sixteenth century and were under Ottoman and European colonial rule for several centuries, thus have weighty reasons for feeling inferior, helpless, worthless, and narcissistically injured.

We Israeli Jews hark back to our glorious Biblical past, however fantastic some of it may be. We boast of our great achievements throughout history, especially in the twentieth century, when we made the Palestinian desert bloom and built a wonderful country and nation in the incomparable Land of Israel—the Land of Milk and Honey. We seem to be trapped in our own ethnocentrism and national narcissism, in our myth of election as the Chosen People, in our grandiose group self, which is an unconscious defense against feelings of historical defeat and failure. The Muslim Arabs similarly hark back to the glorious past of having conquered half the world during the seventh and eighth centuries, of having invented modern mathematics and medicine, of the great victory of Salah ad-Din Yusuf ibn-Ayyub (Saladin, 1137–1193) over the Crusaders. Saladin, whom the Arabs fondly call *Sultan al-Malik an-Nasir* (the Victorious Ruler King), was a Kurdish Muslim warrior from the Mesopotamian city of Tikrit—Saddam Hussein's birthplace—who pushed the Christian Crusaders out of Palestine in 1187. The fact that Tariq ibn-Ziyad (died circa 720 c.e.), the Muslim general who conquered Spain, was an Arabized Berber, and that Saladin was an Arabized Kurd, does not seem to interfere with the Arab visions of past glory. It may be asserted that national narcissism in the Middle East—and everywhere else—is often pathological and dangerous.

Zonis and Offer (1985) studied the role of both the individual self and the group self in the Middle East conflict. While most charismatic political leaders are deeply narcissistic, using Kohut's ideas, Zonis and Offer distinguished four types of charismatic leaders: the wise, the impulsive, the megalomaniacal, and the messianic. These scholars considered the Egyptian President Anwar as-Sadat a wise leader, the Israeli

Prime Minister Menachem Begin and the Libyan president Muammar Qaddhafi impulsive leaders, the Iranian king Muhammad Reza Shah Pahlavi a megalomaniacal leader (Zonis 1991), and the late Ayatollah Khomeini of Iran a messianic leader. These scholars believed that leaders have a great influence on the Arab-Israeli conflict and should be closely studied.

In the early 1970s, concerned with the deepening Arab-Israeli conflict and wishing to help humanity understand and resolve it, the Group for the Advancement of Psychiatry, known by its acronym of GAP, set up a Committee on International Relations to study the psychological causes of international conflicts, beginning with the most intractable one—the Arab-Israeli conflict. From 1972 to 1977 the American members of GAP's Committee on International Relations conducted numerous interviews with Israeli Jews and Palestinian Arabs. At the end of its interviews and deliberations the Committee published a report on the Middle East conflict. The thrust of the GAP report was that much of the Arab-Israeli conflict derived from problems each side had with its own group self, from each side's attempt to repair severe *narcissistic injuries* to its self, and from each side's *inability to mourn* its historical losses. The GAP report on the Middle East conflict argued that the narcissistic system of each party to the conflict is not fixed but keeps changing with its political, military and economic ups and downs (Group for the Advancement of Psychiatry 1978).

Seven years later, Zonis and Offer (1985) argued that the Arab-Israeli conflict actually encompassed four distinct sub-conflicts: the interstate conflict, the Israeli-Palestinian conflict, the Palestinian-Arab conflict, and the internal conflicts within Israel and the Palestinians. The nature of these four subconflicts keeps changing dramatically, but is always tied to issues of self-esteem, the self-systems, and the group self. The Israeli-Egyptian peace treaty is a case in point. Each side has many internal problems and is far from monolithic. To understand the conflict, one must grasp the internal emotional reality of each side, not only the external reality. Muslim Arabs live in a very different psychological reality from Israeli Jews and Western people in general. They see themselves as the victims of colonialism and imperialism, personified by the United States and Israel (Zonis & Offer 1985).

From their comfortable vantage point in Chicago in the 1980s, Zonis and Offer (1985) believed that historical processes were leading to a lessening of the narcissistic injuries, an improvement of the self-image, and a more realistic perception of reality on both sides. If we have leaders who can rise above their own social and political culture and find new solutions to old problems, peace is bound to come. Even though President Sadat of Egypt was assassinated shortly after signing the peace treaty with Israel, "the structure for the possible transformation of past hates and fears was, nonetheless, erected" (Zonis & Offer 1985, p. 296). Writing in Jerusalem from 2002 to 2004, with suicide bombings a daily occurrence and hundreds of innocent civilians killed on both sides, it is hard for me to be quite as optimistic.

The GAP report of 1978 claimed that our land, nation, country, army, and state are part of our extended self. Damage to our country is felt as damage to our own self. Each side in the conflict feels and believes that its hurts were caused by the other side but in reality is also mired in a conflict with its own self. The group narcissism of each side is badly injured, and each side strives to repair its own self-image. The GAP report agreed with Fornari's psychoanalytic theory of war, which searches for the root cause of the conflict in the internal conflicts of each side, not in external circumstances (Fonari 1974; Group for the Advancement of Psychiatry 1978).

The Palestinian Arab *Intifada* and the Palestinian Arab Group Self

The seemingly intractable and interminable conflict between the Israeli Jews and the Palestinian Arabs who live in the occupied West Bank of the Jordan River and in the Gaza Strip bordering on the Egyptian Sinai peninsula has been simmering for a very long time (Reich 1984). The first uprising of the Palestinian Arabs in the territories occupied by Israel since 1967 began in 1987 and is known as the first *intifada*. The second *intifada*, also known as the *Al-Aqsa Intifada*, began in 2000 after a visit by right-wing Israeli leader Ariel Sharon to Jerusalem's Temple Mount, site of two Islamic shrines, the Dome of the Rock and Al-Aqsa Mosque. At that time Sharon was not a member of the Israeli government, which was headed by Ehud Barak. Sharon is deeply hated by most Palestinian Arabs, who blame him for the Sabra and Shatila massacres of their brethren in Lebanon in 1982. During the *Al-Aqsa Intifada*, suicide bombings, which the Palestinian Arabs called martyrdoms, have become commonplace.

The crucial psychological motive of the Palestinian-Arab *intifada* is not only their hatred of the Israelis but also the profound need of the Palestinian Arabs to improve their self-image. For several decades they felt shamed, humiliated, despised, oppressed, without honor, rights, and self-worth. Now they seemingly feel proud, important, and with honor. Grosbard (2003, p. 124) thought that our negative feelings of contempt for the Palestinian Arabs could not have changed without the *intifada:*

> We feel contempt toward them, their poverty, and their help-
> lessness, and see them as a mob with no rights, in whom we
> have no interest unless they are committing terrorist attacks,
> and we are not really willing to help them. Indeed, only the *In-
> tifada* made us view them and their wishes with more consid-
> eration and respect. Alternately, we see them as a cheap labor
> force, lowly workers we can exploit for our benefit . . . our ar-
> rogant stance toward them comes, like any arrogance, from the
> emotional hurt we feel, that we are trying to protect.

The leadership of the Palestinian Arab uprising publishes Arabic-language leaflets that it circulates among the Arabs of the West Bank and Gaza Strip. The leaflets call upon all Palestinian Arabs to boycott Israeli products, join the armed struggle, and become martyrs in the cause of liberating their holy land of Palestine. What seems like political, military, and economic warfare is also a struggle for honor and self-worth. The psychology of the *intifada* is related to that of the Palestinian Arab refugee families from which the young leaders and rioters of the uprising originate. These family dynamics will be discussed in Chapter 12.

Nationalism, Patriotism, and Ethnocentrism

Nationalism is one of the great afflictions of our species. It has led to terrible human catastrophes. We think of our nationalism as natural, honorable, and admirable. We do not think of it as a disease, nor do we seek to cure ourselves of it (Group for the Advancement of Psychiatry 1987). Healthy identification with our national group must not be confounded with fanatical and pathological fusion with it. The distinction between nationalism, patriotism, and chauvinism raises both a semantic and a psychological problem. The English word *nation* derives from the Latin word *natio* (birth), while the word *patriotism* derives from the Latin word *pater* (father). The Romans called their country *patria*, the Germans call theirs *das Vaterland,* and the French call their country *la patrie* (the fatherland). Nationalism involves the powerful feeling that our own nation is unique, better than other nations, and worth laying down our lives for.

Because our nation is part of our extended self, and plays the unconscious role of our Early Mother, nationalism is in any event an immature feeling by its very nature (Volkan 1979, 1988). The key question involves the nature of the feelings fueling nationalism. It can be argued that the fanatical Palestinian terrorists of the *Islamic Jihad, Hamas,* and *Fatah* who send suicide bombers to kill Israeli civilians suffer from pathological narcissism and a grandiose sense of their selves. National group narcissism—from nationalism, patriotism, and chauvinism to fascism and Nazism—may result from an unconscious displacement of the personal narcissism of each of the individuals belonging to the group onto the national group, and of an identification with the group as a mirror image of one's own grandiose self. After the Six-Day War, when Israel suddenly quadrupled in size, some Israelis personally felt bigger and stronger.

Mack (1983) thought that the emotional hurts and the respective feelings of victimization of the two parties to the Arab-Israeli conflict have played a key role in its becoming chronic. The lack of empathy on both sides is another factor. At the heart of the tragedy lies the refusal of the Arabs to recognize Israel and that of the Israeli leaders to recognize the Palestinians. Each side is fixated on its own historical hurts, losses, and injuries. Our national group is the largest and most abstract of all the groups to which we belong, barring humankind itself. We jealously guard its ethnic and geographic boundaries. Our group-narcissistic myth of election—which most tribes and nations have about themselves—claims that our people are God's chosen one and that we are better than all other peoples on this earth. We Israelis feel that our Holy Land is incomparably more beautiful and glorious than all others. Some of us think that our army is not only the best and strongest in the Middle East but that it is also among the best and strongest in the whole world. Between the Six-Day War of 1967 and the Yom Kippur War of 1973 we felt like a regional power, if not a superpower. The Israel Defense Army—its official name—is the most important, most central, and most sensitive vehicle of our national narcissism and grandiose group self—along with the national flag, the national anthem, the government, and the Knesset. The victories of the Israeli army in the wars of 1948, 1956, and 1967 reinforced our grandiose self.

Nationalism can be viewed as defensive group narcissism. Our national group unconsciously plays the role of the Great Early Mother reflecting our own self. Just as the infant feels its mother as part of itself, and lives in fusion with her, so we all feel ourselves to be part of our nation and vice versa. The big question is the degree of emotional fusion of individuals with their nation. The more one is fixated on one's early emotional development, symbiotically tied to one's early mother, the more one is likely to be a chauvinist, fuse oneself emotionally with one's nation, and idealize its power and glory, just as the little child idealizes its mother or father.

Imagined Communities and Ethnic Tents

Nations are the largest human groups on this planet. Some of them, like China and India, have over a billion members. Are such nations real communities, or psychological entities? Is a nation tangible, or does it exist only in our imagination? Are the national flag, army, anthem, and other national symbols proof of the real existence of the nation?

One American historian has called nations "imagined communities" because they are not communities in the same sense as small local communities and because the creation of a national consciousness requires both the invention of a fantasied past and the repression of the many actual ethnic, sectarian, and linguistic differences of origin of the component peoples of a nation (Anderson 1983, 1991; Loewenberg 1994, p. 8). Indonesia, for example, has fourteen thousand islands, over one hundred languages, five religions, and many different ethnic groups. Making it into one nation required the invention of a mythical common past and the adoption of a Malay trading dialect as Indonesia's national language (Anderson 1991, pp. 120–121). This scholar thought that the profound changes of consciousness required in creating modern national identities were psychologically like childhood amnesia because national groups forgot actual events and invented national myths (Anderson 1991, pp. 204–205).

Peter Loewenberg, a well-known American Jewish psychohistorian, thought that Anderson had overlooked a key psychological fact:

> When all has been said of the fantasied quality of nationalism, what Anderson is overlooking is that affectual context and environment (family socialization), and historical events and traumas ("community of fate"), make familiarity, comfort, and common political allegiance "natural" for people sharing the same historically constructed experience. Anderson's "imagined community" is certainly artificial; but it is also a psychological reality. As Freud discovered and taught us, fantasies are also facts, they are operational data upon which people act and stake their lives. (Loewenberg 1994, p. 9)

Despite his criticism of Anderson's method, Loewenberg followed Anderson's approach, which, he thought, had "much value, but only partial truth." Loewenberg called the United States, Brazil, *and Israel* "synthetic nations." He believed that they were "invented nations, each with an aggressive, self-worshipping and aggrandizing nationalism, and each worthy of special attention, study and interest" (Loewenberg 1994, pp. 8–9). Loewenberg thought that Israel was a synthetic nation because it had brought together Jews from many different countries, cultures, and races to create an artificial national group.

This scholar, however, who thought that Anderson had overlooked a key psychological fact, overlooked one himself: unlike the United States and Brazil, neither of which had an ancient history common to all their diverse people, Israel imagines itself as the natural culmination of over three thousand years of Jewish history. How much of this history is real or imaginary has been the subject of much debate. In this sense, Israel is not a synthetic nor an invented nation, although it is true that Israel, too, has forged a common national identity out of diverse groups of Jews from dozens of cultures with enormous differences between them.

In his pioneering studies of large-group psychology, Vamık Volkan, a Muslim Turkish-Cypriot-born American psychoanalyst, an expert on large-group psychology, coined the term "ethnic tent" (Volkan 1999, 1999a). This tent is made up of a psychological "canvas" that "covers" all the members of an ethnic group and forms their collective identity. Its complex nature is better understood by dividing it into its seven components, the "threads" that make up the canvas: the large group's shared identifications; its shared suitable "reservoirs" for self and object images associated with positive emotions; its absorption of the "bad" qualities of others (unconsciously externalized, projected, and displaced); its absorption of the internal demands of "transforming" leaders; its chosen glories; its chosen traumas; and its formation of symbols that may develop their own autonomy, which he called "proto-symbols" (Volkan 2003, pp. 51–61).

Volkan thought that threats to large-group identity cause the members of the ethnic group to try to fortify their ethnic tent, "to become more preoccupied in repairing the wear and tear in the [ethnic] canvas and maintaining their large group identity. " One of the most obvious threats to large-group identity is the instability of the group's political borders, as in the case of Israel and Palestine. The collective psychological processes that occur in such cases are coexistence, integration, and absorption (Volkan 2003, p. 61). Volkan applied his notions to three countries that he knows well—Israel, Cyprus, and Germany. Citing Loewenberg's questionable characterization of Israel as a synthetic nation, Volkan thought that the three collective processes of coexistence, integration, and absorption are very evident in the case of Israel, whose borders have never been stable nor final (Volkan 2003, p. 62). In the following chapter we shall look at the unconscious meaning of such borders and its effect on the Arab-Israeli conflict.

6

Psychogeography
The Unconscious Meaning of Geographical Entities

It has long been observed that one's country has an unconscious maternal meaning for most people. The French call their country *la patrie* (a feminine noun meaning the fatherland) and personalize their republic as a woman named Marianne. French colonists have called France *la mère patrie* (the mother fatherland). Israeli Jews call their country *moledet* (a Hebrew feminine noun meaning land of birth) and English speakers call theirs the motherland or mother country. In Turkey, a major political party is called *ANAP* (The Motherland). Many people are prepared to die for their motherland, and even the name *America*, with its many maternal connotations, is a feminized version of an Italian explorer's first name (Niederland 1971).

Geopolitical boundaries, borders, frontiers, state lines, and so on also have a special emotional meaning for most people. I have interpreted the unconscious meaning of geopolitical borders as symbols of internal boundaries such as the incest taboo and the boundaries of the self (Falk 1974, 1983, 1987). Large groups such as nations need psychological boundaries to maintain their group self and psychological existence (Volkan 2003). Other aspects of our physical world, such as rivers, lakes, oceans, mountains, and cities all have unconscious emotional meanings and are often conceived of in human terms such as the "mouth" of the river. The discovery of the hidden meanings of these entities has led to the development of a special field of applied psychoanalysis called psychogeography, the unconscious meaning of geographical entities.

This chapter summarizes these findings and discusses the psychological significance of the perennially fluid boundaries between Israel and Palestine.

Like beauty and truth, politics, history, and geography are also in the eye of the beholder. Our lives are a vast *Rashomon* story. East and West are relative terms depending on where you stand. Several scholars have noted the extraordinary power of our unconscious feelings and fantasies about the geographical entities in which we live—our countries, cities, lakes, rivers, mountains, and borders, which are often construed in terms of the human body—including its intimate sexual parts—and have interpersonal symbolism (Stein 1987; Stein & Niederland 1989). These are called *psychogeographical fantasies*.

The psychogeographical issue of land is crucial to the Arab-Israeli conflict. In a tiny area like the Holy Land of Israel and Palestine, with its complicated history dating backs several thousand years, every square inch of land seems to have enormous emotional significance, and the attachment to the motherland has the emotional qualities of a yearning for an idealized Early Mother. Most people in Israel and in the rest of the world treat the Palestinian Arab territories of the West Bank and Gaza Strip, inhabited by millions of Palestinian Arabs and by some two hundred thousand Israeli Jewish settlers, as under foreign occupation by Israel. The Palestinian Arabs themselves call those territories *Falastin,* and to some of them this term includes all of Israel as well. Ironically, like "Palestine," the Arabic name *Falastin* (also pronounced *Filastin* or *Filistin*) derives from the Biblical Hebrew name for the ancient Philistines, an ethnic group that had nothing in common with the Arabs, while the Hebrew name *Israel* comes from the Canaanite Hebrew "El shall reign," El being the ancient father-god of the polytheistic Canaanites. Many far-right Israeli Jewish nationalists and religious fanatics, however, including Israeli Prime Minister Ariel Sharon, claim that these territories—which they call Judea, Samaria and Gaza—are not "occupied" at all, because they belong by historical and juridical right to the Israeli Jews.

Saracens, Moors, and other Psychoethnic Fantasies

History and geography are in the mind of the beholder, and so are the names that ethnic groups give one another. The ancient Romans called any member of the nomadic tribes on the Syrian borders of their empire *saracenus*. During the middle ages, the European Christians, especially the Crusaders, used the same name, Saracens, for all the non-Christian peoples of the East, lumping together Arabs, Persians, Turks, and Muslims of all kinds. As late as 1575, when the great Italian poet Torquato Tasso (1544–1595) wrote his epic poem *La Gerusalemme liberata* (Jerusalem Liberated) about the crusades, he still used the word *saraceni* for the Arabs. Tasso's Tancredi, the Crusader prince, unknowingly kills his lover, the Saracen princess Clorinda.

Another example is the English name Moors for the North African invaders of Spain. The English word Moor derives from the Middle English More, which comes from the Old French Maure, which derives from the Latin *maurus*, which comes from the Greek *mauros*. The ancient Romans gave the name *mauri* to the inhabitants of their North African province of Mauretania, in what are now Algeria and Morocco. In the Middle Ages the Spanish Christians gave the name *moros* to their Muslim conquerors from North Africa. Modern Mauritanians are called *maures* in French, but the modern Islamic Republic of Mauritania lies in another geographical area than the ancient Roman province of Mauretania—in the Sahara desert, between Morocco, Senegal, and Mali.

We can see how the names that ethnic groups give one another are the product of their own imagination. The ancient Greeks called anyone who could not speak their language *barbaros*—the origin of the word "barbarian"—because he sounded to them as if he were repeatedly saying "bar, bar . . ." The Slavic peoples call the Germans *niemci*, meaning "mute," because the Germans could not speak their language. The medieval Arabs called all the European Christians *franji* well after the Franks had ceased to exist as an ethnic or political entity, whereas the medieval Christians used the old Latin name *saracens* for all Muslims, Arabs, Persians, Turks—anyone who was Middle Eastern, foreign, strange, non-European, and non-Christian.

Many fundamentalist Muslims, and many ordinary Arabs today, wish to restore what they see as the glory of their lost empire. From 1361 to 1541 the Muslim Ottoman Turks, originating in central Asia, conquered the entire Byzantine empire, the Arab world, and the Muslim caliphate. In 1492, after more than seven centuries of Spanish Christian *reconquista*, the Moors—Muslim Arabs and Berbers from North Africa—were finally defeated and driven back to Africa by the Spanish Christians. The Moors had ruled *Al-Andalus*—the Arabic name for Muslim Spain—for almost eight centuries. The name *Al-Andalus* is an Arabic corruption of the Roman name for the Vandals, a Germanic people that had sacked the Roman provinces of Gaul and Spain in the early fifth century C.E., crossed from Spain to Africa—the reverse direction from the later crossing of the Moors—maintained a kingdom in North Africa from 429 to 534 and sacked Rome in 455. In the West, vandalism has remained a synonym for willful desecration or destruction.

The Moorish elements of Muslim Spain were native North African Berbers converted to Islam by the conquering Arabs in the seventh century. The Spanish Catholics called them *moros*. The year 1492 was a historical watershed for the Spanish Catholics, Muslims, and Jews. After the Spanish Catholic king Fernando and his wife Isabel had succeeded in completing seven centuries of *reconquista* and driving the Moors out of Spain, they also expelled the Spanish Jews. Facing religious persecution and death at the hands of the Inquisition, some Muslims and Jews force-converted to Christianity. The Muslim Moors who converted to Catholicism were derogatorily called *moriscos* (Little Moors), while the Jews who converted to Catholicism—as early as the mid-fifteenth-century—were abusively called *marranos* (an obscure word probably meaning "pigs") (Netanyahu 1966; Lea 1968; Webb 1980; Chejne 1983).

Like many Muslim immigrants in present-day Europe, the *moriscos* had great trouble assimilating into Spanish Christian society. From 1609 to 1614 some 300,000 *moriscos* were expelled from Spain, settling in North Africa, from which their ancestors had come, but there they were tragically considered Christians and were discriminated against by the Muslim majority. Most of the *marranos* secretly practiced their Jewish faith. Many *marranos* eventually emigrated from Spain to North Africa and to the Ottoman empire; others emigrated to Western European countries (Falk 1996, pp. 507–522).

While to most Iberian Jews their expulsion from Spain in 1492 (and from Portugal in 1497) was a traumatic catastrophe and rude awakening, sparking a new wave of reality-based Jewish historiography (Yerushalmi 1982, pp. 53–57), most Arabs and Muslims seem to have reacted the opposite way, escaping into fantasies of the glorious past (Laroui 1976). Many Arabs could not mourn their losses or accept the blow to their collective narcissism, and they have been denying their great historical losses ever since. Many believe that during their Golden Era, which coincided with the European Dark Ages, they ruled a great empire comprising the entire Middle East, North Africa, and Spain from the seventh to the fifteenth century. The Arabs also believe that they were the world's leading mathematicians, physicians, and artists. In reality the medieval "Arab" empire was Islamic rather than Arab, as many parts of it were non-Arab. Moreover, this "empire" was far from united. There were perennial wars between tribes, clans, sects, and dynasties in the Muslim world. Several caliphates—in Baghdad, Cairo, and Córdoba—vied with one another for control, while several clans and dynasties assassinated one another to take control of these caliphates.

White Moors and New Moors

Like history, geography, and politics, ethnicity, too, is in the eye of the beholder. The medieval Moors were Arabized North African Berbers force-converted by the conquering Muslim Arabs to Islam. While the monotheistic Jews and Christians were not force-converted by the Muslims, who called them "the people of the book" and let them keep their religions, they were treated as second-class *dhimmi* (protected people) and forced to pay special taxes and special reverences to the Muslims. The Berbers, however, were polytheistic descendants of the ancient people whom the Romans called "Numidians." The Arabs called them *qaba'il*, meaning "tribes," hence the name Kabyle. The name *Berber* derives from the Arabic version of the the the Greek word *barbara* (one who could not speak Greek), but the Berbers' own name for themselves, *imazighen*, means "free and noble men." They had been practicing a religion involving the worship of numerous saints and their tombs (a practice still common among North African Jews and Muslims). The Muslim Arabs force-converted the Berbers to Islam and imposed their culture and language on them. Within less than a century, some of the Arabized and Islamized Berbers became the conquerors of Spain.

The French now call their Christian converts to Islam *les Maures blancs* (White Moors). This appellation originates in the former French African colony of Mauritania, where the Arabized Berbers called *les Maures blancs* or *Beydanes* dominate the *Maures noirs* (Black Moors) and *négro-Mauritaniens*. The name *Maures blancs* has taken on a new meaning in France. In late 2001, after *Al-Qaeda*'s suicide terrorists flew their hijacked planes into New York's World Trade Center and destroyed it along with some three thousand innocent lives, some French converts to Islam joined a militant French Muslim group plotting to blow up the U.S. Embassy in Paris. When American journalists interviewed French police officials about these plotters, they were told that there were *Maures blancs* among them (Hedges 2001; Erlanger & Hedges 2001). "The plotters, " the officials said, "were students, fathers and delinquents. Some came from middle-class households that embraced modernity. Many grew up in Europe and did not even speak Arabic. There were converts to Islam, called 'white Moors.' Others came from the underclass in the Middle East that found its solace in militant Islam" (Hedges 2001).

Nancy Kobrin (2003, p.157) coined the term "New Moors" to denote the modern Western converts to fanatical Islam and *jihad*. This psycho-analytic scholar made much of the psychological meaning of *Al-Andalus* to the Muslims (Kobrin 2003, p. 176). As we have seen, the Arabic name *Al-Andalus*, which the medieval Moors had given to Spain when they ruled it, derived from the fifth-century Germanic tribe of the Vandals, who had overrun Rome and its western province of Hispania, then crossed the Straits of Gibraltar into North Africa—the reverse direction from that traveled by the Moors themselves when they conquered Spain in the early eighth century, and the same direction they would take in the late fifteenth century after they were driven out of Spain by the Spanish Christians. The name Gibraltar derived from the Arabic *Jibl al-Tariq* (Mount Tariq) after the Berber conqueror Tariq ibn Ziyad, who invaded Spain from Morocco in 711 c.e. and conquered Toledo and most of Spain during the next four years (Falk 1996, p. 387). Ironically, Tariq did so at the request of the two sons of the Visigothic king of Spain, Witiza, who died in 710 c.e. Rather than let Witiza's sons assume the crown, the Visigothic nobles had elected as their new king a duke named Rodericus or Rodrigo, dispossessing Witiza's two orphan sons. These sons, enraged at being dispossessed and disinherited, appealed for military help to the Moroccan Muslims, thus precipitating the Muslim conquest of Spain.

In her study of the New Moors, this psychoanalyst pointed out the unconscious Good Mother aspects of *Al-Andalus* in the Muslim convert's mind, as opposed to the depriving and ungiving Bad Mother aspects of the Arabian desert:

> The loss of Al Andalus is *as if* the Muslim group self has experienced the sudden untimely death of its good nurturing mother represented by the psychogeography of Spain. She is repeatedly described as a blissful lush paradise—the garden of delights. . . . It is as if the Moors felt that they had been orphaned, cast back into the unforgiving desert of the Maghreb without provisions or supplies, left to starve to death. A preexisting [Koranic] theme of the desert's unforgiving deprivation has been noted. . . . It re-enforces the group self's fear. It

> also contributes to and compounds its own communal rage. . . .
> Conversion is the psychological hunt for the long lost early
> good mother. (Kobrin 2003, pp. 176–177)

The conquest of Spain by the Moors was not only due to their invitation by the disinherited Visigothic kings. In yet another psychogeographical fantasy, the Muslims had split their world into two opposing parts: the good *Dar al-Islam*—House of Islam, and the bad *Dar al-Harb* or *Dar al-Kufr*—House of War or House of Unbelief, inhabited by the infidels. This fantasy, which was due to the unconscious infantile splitting of the world into all-good and all-bad parts, has characterized most human religions and cultures. Islam made it the duty of all Muslims to expand the *Dar al-Islam* at the expense of the *Dar al-Harb*—that is, to convert the infidel to Islam, either by conviction or by force.

> Like every other civilization known to human history, the
> Muslim world in its heyday saw itself as the center of truth
> and enlightenment, surrounded by infidel barbarians whom it
> would in due course enlighten and civilize. But between the
> different groups of barbarians there was a crucial difference.
> The barbarians to the east and the south were polytheists and
> idolaters, offering no serious threat and no competition at all
> to Islam. In the north and west, in contrast, Muslims from an
> early date recognized a genuine rival—a competing world re-
> ligion, a distinctive civilization inspired by that religion, and
> an empire that, though much smaller than theirs, was no less
> ambitious in its claims and aspirations. This was the entity
> known to itself and others as Christendom, a term that was
> long almost identical with Europe. (Lewis 1990, p. 49)

Therefore, the Muslims set out to conquer Christian Europe, and their invitation by the sons of the Visigothic king in 710 gave them the opening. Their sights were set on all of Europe. Less than 20 years after Tariq ibn Ziyad had taken Spain, Abd ar-Rahman, the Muslim governor of Córdoba, advanced on west-central France. In 732 he was defeated between Tours and Poitiers by the Frankish Christian leader Carolus Martellus (Charles Martel, or Charles the Hammer, 688–741), the "mayor of the palace" of the eastern Frankish kingdom of Austrasia. While some historians regard the battle of Poitiers as a minor skirmish, Charles Martel united the entire Frankish realm and stemmed the Muslim invasion. There were no further Muslim invasions of Frankish territory, and Charles's victory has often been regarded as decisive for world history, since it preserved western Europe from Muslim conquest and Islamization.

The Muslims ruled large parts of Spain from the eighth to the fifteenth centuries, but their great Islamic empire was lost forever when the Spaniards drove the Moors out of Spain in 1492, and they have not been able to mourn its loss properly. Many Arabs still wish to turn back the historical clock and restore the medieval Arab glory, and are searching for the elusive Arab unity. All over the world, fanatical Muslims are plotting to destroy America and re-establish the glory of Islam. The Arabs have similarly been unable or unwilling to accept their defeats by Israel and to mourn their losses, unconsciously inventing all kinds of excuses and pretexts for their defeat, which some scholars have called myths, and which are known in psychoanalysis as rationalizations (Davis 1981; Bard 2001).

Lewis thought that the rage of the Muslims against the West had deep historical roots. The struggle between Islam and Christendom has lasted 14 centuries and is still being waged. During the first millennium of this struggle Islam was mostly victorious. They ruled not only most of Spain but also large parts of southeastern Europe. But in 1492 the Muslim Moors were ousted from Spain, and in 1683 the Muslim Ottomans were driven out of Eastern Europe. These two humiliations have been etched into Muslim consciousness and have fueled Muslim rage (Lewis 1990). In fact, while the Ottoman defeat at Vienna in 1683 marked the beginning of the end of Ottoman domination in Eastern Europe, it took Prince Eugene of Savoy and the Habsburgs of Austria until 1699 to get a treaty with the Ottomans that cost the latter some territory, and the Ottomans ruled large parts of the Balkans until the twentieth century.

The defeat of the Ottomans at Vienna in 1683 was especially galling to the Muslims. Acting on an appeal from the Hungarian Calvinists to attack the Austrian Habsburg capital of Vienna, the Ottoman grand vizier, Kara Mustafa (1634–1683), and his army of 150,000 laid siege to Vienna after capturing its outer fortifications. Fearing no less than the fall of Christian Europe to the Muslims, Pope Innocent XI, "the Blessed" (1611–1689), convinced Poland's King Jan III Sobieski (1629–1696) to lead a combined Catholic army of 80,000 to relieve the siege. Aided by the young Catholic duke of Lorraine and Bar, Charles IV Leopold (1643–1690), Sobieski led the attack from the surrounding hills and after a pitched 15-hour battle drove the Ottomans from their trenches around the city. Thousands of Ottoman soldiers were slaughtered or taken prisoner. Charles of Lorraine pursued the Ottomans east into Hungary and drove them back to Turkey. The event marked the beginning of the decline of Ottoman Turkish domination in Eastern Europe and the second point in the decline of Muslim civilization and power after the Spanish expulsion of the Moors in 1492. Chapter 10 looks at the debate between three prominent scholars—Bernard Lewis, Samuel P. Huntington, and Edward William Said—about the conflict between Islam and the West.

7

Denial Is Not a River in Egypt

The Americans, who have made psychoanalytic terms part of their language, often say, "I am in denial." Back in 1935 the American comedian Jimmy Durante (1893–1980) stopped the show in Billy Rose's popular stage musical *Jumbo* with a blatant example of denial. Playing a bankrupt circus owner who tries to escape his creditors, Durante was leading a live elephant away from the circus when he was stopped by a policeman. "Where are you going with that elephant?" demanded the cop. Durante looked askance and bellowed, "What elephant?" This blatant denial of reality struck a deep chord in the unconscious emotions of his delighted viewers.

Unconscious denial is common in everyday life. We often deny the painful aspects of both our outer reality and our inner feelings. In interethnic conflict, we deny the humanity and suffering of our enemies and demonize them. This makes it easier for us to fight them, hurt them, or kill them as part of the conflict, which we rationalize in terms of the public good and sublime ideals. This chapter analyzes the development of unconscious denial in our very early lives and its evolution into massive, large-scale denial in interethnic conflict.

People unconsciously tend to deny both their outer reality and their inner reality—their own emotions—especially when these are painful or scary. In 1983 an Austrian-born Israeli psychiatrist and his two American colleagues organized an international conference on denial in Jerusalem, the best papers from which they later published (Edelstein, Nathanson, and Stone 1989). Reality, however, is not a clear-cut matter. We have seen the enormous differences between the psychological realities of the Israeli Jews and Palestinian Arabs. Each side seems to live in its own reality, to deny the reality of the other, to be unable to see the world from the other's viewpoint, and to be able to see it only from his own. The history of the conflict from the late nineteenth century to the present day indicates that this was due to a massive and continual denial of reality on both sides. Let us examine some instances of this denial.

The early Jewish Zionists in the 1890s did not take seriously the Arab question in Ottoman Palestine. Most of them denied the reality of the Arab population of Palestine. The favorite Zionist catch phrase was "a land without a people for a people without a land" (Zangwill 1901, p. 627). Like their ancestors for many centuries, they regarded the neglected backwater of Palestine, which was part of the Ottoman province of Syria, as the Land of the Jews, calling it by the Hebrew name of *Erets Yisrael* (the Land of Israel). This name implied that Palestine was the ancient Land of the Jews, that it did not harbor hundreds of thousands of non-Jewish Arabs. The early Zionists were astonishingly blind to the existence of the Arabs. Eager to see Palestine as the promised Jewish homeland, they did not wish to see its demographic realities. Even today, some Israeli maps show the West Bank and Gaza as part of the territory of the state of Israel (Laqueur 1972, pp. 209–210).

On the other side of the fence, as the Palestinian Arabs initially denied the political and demographic danger that Jewish immigration to Palestine posed to them, they have similarly denied the political existence of Israel and its military might since it became a state in 1948. To this day, most maps of Palestine in Arab schools, libraries, and government offices do not show Israel at all. The name Palestine is written across the entire area between the Jordan River and the Mediterranean Sea. Most Arab governments refer to the Israeli government in Jerusalem as "the Zionist government of Tel-Aviv." The massive denial of Israel's military power and the wishful thinking that Israel is a transitory state has cost the Arabs many military defeats, losses, and humiliations.

Denial is an unconscious defense that we develop in our infancy. The baby shuts its eyes to anything unpleasant that it does not wish to see. It imagines that what it does not see does not exist. This process persists into adulthood. The denial of reality was current not only among the early Jewish Zionists but also among some nineteenth-century Christian Zionists. For example, the English pre-Raphaelite painter William Holman Hunt (1827–1910) visited Palestine in 1854 and 1855 to seek inspiration for his religious illustrations of the life of Jesus Christ. Hunt believed that the Arabs should be "the natural drawers of water and hewers of wood" for the Jews, just as the Biblical Gibeonites had been for the Israelites (Joshua 9). It was therefore unnecessary for the Zionists to displace the Arabs from Palestine. "They don't even have to be dis-possessed, for they would render the Jews very useful services," wrote Hunt. The Arabs could do all the menial labor and serve the Chosen People. Arab-Jewish relations would be fine when each side knew its place (Hunt 1905–1906; Coombs et al. 1986; Elon 1975, p. 179).

The founder of modern political Zionism, Theodor Herzl (1860–1904), imagined Palestine as an orderly, beautiful, cultured, lush green land like Austria or Switzerland, with German as its official language and a Central European way of life. Unconsciously, Palestine, the Land of Milk and Honey, was Herzl's idealized mother, just as a baby imagines his mother's breasts to be endlessly bountiful, or as the ancient Romans imagined their cornucopia. When Herzl visited Jerusalem in 1898 to see the German emperor, Wilhelm II (1859–1941), he was so appalled by the poor and dirty sight of Jerusalem that he wanted to tear down the entire filthy city and replace it with a new one patterned after Vienna (Herzl 1960, pp. 745–746; Falk 1993, p. 352).

From a psychoanalytic viewpoint, these psychogeographical fanta-sies betrayed the powerful denial and idealization that propelled them. Before creating political Zionism at a time of deep crisis and despair in his personal life, Herzl had had fantasies of solving the Jewish question in Austria by fighting duels with its anti-Semitic leaders, such as Georg von Schönerer (1842–1921), Karl Lueger (1844–1910), and Aloys von Liechtenstein (1846–1920), or by leading the Jews into mass conversion to Christianity in Vienna's *Stephansdom* (St. Stephen's Cathedral). On a deeper personal level, each fantasy unconsciously represented another "solution" to Herzl's fusional relationship with his domineering and engulfing mother, with Herzl himself symbolized by the Jews and his impossible mother by Christian Europe (Falk 1993, p. 90).

Other early Jewish Zionists were obsessed with turning semiarid Palestine into a green land of plenty. Herzl himself preferred to stay in Vienna, except when forced into a brief visit to Palestine in 1898 to see the German emperor. The First Zionist Congress took place in Basel, Switzerland, in July 1897. In April 1898 the Zionist Executive, the gov-erning body of the Zionist Organization, dispatched the 30-year-old Leo Motzkin (1867–1933), one of the early Russian Jewish Zionist leaders, to Ottoman Palestine to investigate the conditions of the handful of Jews then living there. Motzkin had visited Palestine six months before Herzl. From Palestine, Motzkin wrote the Zionist Executive that the most fer-tile parts of the land were settled by 650,000 Arabs, that there was con-siderable tension between them and the handful of Palestinian Jews, and that innumerable violent confrontations between Jews and Arabs had already taken place in Palestine. Motzkin added, however, that the number of Palestinian Arabs had not been verified, and that Palestine was a colorful mixture of desert, tourism, pilgrims, East, and West. In fact, Motzkin had exaggerated both the number of violent confrontations and his idyllic portrait of Palestine. Despite his accounts of violence in Palestine, both he and other Zionist envoys wished to believe that the Jews had nothing to fear in their land (Laqueur, 1972, p. 211).

Like the Christian idea of Ottoman Palestine as the Holy Land of Jesus Christ, the Zionist belief that Ottoman Palestine was the Land of Israel was wishful thinking. It was a belief in the right of the Jews to the Land of Israel, yet it led the Zionists to act as if in fact that land was really theirs. In 1898 this was, to say the least, exaggerated, if not downright fantastic. Some of the early Zionists thought that if the Christian Arabs of Palestine were anti-Zionists, the Muslim Arabs were potentially friendly. They ignored the warnings of the German Jewish Zionist envoy Arthur Ruppin (1876–1943) and other Jews in Palestine who argued that the Muslim Arabs were more hostile to the Jews than the Christian ones.

Until 1933, however, most European Jewish Zionists remained in Europe, whence they could imagine faraway Palestine as they wished. Adopting ancient Biblical Hebrew terms, they called their immigration to Palestine *aliyah* (ascent), as if Palestine were some heavenly land, set above all other countries. This idea of *aliyah* reminds the psychologically oriented observer of the way a little infant looks up at its huge mother, set high above it. During the first *aliyah*, from 1881 to 1904, no more than a few hundred (mostly Russian) Jews came to Palestine. The second *aliyah*, from 1905 to 1914, brought 40,000 Jews to Ottoman Palestine, but there was a great turnover among them, as many went back to Russia or left for America.

One of the early Jewish Zionists who settled in Palestine during the second *aliyah* was Dr. Elias Auerbach (1882–1971), a young German Jewish physician. In 1909 Auerbach founded the first Palestinian Jewish hospital in the Palestinian Arab port city of Haifa, which opened in 1911. A greater realist than his colleagues, Auerbach wrote in 1910 that the Arabs owned Palestine by virtue of their being the majority there, and that they would remain Palestine's owners because of their natural population increase. When the Great War broke out in 1914, Auerbach returned to his German fatherland to serve in its army medical corps. In 1931 Auerbach wrote that it had been a fatal Zionist error to ignore the

Arabs at the outset, but added that even had the Zionists taken the Arabs into account, it would not have changed matters, because the Arabs were hostile to the Jews in Palestine and would remain hostile no matter how nicely the Jews treated them (Auerbach 1910, 1912, 1969; Laqueur 1972, pp. 213–214).

The Zionist denial of the reality of the Palestinian Arabs was a pathological defensive unconscious process, and we Israelis have paid a very tragic price for it—over 20,000 of our young men killed during the interminable Arab-Israeli wars, hundreds of innocent victims murdered by Palestinian Arab suicide bombers, hundreds of thousands of us wounded, maimed, crippled, widowed, orphaned, bereft of our children, and traumatized. When the Arabs reacted with rage and violence to the Zionists' ignoring them and attempting to build a Jewish homeland in what they regarded as their country, the idealistic and self-righteous Zionist settlers became enraged and violent in their turn at this Arab assault, which seemed to them so utterly vicious and unjustified.

Many Israeli and Jewish scholars believe that the Arabs would never have accepted a Jewish state in Palestine, whatever the Zionist empathy for their feelings or lack of it. Yet some Arab states—Egypt, Jordan, and the Palestinian Authority—have grudgingly recognized Israel, whereas Israel has so far rejected the formal creation of a Palestinian state. As a result of the mutual lack of recognition and empathy, a violent, murderous conflict has been raging between Israelis and Arabs for over a century. In fact, many of us Israelis still tend to deny the reality of the Arabs and of their deep hostility for us. This is obvious in the "Jordan is Palestine" fantasies of the extreme right-wing Israeli political parties that wish to transfer the Palestinian Arabs to Jordan (Sprinzak 1991).

The Zionist denial of reality was by no means the only cause of the Arab-Israeli conflict. Already in the 1970s, Abdallah al-Arawi (Laroui), an astute Moroccan Arab scholar, pointed out the extreme distortions of reality in Arab historiography and the inability of the Arabs to adapt to modern culture (Laroui 1974, 1976, 1987, 1999). Classical Arab historiography was permeated with Islamic religious thought, its seeming objectivity and emotional neutrality masking an inability to comprehend the past in its historical continuity and complexity. Every event of Arab history had to conform with the sayings of the Prophet and no event existed in its own right. It was only a matter of time, the Muslims believed, until the entire world became *Dar al-Islam*. This classical religious distortion was compounded by a modern nationalistic and ideological

Arab historiographic tendentiousness, which attempts to ascribe all Arab failures, defeats, losses, and humiliations to the diabolical plots of the colonialist nations. Fanatic Islamists still fervently believe in these notions. From our Western viewpoint, then, classical Arab historiography betrays massive denial and idealization.

Most scholars of the Arab world and Islam think that the Muslims and Arabs have had considerable psychological difficulty adapting themselves to modern Western culture, which is dominated by European-American, Christian, scientific, and technological values. These scholars speak of a bitter and extended clash of civilizations between traditional Muslim Arab culture and Christian Western culture (Laroui 1976; Tibi 1981; Ajami 1981; Rahman 1982; Tibi 1988; Lewis 1990; Ahmed 1992; Ahmed & Donnan 1994; Viorst 1994; Hanif 1997; Ewing 1997; Khuri 1998; Cooper et al. 1998; Rejwan 1998; Khundmiri 2001; Viorst 2001; Lewis 2002; Malik 2003; Berry 2003). The Palestinian-American scholar Edward William Said, however, has derided this view as "the clash of ignorance" (Said 2001).

Another Arab-American scholar, however, and his Pakistani Muslim colleague thought that because the Arabs and Muslims have suffered many humiliations in their conflict with the West in general and with the Israeli Jews in particular, they have a deep-seated and painful sense of inferiority and failure (Ajami 1981; Ahmad 1998). One way to deal with this pain is to deny the reality of the dominant culture or to make endless war on it, as the Islamic extremists of *Al-Qaeda* have been doing. By thinking of the Americans as the medieval Crusaders and of themselves as Saladin's medieval warriors, these fanatics manage to believe that *ansar al-Islam* (victory of Islam) over the Christian infidel is only a matter of time and patience. In fact, one of the major Islamic terrorist groups in Iraqi Kurdistan is called *Ansar al-Islam.* Despite Saddam Hussein's gassing of their fellow Kurds at Halabja, *Ansar al-Islam* supported the Iraqi tyrant as a great hero, along with Saladin and Nasser, and continued to fight for him even after his capture by the "infidel invaders and occupiers."

In Chapter 10 we shall discuss in some detail the aspects of Arab and Muslim culture and psychology which have made it so hard for the Arabs and Muslims to accept the realities of their modern world.

8

Splitting, Projection, and the Need for Enemies

Having discussed the pervasive and pernicious role of denial in the Arab-Israeli conflict, I now turn, in this chapter, to the other unconscious defensive processes operating in interethnic conflict: splitting, projection, projective identification, and externalization. Tragically, Zionist ideology, which led to the creation of the Jewish state of Israel, also involved these infantile and pathological defensive psychological processes, which distorted external reality and contributed to the Palestinian Jews' prolonged and tragic conflict with the Arabs. Zionism's success at altering Jewish political reality by creating the Jewish community of Palestine and later establishing the Jewish state of Israel came at a very high cost. Let's look at these pathological unconscious processes.

Unconscious Splitting and Projective Identification

After the tragic destruction of the Twin Towers of New York's World Trade Center by suicidal *Al-Qaeda* terrorists on September 11, 2001—a tragedy that the Americans, perhaps not only for brevity's sake but also to alleviate their painful feelings about it, refer to as "9/11"—President George W. Bush declared his "crusade" on terrorism. Bush told all the world's leaders, "You're either for us or against us," and denounced the "Axis of Evil" consisting of Iraq, Iran, and North Korea. The United States of America, obviously, was the "Axis of Good." The American Jewish psychoanalyst John Mack thought that Bush's declaration, "This is a war of good against evil," expressed his infantile dualistic thinking no less than the Iranian ayatollahs' war cry, "We must destroy America, the Great Satan," expressed theirs (Mack 2002, p. 177).

Bush's black-and-white thinking has made him commit tragic errors. His former anti-terrorism adviser, Richard Clarke, has claimed that he had resigned his post in early 2003 in order to protest the fact that from January to September 2001 Bush and his National Security Adviser had ignored his warnings about the urgency of the *Al-Qaeda* threat and focused on the much less urgent one of Saddam's non-existent "weapons of mass destruction" (Clarke 2004). Clarke himself, however, has been described as having a "dual personality" (Ripley 2004).

Indeed, without being aware of it, the most powerful man in the world, U.S. president George W. Bush, has treated his world as an infant treats his. A baby is unable to integrate within himself his good experience of his nurturing mother with his bad experience of the same mother when she is unavailable to him. This creates an inner chaos of sensations and feelings and raises the anxiety of the infant to unbearable levels. To defend against this inner chaos and anxiety, the infant unconsciously splits his mother—that is, his whole world—into an all-good and an all-bad part. This is the psychological origin of fairy tales like *Snow White*, in which the heroine has two mothers, one all-good, the other all-bad.

In 1976 the 30-year-old George W. Bush was arrested for driving under the influence of alcohol in Midland, Texas, where his father, George Herbert Walker Bush, had settled and started his oil business. He was tried and convicted of drunken driving, yet went on drinking for another ten years. He claims to have stopped and to have become a born-again Christian on his 40th birthday in 1986. (We shall discuss the relation of rebirth fantasies to violence, death, and suicide in Chapter 11.) Age 40 is often a time of crisis in the life of a man. Bush's black-and-white thinking is an unconscious defense against anxiety and emotional trouble. It is the pernicious unconscious process of *splitting* that Czech president Václav Havel, in an address to the United States Congress on February 21, 1990, called "the antiquated straitjacket of the bipolar view of the world" (Havel 1997), and what Mack (2002) has called "dualistic thinking."

Shortly after the terrible tragedy of September 11, 2001, the Indian writer and political activist Arundhati Roy had this to say about George W. Bush and Osama bin Laden:

But who is Osama bin Laden really? Let me rephrase that. What is Osama bin Laden? He's America's family secret. He is the American president's dark *Doppelgänger*. The savage twin of all that purports to be beautiful and civilized. . . . Now Bush and Bin Laden have even begun to borrow each other's rhetoric. Each refers to the other as "the head of the snake." Both invoke God and use the loose millenarian currency of good and evil as their terms of reference. Both are engaged in unequivocal political crimes. Both are dangerously armed—one with the nuclear arsenal of the obscenely powerful, the other with the incandescent, destructive power of the utterly hopeless. The fireball and the ice pick. The bludgeon and the axe. The important thing to keep in mind is that neither is an acceptable alternative to the other. (Roy 2001, p. 2)

The prominent Palestinian-American scholar Edward William Said made a similar point. A few weeks after the tragedy of September 11th, this Christian Arab intellectual pointed out that the spectacularly destructive acts of Osama bin Laden's *Al-Qaeda* had mirror images in the spectacularly self-destructive acts of esoteric cults like the Branch Davidians of Waco, Texas, the disciples of the Reverend Jim Jones in Guyana, and the Aum Shinrikyo cult in Japan (Said 2001, p. 12). Calling the September 11th tragedy "the carefully planned and horrendous, pathologically motivated suicide attack and mass slaughter by a small group of deranged militants," Said called the mass-murderous act of Osama bin Laden's *Al-Qaeda* "the capture of big ideas . . . by a tiny band of crazed fanatics for criminal purposes." Instead of seeing it for what it was, however, Said complained that "international luminaries . . . have pontificated about Islam's troubles" and used the tragedy to confirm the dubious theories of the American political scientist Samuel P. Huntington (1993) about "the clash of civilizations." In Said's view, one of the worst offenders was the Italian prime minister Silvio Berlusconi, who used Huntington's ideas "to rant about the West's superiority" to Islam (Said 2001, p. 12).

The crucial psychological point—that Western culture is not all-good, that Islamic culture is not all-bad, and that George W. Bush unconsciously sees the unacceptable parts of his own self in Osama bin Laden—was strikingly illustrated (perhaps unintentionally and unwittingly) by a clever photo-montage circulated on the Internet in 2002, shortly after the beginning of Bush's war on bin Laden's *Al-Qaeda* and

the Afghan *Taliban*. The picture was variously titled "George W. Bush Goes Undercover to Find Osama" or "Bush Undercover in Afghanistan," and showed the President disguised as Osama bin Laden.

The same point was made again in February 2003, as the United States was preparing itself and the rest of the world for war on Iraq. A pair of American psychotherapists posted an open letter to their president on the Internet. Upset about the upcoming war in particular, and about President Bush's emotional health in general, these two mental-health professionals pointed out Bush's unconscious splitting and projection:

Every day that passes someone in your administration reminds us that some person or some other country is evil. Using language such as the Axis of Evil comes from a part of us that sees us as being good and living lives of righteousness and all darkness as living "out there" in the world. That part of us doesn't realize that each of us has darkness and evil—as well as good—within. It doesn't realize that the battle on the outside is a reflection of the battle that we all must wage within our own souls. We are less concerned about the issue of whether we go to war than we are about the issue of what parts of you and what parts of Mr. Rumsfeld are moving us towards this war. What we hear from your core administrative group is a constant barrage of emotionally charged judgments of others. *In psychological terms, you are disowning your own evil and projecting it out onto the world around you* [italics added]. This makes us more and more distrustful of your judgment, and makes us wonder about which selves are operating in you in such an "automatic pilot" kind of thinking and reacting. This is having a terrible effect on much of the world. It pulls forth an equal and opposite reaction in others. The more they look evil to you, the more you look evil to them. It is a mathematical relationship. It is evenly balanced. It is a recipe for disaster! (Stone & Stone 2003)

Did these "thoughtful, professional, competent" psychotherapists, as they called themselves in the preamble to their letter, delude themselves that their letter would have a psychological effect on George W. Bush or a political effect on his administration? As they could have known, open letters, however well-intentioned, thoughtful, and sincere, cannot modify psychological defenses. These can only be modified in psychotherapy—if the patient seeks psychotherapy, wants to change, and has the ego strength and psychological mindedness required to deal with the anxiety in the process. Politicians, however, whose key psychological defenses are usually splitting and projection, rarely seek psychotherapy. The psychotherapists' key point, at any rate, was that the self-righteous Bush unconsciously splits off the unacceptable and disowned parts of his own self-image and projects it upon the master terrorist Osama bin Laden—whom Bush hates with a passion, but who mirrors Bush's dark side. The same point had been made in a literary way by Roy (2001, p. 3), when she called bin Laden "the American president's dark *Doppelgänger*."

How did George W. Bush become the severe, self-righteous black-and-white-thinking judge and policeman of the world that he is? An

American magazine article (Fineman et al. 2003) examined Bush's born-again religious faith and noted that he was "a quick-to-judge son of a quick-to-judge mother." On April 4, 2003, when George's mother, Barbara Pierce Bush, was a guest speaker at Ohio's Ashland University, she said that as she watched her son "guide our country through this very difficult time," she could not help but wonder, "Is this the same kid I used to spank?" (Schechter 2003).

Perhaps those who need to be born-again were not born by the right mother the first time around. One American Jewish scholar thought that Bush had unconsciously identified with his judgmental mother:

> "George W. may have followed in his father's footsteps to prep school, Yale, the oil business, politics, the presidency, and war in Iraq," said Paul Elovitz, editor of the psychohistory journal *Clio's Psyche* and a professor at New Jersey's Ramapo College, "but his personality is most like that of his mother, with whom he spent an enormous amount of time." It was tragedy that made mother and son extremely close. In February 1953, Bush's little sister, Robin, was diagnosed with leukemia at the very same time that his father began building his oil business in Midland, Texas. She died by the fall of that year, a tough blow for six-year-old George. "Mother and son were quite close as part of the legacy of the trauma of Robin's death at a time the family breadwinner was absorbed building his business," said Elovitz, who will be publishing a biography of Bush. (Schechter 2003; see also Frank 2004; Renshon 2004)

Needless to say, George W. Bush's mother Barbara was not the only emotional influence in his life. His remarkable father, former U.S. President George Herbert Walker Bush (born 1924), had a considerable effect on the son's character as well. Yet it was in George's early relationship to his mother that his dualistic and projective character was initially formed. His unconscious Oedipal wish to outdo his father, to take his symbolic mother—America—from him, and his conscious wish to avenge what he saw as his father's humiliation by Saddam Hussein— Bush senior had not successfully completed the Gulf War of 1991 and had almost been assassinated by Saddam—also played a role in George W. Bush's decision to make war on Saddam's Iraq. In fact, Saddam had tried to do to George's father what George himself had unconsciously wished to do to him. At the same time, unlike other alcoholics, George W. Bush had absorbed enough ego strength from his mother and father to be able to overcome his addiction and to channel his aggressive and self-destructive energies into a presidential campaign that won him the White House.

It is not only born-again politicians like George W. Bush, religious fanatics like Osama bin Laden, and suicidal terrorists like the Palestinian-Arab "freedom fighters" of *Hamas* and *Islamic Jihad* who unconsciously split their world into all-good and all-bad parts and project the disowned parts of themselves upon their enemies as a psychological defense against anxiety. Eminent scholars do so too. While Roy (2001, p. 3) wrote after September 11, 2001, that "it's absurd for the U.S. government to even toy with the idea that it can stamp out terrorism with more violence and oppression," a well-known American Jewish political scientist attacked the American political left's "culture of excuses" for the behavior of suicidal terrorists: "As Americans, we have our own brutalities to answer for—as well as the brutalities of other states that we have armed and funded. None of this, however, excuses terrorism; none of it even makes terrorism morally understandable" (Walzer 2001, p. 17). Backhandedly dismissing the psychological understanding of suicidal terrorism, and artificially divorcing psychology from politics, this scholar concluded tartly: "Maybe psychologists have something to say on behalf of understanding. But the only political response to ideological fanatics and suicidal holy warriors is implacable opposition" (Walzer, p. 17).

In response to Walzer's "implacable opposition," an equally eminent American Jewish psychiatrist observed that Walzer had displayed "dualistic thinking, the separation of politics from psychology," overlooking the fact that his political stance of "implacable opposition" to suicidal terrorism was in fact a psychological position (Mack 2002, p. 174). This psychiatrist pointed out that explaining and understanding terrorism are not the same as excusing or legitimizing it. On the contrary, understanding suicidal terrorists is essential to the prevention of their terrifying acts, just as understanding any type of human behavior is essential to dealing with it effectively. This fact was well understood by Mario Cuomo, the former governor of New York, who after September 11, 2001, said that "the only way to solve the terrorist problem is to change the minds of those who practice terrorism" (Cuomo 2001, Mack 2002, p. 174). We shall examine the psychology of suicide terrorists in Chapter 11.

The unconscious dynamics that we have seen above between George W. Bush and Osama bin Laden, each of whom consciously hates the other with a passion, yet each of whom unconsciously sees the disowned parts of himself in the other, also operate on the collective level. Ethnic and religious groups that share a geographical or political entity tend to trade unconscious dissociations. From early childhood, the members of each group learn to attribute all bad traits of character to those of the other groups, and all good traits to themselves. This is one of the reasons why we need not only allies but also enemies: they unconsciously serve as a container for the unacceptable and disowned— that is, split-off, projected and externalized—aspects of our own selves (Volkan 1988).

According to the Austrian-British psychoanalyst Melanie Klein (1882–1960), the unconscious infantile process of splitting is part of the larger defensive process of *projective identification*—a combination of unconscious *projection* and *introjection*—the latter being the psychoanalytic term for unconscious identification, the incorporation of an emotional object into the self. The term "projective identification" was coined by Melanie Klein, who defined it as an unconscious splitting off [of unbearable] parts of the self and projecting them onto another person (Klein 1946). She described the process as a complex interplay between unconscious introjection and projection:

> As regards normal development, it may be said that the course of ego development and object relations depends on the degree to which an optimal balance between introjection and projection in the early stages of development can be achieved. This in turn has a bearing on the integration of the ego and the assimilation of internal objects. Even if the balance is disturbed and one or the other of these processes is excessive, there is some interaction between introjection and projection. For instance, the projection of a predominantly hostile inner world which is ruled by persecutory fears, leads to the interjection— a taking back—of a hostile external world. *Vice versa,* the introjection of a distorted and hostile external world reinforces the projection of a hostile inner world. (Klein 1946, pp. 103–104)

Toward the end of her life, Klein developed her notions into a general theory of how we unconsciously construct our adult world out of our infantile experiences (Klein 1959). The relationship of unconscious splitting to projective identification has been explored in detail by one of her followers (Grotstein 1981).

One might ask what all this has to do with the Arab-Israeli conflict. Surprisingly, the answer is: everything. The unconscious processes of splitting and projective identification occur in our everyday

life, especially in our relations to our enemies. We tend to think of ourselves as virtuous and of our enemies as villainous. The GAP report of
1987 entitled *Us and Them* focused on the early unconscious defensive
processes in our lives such as splitting, externalization, projection, denial, and projective identification, all of which play a crucial role in the
primitive and violent feelings of ethnic nationalism (Group for the Advancement of Psychiatry 1987). The main point of the report is that our
earliest feelings for our mother are unconsciously displaced onto the
ethnonational realm. The national group—or the motherland—plays
the unconscious psychological role of our early mother, and our wish to
fuse with it and to be part of it derives from our regressive but persis-
tent lifelong wish to fuse with the Early Mother.

Us and Them claimed that the problem with national feelings was not
only their intensity but also their quality. National, especially nationalist, emotions are undifferentiated, primitive, and irrational, and lack any
intellectual control. The members of the GAP's Committee on International Relations were divided among those who felt, like Kohut, that
ethnic feelings were a normal aspect of human development, and those
who argued, like Kernberg, that nationalist feelings were basically
pathological. In any event, ethnonationalist feelings derive from the
process of splitting between good and bad, and the externalization of
evil upon the enemy. These processes occur already in early childhood
in the family. The GAP report sadly found all these processes to occur
pervasively in the Arab-Israeli conflict.

Finally, of course, each national group has its own reality. It is obvious that the Israeli Jews and the Palestinian Arabs live in different
psychological realities. Each group sees the world very differently. It is
extremely difficult under such circumstances to find any common
ground. Moreover, under conditions of prolonged emotional stress,
such as during violent conflict and war, people tend to dehumanize and
demonize their enemies. This phenomenon was observed by Volkan
(1988, pp. 120–122) as well as by Moses (1990). I have studied the unconscious role of geopolitical borders in this process (Falk 1974, 1983),
and Volkan (2003) has developed this subject further.

In the unconscious mind of U.S. President George W. Bush, America is the idealized all-good mother, while her enemies—the Axis of
Evil—are the all-bad mothers, and are demonized. Bush could not
stand the North Korean leader, Kim Jong-Il, because he starved his
own people. Symbolically, to Bush, Kim was the image of the depriving mother. America is the greatest country, she and her allies are

good, their enemies are evil. This black-and-white view of the world is similar to an infant's division of his or her world into all-good and all-bad parts. This infantile defensive process is known as splitting in psychoanalysis, and it persists in varying measures into our adulthood. We idealize ourselves and demonize our enemies. In addition, the unconscious processes of projection and externalization, which also develop in our early life, help us to ward off from our consciousness the painful aspects of our feelings and self-image. The enemy serves as a container for the unacceptable aspects of ourselves.

In the mid- and late-1970s, following the violent Turkish takeover of northern Cyprus in 1974, Volkan (1979) carried out a fascinating psychological study of the Greek-Turkish conflict in his native Cyprus. As we shall see, many of the points made by Volkan about that conflict are valid for the Arab-Israeli conflict as well. In the late 1980s the same scholar also published a very important study of the universal human need for enemies and allies (Volkan 1988). Our unconscious need for enemies derives from the unconscious defensive processes of *externalization* and *projection*.

Externalization is an unconscious defensive process that develops earlier than projection. The infant externalizes the painful parts of itself, imagining them to exist in the outside world. Later the child unconsciously projects upon others its own forbidden feelings or drives, imagining others to harbor them. For instance, when I was a child growing up in Tel-Aviv, the adults around me—beginning with my parents, who are all-important to a growing child—told me that the Arabs were mean and dirty and that we Jews were good and clean. A Palestinian Arab child of my age growing up in an Arab society was told exactly the same things in reverse about the Jews. The process of splitting and externalization is clear. Each side unconsciously splits up its world into all-good and all-bad, the all-good Us and the all-bad Them, externalizing upon the enemy everything it cannot bear in itself and projecting upon the enemy its own bad feelings. The actual behavior of the enemy may or may not reinforce one's image of that enemy, but the defensive process distorts our feelings.

The need for enemies is clear from the violent *internal conflicts* that beset each party in the Middle East conflict. Far from being united, the Arab world is riven by innumerable bloody conflicts between Muslims and Christians; Sunnis, Shiites, Alawites, and Druze; *Amal* and *Hizballah*; leftist revolutionaries and rightist royalists; rulers of Syria, Egypt, and Iraq striving for Arab hegemony; fundamentalist Muslim Brethren and Baathists. Even the fanatical Islamic terrorists in the Palestinian Arab community are split between the rival *Hamas* and *Islamic Jihad*. The Israeli Jews are split into secular and religious; socialists and nationalists; left-wing peace activists and right-wing settlers; Western Ashkenazi and so-called oriental or Sephardic Jews, many of whom are actually Arab Jews; the *Likkud* and Labor and dozens of other political parties. Israeli Jews coming from Arab countries speak a kind of Judeo-Arabic which is different from the spoken Arabic of their lands, just as Yiddish differs from German, or Ladino from Spanish. Nothing unites each party to the conflict better than the enemy.

We Have Met the Enemy—And He Is Us

Several scholars have pointed out that the worst wars occur between ethnic groups that are very similar to one another (Zonis & Offer 1985; Volkan 1988). A similar point had been made in 1950 by the French film director René Clair (René Chomette, 1898-1981) in his elaboration of the old Faust legend, *La Beauté du diable* (The Beauty of the Devil). In that classic film, the Devil's messenger, Mephistopheles, who tempts Dr. Faust into selling his soul in exchange for regaining his youth, is none other than Faust himself, played by the homely Michel Simon (1895-1975), while the rejuvenated Faust is played by the same handsome actor who plays the Devil, Gérard Philippe (1922-1959). As the American cartoonist Walt Kelly (1913-1973) put it in his classic comic strip *Pogo*, "We have met the enemy, and he is us" (Kelly 1972).

We Israelis resemble our Arab enemies in more ways than we care to know. The enemy makes it possible for us to externalize the unacceptable aspects of our group self upon it. All the evil figures of our childhood, witches and demons, are projected upon the enemy. The Arabs see Israel and Zionism as the symbol of Evil. Grand Ayatollah Ruhollah Khomeini of Iran (1900-1989), whose father (a Shiite *mullah*, or religious leader) was killed on the orders of a local landlord when Ruhollah was five months old, saw the United States as the Great Satan. Some Turks and Greeks on Cyprus still see each other as the embodiment of Evil: their mutual fears, suspicions, and hatreds have foiled many attempts at reunifying the island. This also happens between Muslims and Hindus in India, Catholics and Protestants in Ulster, Flemings and Walloons in Belgium, Viets and Khmers in Indochina, and so on throughout the world—as this book amply demonstrates. The enemy, the stranger, the foreigner, all make ideal objects for unconscious projection and externalization (Volkan 1988).

The more two neighboring groups resemble one another culturally or physically—in their character traits, customs, food, dress, and other cultural aspects, while differing from each other in some minor aspects—the more they unconsciously project and externalize upon, and hate, the other group. This is very much the case in the Israeli-Palestinian conflict, in which the two national groups have much in common and have lived in close proximity for over a century. Add to this the fact that almost half of the Israeli Jewish population came from Arab or Muslim countries, that many of them are culturally and linguistically Arab, and that Jews and Arabs had close if unequal relations in medieval Spain and all over the medieval Muslim world, and you can see how easy it is for the Israeli Jews and Palestinian Arabs to trade unconscious dissociations, projections and externalizations. At the same time, this is not the case in the American-Canadian relationship, which is basically an amicable rather than a hostile one. Sigmund Freud called this fascinating yet tragic phenomenon "the narcissism of minor differences" (Freud 1955–1974, vol. 11, p. 199; vol. 18, p. 101 note 4; vol. 21, p. 114; and vol. 23, p. 91 note 1). This narcissism plays a key role in inter-ethnic conflict. Still deeper under it lurk the unconscious fear of fusion, the fear of loss of identity, and the fear—and wish—of merging with the other and losing one's separate existence. It is such fears that hinder the resolution of the Arab-Israeli conflict.

9

War and the Inability to Mourn

This chapter deals with the crucial issues of loss and mourning in our individual and collective lives. None of us can escape important emotional losses throughout his or her life, and every one of us must learn how to mourn his or her losses without remaining stuck in the past. We shall see that the large group's collective inability to mourn its losses and to give them up is a major cause of human warfare.

The psychoanalytic literature on the causes of war has developed considerably since Freud wrote Einstein his famous letter "Why War?" (Freud 1933). The early British psychoanalysts Edward Glover (1888–1972) and Alix Strachey (1892–1973) tried to explain human warfare mainly in terms of Freud's notions of infantile drives or instincts, aggression, and regression (Glover 1933; Strachey 1957). Taking a very different avenue, the Italian psychoanalyst Franco Fornari (1921–1985), who followed Melanie Klein's notions of child development, thought that war was "the paranoid elaboration of mourning" (Fornari 1974). After Fornari, two German psychoanalysts studied the inability to mourn as a key problem underlying large-group behavior (Mitscherlich & Mitscherlich 1975). By the last decade of the twentieth century, the psychoanalytic literature on the causes of war had expanded considerably (Caspary 1993).

Fornari's notion of war as "the paranoid elaboration of mourning" itself requires some elaboration. The connection between war and mourning is not immediately obvious. Fornari used the word "elaboration" in the sense of "working through." Mourning the loss of a person who was dear to us—or, for that matter, mourning any serious loss in our lives—is a prolonged and painful process, which we naturally do not wish to experience. Yet without going through this process we cannot move forward. One of the common unconscious defenses against the pain of mourning is the denial of the loss. We behave as if the loved person has not died, as if he or she were still there, and as if we had not suffered the painful loss. We do not allow ourselves to feel the pain of our loss.

While on the individual level, partial or incomplete mourning is common, on the collective level it is almost universal. Most nations, rather than mourn their collective losses, immortalize them through memorial days, monuments, national cemeteries, sacred battlefields, and other instruments of commemoration. The national past is idealized and glorified. In the case of the Jews, this is obvious in the perennial longing to resettle the Land of Israel and to rebuild the Temple of Jerusalem, last destroyed in 70 C.E.. In Israel, it comes through in the Holocaust memorial projects, fallen soldiers' remembrance days, and the so-called *mifaley hantsakhah* (eternalization projects)—the Israeli monuments, physical, archival, and literary, commemorating those who were killed in the *Shoah* or in Israel's wars. In the case of the Arabs, the loss of their medieval empire has never been properly mourned, the past is glorified, and fanatical Islamists fervently desire the restoration of Islamic hegemony in the world. The inability to mourn one's losses on the collective level also involves the inability to let go, make painful but indispensable concessions, and sign peace treaties. As the Cypriot-Turkish-American psychoanalyst Vamık D. Volkan has observed, each large group has its "chosen traumas" and its "chosen glories" and no group will give them up easily unless some collective crisis brings up a profound change (Volkan 2004, pp. 47–52).

I have mentioned above the inability to mourn historical losses on both the Israeli Jewish and Palestinian Arab side. An American Jewish psychiatrist thought that if only the Israeli Jews and Palestinian Arabs could resign themselves to their losses, their intractable conflict would soon be resolved (Reich 1991). Such resignation, however, first requires going through the extremely painful mourning process. The problem of why and how people mourn—or will not, or cannot, mourn—their losses, both individually and collectively, was first tackled by Sigmund Freud (1955–1974, vol. 14, pp. 243–258) and continued by several modern psychoanalysts (Rochlin 1973; Mitscherlich & Mitscherlich 1975; Volkan 1981; Pollock 1989). Other scholars have pointed out the adaptive, creative, and regenerative role of mourning in our lives (Dietrich & Shabad 1989). Those who cannot—or will not—mourn their losses are stuck in the past and cannot move on. The Mitscherliches argued that the Germans could not mourn the heavy losses of their Führer, their

Reich, the millions of German dead, the devastation of their country, and the death of their aspirations. They plunged instead into the postwar *Wirtschaftswunder* (economic miracle). I believe that the inability to mourn is a key psychological problem in the Arab-Israeli conflict as well.

The problem of mourning arises very early in our lives, when we emerge from the stage of psychological fusion with our mother into the stage of separation and individuation. This painful, difficult, and complicated process has been called "the psychological birth of the human infant" (Mahler, Pine, & Bergman 1975). We have to mourn the loss of the blissful paradise of union, the loss of the Great Early Mother. Our entire life thereafter may be viewed as a succession of separations and losses, with the perennial craving for the paradise lost of our infancy. Many people are unable to mourn properly, because their mother experienced their early attempts to separate and individuate as an abandonment of her. She reacted with fear, rage, or depression to such attempts, which made the infant feel helpless, lost, and overwhelmed with fear. These problems persist throughout life.

As we have seen, the pioneering Italian psychoanalyst Franco Fornari advanced a psychoanalytic theory of the unconscious causes of war, which he thought was "the paranoid elaboration of mourning" (Fornari 1974). Our war-making derives from our inability to mourn our losses, beginning with the loss of the paradise of our early fusion with our mother. Fornari was influenced by the theories of Melanie Klein (1950) about early human development. Klein had stressed the overwhelming power of our feelings for our mothers during the first year of our lives, when we are very little and helpless: the fear of being devoured by the mother, the wish to destroy her, the persecutory and depressive feelings, and the splitting of our own selves and of our internal image of the mother into all-good and all-bad parts. Klein—and Fornari—believed that, irrationally but powerfully, we feel guilty for having damaged our Early Mother, whom we abandoned when we began to separate and individuate from her. The motherland and nation unconsciously stand for our idealized Early Mother. We unconsciously displace our guilt feelings from mother to country and project them upon our enemy. We are certain that the enemy wishes to destroy our mother country, and to rape our mothers, wives, sisters, and daughters. We are filled with righteous rage at this enemy and wish to annihilate him. Feeling unconsciously guilty for having damaged or destroyed our Early Mother, whom we unconsciously identify with our motherland or nation, we unconsciously project our guilt feelings upon our enemies. Projection and externalization are the key processes in this "paranoid elaboration of mourning."

If I have given an oversimplified review of Fornari's psychoanalytic theory, nevertheless this is its basic thesis, and it constitutes a minor revolution in the psychological view of war. Admittedly, Klein's theories about early infant emotions—and Fornari's theories about the psychological causes of war—are emotionally difficult to accept, and have given rise to controversy and schisms among psychoanalysts (Hughes 1989). The unconscious motives for war advanced by Fornari have been disputed by rationalistic scholars, who argue that there is no need to look for unconscious motives, as there are real and material causes of war, such as the greed of nations for territory, profit, and domination, and that destructive feelings are not only projected by us on our enemies but really exist in them. Volkan (1988) has shown how we use our enemies for our psychological survival.

Is Collective Mourning Possible?

We have seen that the collective inability of a national or ethnic group to mourn its historical losses and overcome its narcissistic injuries is a major cause of conflict and war. To my mind, *whether collective mourning is at all possible* remains an open question. In my study of Jewish history I have shown how difficult it has been for the Jews to mourn their historical losses and how their inability to mourn has complicated their history and caused additional historical tragedy. If we consider the painful historical losses suffered by both Jews and Arabs, and their difficulty in mourning them, we may sense Fornari's meaning. The *Shoah* is a recent example of Jewish losses, while the partition of Palestine and the creation of Israel in 1948 is a recent example of Arab losses. Rather than mourn its losses, each side has dealt with them through unconscious projection and denial.

I believe that both Jews and Arabs have been unable to mourn their historical losses. This is one reason for the astonishing absence of scientific and chronological Jewish historiography from the first to the sixteenth century, and for the equally astonishing non-historicity of the Arabs—the apparent timelessness of their way of remembering and writing their own history (Laroui 1976, 1999; Yerushalmi 1982; Carlebach, Efron, & Myers 1998). Those who argue that Jewish religious and Israeli national life are permeated with mourning do not use the term "mourning" in the sense of grieving and accepting one's losses, but rather in the opposite sense of bemoaning them and wishing to restore them.

The pervasive feeling of righteous rage at one's victimization by the enemy characterizes both sides of the Israeli-Palestinian conflict, each of which feels unjustly victimized by the other. One of the New Israeli Historians used the apt title *Righteous Victims* for his study of the Zionist-Arab conflict (Morris 1999). Twenty years earlier, Mack (1979, pp. xii–xix) had delineated the key psychological aspects of conflicts between neighboring ethnic groups: (a) the identity of self and nation; (b) the problem of historical grievances; (c) the intergenerational transmission of attitudes toward the "other"; (d) splitting, externalizing, and mirroring: the demonization of the "other"; (e) the egoism of victimization; (f) war as therapy; (g) aggression and the inability to mourn. While all these aspects apply to the Arab-Israeli conflict, no scholar seems to have stressed the crucial importance of the last aspect.

In order to live healthily in present reality, rather than in dangerous unhealthy fantasies, one must first mourn one's past losses and give them up. The Jews have been unable to mourn their great historical losses: the losses of land, independence, holy city, temple, their exiles, expulsions, humiliations and persecutions, and the millions of their people massacred and murdered. The collective mourning process has been too painful. After the destruction of the Second Temple in 70 C.E., the Jews unknowingly closed themselves up inside a kind of ahistorical bubble and refused to write their chronological history. Instead, they produced a vast body of historical legends and religious fantasies (Ginzburg 1909–1938). In 1574 the Italian Jewish scholar Bonaiuto de' Rossi (1514–1578), under the Hebrew version of his name, Azariah min Ha-Adumim, published his Hebrew book *Meor Enayim* (Light for the Eyes), in which he translated the major classical Greek and Latin historical writings, both Jewish and non-Jewish, into Hebrew, and wrote the first scholarly Jewish history since Flavius Josephus (37–100). The Italian Jewish rabbis banned his book, fearful of having the ahistorical bubble in which they lived burst by it. The Jews continued to live in the past and in fantasy.

To my mind, the inability to mourn is a key psychological factor in the Arab-Israeli conflict. The two parties to our tragic conflict have not been able to resign themselves to their historical losses. Some Israeli Jews still wish to rebuild the Third Temple of Yahweh on the site of the mosque of the Dome of the Rock in Jerusalem and restore the glories of the Kingdom of Solomon. Most Palestinian Arabs—and many non-Palestinian Arabs—have not made peace with their loss of Palestine, their status as refugees, the frustration of their national ambitions, and their military defeats by Israel. They seize upon the Yom Kippur War of October 1973 as a symbol of a great Arab victory and of the restoration of Arab honor. Although they publicly aspire to a Palestinian state within the occupied territories, they privately wish to recapture all of Palestine and to do away with the existence of Israel.

For many years, the Palestinian National Covenant (or Charter), adopted in 1964 and expanded in 1968, called for the Arab recovery of all of Palestinian land—including Israel (Kadi 1969, pp. 137–141). In 1996, honoring a pledge made to the United States the year before, the Palestinian National Council voted to revoke the sections of the Palestinian National Covenant that called for the destruction of the State of Israel. But the extremists of *Hamas, Islamic Jihad,* and *Fatah* have not accepted the loss of any part of their country. They live more in fantasy than in reality, more in the past than in the present. They seethe with murderous narcissistic rage. Our personal and national narcissism is directly related to our inability to mourn, to let go of the past, to separate from the lost object of our love, whether Early Mother or early motherland. The more individuals or groups are stuck in a symbiotic relationship with their early love object, the more they need to compensate themselves for its loss with self-love. Those who are unable to separate and individuate from their Early Mother will find it harder to mourn the loss of their motherland when they are forced to leave it.

We Israeli Jews have not properly mourned our unthinkable losses of 6,000,000 Jews in the *Shoah,* and it may be psychologically impossible for any large group to mourn the incomprehensible murder of so many of its people. Every year we mark a memorial day named *Yom HaZikaron LaShoah velaGvurah* (Holocaust and Heroism Memorial Day). This day of remembrance is observed in Israel on the 27th day of the Hebrew month of Nissan. If this day falls on a Friday, then the observance is advanced one day to the preceding Thursday. This date was chosen in a resolution passed by the Israeli Knesset in 1951; it falls between that of the Warsaw Ghetto Uprising, which began on the first day of the Jewish Passover, and Israel's Memorial Day for the War Dead. Holocaust Day therefore occurs during the traditional Jewish mourning period of the Counting of the Omer between Passover and Shavuot. In 1959, the Knesset passed the Holocaust and Heroism Memorial Day Law, which required tribute to victims of the Holocaust and ghetto uprisings to be

paid in public observances. In 1961, an amendment to this law required
that all Israeli places of entertainment be closed on the eve of Holocaust
Day as well as on Holocaust Day itself.

To my mind, the inclusion of heroism—the Jewish resistance to
the Nazis, the ghetto uprisings, the Jewish partisan fighters—in the
commemoration of the unthinkable catastrophe of the *Shoah* may be an
unconscious attempt to escape the unspeakable pain of our losses and
deny the enormity of the catastrophe by telling ourselves that the Jews
of Europe were not led like lambs to the slaughter. Even professional
Israeli mental health workers denied the disaster for a long time. The
psychiatric literature about Holocaust survivors began to be published
only in the 1960s, twenty years after the end of the *Shoah* and after the
Eichmann trial.

During the late 1960s and 1970s, in the intoxication following the Six-
Day War of 1967, we Israeli Jews thought of Egypt's Sinai peninsula, as
well as of the Palestinian West Bank and Gaza Strip, as an integral part
of our land. Our prolonged, tragicomic conflict with Egypt over its one
square mile of real estate on our border called Taba, which was finally
resolved by Taba reverting to Egypt, may be another indication that we
Israelis have not properly mourned our loss of the large territory we
gave back to Egypt, namely the Sinai peninsula. It may also be proof of
our need for enemies. Nor must we forget that all Israeli Jews who immigrated to Israel from other countries have had to undergo a process
of mourning over their native lands, where they were born and grew
up, and which they lost by immigrating to Israel, however sincere their
Zionist feelings.

From 1970 to 2000, about 1,000,000 people—Jews and non-Jews—
immigrated to Israel from the former Soviet Union, most of them for
economic reasons, some because they could not get visas to the United
States. Israel is an adoptive motherland for these immigrants, whom
we native Israelis call *olim* (literally "ascenders"), betraying the striking
fantasy that Israel is set above all other lands. Our Zionist slogans call
Israel the natural motherland of every Jew. But to integrate into Israeli
society, the Russian immigrants must first mourn the loss of the country
of their birth and adopt their new country. This is a painful process that
many of them will not or cannot go through. Nostalgia for their native
land is common among immigrants everywhere (Zwingmann & Pfister-
Ammende 1973). Many foreign-born Israelis still speak their mother
tongue rather than Hebrew, are emotionally and culturally tied to their
country of origin, read newspapers and books in their native tongue,

and live among immigrants from the same countries. Many Israelis hold two passports, one from their native country and the other from Israel. More than 125,000 German-born Israelis and their children and grandchildren have requested and accepted German citizenship.

One prominent Anglo-Jewish Arabist thought that the roots of Muslim rage against the West, which have since given rise to murderous terrorism, involved the search for scapegoats among the non-Muslim nations (Lewis 1990). Psychologically, our collective inability to mourn our losses and to give up what we have lost increases our aggression against the out-group, against the enemy, whereas the painful but vital process of mourning decreases it. Franco Fornari (1974) made a similar point in his study of war. This may also be true of individuals—those who can tolerate the pain of weeping and mourning their losses are no longer filled with righteous warlike rage. They are free of unconscious guilt feelings for having abandoned their mother, or for damaging their motherland, and no longer need to project their guilt upon others. The unconscious projection of guilt feelings upon the enemy produces murderous rage and is most dangerous.

10

The Arab Mind

Over the centuries, there have been many studies of the particular psychology and character of the Arabs, which seem so very different from those of Europeans and other Westerners. When Westerners watch a crowd of young Palestinian Arabs in Gaza demonstrate, shout, and run wild at the funeral of one of their leaders who has just been killed by Israeli security forces following a suicide bombing in Israel, these Arabs may seem to those Westerners inordinately excitable, hyperemotional, overreactive, violent, and irrational. On the other hand, to themselves, these young Arabs seem totally normal, and their violent reactions to the assassination of their leaders absolutely comprehensible and justified.

Can non-Arabs understand the emotional make-up of the Arabs? Can the Israeli Jews understand the Palestinian Arabs—and vice versa? The psychology and character of the Arabs have preoccupied non-Arab historians, psychologists, psychiatrists, and anthropologists over the centuries. It has also preoccupied Arab and Muslim historians in what Westerners call the Dark Ages, which were a time of great flowering for Muslim and Arab culture. From the late-medieval Arab historian Ibn Khaldun to twentieth-century scholars like the Egyptian sociologist Sania Hamady and the American Jewish anthropologist Raphael Patai (1910–1996), who spent his youth in Palestine, Arab and non-Arab scholars have tried to describe and explain what two non-Arab scholars have called "the Arab Mind" (Patai 1973; Laffin 1974).

Most of these studies have emphasized the key role of honor and how unbearable the feeling of shame is in the minds of the Arabs. Most of these scholars observed that an Arab male will do anything to preserve his honor, including performing honor-killings within his own family. However, the Arabic language has no word for "honor killing," as it has no word for "suicide bomber." Scholars have also noted the Arab tendency to exaggerate, to live in fantasy, to display extreme emotional reactions, to harbor feelings of revenge, to hate authority, and to ignore private physical space. This chapter discusses the validity of these national-character studies and their possible contribution to the understanding of the Arab-Israeli conflict. While some scholars have criticized the national-character model for understanding this conflict (Zonis & Offer 1985), other scholars believe that the psychology of the Arabs is very different from that of Westerners, and that the Muslim Arabs live in a considerably different reality from ours.

One of the greatest Arab historians was the fourteenth-century Tunis-born chronicler Ibn Khaldun (1332–1406)—his full name was Wali ad-Din Abd-ar-Rahman ibn Muhammad ibn Muhammad ibn Abi-Bakr Muhammad ibn al-Hasan abu-Zaid ibn Khaldun. As a young man, Ibn Khaldun was a politician and diplomat under various North African and Spanish Muslim rulers, but his restless and difficult character repeatedly got him in trouble and he kept changing employers. In 1375, at the age of 43, craving solitude and peace, he sought refuge with the desert Arab tribe of Awlad Arif, who lodged him and his family in the safety of a castle, *Qalaat ibn Salamah*, near what is now the town of Frenda, Algeria. There Ibn Khaldun spent four years, "free from all preoccupations," and wrote his massive masterpiece, *Al-Muqaddimah*, an introduction to history. Ibn Khaldun's ambition was to write a universal history of the Arabs and Berbers. Before doing so, however, his obsessive mind found it necessary to discuss and discover a general historical method and find the criteria necessary for distinguishing historical truth from error.

Ibn Khaldun's achievement was admired by both Arab and non-Arab historians. More than three centuries after Ibn Khaldun, the Italian historian Giambattista Vico (1668–1744) became the European founder of cultural anthropology. In his *Scienza nuova* (New Science) Vico sought to integrate history with the social sciences so as to create a single science of humanity (Vico 1725). The nineteenth-century Scottish historian Robert Flint (1838–1910) considered Ibn Khaldun as great as Vico:

> Whether [Ibn Khaldun] is to be regarded or not as the founder of the science of history . . . no candid reader of his 'Prolegomena' [*Muqaddimah*] can fail to admit that his claim to this honor is more valid than that of many other authors previous to Vico. . . . [T]he work he left is sufficiently great and valuable to

preserve his name and fame to latest generations. . . . As a theo-
rist on history he had no equal in any age or country until Vico
appeared, more than three hundred years later. Plato, Aristotle
and Augustine were not his peers. (Flint 1893, pp. 157, 171)

Outdoing Flint, the controversial twentieth-century English historian Arnold Toynbee (1889–1975) considered Ibn Khaldun's *Muqaddimah* "undoubtedly the greatest work of its kind that has ever yet been
created by any mind in any time or place" (Toynbee 1962, vol. 3, p. 322).
Toynbee, however, who had grandiosely set out to write a universal
history of mankind, was given to exaggeration and extremism. For example, he called the tragic massacre of about one hundred Palestinian
Arabs at Deir Yassin by an extreme right-wing Palestinian Jewish terrorist group in 1948 a crime "comparable to crimes committed against
the Jews by the Nazis" (Toynbee 1962, vol. 8, p. 290). Even the Palestinian Arabs themselves have never claimed more than 350 casualties at
Deir Yassin, and the actual figure is probably around 100 (Morris 1999,
p. 209). The American Jewish philosopher Eric Hoffer (1902–1983) in
turn exaggerated Toynbee's statement in order to be able to accuse him
of violent anti-Semitism: "Arnold Toynbee calls the displacement of the
Arabs an atrocity *greater than* any committed by the Nazis" (Hoffer
1968). In any event, Toynbee was a supporter of the Arabs and an
enemy of Israel (Toynbee 1970).

It should be pointed out that the term "anti-Semitism" is a euphe-
mism invented in 1879 by the Jew-hating German political agitator and
gutter journalist Wilhelm Marr (1819–1904) in order to make Jew-hatred
respectable (Marr 1879, 1880; Falk 1996, p. 637). Like many present-day
Arabs and Muslims, Marr ascribed all of Germany's woes to its defeat
in an imaginary battle with world Jewry. The term anti-Semitism has
become so popular that most Jews use it unthinkingly. Some scholars
prefer the term "Judeophobia" which literally means "fear of Jews"
(Schäfer 1997; Perednik 2001). To my mind, Jew-hatred is still the best
and most accurate term for this pathological phenomenon.

In this *Muqaddimah*, the city-bred Ibn Khaldun derided the rural and
nomadic Arabs as "wild, savage, destructive, uncivilized, rude, proud,
ambitious, haters of government and enemies of culture" (Ibn Khaldun
1958, vol. 1, pp. 299–305; Patai, 1973, pp. 19–20). In trying to understand the causes of such character traits, Ibn Khaldun thought that
the Arabs were savage, wild, and destructive *because of* their pride,
strength, hardness, ambition, and constant wish to lead and rule. The

Arabs love freedom, he wrote, and hate authority and government. They cannot stand to be ruled by others. Was Ibn Khaldun unconsciously projecting his own unpleasant personal traits on all the Arabs?

Ibn Khaldun's disciple, Ahmad ibn-Ali Taqi ad-Din Abul-Abbas al-Maqrizi (1364–1442), also described the national character of the Egyptian Arabs in a most unflattering manner. He called the Arabs unreliable, cowardly, stingy, lying, cheating, fanatical, libelous, traitors, and thieves (Al-Maqrizi 1895–1900, volume 17, pp. 121–138; Patai 1973, pp. 20–21). All of this can obviously not be true of all Arabs at all times. At the same time, it may have characterized the behavior of some Arabs in the fourteenth and fifteenth centuries. It is ironic, and may be psychologically significant, that both of these Arab historians were not purely Arab. Ibn Khaldun was of Moorish-Berber descent, and Al-Maqrizi was an Egyptian Mameluke.

The Primacy of Honor and Shame among the Arabs

As we have seen above, what the Palestinian Arabs see as their *naqba* (catastrophe) of 1948 is to them a perennial source of loss of honor, shame, and need for vengeance. Understanding the Arab notions of *sharaf* (honor), *ird* (sexual honor), *wajh* (face saving), *ayb* (shame), and *qadhah* (disgrace, rebuke, or slander) is crucial to the understanding of Arab culture and society. To most Arabs, preserving their honor is indispensable while the feeling of shame is unbearable (Patai 1973, pp. 106, 120–123; Laffin 1974). Sania Hamady, a female Arab sociologist, called this "the culture of shame" (1960, pp. 5, 36, 62–63, 217). She found that shame was the worst and most painful feeling for an Arab, and that the overwhelming need to erase one's shame, to preserve one's own honor, and the honor of one's family, clan, and tribe—in other people's eyes—was psychologically crucial. Any injury, real or imaginary, to one's honor causes the Arab an unbearable feeling of shame that must be wiped out or repaired by an act of revenge that injures those who have damaged one's honor. This code of honor can lead to interminable blood feuds between Arab clans and to the so-called honor killing of one's own daughter or sister if she has dishonored her family by becoming pregnant out of wedlock. Hamady thought that the Arabs lived in fantasies of their glorious past rather than in their painful present and that they had no compunction about lying to achieve their goals.

Why have the Arabs lost most of their wars against tiny, outnumbered Israel? Hamady thought that it was their fear of facing their painful

reality. To lessen the burning pain of what they felt to be their sham-
ing and humiliation by the Jews, the Arabs of Palestine, Syria, Jordan,
Egypt, Iraq, and Lebanon have talked themselves into believing that it
was not the weak and cowardly Israelis who had defeated them but the
mighty Americans, and that the Israelis would last no longer than the
medieval Crusaders and their Latin Kingdom of Jerusalem, established
in 1099 and defeated in 1187 by the Kurdish Muslim leader Salah ad-
Din Yusuf ibn-Ayyub, known to Westerners as Saladin. A key part of
the Arab concept of *sharaf* is the freedom from being ruled by others. An
Arab proverb says that nothing is more humiliating than being under
another man's authority. At the same time, in the traditional Arab family the father has absolute authority, and the son must submit to him.
Can this be the reason why the Arabs hate government so badly? The
harsh rule of the father at home may cause the son to rebel and to displace his patricidal rage onto political governors. The father's honor
depends on his ability to maintain his authority in the family. What
about the son's honor? This question will be examined later in this
chapter in the context of the Palestinian Arab family (Hamady 1960;
Patai 1973; Laffin 1975).

From a Western psychoanalytic viewpoint, the painful feeling of
shame begins at an early stage in our development, during the second
year of our life, when we must wrestle with the issues of separation, individuation, and differentiation from our mother and develop a sense
of autonomy, separateness, and self. Our toilet training may cause us to
feel shame when we soil ourselves with feces or wet ourselves with
urine. The sense of lack of autonomy is tied in with the feeling of shame.
Honor, pride, and *amour-propre* are aspects of narcissism, the maintenance of self-worth, self-respect, and self-love. The painful feelings of
shame and humiliation are naturally not limited to Arab culture; they
have led Western politicians to fateful and even tragic decisions (Kaufman 1989; Steinberg 1996).

The Egyptian sociologist Hamid Ammar (born 1921) coined the term
"fahlawi personality" to describe Arab culture. The Arabic term *fahlawi*
is derived from the Persian word *pahlavi* meaning "clever or sharp-
witted." Ammar's fahlawi personality is characterized by his seeking
the easiest and quickest way to his every goal, shirking hard work and
effort, boasting of his own achievements and deriding his fellows, flat-
tery, cheating, bribery, and lies. He covers up his failures and defeats,
becomes quickly excited and violently daring when it seems to him he
will easily achieve his wishes, and cools down very fast when he faces

obstacles. The fahlawi personality has exaggerated self-confidence and arrogance and always assigns responsibility for his failures to others. Ammar believes that the Fahlawi suffers from a profound feeling of inferiority, a burning feeling of shame, and a terrible fear of humiliation should his true deeds become public knowledge. He makes a great show of chivalry, manliness, honor, daring, and courage because deep down he fears the reverse: that he is without honor, shameful, cowardly, and helpless (Patai 1973, pp. 107–111).

A Syrian Arab philosopher, Sadiq Jalal al-Azm, thought that one of the chief causes of the Arab defeats in their wars with Israel was the extreme Arab tendency to project and externalize all sense of guilt and responsibility upon others, to boast, to live in fantasy, to deny painful reality (Haim 1971, p. 6; Patai 1973, pp. 60, 111–112). Both Al-Azm and Ammar stressed that the old-fashioned Arab society encourages rigidity and conservatism. Arab commanders cannot adapt themselves to the rapidly changing conditions in wartime and are unable to find new solutions or moves to counter the problems they keep facing. They are fearful of reporting their failures and defeats to their superiors, which causes the high command to lack vital information needed to conduct the war. This description is strikingly similar to Norman Dixon's view of military incompetence. This psychologist found that the rigidity of the bad commander and his fear of losing the love of his superiors, who unconsciously stand in his mind for his early parents, cause terrible catastrophes in time of war (Dixon 1976).

Several Israeli Jewish and Muslim Arab scholars have rejected the notion of the basic Arab personality (Beit-Hallahmi 1976; Moughrabi 1978). Zonis and Offer (1985) rejected "the national-character model" in analyzing the Arab-Israeli conflict. Other scholars, however, have insisted on the existence of a special Arab psychopathology. Robert Glidden, an American diplomat who spent many years in Egypt and translated the memoirs of King Abdullah of Transjordan from Arabic into English, considered Arab culture psychopathological by Western standards (Glidden 1972). This diplomat carefully warned his readers that Arab culture must be examined from the viewpoints of Islam and of the Middle East rather than from those of Christian Europe and America. As Glidden saw it, Arab notions of politeness, property, honor, privacy, personal space, truth, lies, compromise, peace, and many other values are radically different from Western notions of the same. It is normal for Arabs to touch each other, interrupt each other, invade each other's privacy, lie, cheat, and act altogether differently from

Europeans. Vengeance for humiliations is much more important to Arabs than peace. Hence, from Glidden's point of view, the Arabs will continue to make war with Israel for a very long time.

One of the critics of Glidden's views of Arab psychopathology was the well-known Palestinian-American scholar Edward William Said, who considered most of Western Christian scholarship of Arab culture racist and misguided "Orientalism" (Said 1978). With cutting irony, Said called Glidden's attitude toward the Arabs' character a form of "respectable Orientalism":

> It is a notable fact that while [Glidden believes that] the Arab value system demands absolute solidarity within the group, it at the same time encourages among its members a kind of rivalry that is destructive of that very solidarity; in Arab society only "success counts" and "the end justifies the means"; Arabs live "naturally" in a world "characterized by anxiety expressed in generalized suspicion and distrust, which has been labeled free-floating hostility"; "the art of subterfuge is highly developed in Arab life, as well as in Islam itself"; the Arab need for vengeance overrides everything, otherwise the Arab would feel "ego-destroying" shame. Therefore, if "Westerners consider peace to be high on the scale of values" and if "we have a highly developed consciousness of the value of time," this is not true of Arabs. "In fact," we are told, "in Arab tribal society (where Arab values originate), strife, not peace, was the normal state of affairs because raiding was one of the two main supports of the economy." (Said 1978, pp. 48–49)

Like other matters, however, Arab psychopathology or normality are in the eye of the beholder. Western Christian misinterpretation of Arab culture has a long history. In 1844, an English traveler named Alexander William Kinglake published his personal impressions of the Middle East, *Eothen*, a much-reprinted and very popular book in the West, which contains an early example of Said's Orientalism—the culture-biased view of the Arabs and Islam as "fallacious nonsense":

> A man coming freshly from Europe is at first proof against the nonsense with which he is assailed; but often it happens that after a little while the social atmosphere of Asia will begin to infect him, and, if he has been unaccustomed to the cunning of fence by which reason prepares the means of guarding herself against fallacy, he will yield himself at last to the faith of those

around him; and this he will do by sympathy, it would seem,
rather than from conviction. (Kinglake 1844, quoted in Kaplan
1993, foreword)

The famous English adventurer Thomas Edward Lawrence (1888–
1935), popularly known as Lawrence of Arabia, who seemingly loved
the Arabs and their culture, wrote his well-known *Seven Pillars of Wisdom* to explain the Arab mind. Lawrence was a very complex character
with much inner conflict and ambivalence (Mack 1976). One scholar
thought that his book contained "perhaps the most famous Arabist
analysis of the Arab mind, considered brilliant by some and racist by
others" (Kaplan 1993, p. 52).

> In the very outset, at the first meeting with them, [Lawrence]
> found a universal clearness or hardness of belief, almost math-
> ematical in its limitation, and repellent in its unsympathetic
> form. . . . They were a people of primary colours, or rather of
> black and white, who saw the world always in contour. They
> were a dogmatic people, despising doubt, our modern crown
> of thorns. They did not understand our metaphysical difficul-
> ties, our introspective questionings. . . . They were at ease only
> in extremes. They inhabited superlatives by choice[:] . . . they
> never compromised, they pursued the logic of several incom-
> patible opinions to absurd ends, without perceiving the incon-
> gruity. . . . They steered their course between the idols of the
> tribe and the cave. (Kaplan 1993, p. 52)

An American Christian traveler, the Reverend John Haynes Holmes,
visited Palestine in 1929, a time of trouble between Jews and Arabs.
Holmes admired the Jewish settlers, while their Arab enemies re-
minded him of the "savage" American Indians:

> As I met and talked with these toilers on the land, I could think
> of nothing but the early English settlers who came to the bleak
> shores of Massachusetts, and there amid winter's cold in an
> untilled soil, among an unfriendly native population, laid firm
> and sure the foundations of our American Republic. For this
> reason I was not surprised later, when I read Josiah Wedge-
> wood's *The Seventh Dominion*, to find this distinguished Gen-
> tile Zionist of Britain speaking of these Jewish pioneers as "the
> Pilgrim Fathers of Palestine." Here is the same heroism dedi-
> cated to the same ends. . . . It is obvious that the native Arabs,

while no less stubborn and savage than the American Indians,
cannot be removed from the scene. (Holmes 1929, pp. 89, 248;
Sharif, 1983, p. 135)

Edward Said detected the Western intellectual racism toward the
Arabs that he called "Orientalism" among his contemporary statesmen
and scholars. One of them was Henry Alfred Kissinger (born 1923), the
German-born American Jewish political scientist and secretary of state
under U.S. Presidents Nixon and Ford (AlRoy 1975; Golan 1976; Hersh
1983; Kissinger 1997; Stein 1999). Kissinger had used the linguistic notion of binary opposition to divide the world into two opposing parts,
the developed post-Newtonian and the developing pre-Newtonian
world (Kissinger 1969). Kissinger idealized the post-Newtonian world
of the West and denigrated the Pre-Newtonian world of the Arabs. Said
thought that "both the traditional Orientalist . . . and Kissinger conceive
of the difference between cultures, first, as creating a battle front that
separates them, and second, as inviting the West to control, contain,
and otherwise govern (through superior knowledge and accommodating power) the Other" (Said 1978, pp. 47–48). In fact, Kissinger's binary
opposition—like Said's own Orientalism—was yet another example of
the unconscious splitting process through which we view our world in
black-and-white terms to defend ourselves against the anxiety provoked by the realization that we are not really that different from our
hated enemies.

The Conflict between Islam and the West

Glidden's views of Arab psychopathology have given rise to heated
controversy about Arab culture and character in general, as well as
about the apparent struggle between Islam and the West. Six years after
Glidden's article, Said coined the derogatory term "Orientalism" to describe most Western Christian scholarship of the Arabs and Islam (Said
1978). With great personal animosity, Said singled out for attack one
of his prominent elder colleagues, the Anglo-Jewish Arabist Bernard
Lewis, calling him "full of condescension and bad faith" toward an Arab
world that he had spent his lifetime studying and writing about. Said
called Lewis "the perfect example of the Western Arabist whose work
purports to be liberal objective scholarship but is in reality very close to
being propaganda *against* his subject material . . . [meant] to debunk, to
whittle down, and to discredit the Arabs and Islam." Lewis defended

himself publicly against Said's accusations, but that in no way ended the debate set off by *Orientalism,* a book that labeled a century and a half of Western scholarship about the Arab world a disguised form of intellectual racism and colonialism.

Indeed, Said's accusations of racist Orientalism gave rise to a ferocious controversy. One of Said's supporters described Orientalism as "a gross form of Western superiority complex, expressed in a literature and a scholarship that imposed its own false portrayal on the East and refused to care sensitively for the East's own evaluation of itself. By distortion it had its own way with its eastern versions and made these the instrument of control and, indeed, of denigration. . . . Orientalism is thus found uniformly culpable, and a conniver with misrepresentation" (Cragg 1991, p. 297). Said's foes, on the other hand, have charged him with being as biased against the West as his Orientalists were supposed to be against the Arabs. Was Said ashamed, as one critic speculated, of the fact that all major scholarship on Arab culture had been done by non-Arabs and non-Muslims? In fact, Said was deeply ambivalent about Western culture, of which he was an integral and important part, while at the same time being an Arab with roots in the Middle East.

The psychology and culture of the "Oriental" Arabs are still a matter of intense controversy between Muslim, Arab, Jewish, and other scholars (Beit-Hallahmi 1980; Cohen 1983; Ahmad 1991; Lewis 1990, 1998, 2002, 2003). The subject obviously stirs very deep and powerful emotions. Three prominent scholars have debated the clash between Islam and the West and the powerful emotions of rage, envy, hatred, and also fascination and attraction found in the Arab and Muslim world toward America and the West in general. Bernard Lewis (1990), in seeking "the roots of Muslim rage" toward the West, coined the phrase "clash of civilizations." He was followed by the American Christian political scientist Samuel P. Huntington, who borrowed the phrase from Lewis and made it the basis of his own fame (Huntington 1993, 1996). Lewis and Huntington were bitterly attacked by Said, who called their theories "the clash of ignorance" (Said 2001).

Lewis (1990) thought that the Muslims were enraged at the West for the humiliations it has inflicted upon them:

> For a long time now there has been a rising tide of rebellion against this western paramountcy, and a desire to reassert Muslim values and restore Muslim greatness. The Muslim has suffered successive stages of defeat. The first was his loss of

domination in the world, to the advancing power of Russia
and the West. The second was the undermining of his authority in his own country, through an invasion of foreign ideas
and laws and ways of life and sometimes even foreign rulers
or settlers, and the enfranchisement of native non-Muslim
elements. The third—the last straw—was the challenge to his
mastery in his own house, from emancipated women and rebellious children. It was too much to endure, and the outbreak
of rage against these alien, infidel, and incomprehensible
forces that had subverted his dominance, disrupted his society, and finally violated the sanctuary of his home was inevitable. It was also natural that this rage should be directed
primarily against the millennial enemy and should draw its
strength from ancient beliefs and loyalties. (Lewis 1990, p. 49)

Lewis thought that the Muslims had an endless list of grievances and
accusations against the West—its colonialism, racism, imperialism,
slavery, secularism, and sexism; its exploitation of their oil, its violation
of their culture, its disrespect for their wives and daughters, and, above
all, its support of Israel, the principal enemy of the Arabs. Yet Lewis
thought that each of the crimes with which the Arabs accuse the West
had an even worse parallel in the Arab world itself. The Western treatment of women, however unequal and oppressive, has been vastly better than "the rule of polygamy and concubinage that has otherwise
been the almost universal lot of womankind on this planet" (Lewis
1990, p. 53). Slavery was much more widespread and cruel among the
Arabs than in the West. And, irrationally, Muslim hostility to Western
imperialism is much deeper and stronger than to Russian imperialism,
even though Russia "still rules, with no light hand, over many millions
of reluctant Muslim subjects and over ancient Muslim cities and countries" (Lewis 1990, p. 54).

Lewis (1990, pp. 56, 59) thought that while the Muslims at first re-
sponded to the advent of Western civilization with immense admiration and emulation, in our own time these feelings have turned into
their opposite—hostility and rejection. Muslim fundamentalists fight
against what they see as their two chief enemies: Western secularism
and modernism. Lewis called this struggle "a clash of civilizations."
Three years later the American political scientist Samuel Huntington, in
an article entitled "The Clash of Civilizations?" grandiosely predicted a
cultural war between Islam and the West:

It is my hypothesis that the fundamental source of conflict in this new world will not be primarily ideological or primarily economic. The great divisions among humankind and the dominating source of conflict will be cultural. Nation states will remain the most powerful actors in world affairs, but the principal conflicts of global politics will occur between nations and groups of different civilizations. The clash of civilizations will dominate global politics. The fault lines between civilizations will be the battle lines of the future. (Huntington 1993, p. 22)

Huntington believed that world history was entering a new phase in which the great divisions in humankind and the chief sources of international conflict would be cultural rather than economic, military, territorial, or political. Huntington thought that civilizations were the highest cultural groupings of people, and that they differed from one another by four elements: religion, history, language, and tradition. These divisions, he wrote, were deep and increasingly important.

Arnold Toynbee had distinguished 21 different civilizations in the course of human history (Toynbee 1962). Huntington thought that there were only seven or eight civilizations in our modern world: the Western (Judeo-Christian), Eastern Orthodox (Slavic), Latin American, Islamic, Japanese, Confucian (Chinese), Hindu, and "perhaps" the African civilization. He thought that in this emerging era of cultural conflict the United States must forge alliances with similar cultures and spread its values wherever possible. With alien civilizations the West must be accommodating if possible, but confrontational if necessary. In the final analysis, however, all civilizations will have to learn to tolerate each other (Huntington 1993, 1996).

In an article published shortly after September 11, 2001, Edward William Said had some scathing things to say about Huntington, who, after all, had drawn his notion of the clash of civilizations from Said's arch-rival, Bernard Lewis. Both Huntington and Lewis, wrote Said (2001, page 12), had recklessly affirmed "the personification of enormous entities," which they call the West and Islam, turning "hugely complicated matters like identity and culture" into cartoon-like Disneyland characters like Popeye and Bluto who "bash each other mercilessly, with one always more virtuous pugilist getting the upper hand over his adversary." Said accused both Lewis and Huntington of having ignored three keys issues: the internal dynamics and plurality of every civilization, the fact that "the major contest in most modern cultures concerns the definition or interpretation of each culture," and the fact that presuming to speak for a whole religion or civilization involves "a great deal of demagogy and downright ignorance."

Said also called Huntington a rigid ideologist who wanted to turn multifaceted civilizations and identities into "shut-down, sealed-off entities that have been purged of the myriad currents and countercurrents that animate human history." That history, to Said, was not only one of religious wars and imperial conquest but also one of cultural exchange, cross-fertilization and sharing. Huntington, he charged, had ignored this far less visible history in his rush to highlight "the ludicrously compressed and constricted warfare" that his "clash of civilizations" took to be historical reality (Said 2001, p. 12). Given Said's aggressive style, it is no wonder that both Said's *Orientalism* and Huntington's *Clash of Civilizations* have given rise to heated scholarly polemics (Huntington et al. 1996).

Four months after the tragedy of September 11th, Lewis (2002) published an article entitled "What Went Wrong?" which he followed with a book of the same title (Lewis 2002a). Seeking to explain the Muslim mind, Lewis described the decline of Muslim civilization after the expulsion of the Muslims from Spain in 1492, and especially after their defeat at Vienna in 1683. Those defeats had caused the Muslims to search for the causes of their humiliation. Some blamed the devastating thirteenth-century Mongol invasion that destroyed most what are now Iran and Iraq, only to discover that "the greatest cultural achievements of Islam, notably in Iran, came after, not before, the Mongol invasion" (Lewis 2002, p. 44). Moreover, the Mongols had overthrown a Muslim empire that was already fatally weak and crumbling from within.

When nationalism was exported from Europe into the Muslim world, Lewis thought, the Muslims began to split into ethnic groups. The Arabs blamed the Ottoman Turks for the decline of their power and influence; the Turks blamed the Arabs; and the Persians blamed the Arabs, the Turks, and the Mongols. After the British and French had colonized much of the Muslim world, Western imperialism and colonialism were blamed for all its ills. Lewis (2002, p. 44), however, thought that "the Anglo-French interlude was comparatively brief, and ended half a century ago; Islam's change for the worse began long before and continued unabated afterward." In our own time, the Muslims blame their ills on the colonialism and imperialism of the United States as well as on Israel and "the Jews." Lewis, however, thought that Western rule and influence in the Muslim world was the result of the latter's inner weakness rather than its cause (Lewis 2002, p. 44).

This scholar understood that the unbearable feelings of shame and humiliation play a key role in the Arab attitude toward Israel and the Jews. The defeat of several Arab armies by the outnumbered Israeli forces in 1948 was too much: "As some writers observed at the time, it was humiliating enough to be defeated by the great imperial powers of the West; to suffer the same fate at the hands of a contemptible gang of Jews was intolerable. Anti-Semitism and its image of the Jew as a scheming, evil monster provided a soothing antidote" (Lewis 2002, p. 44). Arab anti-Semitism had begun to take root after 1933, following Hitler's rise to power. It became more deeply rooted after the creation of Israel in 1948. Since then, the Arab mass communications media have been seething with anti-Semitic propaganda.

One of the prominent Palestinian Arab anti-Semites was the Muslim grand mufti of Jerusalem, Amin al-Hussaini (1897–1974). This fanatical Muslim hated the Jews and the British with a passion and wanted to drive both out of Palestine (Elpeleg 1993). He became a close friend and admirer of Adolf Hitler. Hussaini waged a bitter power struggle against other Palestinian Arab nationalist elements, especially the Nashashibi clan. During most of the British mandate in Palestine (1920–1948), constant personal bickering between these groups seriously weakened the effectiveness of Palestinian Arab efforts.

In 1936 Hussaini and the Nashashibis achieved a semblance of unity when all the Palestinian Arab groups joined in the Arab High Committee under Hussaini's leadership. The committee demanded the cessation of Jewish immigration to Palestine and a prohibition of land transfers from Arabs to Jews. An Arab general strike in Palestine developed into a rebellion against British authority. The British removed Hussaini from the Committee's presidency and declared the committee illegal. In 1937 Hussaini fled to Lebanon, where he reconstituted the Committee under his domination. Hussaini retained the allegiance of most Palestinian Arabs, using his power to punish the Nashashibis.

In 1939 the Palestinian Arab rebellion forced Britain to make substantial concessions to Arab demands. The British issued a white paper abandoning the idea of establishing Palestine as a Jewish state, and, while Jewish immigration continued for another five years, it thereafter depended on Arab consent. Hussaini, however, felt that the British concessions did not go far enough and repudiated the new British policy. This was a serious error which badly damaged the Palestinian Arab

cause: Arab support for Britain might have prevented the establishment of Israel in 1948. Ceasing to play an active role in Palestinian affairs, Hussaini spent most of World War II with Adolf Hitler in Germany. At the war's end he fled to Egypt, and finally to Lebanon.

Arab Anti-Semitism is still rife. The Palestinian Arab media are dis-
torting reality in order to demonize the Israeli Jews. A U.S.-trained Palestinian Arab scholar, Mohammed Dajani, thought that the Palestinian
media coverage of the Israeli operation against suicide bombers in
Jenin has been biased, emotional, exaggerated, inconsistent, sloppy and
jingoistic (Dajani 2003). Dajani felt that there was no deliberate Palestinian Arab malice involved, but rather that the situation is the result of a
lack of professional, well-trained, qualified reporters. Unprofessional
Palestinian Arab journalists force-feed the Palestinian public with emotional material reminiscent of the coverage of the Sabra and Shatila
massacres. In covering the events occurring at the Jenin refugee camp,
the Palestinian media trained its sights on the fears and suspicions of
the Palestinian public and did not report what really happened (Dajani
2003). Dajani believes that most Palestinian Arabs are still living in the
past, and that, unless they begin to live in the reality of the present, the
tragic conflict will not end.

The Protocols of the Elders of Zion, a virulently anti-Semitic Russian forgery from 1905, probably plagiarized from two mid-nineteenth-
century French and German works (Segel 1934; Falk 1996, p. 643), has
become so popular in the Arab world that most Arabs seriously believe
it to be a secret Jewish tract describing the Jews' plans to conquer and
dominate the world. In the fall of 2002, during the Muslim holy month
of *Ramadan,* the fabricated *Protocols* became the key theme of *Horseman
Without a Horse,* a 41-part Egyptian anti-Jewish television series that
purported to portray the history of the Middle East from 1855 to 1917,
but was actually a venomous attack on the purported Jewish world
government, as viciously anti-Jewish as the original Russian fabrica-
tion. A year later, at the meeting of the Organization of the Islamic Conference, the Malaysian leader Mahathir Mohammed, who had jailed his
rival, Anwar Ibrahim, on trumped-up charges of "sodomy," publicly
accused the Jews of "running the world by proxy." *Al-Manar,* the Lebanese Hizballah-run television station, followed this during the next
Ramadan with *The Exile* or *The Disapora,* a 30-part, viciously anti-Jewish
Syrian television series that purported to describe the history of Zionism from 1812 to 1948, but was yet another attack on the purported Jewish world government.

In the Muslim world, however, blaming the Western colonialists, imperialists, Jews, and Americans for the ills of Muslim society is not universal. Some Muslims blame modern Islam itself. Fundamentalist Islamists blame all the ills of Muslim society on the Muslims' adoption of foreign ideas and practices. Liberal, modernist, and pro-reform Muslims blame them on the Islamic fanatics themselves, who refuse to adopt modern ways and stubbornly cling to ancient ones, and on "the inflexibility and ubiquity of the Islamic clergy" (Lewis 2002, p. 45), who insist on regressive and dysfunctional thousand-year-old practices and beliefs (Laroui 1976; Ahmad 1998, 1999, 1999a, 2000).

Lewis thought that this "blame game" leads the Muslims to offer two different answers to the ills of their society (Lewis 2002, p. 44). One answer is that of the Iranian Muslim revolution of Grand Ayatollah Ruhollah Khomeini and of the fundamentalist Islamic movements. It blames all evil on the Muslims' abandonment of Islam's divine heritage and advocates the return to a real or imagined past—the glorious past of Islam. The other answer is that of the modernist, pro-reform, and liberal Muslims. Seeing the root of evil as the Islamic fundamentalists' refusal to accept reality, they advocate the kind of secular democracy that was brought to Turkey by Mustafa Kemal Atatürk in 1923 (Lewis 2002, p. 45; cf. Volkan & Itzkowitz 1984). So far, however, Western attempts to install democracy in Arab and Muslim countries have not met with great success.

Child Abuse and Childhood Trauma in the Arab Family

Some scholars have attempted to explain the special emotional makeup of the Arabs as arising from the original way of life of the desert Arab nomads or Beduin—the word comes from the Arabic *badaween*, meaning "men of the desert" (Patai 1973; Gonen 2002). The Beduin value sons vastly more than daughters because men can fight other tribes for survival, avenge insults, and thereby save the tribe from shame and humiliation, whereas women can do none of these things. The Beduin used to bury some of their newborn female infants alive in the desert sand because they were seen as simply another useless mouth that would have to be fed.

Several scholars of Arab psychology, both Arab and non-Arab, thought that severe emotional blows befall the Arab boy at a tender age, when he ceases to be the object of the love and adulation of his mother and sisters and becomes the direct object of his father's aggression

(Hamady 1960; Glidden 1972). Three scholars, one Jewish, one Christian, and one Hindu, whose books bear the same title, *The Arab Mind*, stressed the fact that in Arab culture the son, unlike the daughter, enjoys an overindulgence of his wishes and is spoiled by the women of his family (Patai 1973; Laffin 1975; Sharma 1990). At first the son receives much care from his mother, who is grateful to her son for being born, because Arab society values a woman who has sons more than one who has daughters. When the son reaches a certain age, however—usually the age of seven years—he is suddenly and abruptly forced to be self-sufficient, to work, to serve, to give, to obey his father, to submit to him, and to keep silent in his father's presence.

To add insult to injury, the Muslim Arab boy is circumcised—some time between the age of seven and the age of thirteen. This violent circumcision, a direct attack on his sexual organ, is a traumatic event, psychologically akin to a castration. Sigmund Freud, the father of psychoanalysis, considered it an unconscious substitute for castration (Freud 1955–1974, vol. 15, p. 165, vol. 17, pp. 86–88, vol. 22, pp. 86–87, vol. 23, pp. 91, 92 note 1, 122, 190). Losing the protection and care of his mother, passing under the harsh control of his rival-father, and being circumcised by the latter constitute a sharp, traumatic turn of events in the life of the Arab boy, even in the best of cases.

The young Arab boy therefore harbors a deep feeling of rage against his father. This can become even worse if the furious father beats up his son when the latter does not obey him or does not respect his honor as the father wishes. Father and son become chronically enraged at each other, but the son must repress his rage, while the father may give vent to it physically. In some cases the son suffers narcissistic injuries from his mother as well. The mother, whose social standing in Arab society is low, may herself feel hurt or oppressed, and may not be able to give her son the love, warmth, understanding, and separate existence that he so badly needs.

Wife abuse is also common in Arab society (Haj-Yahia 1999, 1999a, 2000). Abused wives fail to make good enough mothers, further traumatizing and enraging the Arab child. Feelings of impotent rage at both parents overwhelm the Arab boy from a very young age. The Arab boy's rage at his mother for abandoning him at the age of seven may consolidate and crystallize much earlier infantile rage at the mother for much earlier psychological abandonments. The rage at his father for abusing him physically and emotionally fuels the inner volcano. In the best of cases the Arab boy unconsciously channels his rage into constructive or creative avenues. In the worst cases, he may unconsciously displace them onto the Israeli enemy who, as he thinks and feels, has robbed him of his motherland—the symbolic mother.

The Palestinian Arab Refugee Family

The matter of the father's honor and respect in the traditional Arab family is of great psychological importance. We need to examine the psychological fate of the Palestinian Arab refugee families who fled their homes, or were expelled, in the war of 1947 to 1949 and settled in 61 squalid refugee camps on both sides of the Jordan River and in all the surrounding Arab countries—Lebanon, Syria, Jordan, even Iraq. One journalist has observed that "the phenomenon of the refugee camp . . . has become so central to the Palestinians' sense of duty and identity that the political leaders of Dheisheh, a militant Palestinian camp on the West Bank, reacted with alarm and protest to an Israeli suggestion in 1984 that its residents be dispersed into new, modern housing" (Shipler 1986, p. 55). While cynics might say that those leaders wish to exploit the victimization of the refugees for political ends, a psychologist might agree that being camp refugees has become a key part of their identity.

It would be interesting to know how many of the young Palestinian Arab men throwing rocks and firebombs at Israeli soldiers in the occupied territories, or how many of the suicide bombers, come from such families. The small group of Israeli Jewish historians, known in Israel—admiringly or derisively, depending on who is discussing them—as the New Historians, has found that most of the Palestinian Arab rock throwers and fire-bombers in the occupied territories are sons of Arab refugees who either fled or were driven from their homes as children in the war of 1947 to 1949 (Morris 1987, 1990, 1993, 1999, 2004; Pappé 1988, 1992, 1999, 2004; Shlaim 1988, 1994, 1999). The undeclared, civil part of the war between the Palestinian Arabs and Jews began on November 30, 1947, following the adoption of U.N. General Assembly Resolution 181 on the Partition of Palestine the day before, and lasted until May 14, 1948, when the State of Israel was declared by the Palestinian Jews. The declared, conventional part of the war, in which several Arab armies invaded Israel, lasted from May 15, 1948, until early 1949 (Morris, 1999, p. 191).

More often than not, the Palestinian Arab refugee who had to abandon his home lost his status in his family and, what is worse, his honor. He suffers from a deep, burning feeling of shame and an equally painful sense of humiliation. His sons, members of a new generation, no longer respect his wishes nor obey his commands, as he had done his own father's. To repair his self-image, regain the respect of his family, and restore his honor in his society, the father often resorts to being violent with his sons, just as his own helplessly enraged father may have been with him. When the sons disobey or disrespect their father, as he sees it, the father is filled with murderous narcissistic rage and explodes violently at his sons, who, he feels, have injured his honor. The sons in turn feel humiliated by, and enraged at, their father, and suffer damage to their own sense of self. Their rage at their father unconsciously seeks an outlet via displacement.

In those Palestinian Arab refugee families, there is much tension and rage between fathers and sons, which must be unconsciously displaced to find an acceptable outlet. Since the Israelis are perceived as the brutal oppressors—just like the bad father—it is quite likely that the aggression and rage of these sons at their fathers are unconsciously displaced onto the Israeli enemy. Before these young Palestinian Arabs of the *Al-Aqsa Intifada* were humiliated by the Israelis, they had been humiliated by their own fathers. Rationally, the *intifada* seems to be a natural, obvious response to occupation, oppression, and humiliation. Yet this *intifada* only erupted in 1987, after twenty years of Israeli occupation of the Palestinian Arab West Bank and Gaza Strip. The uprising of the young Palestinian Arabs is first and foremost an attempt at repairing their damaged self-image. The feelings of shame and humiliation are so painful that they make the young Palestinian Arabs explode in violent rage. The guilt feelings of their fathers at having lost Mother Palestine are displaced and transferred onto the Israeli enemy, who is seen as the embodiment of evil.

Issues of Separation and Individuation

Volkan (1979) thought that, more often than not, the process of separation and individuation from the mother among the Turks is incomplete. The Turkish family rewards the child for obedience, imitation, conformity, and passivity, and punishes it for activity, independence, curiosity, and rebellion. In Turkish society, the family, clan, or tribe are supremely important, rather than the individual. This may also be true of the Arabs, among whom family and clan are all-important (Patai 1973). Among the Arabs, too, I believe, separation and individuation are often incomplete; there is no full emotional autonomy and maturity, and a deep feeling of shame pervades the soul. There is also a strong tendency to split one's world up into all-good and all-bad objects.

The fighting stance in the Arab world is endemic. An old Arab saying goes, "Me against my brother, me and my brother against our cousin, me, my brother and our cousin against the stranger." This warlike attitude among the Arabs may derive not only from their history of fighting other tribes in the desert for survival, but also from the unconscious processes of projection and externalization. These two concepts are similar, but projection refers to unconscious feelings such as rage, hostility, hatred, and death-wishes against loved ones, whereas externalization refers to aspects of the self such as weakness, greed, stinginess, meanness, stupidity, or sloth. Arab culture has numerous examples of the attribution of unpleasant traits to non-Arab minorities such as Jews. The Koran itself includes many unfavorable references to Jews and to other ethnic and religious groups.

With Glidden's caveats in mind, from a psychoanalytic viewpoint the personality traits of the Arabs discussed by Hamid Ammar and Sadiq Jalal al-Azm are those of a narcissistic child who is unable or unwilling to face the difficulties of its life, internal and external. The child unconsciously falls back on emotionally regressive defenses such as denial, projection, and externalization, being dishonest with both itself and the outside world. The effects of such character structure on the Arab-Israeli conflict are disastrous. The massive externalization of everything it cannot stand in itself brings about a blind hatred of the Jews and of Israel, over and beyond whatever real injustice may have been done to the Arabs by these enemies, which makes peace seem impossible.

As we have seen, Franco Fornari (1974) thought that unconscious projection is a factor in the causation of all wars, while Vamık Volkan (1988) has shown us our deep psychological need for enemies. The Israeli-Palestinian conflict is no exception. Nothing unites the Palestinian Arabs—and the Arabs as a whole—as much as their hatred of their common enemy, Israel. The Israeli enemy is as psychologically necessary to the Arabs as the Arab enemy is to us Israelis. Without Israel, the Arabs would have been mired in their own bloody internal struggles. The horrific Sabra and Shatila massacre of 1982 was carried out, after all, by Christian Arab Lebanese against Muslim Arab Palestinians, even if the Israeli defense minister of that time made it possible for this massacre to take place (Zaitoun 1983; Kapeliouk 1984). Naturally, as we have seen, the same is true of the Israelis, with their numerous, interminable, and at times violent internal conflicts.

Bernard Lewis thought that the lack of freedom in the Arab and Muslim world "underlies so many of the troubles" of that world. The only cure, from a Western point of view, therefore, is democracy and freedom. "But the road to democracy, as the Western experience amply demonstrates, is long and hard, full of pitfalls and obstacles" (Lewis 2002, p. 45). As we have seen, however, Western attempts to install democracy in Arab and Muslim countries have not done very well. If the Western road to democracy has been difficult and painful, the Arab and Muslim road is going to be that much harder. Arab family structure is autocratic rather than democratic, and so are most Arab societies and political systems. As we can see in Iraq now, it will take a very deep and painful psychological change on a very large scale to bring democracy into the Arab and Muslim world.

11

The Psychology of Suicide Bombers

While some extreme right-wing Israeli Jews deny that their country is occupying another people's land, and see their country's presence in the Palestinian Arab lands as a legitimate Jewish settlement in ancestral Jewish lands, many other Israelis, the Palestinian Arabs themselves, and most of the rest of the world see it as a straightforward military occupation of one country by another. To most Palestinian Arabs, this is an illegal and unjust occupation, which they deeply resent and wish to "shake off." The Palestinian Arab feelings of helpless rage and despair have engendered two major uprisings. The first Palestinian Arab *intifada* against the Israeli occupation erupted in 1987 and lasted several years (Aronson 1987; Leach & Tessler 1989; Lockman & Beinin 1989; Nassar & Heacock 1990; Peretz 1990; Schiff & Ya'ari 1990). The second Palestinian Arab *intifada* against the Israeli occupation, the *Al-Aqsa Intifada,* erupted in the fall of 2000, after what most Palestinian Muslim Arabs saw as Ariel Sharon's provocative visit to the *Haram ash–Sharif.* Since that time, the extremist Islamic Palestinian groups of *Hamas* and *Islamic Jihad* have used suicide bombings as a key weapon in their relentless war on Israel (Edlinger 2001; Bregman 2002; Peri 2002; Jones & Pedahzur 2004).

While the *intifada* itself has rational emotional causes as well as irrational and unconscious ones, fanatical terrorism, and especially suicide terrorism, is so irrational and tragic that it cries out for a psychological investigation, understanding, and explanation. This latest and most horrifying brand of terrorism in the Arab-Israeli conflict, and in *Al-Qaeda*'s war on "the infidel Crusaders," involves murderous rage, fusional longings, and the infantile unconscious defensive processes of splitting, projection, and denial. One of the first writers to investigate the psychology of terrorists was the Polish-English writer Józef Teodor Konrad Korzeniowski (1857–1924), better known as Joseph Conrad. This insightful author understood that the sharp lines separating savagery from civilization can become blurred under extreme circumstances, and that ideological terrorists, who are so fond of citing abstract and lofty ideals, unconsciously rationalize their murderous acts as intellectual abstractions (Conrad 1902, 1907; Said 2001, p. 13).

As we have seen, some scholars reject the need for a psychological understanding of terrorism. Thus, after the tragedy of September 11, 2001, an American political scientist concluded his attack on "left-wing excuses for terrorism" with a backhanded dismissal of psychological understanding: "Maybe psychologists have something to say on behalf of understanding. But the only political response to ideological fanatics and suicidal holy warriors is implacable opposition" (Walzer 2001, p. 17). The correct reply to this black-and-white thinking was made by an American psychiatrist: "The proper place to begin our effort to understand (not to excuse), it seems to me, is with the question of causation. For no matter how loathsome we may find the acts of 'fanatics,' without understanding what breeds them and drives them to do what they do in a particular time and place, we have little chance of preventing further such actions, let alone of 'eradicating terrorism'" (Mack 2002, p. 174).

This psychiatrist proposed three levels of causation in the phenomenon of suicidal terrorism: (a) the *immediate causes,* which include the "purposive actions of men who are willing to die as they destroy other lives"; (b) the *proximate causes,* including the personal pain and the unhappy political, social and economic conditions that breed such desperate acts; and (c) the *deeper causes,* which derive from "the nature of mind, or consciousness itself" (Mack 2002, p. 174).

The immediate causes are obvious enough. The implacable hatred of the Palestinian Arab suicide bombers for their Israeli Jewish oppressors—as they see them—matches the "implacable opposition" of the political scientist to "ideological fanatics and holy warriors." Any journalist writing about the Middle East conflict will tell you about those immediate causes of suicidal terrorism: unemployment, despair, vengeance, and rage—all due to the Israeli occupation of Palestinian Arab lands and the deadlock in the Israeli-Palestinian negotiations.

Mack's proximate causes of suicidal terrorism are somewhat more complex. Here is how Mack described these historical, social, economic, and political causes of the conflict that have created the suicide bombers, citing the Indian writer Arundhati Roy:

Listening to the pronouncements of President Bush and other
American leaders in the weeks after the events of September
11th, one could get the impression that the rage that leads to
the planning and execution of terrorist acts arises from a kind
of void, unconnected with history, without causation other
than pure evil fueled by jealousy. Yet it is not difficult to discover that the present conflict has complex historical and economic roots. It has grown out of *the affliction of countless millions of people in the Middle East and elsewhere who perceive
themselves as victims of the policies of a superpower and its allies
that have little concern for their lives, needs, or suffering* [italics
added], and of the actions of multinational corporations that,
in the words of an Indian writer, "are taking over the air we
breathe, the ground we stand on, the water we drink, the
thoughts we think." (Mack 2002, p. 175, citing Roy 2001, p. 2)

Mack further underscored this point: "For these millions, a figure like
Osama bin Laden, who we see only as the mass murderer that he is, can
become a hero for moving beyond helplessness to action against the
seemingly indifferent and invincible oppressor."

Since the superpower that the American-Jewish psychiatrist had in
mind was obviously the United States, and since one of its allies was
clearly Israel, this psychiatrist, while seeking a psychological understanding of suicidal terrorism, was identifying with—and taking the
side of—what he saw as the countless millions of Palestinian Arab victims against their Israeli Jewish oppressors. The unconscious process of
splitting which this psychiatrist had detected in the political scientist
may have been operating in him as well.

Mack (2002) went on to explain why these "countless millions" of
self-perceived Arab and Muslim victims of American and Israeli oppression adore terrorist masterminds like Osama bin Laden:

It is inconceivable that terrorism can be checked, much less
eradicated, if these [proximate] causes are not addressed. This
would require at the very least a reexamination of U.S. government policies that one-sidedly favor Israel in relation to the
Palestinians (not to mention U.S. support of Saddam Hussein
against Iran, before he started a conflict a few years later that
continues to take the lives of tens of thousands of innocent
Iraqi men, women, and children). It would require further
help with the growing refugee problem and a turning of our
attention to the toll that poverty and disease are taking in the
Middle East and other parts of the globe. (Mack 2002, p. 175)

While the difference between Mack's "immediate causes" and "proximate causes" is not readily apparent, it would seem that by "proximate causes" he was referring to the "complex historical and economic roots" of this conflict (Mack 2002, p. 175).

The "deeper causes" of suicidal terrorism outlined by Mack comprise conflicting worldviews, dualistic thinking, and "augmenting dualistic thinking." The word "worldview" is a rendering of the German *Weltanschauung,* which literally means "looking at the world." Mack described a worldview as "a kind of mental template into which we try to fit events" (Mack 2002, p. 176). We have seen the great differences between the worldviews of the Israeli Jews and the Palestinian Arabs, who live in different psychological realities, and even more so between those of the far-right religious Jews and the fanatical Islamic suicide terrorists. Upon closer examination, however, one view may be a mirror image of the other. This psychiatrist contrasted the splitting, black-and-white view of the world as divided into good and evil, us and them, for-us or against-us, with the idealistic world view of universal love and oneness which, he admitted, "has its own rigidities." Nationalism and religion augment dualistic thinking, the psychiatrist thought, although he did not use the psychoanalytic term of unconscious splitting (Mack 2002, p. 177).

The trouble with the "deeper causes" proffered by Mack is that they are not deep enough. He repeatedly referred to "the nature of human consciousness" and to the need to change it if we are to "transcend the mind of enmity," but mentioned the unconscious mind only once in his entire study: "Although nationalists tend to resist looking at the harmful actions in their nation's history, they may, nevertheless, fear unconsciously that retribution for the crimes of the past lies just across the next border" (Mack 2002, p. 177). While this may be true, the unconscious mind of the nationalist in general, and of the suicidal terrorist in particular, harbors much more than this: murderous rage against an engulfing mother and a punitive father, wishes for fusion with the early mother, the fear of this fusion, splitting, projection, externalization, and idealization. I shall examine all of these below.

Before analyzing further the psychology of suicidal terrorists, we need to understand that of religious extremism and fundamentalism, the breeding grounds for such terrorists. The psychoanalytic literature on religion in general is large (Freud 1927; Fromm 1950; Reik 1951; Zilboorg 1962; Beit-Hallahmi 1978; Smith & Handelman 1990; Symington 1994, Beit-Hallahmi & Argyle 1997). The founder of psychoanalysis,

Sigmund Freud, thought that all religious belief—whether in God, the Devil, angels, demons, or any other supernatural beings—was a neurotic illusion and compared it to an individual patient's obsessional neurosis (Freud 1955–1974, vol. 21, pp. 42–44). At least one modern psychoanalyst, however, thought that religious belief derives from normal processes of human development:

> The image of God incorporates inputs from different sources as the child grows and it is modified according to an individual's own psychology—early identification and unconscious fantasies, for example—as well as socio-cultural experiences, education, and the use of religious symbols. For each individual, the image of God becomes a source of various significant images, such as maternal or paternal images. It also becomes a source of psychological nourishment, anxiety of punishment, omnipotence, hatred, and so on—including, very significantly, the sense of belonging to a family, clan, and/or large group. (Volkan 2001, p. 157)

Whether moderate religious belief is normal or not, religious extremism, fanaticism, and fundamentalism conceal psychopathological processes. The religious fanatic displays a marked psychological regression. Like an anxious and unhappy infant, he unconsciously denies reality, projects and externalizes the unbearable aspects of his own self upon his enemies, and splits his world into all-good and all-bad parts— a black-and-white picture with no shades of gray. Religious extremism and fanaticism have occurred throughout history and in every religion and sect. An American theologian and his historian colleague have noted "the tendency of some members of traditional religious communities to separate from fellow believers and to define the sacred community in terms of its disciplined opposition to non-believers and 'lukewarm' believers alike" (Marty & Appleby 1995, p. 1).

Fantasies of Rebirth through Violent Death

Religious fanaticism and extremism are by no means limited to Muslims. Fanatical American Christian fundamentalism is well-known. A prominent American historian and psychoanalyst spent five years attending fundamentalist Christian religious services and interviewing apocalyptic fundamentalist Christians who believe in the coming End of Days. His colorful interviewees included an ex-prostitute, a multi-millionaire entrepreneur turned missionary, a fiery preacher, and a

Wall Street broker. All of them were born-again Christians who regarded their past lives as sinful and worthless. The scholar concluded that their born-again experiences represented unconscious attempts to heal their traumatized and fractured selves (Strozier 1994). The key role of violent fantasies or acts in millennial and messianic movements has been explored as well (Robbins & Palmer 1997).

Fantasies of rebirth—whether actual or symbolic—are common among fundamentalist religious extremists, such as born-again Christians, apocalyptic movements, millenarians, destructive cults and sects, and religious terrorist groups. There is a massive individual and collective psychopathology in these groups. Fantasies of rebirth are often tied to fantasies—and acts—of violent death, including suicide or murder. An American Jewish anthropologist tried to explain human civilization as our unconscious denial of the unbearable idea of our mortality (Becker 1973, 1975). An Israeli Jewish psychologist thought that "rebirth is *always* tied to imagined death and violence" and that "the [belief in the] apocalypse is first the denial of [one's own] death" (Beit-Hallahmi 2002, pp. 166, 173).

To illustrate the connection between the craving for rebirth and the wish for violent death, Beit-Hallahmi cited the examples of the People's Temple, the Branch Davidians, the Aum Shinrikyo, the Solar Temple, and Heaven's Gate. Each of those cults had a very disturbed, psychotic or borderline charismatic leader. The People's Temple of Jonestown, Guyana, was led by the borderline Reverend Jim Jones (1931–1978), who drove over nine hundred followers to commit suicide (Ulman & Abse 1983; Chidester 1988). The Branch Davidians of Waco, Texas, were disciples of the paranoid psychotic Vernon Wayne Howell (1959–1993), who called himself David Koresh, alternately believed that he was Jesus Christ and God Himself, and led dozens of followers to their violent death by fire (Wright 1995; Tabor & Gallagher 1995; Hall 2002). The Aum Shinrikyo cult of Japan was headed by the paranoid Chizuo Matsumoto, who called himself Shoko Asahara and caused the death of many innocent people by sarin gas poisoning (Brackett 1996; Mullins 1997; Lifton 1997, 1999; Reader 2002). In each case, the charismatic leader owed his charisma to some physical defect or foreignness that evoked the infantile fantasies of his followers (Schiffer 1973).

The French-speaking *Ordre du Temple Solaire* was led by a bizarre Italian Canadian named Joseph di Mambro (1924–1994) and his equally bizarre Belgian partner Luc Jouret (1948–1994). They were a *folie-à-deux* "father-and-son" team who ultimately murdered their 46 followers and committed suicide. Thirteen additional members of the cult killed themselves the following year (Hall & Schuyler 1997; Introvigne & Mayer 2002). The Heaven's Gate cult of the United States was led by Bonnie Lu Trousdale Nettles (1927–1985), who called herself Ti or Peep, and Marshall Herff Applewhite (1932–1997), who called himself Do or Bo. In yet another case of *folie-à-deux*, this psychotic couple believed that they were the two End-Times witnesses in Chapter 11 of the New Testament book of Revelation or the Apocalypse. They led a few dozen equally disturbed individuals who kept moving, designed Internet web sites, and believed in aliens from outer space. In 1997, thirty-nine cult members committed suicide in the belief that a spaceship following the Hale-Bopp comet was about to take them to a better life on another planet (Balch & Taylor 2002).

Religious madness is not restricted to Christian apocalyptics. The unconscious quest for psychological rebirth and a new Good Self to replace the unbearable Bad Self also characterizes fundamentalist Islamic fanatics and terrorists. The prominent Pakistani Muslim scholar Eqbal Ahmad (1932–1999) thought that Islamic fanatics were obsessed with controlling people's personal behavior, seeking "an Islamic order reduced to a penal code, stripped of its humanism, aesthetics, intellectual quests, and spiritual devotion" (quoted in Said 2001, p. 13). They try to promote and enforce "an absolute assertion of one, generally decontextualized, aspect of religion and a total disregard of another. The phenomenon distorts religion, debases tradition, and twists the political process wherever it unfolds" (Ahmad 1999, quoted in Said 2001, p. 13). This respected Pakistani Muslim scholar thought that fundamentalist Islamists were concerned with power, not with the soul, and that they sought to exploit people for their political ends, rather than alleviate their sufferings (Ahmad 1999, quoted in Said 2001, p. 13).

Volkan (2001, p. 157) thought that the identity of religious extremists involved "the regressive use of religious beliefs and feelings." This psychic regression displays the following characteristics: an absolute belief that one is in possession of the true divine text and/or rule; a supreme leader as the sole interpreter of the divine text; the exhibition of magical beliefs; a pessimistic attitude, paradoxically coexisting feelings of victimization and omnipotence; the construction of psychological (and sometimes physical) barricades between the group and the rest of the world; the expectation of threat or danger from people and things outside the group's borders; altered gender, family, child-rearing, and sexual norms, often including the degradation of women; a changed group morality, which may accept the destruction of monuments, buildings, or other symbols perceived as threatening to the group's beliefs; and attempts at mass suicide or mass murder in order to enhance or protect the large group identity (Volkan 2001, p. 158).

These collective psychopathological processes occur in fanatical religious cults led by disturbed charismatic leaders, as well as in large religious groups. They can be found in all major religions. In extreme cults, collective psychological regression to infantile modes of feeling and behavior is obvious (Ulman & Abse 1983; Chidester 1988). These processes also occur in modern fanatical Muslim groups like the Afghan *Taliban*, whose charismatic and paranoid leader, Mullah Mohammed Omar (born 1959), in an unconscious Oedipal act, donned "the sacred cloak of the Prophet Muhammad," and whose followers display signs of collective psychic regression (Volkan 2001, pp. 158–160).

The most terrible offspring of fundamentalist Islamic extremism, suicidal terrorism, was not invented by the Palestinian-Arab Islamic fanatics. The ancient Celts reportedly staged suicidal hunger strikes at the doors of their enemies to shame them (Fields et al. 2002, p. 193). In the eleventh century C.E., the Muslim Abbasid caliphate was based in the former Persian village of Baghdad (the original Persian name means God's Gift), which the eighth-century Abbasid Caliph Al-Mansur had made into his capital city and renamed *Madinat as-Salaam* (city of peace). It was occupied by the Turkish Seljuks in 1055. In 1090 a fanatic young Ismailite Muslim named Hasan-i Sabbah (died 1124 C.E.), who had studied in Egypt and claimed royal descent from the Himyarite kings of Arabia, seized the mountain fortress of Alamut (the name probably means Eagle's Nest), in the Seljuk province of Daylam, on the southern shore of the Caspian Sea, and launched suicide terror against his enemies. Hasan established a power base among the outer tribes and mountain people, far from the centers of established political and economic power. Hasan-i Sabbah became a Muslim *imam* and founded the fanatical sect of the Nizari Ismailites, who used suicide terror against their enemies, including self-drugging with hashish, a practice which the late-medieval travelogue *Il milione* by Marco Polo (1254–1324) introduced into Italian and other European languages in the word "assassins" (Polo 1928; Falk 1996, pp. 381, 476). While the Anglo-Jewish scholar Bernard Lewis described the Nizari Ismailis as history's first terrorists (Lewis 1967), a curious characterization in view of the numerous political assassinations in ancient times, the Anglo-Iranian scholar

Farhad Daftary believed that Marco Polo's story about the Ismaili Nizaris using hashish was a myth, and that the "assassins" would not have been so effective in their deadly and often patient work had they been high on drugs (Daftary 1994). While Daftary's account is biased in favor of the Ismailis, Western accounts since Marco Polo have been biased against them. It would seem that, as with beauty, an assassin is in the eye of the beholder.

Like a medieval *ayatollah,* the fanatical and autocratic *imam* Hasan-i Sabbah led an ascetic existence and imposed a puritanical regime. When one of his sons was accused of murder and the other of drunkenness, he had them both executed. After Hasan-i Sabbah died in the Year of the Hijrah 517 (1124 C.E.), he was succeeded by one of his lieutenants, Dai Kiya Buzurg Ummid, who came from a peasant family in the district of Rudbar, in the immediate neighborhood of the castle of Alamut. Buzurg Ummid's grandson, also named Hasan, became the *imam* of Alamut in 1162 C.E. Two years after Hasan's ascension to the imamate of Alamut, he assembled all of the religious leaders of the area and announced "to all demons, angels, and men," that their salvation lay in obeying his commands and that the religious law of Islam was hereby abrogated. He then made two bows signifying the premature end of *Ramadan* and celebrated by drinking and feasting and holding a festival to mark the shattering of the sacred law. On the door of his library were the words, "With the aid of Allah, the ruler of the universe destroyed the fetters of the law."

During the Second World War, Japanese military commanders used suicide pilots whom they called *kamikaze* to fly their planes into the American enemy's ships. The Japanese word *kamikaze* means "divine wind." The term harks back to a "miraculous" Japanese victory against the invading Mongols in 1281, which the Japanese attributed to a divine typhoon that sank the Mongols' ships. The Americans, however, used the word *kamikaze* to describe violent, reckless, and suicidal people. On the other hand, the European mass communication media, especially the French, have used the word *kamikaze* to refer to the modern Palestinian Arab suicide bombers, often with respect and admiration. An Egyptian-born Jewish scholar has called this submissive European attitude to the Muslims "psychological dhimmitude" (Bat Ye'or 1996, 2002). A Moroccan-born Israeli Jewish scholar, who had personally suffered abuse at the hands of Muslim Arabs as a child, has coined the word "Islamikaze" to replace the commonly used term suicide bomber, which he rejects (Israeli 1997, 2002, 2003).

Suicidal terrorism is widespread. In Sri Lanka, the Buddhist Sinhala are the majority and the Hindu Tamils are the minority. Most Tamils live in peace with the Sinhala, but some are full of rage and hate. The Liberation Tigers of Tamil Eelam, one of the world's most sophisticated and tightly organized terrorist groups, have used suicide terrorism against the governments of both Sri Lanka and India. In 1991 a Tamil Tiger suicide bomber killed India's prime minister Rajiv Gandhi (1944–1991). In 1993 another Tamil Tiger blew himself up together with the Sri Lankan president Ranasinghe Premadasa (1924–1993) a few days after his chief opponent, Lalith Athulathmudali (whom I had met in the 1960s when he was a young student in Israel), had been murdered by gunmen. His assassination was attributed to the Tamil Tigers, who hotly disputed this charge.

A specialized Tamil Tiger unit called the Black Tigers carries out the suicide attacks on the Sinhalese government. If faced with capture by the Sri Lankan authorities, the Black Tigers commit suicide by swallowing cyanide capsules that they wear around their necks. The ruthless and overweight Tamil Tiger leader, Velupillai Prabhakaran (born 1954), has been addicted to violence—and food—since his childhood. His fusional mother was "deeply religious and very fond of him" (Goertzel 2002, p. 104) while his father was a strict and punitive disciplinarian who demanded absolute obedience from his children and was also clinging and intrusive. It is not hard to imagine the murderous rage at his parents in Velupillai's unconscious mind (Swamy 1994, pp. 49–69).

In 2000 the Palestinian leaders of *Hamas* and *Islamic Jihad* began copying the effective methods of the Tamil Tigers, and found a willing pool of disaffected youths ready to assume the role of martyr. Let us now look at the psychological literature on suicide bombers and attempt to link it with what we know of borderline personality disorders and collective psychopathology.

Are Suicide Bombers Normal Individuals?

There has been much debate in the psychological literature as to whether terrorists in general and suicide bombers in particular are normal or disturbed individuals, whether they act out of rational motives or out of a distorted perception of reality. One scholar believed that terrorist behavior "displays a collective rationality" and that it is often effective in achieving its goals (Crenshaw 1998, p. 9). Another expert thought that "terrorists are driven to commit acts of violence as a consequence of psychological forces, and that their special psycho-logic is [unconsciously] constructed to rationalize [murderous] acts [that] they are psychologically compelled to commit" (Post 1998, p. 25). A third writer thought that while all behavior is "a combination of rational and emotional responses," terrorists typically court death, torture, or imprisonment, and these self-destructive sacrifices are irrational (Goertzel 2002, p. 97–98).

In studying a particular type of terrorist, the political assassin, I found that more often than not these are late adolescents who suffer from severe psychopathology, especially borderline personality disorder (Falk 2001). An American anthropologist, however, believed that suicide terrorists had no serious psychopathology and were basically normal people (Atran 2003). In the West, this scholar said, suicide terrorists from the Middle East are deemed crazed cowards who thrive in poverty and ignorance and are bent on senseless destruction. Atran thought that this was a serious misperception: suicide terrorists are neither poor nor ignorant; they have much to lose, and many of them are as educated and economically well-off as their surrounding population (which is often poor and uneducated). This scholar thought that a first line of defense against suicide bombers was to get the communities from which they stem to stop the attacks by learning how to minimize the receptivity of mostly ordinary people to recruiting organizations.

Volkan (2001a) seemingly shared Atran's opinion about the normality of suicide bombers: "Suicide bombers are not psychotic. In their case, the fabricated identity fits soundly with the external reality, and, significantly, is approved by outsiders. Thus, future suicide bombers, like the Sabra and Shatila children at play in a team, by all outward indications are 'normal' and often have an enhanced sense of self-esteem" (p. 209). Volkan's quotation marks around the word "normal" however, were not accidental. As we have seen, this scholar observed in the same breath that suicide bombers were "young people whose personal identity is already disturbed" and youths who seek an outer element to internalize in order to stabilize their unstable internal world (Volkan 2001a, p. 209). The heated controversy over the psychopathology of suicide bombers is reminiscent of—and tied to—the excited controversy over the Arab mind itself.

Suicide Terror As an Unconscious Fusion with the Mother

In my study of political assassination, I attempted to show that in the person of the political leader whom he murders the political assassin unconsciously seeks to kill his bad early mother and to fuse with her at the same time (Falk 2001). Nancy Kobrin, an American-Jewish psycho-analyst, thought that suicide bombers, as well as yearning for death and rebirth, unconsciously seek the deeply coveted fusion with the early mother, which she called "the maternal fusion." Because the suicide bomber dies along with his victims, he desires fusion with them. Rather than wish to kill the sadistic father, she wrote, "the assassin wishes to kill the sadistic pre-Oedipal mother" (Kobrin 2002, p. 182).

One of the ways scholars deal with complex material that makes them feel helpless, provokes their anxiety, and makes its study painful for them, is to divide the subject they are studying into manageable entities. As we have seen, Zonis and Offer (1985, pp. 268–287) stipulated three models for the Arab-Israeli conflict—the national-character model, the psychopathology model, and the self-system model, and Mack (2002, p. 174) distinguished three levels of causation for suicidal terrorism—the immediate, proximate, and deeper levels. Similarly, an American scholar and her Arab collaborators, in an attempt to integrate and reconcile the seemingly-contradictory studies of suicide bombers, outlined four different models or conceptual frameworks for understanding this tragic phenomenon: the psychological, sociological, psychiatric, and religious models (Fields et al. 2002, p. 219).

The psychological model proposed by these scholars focuses on the bombers' personality profiles; the sociological model on their marginality, unemployment, and poverty; the psychiatric model on their psychopathology; and the religious model on their religious belief system. Claiming that none of these models was sufficient to explain the phenomenon, these scholars proposed a "multilevel ecological/dynamic" and a "transactional/ecological" model. As they put it, "the sociopolitical matrix interacting with gender identity and personal and interpersonal loss, with religious sentiment fed by symbolic gratification, and the death of optimism as [a] result of the political situation all must be considered as operational factors in the phenomenon of the Palestinian suicide bomber." These scholars attempted to present their "multilevel, ecological, dynamic and transactional" model in a later study (Fields et al. 2002, p. 219).

The collective psychology of the suicide bombers is just as complex and intriguing as their individual psychology. The psychoanalyst Vamık Volkan believed that terrorist groups were like any other youth group: "The mechanisms that pull together a football team or boy scout group are similar to those used to create a terrorist group, but in the latter, secrecy binds the recruits" (Volkan 1997, p. 165). Nevertheless, some group dynamics are specific to Muslim Arab culture and even more so to extreme fanatical Islamic groups.

> According to fundamentalist Islamic tradition and correspond-
> ing cultural norms, most of these teenagers suppress their sex-
> ual desires; some even refrain from watching television to
> avoid sexual temptation. Indoctrination creates a severe—but
> external—superego, which demands adherence to restricted
> ways of thinking and behaving. But as a counterweight—or
> incentive—there is the suggestion of unlimited pleasures in
> heaven, where their stomachs will be filled with scrumptious
> food and they will receive the love of houris (angels). After the
> death of a suicide bomber, members of a terrorist group actu-
> ally hold a celebration (despite the family members' genuine
> grief) and speak of a martyr's death as a "wedding." With the
> examples of those who died before, recruits are given hope
> and a belief in immortality, as well as assurances that after
> their demise their parents and siblings will be well taken care
> of by the terrorist group. In fact, relatives receive compensa-
> tion. (Volkan 1997, p. 166)

The leaders of these fanatical Islamic groups, who blindly worship Allah and hate the "occupying infidel" with a murderous passion, typi-cally recruit a troubled late-adolescent youth who has failed in his stud-ies, his work, or his personal life, and brainwash him to become a *sha-heed*, to sacrifice himself for Allah in the war of liberation against the hated infidel. (There have also been a few atypical cases of women and older men becoming suicide bombers.) Volkan has described this pro-cess as consisting of two stages:

> The typical technique of creating Middle Eastern Muslim sui-
> cide bombers includes two basic steps (Volkan, 1997): first, the
> "trainers" find *young people whose personal identity is already dis-*
> *turbed* [italics added] and who are [unconsciously] seeking an
> outer "element" to internalize so they can stabilize their inter-
> nal world. Second, they develop a "teaching method" that
> "forces" the large-group identity—ethnic and/or religious—
> into the "cracks" of the person's damaged or subjugated indi-
> vidual identity. Once people become candidates to be suicide
> bombers-in-training, normal rules of behavior and individual
> psychology no longer fully apply to their patterns of thought
> and action. The future suicide bomber is now an agent of the
> large-group identity—which is perceived as threatened—and

will attempt to repair it for himself or herself and for other members of the large group. Killing one's self (and one's personal identity) and "others" (enemies) does not matter. What matters is that the act of bombing (terrorism) brings self-esteem and attention to the large-group identity. (Volkan 2001a, p. 209)

The prospective *shaheed* is told that he will enjoy the sexual favors of the 72 *houris* (angelic maidens) in Heaven. There are many Muslim myths and legends about these *houris*. The Koran (Surah 55) says, "In the Gardens of Paradise will be fair *houris*, good, beautiful . . . restrained (as to their glances), in (goodly) pavilions. . . . Whom no man or *jinn* (demon) before them has touched." The fourteenth-century Muslim scholar Ibn Kathir, in his *tafsir* (Koranic commentary) on Surah 55 quoted the Prophet Muhammad as saying, "The smallest reward for the people of paradise is an abode where there are 80,000 servants and 72 wives, over which stands a dome decorated with pearls, aquamarine, and ruby, as wide as the distance from Al-Jabiyyah [a Damascus suburb] to Sana'a [in Yemen]."

In the unconscious mind of the prospective *shaheed*, the imaginary *houris* are projections of his idealized mother, virginal, untouched, the fulfillment of an Oedipal dream. This fulfillment, however, comes at the awful price of "castration" and death, which brings us to the collective psychopathology of extreme terrorist groups:

> Meanwhile, the "teachers" also interfere with the "real world" affairs of the students, mainly by cutting off meaningful communication and other ties to students' families and by forbidding things such as music and television, on the grounds that they may be sexually stimulating. Sex and women can be obtained only after a passage to adulthood. In the case of the suicide bombers, however, the "passage" is killing oneself, not a symbolic castration. The oedipal triumph is allowed only after death. Allah—who is presented as a strict and primitive superego against the derivatives of libidinal drive and a force to be obeyed while the youngster is alive—allows the satisfaction of the libidinal wishes by *houris* (angels) in paradise. Using the Prophet Muhammad's instructions to his followers during the Battle of Badr (624 C.E.) as justification, the "teachers" convince their students that by carrying out the suicide attack, they will gain immortality. In what some consider one of the earliest examples of "war propaganda," Muhammad told his followers that they would continue to "live" in Paradise if they

died during the battle. The bomber candidates are told that life continues in paradise. The death of a suicide bomber is celebrated as a "wedding ceremony," a gathering where friends and family rejoice in their belief that the dead terrorist is in the loving hands of angels in heaven. (Volkan 2001a, pp. 210–211)

While Muhammad's Muslims had defeated the Meccan Qureishis at the Battle of Badr, they lost another battle to the same enemies the following year at Uhud (625 C.E.). However, with an infinite capacity for denying reality, the Prophet declared to his followers that their defeat at Uhud was really a victory, and that their 70 martyrs had gone to Heaven while the twenty-two enemy dead were in Hell. The Arabs used this kind of denial when they were defeated in the Arab-Israeli wars of 1948, 1956, 1967, and 1973.

In the same way, the fanatical leaders of extreme Islamic groups assure their young recruits that their deaths will really be new lives. As every television viewer knows, the mentors of the prospective *shaheed* dress him up in black martyr's garb with a green headband carrying Koranic verses such as, "Think not of those who are slain in Allah's way as dead. Nay, they live, finding their sustenance in the presence of their Lord" (Surah 3). They make a video of the future *shaheed* reading the appropriate declaration for Allah and against Israel, and then send him on his "sacred" mission to blow himself up among as many Israelis as possible, dying a martyr for Allah (unconsciously the Good Father) and for Palestine (the Good Mother).

As we have seen in our discussion of wife abuse and child abuse in the Arab family, in many cases the physical and emotional abuse of the Muslim Arab boy causes him to harbor unconscious murderous rage at his parents, which seeks an avenue of release through displacement. The traumatized young Muslim Arab boy will then join the Islamic terrorist organizations, hurl rocks and firebombs at Israeli soldiers, and even become a suicide bomber, being promised instant martyrdom with a guaranteed seat in Heaven and 72 *houris* for his pleasure. The murderous rage of the young Arab terrorist is thus unconsciously displaced from the original object, father or mother, onto the Jews, onto Israel (Kobrin 2002). Just as the Iranian *mullahs* and *ayatollahs* genuinely believe that the United States is the Great Satan or the Devil himself, so the fanatical Arab terrorist is often genuinely convinced that Israel, the Little Satan, is the embodiment of evil.

12

The Israeli Mind

In the same way as one can debate the existence of a particular national character, psychology or psychopathology of the Arabs, one could ask, is there such a thing as a specific psychology or psychopathology of the Jews? Is there an Israeli mind?

Three years after publishing *The Arab Mind*, Patai (1976) published an important article on Jewish ethnohistory and inner history. A year later this article was incorporated as the third chapter in Patai's book *The Jewish Mind* (Patai 1977). Among other things, Patai pointed out that for fifteen centuries, from Flavius Josephus in the first century C.E. to Bonaiuto de' Rossi in the sixteenth century, the Jews had lived in an ahistorical bubble, writing fantastic history and living in the past. This crucial point was amplified by a prominent Jewish historian five years later (Yerushalmi 1982), but neither scholar gave a satisfactory psychological explanation for this striking phenomenon. In my *Psychoanalytic History of the Jews* I attempted to integrate these insights and provide a psychological explanation for them (Falk 1996). My key thesis was that the Jews had not been psychologically able to mourn their historical losses, and that, in fact, collective mourning is very different from personal mourning, if not altogether impossible.

Patai himself, however, thought that "it is futile to attempt a portrayal of 'the Jewish personality,' for the simple reason that the two millennia of dispersion in the far corners of the world created as many different Jewish modal personalities as there are major Jewish ethnic groups" (Patai 1977, p. 538). If it is impossible to generalize about the psychology of the Jews, it may be possible to make some tentative statements about Israeli psychology.

We Israeli Jews are told from our childhood about our collective historical narcissistic injuries, such as the loss of the Kingdom of Israel in 721 B.C.E., the loss of the Kingdom of Judah and the First Temple in 586 B.C.E., the loss of the Second Temple in 70 C.E., the destruction of Judea in 135 C.E., and the two thousand years of anti-Semitism, persecutions, massacres, and humiliations both in Christian Europe and in the Muslim world, culminating in the *Shoah* in which one-third of the world's Jews were murdered.

From the psychoanalytic viewpoint, the political Zionism of the late nineteenth century was a semiconscious or unconscious attempt to turn back the wheels of Jewish history and to restore the Land of Israel in what was an Ottoman land populated mainly by Arabs. The Zionist longing for the Land of Israel was like that of an infant for its Great Good Mother, which exists only in its fantasy (Gonen 1975). As we have seen, the infant is unable to reconcile the pleasant and painful aspects of its mother, who feeds it milk and gives it love and warmth, but is also at times tired, depressed, exhausted, or angry at it. In defense against this unbearable feeling, the infant unconsciously splits the mother's image inside it into an all-good mother and all-bad one—as if it had two separate and different mothers, a fairy and a witch. The adult continues to idealize his motherland and to denigrate other lands. Those who settled in Palestine longed for a new life in a new motherland flowing with milk and honey. They certainly did not wish to find brothers in Palestine who would be their rivals for the love of their ideal motherland.

Many of the young Jewish immigrants to Palestine of the second *aliyah* between 1905 and 1914 were extremists, fanatics, idealists, and what are commonly called difficult people. They were stubborn and rebellious, could not accept authority, waged interminable power struggles, were unconsciously struggling with fusion-separation issues, and often had tragic personal lives. We Israeli Jews as a group still suffer from emotional problems. The expansionist ambitions of our extreme religious parties and other right-wing political groups spring from an inner feeling of incompleteness that their members carry within them from their early life, feelings arising from disturbances in the early mother-infant relationship, which, as Volkan (2001, p. 157) points out, cause "the regressive use of religious beliefs and feelings" (see also Faber 1981, 2002; Falk 1996, pp. 722–728).

Those of us who feel *whole* inside may not need any *expansion* of our land. Those who feel *damaged* or *incomplete* within themselves try to make themselves whole by expanding their motherland, with which they unconsciously identify and fuse. This does not mean that extreme left-wing parties have only emotionally healthy members. Every extremism, political or otherwise, has an infantile character and may be an unconscious defense against emotional conflict and anxiety. Extreme aggressiveness and hyperactivity may be a defense against feelings of helplessness and worthlessness.

Israeli society is not emotionally healthy. Daily life in Israel is full of aggression, pressure, tension, and strife—psychological, economic, social, communal, ethnic, and religious. In a multicultural society like ours, strife is endemic. The Palestinian Arab terrorists have added external fears to our inner anxieties. The ever-present danger of a suicide bombing makes us live in constant vigilance and fear for our lives. We express our anxiety through aggressive, even violent behavior in the streets, in the stores, in the banks, offices, on the road, everywhere. Tellingly, Israel has a very high rate of road accidents per capita.

In an interesting study of aggression in Israeli life, a Swedish-born Israeli psychologist concluded that the fear of annihilation was related to aggression in the Israeli psyche (Shalit 1994). This scholar thought that after the collectively traumatic *Shoah,* in which six million European Jews were murdered, "death anxiety was deflected into aggressive energy when combating the invading Arab armies" during the Arab-Israeli war of 1947 to 1949. The period prior to the Six-Day War of 1967 revived the fear of annihilation, but Israel's quick and decisive military victory over Egypt, Jordan, and Syria helped the Israelis deny it again and nurse their dangerous illusion of omnipotence (Gonen 1978). This illusion was shattered during the Yom Kippur War of 1973, in which Israel suffered heavy losses, and the Lebanon war of 1982 was, in part, a desperate but futile attempt to reinstate it (Shalit 1994, pp. 422–425).

Another Israeli psychologist discussed the same fear of annihilation in clinical terms, using the concept of "repression" to describe what some might call denial:

> We are repressing the feeling that our own existence is a bluff, that we are living on borrowed time, that the dream is about to vanish with us, that our true weakness will be revealed, and that [that] will be the end. We will give the Syrians the Golan Heights; we will let a Palestinian state be established; there are one million Arabs within Israel's borders; we are splintered and divided; so what is left [for us to hope for]? I admit, *this*

> *way of thinking makes me shudder.* But first, we have to admit to
> shuddering so that we can examine whether it is true. Some
> say Israel lives on the assumption that "everything stays the
> same." That is an inductive proof that says that if we existed
> yesterday and the day before, we will probably exist tomor-
> row. In other words, a feeling that our own existence is a mira-
> cle or magic, and that the only proof of our future existence is
> that it happened before. *That shuddering is a signal of the things
> we repress and do not want to see.* Our fears demand recognition
> and containment, as in therapy, so they do not turn into unde-
> sirable actions. In therapy we call it "acting out"—acts of ag-
> gression manifested toward others that stem from anxiety and
> distress that the individual cannot contain. That is our story in
> a nutshell and the reason why we distort reality and why we
> cannot see the other. (Grosbard 2003, p. 54)

Our Israeli society has many immigrants who secretly or even openly
long to return to their lost homelands. Our hundreds of thousands of
Holocaust survivors and their children are a world of severe emotional
problems unto themselves. As a result of all this, a sizable portion of the
Israeli population is in psychotherapy or other types of psychiatric
treatment, many of them in the public mental health centers. Many others need psychotherapy but do not get it. Israeli daily life is fraught
with aggression, noise, anger, and struggle. Radios blare rock music or
the hourly news bulletins everywhere. There are verbal fights, even
shouting matches, at every step in daily life. Our national myths such
as the Land of Israel, the Chosen People, a Light unto the Nations, and
the "reborn Hebrew nation in its ancient land" are far removed from
the harsh reality of life in Israel, where people often leave their homes
feeling like soldiers going into battle. The wars with the Arabs contribute to the tension, but the tension also contributes to the wars.

Shalit (1994, p. 432) thought that the Palestinian-Arab *intifada* erupted
because the Israelis had denied the problem of the occupied territories
and the rights of the Palestinians, and that it forced Israel to reestablish
the boundaries that it had sought to erase since 1967. In Israel, as elsewhere, individual and collective psychological processes influence and
reflect one another. The Israeli motto "Masada shall not fall again" derives from the ancient story of Flavius Josephus about the Jewish Zealots
who fought the Roman invaders, held their stronghold atop a hill overlooking the Dead Sea (from 70 to 73 C.E.), and, when the Romans were
about to take this fortress, preferred mass suicide to surrender. In the

unconscious mind time does not exist and events long past merge with current ones. Whether the story of Masada is reality or myth, it is a powerful Israeli national symbol and, in the Israeli psyche, the fall of Masada is fused with the annihilation of European Jewry in the *Shoah* (Falk 1996, pp. 309–310).

Modern Israeli Paradoxes

The scholarly and popular literature on modern Israel is vast. Hundreds of volumes and thousands of articles can be found in any good university library dealing with the Jewish state. There are dozens of periodicals in many languages, both inside and outside Israel, that deal with Israeli life. Most of this literature deals with Israel's history, politics, economics, society, and military problems. There is little scholarly literature on Israel's *psychological* history. Volumes could be filled with the stormy political affairs and endless warfare in Israel's fifty-six-year history as a modern state. I shall focus on the *psychological* conflicts and contradictions inherent in Israel's social and political structure.

From 1920 to 1948, after each violent flare-up of the Jewish-Arab conflict in Palestine, the British mandatory government and other organizations sent commissions of inquiry to Palestine, all of which failed to resolve the Arab-Jewish conflict. The British royal commissions were chaired by, among others, Sir Walter Shaw (1929–1930), Lord Robert Peel (1936–1937), and Sir John Charles Woodhead (1938). In 1945, after World War II and the Holocaust, the United Nations came into being in San Francisco. From 1945 to 1948 hundreds of thousands of Jewish survivors of the Nazi death camps, who had been placed in displaced-persons (DP) camps in Europe, attempted to reach Palestine. But British Foreign Secretary Ernest Bevin (1881–1951) ordered the British troops in Palestine to intercept their ships and deport them to Cyprus, or turn them back to Europe. The best-known case was that of the ship *Exodus 1947*, carrying thousands of survivors and refugees (Gruber 1948; Holly 1969; Halamish 1998).

The Jewish terrorist acts in Palestine in 1946 and the harsh British reprisals paved the road for U.N. intervention. An Anglo-American Commission that saw the Jewish Holocaust survivors being turned away by British troops recommended a U.N. trusteeship over Palestine, the repeal of the British government's pro-Arab white paper on Palestine, and the immediate immigration of a hundred thousand Holocaust survivors to Palestine. On November 29, 1947, the U.N. General Assembly voted to partition Palestine into two states, a Jewish one and an Arab one. The Palestinian Jews were jubilant, but the Palestinians Arabs furiously turned down the partition resolution and began a war on the Jews to prevent the creation of the Jewish state, which was nevertheless proclaimed on May 14, 1948. This paved the way for fifty-six years of Arab-Israeli warfare.

When the British left Palestine in May 1948, the first Arab-Israeli war was in full swing. It lasted from late 1947 to early 1949. Some six thousand Jews lost their lives; many more were wounded, physically and emotionally. Hundreds of thousands of Palestinian Arabs lost their homes, living in squalid refugee camps in Transjordan, which had annexed the Arab West Bank of the Jordan River, in Lebanon, and elsewhere. We Israeli Jews gave the 1948 war three different Hebrew names: *Milkhemet Ha'atsmaut* (the War of Independence), *Milkhemet Hashikhrur* (the War of Liberation), and *Milkhemet Hakommemiyut* (the War of Uprightness). These names indicate our prewar and pre-statehood feelings of dependence, subjection, and downtroddenness. While the Israeli Jews were ecstatic, the Palestinian Arabs called this war their *naqba* or catastrophe of 1948, and hated us for it. After two thousand years of "exile" and "diaspora," the Israeli Jews felt that they had found their long-lost motherland and once more become the ancient Hebrews and Maccabees. Like all fantasies, this one too was to end with a rude awakening. In 2003 the Israeli statesman Avraham Burg gave us this awakening with his article on "the end of Zionism" (Burg 2003, 2003a, 2003b).

Modern Israeli history is filled with paradoxes and contradictions. We have already discussed the Israeli notion of Oriental Jews as a euphemistic denial of the fact that most of these were Arab Jews. As we have seen, for fifty-six years Israel has formally maintained the fiction that its Druze Arab minority were not Arabs, even though their language and culture were thoroughly Arabic. In their national identity cards, the Druze Arabs were classified as Druze by nationality. Like the Israeli Beduin Arabs, some of the Israeli Druze Arabs finally gave us another rude awakening by joining their Palestinian Arab brethren and calling themselves Palestinians. Had we Israeli Jews been confident of our own identity, we might not have had to live in fantasy for so long (Falk 1996, pp. 722–728).

The historical fantasies of past greatness and the ever-present fear of annihilation following the *Shoah* have dominated the psychology of the Israeli Jews. If these are mastered and attenuated, we may be better equipped to make peace with the Palestinian Arabs.

Conclusion
Can the Conflict Be Resolved?

Most experts on the Arab-Israeli conflict have concluded their studies with bleak prognoses of its future. One Israeli Jewish scholar, Meron Benvenisti, believed that the two-state solution of separate Israeli and Palestinian states would never work and thought that the only good solution was that of a binational confederation of Israel and Palestine on the whole territory of the Holy Land (Benvenisti 1995). An American Jewish journalist has called this Israeli expert "an oasis of knowledge in the intellectual deserts of the Middle East—deserts where charlatans and ideologues, hucksters and holy men, regularly opine and divine, unencumbered by facts, history, or statistics" (Friedman 1995, p. vii). Unfortunately, however, very few Israeli Jews or Palestinian Arabs accept the idea of an Israeli-Palestinian confederation, and the chances of it becoming a political reality seem very slim indeed.

Historically, however, there have long been small groups of Arabs and Jews working to promote peaceful coexistence between their two communities. In the spring of 1925, during the early years of the British mandate over Palestine, a group of bright-eyed Palestinian Jewish intellectuals gathered in Jerusalem to establish a new association to promote what Martin Buber called *Wirklichkeitszionismus* (Reality Zionism), a Zionism attuned to the reality of the "Land of Israel," which first and foremost included the Palestinian Arabs. This association was called *Brith Shalom*, a Hebrew phrase meaning Covenant of Peace. Its founders and leaders were such luminaries as Arthur Ruppin (1876–1943), the German-born Zionist in charge of Jewish settlement in Palestine, Judah Leon Magnes (1877–1948), the American-born president of the just-founded Hebrew University of Jerusalem, and Martin Buber (1878–1965), the renowned German-born Jewish philosopher. The members of *Brith Shalom* included veteran Jewish residents of Palestine, academics, and socialist, religious and liberal Zionists. They believed in creating an independent binational Jewish-Arab state in Palestine and worked passionately for Jewish-Arab peace. The bloody conflicts that erupted between Palestinian Jews and Arabs in 1929, then in 1936–1939, and throughout the British mandate, however, turned this group into a very small minority among the Palestinian Jews that had no effect on Palestinian Jewish politics and was increasingly isolated from the Palestinian Jewish mainstream. Some Palestinian Jews regarded *Brith Shalom's* members as traitors to Jewish nationalism and Zionism (Ratzabi 2002).

After the creation of the State of Israel in 1948, a few Israeli Jews continued to pursue peace with the Arabs in the face of their implacable hostility. They were pacifists or peace seekers in a nation of military fighters, and were often treated with hostility. Among the Israeli Jewish pacifists of the 1950s and 1960s were Shimon Schereschewsky, Amnon Zichroni, Uri Davis, Joseph Abileah, and Abie Nathan, a flamboyant Iranian-Indian Jewish immigrant to Israel who ran the popular California restaurant in Tel Aviv before flying his light plane to Egypt to seek peace (and publicity). He was prosecuted and jailed by the Israeli authorities but became a popular figure, and later set up a pirate radio station named *The Voice of Peace* on a ship outside Israel's territorial waters.

Uri Avnery, the German-born Israeli Jewish editor of the Hebrew weekly *Ha'Olam HaZeh* and later a member of the Israeli *Knesset*, had been a young Israeli soldier in the traumatic 1948 war. Without endorsing militant pacifism, he single-handedly sought peace with the Arabs. Avnery met with prominent Palestinian Arabs at a time when such meetings were considered treason in Israel (Avnery 1985). The handful of Israeli Jews who refused to serve in the army as conscientious objectors were either jailed or dishonorably discharged on psychiatric grounds. While pacifism may be an unconscious defense against rage, violence, and sadism (Glover 1933), some of the Israeli peace seekers had a more mature and realistic vision of the Arab-Israeli conflict than their militaristic countrymen. However, the attitude of most Israeli Jews toward those early pacifists was represented by the title of a recent article, "Pacifism: A Recipe for Suicide" (Plaut 2004).

Today there are many Israeli Jewish conscientious objectors and they are no longer rejected and ostracized by the majority. Some of them have even become folk heroes and there are frequent demonstrations protesting their treatment by the government. There are also Israeli Jewish peace-seeking groups such as *Shalom Achshav* (Peace Now), *Gush Shalom* (Bloc of Peace), and *Kav Adom* (Red Line). While their political weight may be debated, and while Israeli Jewish nationalist groups like *Gush Emunim* (Bloc of the Faithful) may have more clout, the Israeli Jewish peace movement today is considerably larger and more influential than it was fifty years ago. Many Israeli Jews have become more mature, more realistic, less chauvinist and nationalistic, and more eager for peace in the face of unrelenting terror and implacable hostility.

On the Palestinian Arab side, too, there have been peace-seeking groups, but they are much less conspicuous. Most of these groups are Christian (Bacher 2002). The Palestinian Christian Arab community, however, has been harassed by the Muslim majority, and many of them have emigrated from Palestine (Raheb 1995; Abu El-Assal 1999; O'Mahony 1999). The city of Bethlehem, south of Jerusalem, for example, has lost its Christian majority and is now a mostly Muslim town. Sadly, there is nothing comparable to the Israeli peace movement on the Palestinian side, just as there is nothing comparable to the Palestinian suicide bombers on the Israeli side. Some will argue that this is only natural, because the Israelis are the aggressors and the Palestinians are the victims, but such simplistic, black-and-white views of the conflict are counterproductive, and the only way to resolve this tragic and intractable conflict is to try to understand its complex and unconscious underpinnings—on both sides.

By the end of the twentieth century, one of the leading New Israeli Historians, Benny Morris, thought that despite Israel's peace treaties with Egypt and Jordan things were getting progressively worse for the Jewish state:

> So far the Zionists have been the winners in this conflict . . . the success of the Zionist enterprise has been nothing short of miraculous. . . . But, from a perspective of mid-1999, this victory seems far from final. Islamic or pan-Arab currents may yet undermine those moderate Arab regimes that have already made peace. Moreover, two of the original "confrontation states," Syria and Lebanon, remain outside the process of peacemaking. And beyond the immediate circle of Israel's neighbors lie a cluster of countries—Iraq, Iran, Libya, Sudan— driven by radical philosophies that include among their foreign policy priorities the destruction of the Jewish state.

> Some of these nations are hard at work trying to acquire non-conventional weaponry that might counterbalance Israel's and that might be used to bring Israel to its knees or even destroy the Jewish state. Last, Russia, which with the collapse of the Soviet Union withdrew from the Middle East arena to lick and repair its internal wounds, might yet reassert itself on the world scene and again back radical anti-Western, anti-Israeli regimes. These factors will no doubt be affected by the policies of the new Barak government, elected in May 1999. But there is no certainty that Israeli goodwill or ill-will, flexibility or inflexibility, will decisively temper or resolve this century-old conflict. Islamic fundamentalism, Great Power rivalries or intervention, and nuclear weapons may prove far more telling. (Morris 1999, p. 669)

In early 2004, at the time of the publication of his latest book on the Palestinian Arab refugee problem (Morris 2004), Morris granted a controversial interview to an Israeli daily in which he lamented Israel's failure in 1948 to transfer all the Palestinian Arabs across the Jordan River into Transjordan. Had Israel expelled all the Palestinian Arabs in 1948, Morris said, it would have had the entire territory of Palestine, and the Arab-Israeli conflict would have taken a very different course. In 1948, Morris thought, only three years after tens of millions of people had been transferred across political borders following the Second World War, the world community, sympathetic to the new Israelis, would have accepted such a transfer of populations as an inevitable consequence of the war imposed on Israel by the Arabs. Now, however, such "ethnic cleansing" would be unthinkable. Morris compared the Islamic Arab fanatics to the ancient barbarians who destroyed the Roman Empire from within (Morris 2004a).

The Morris interview drew heavy fire from indignant Israeli liberals and leftists who felt betrayed by him and wrote numerous letters to the daily that published his interview, calling him a fascist and a racist. Morris defended himself in an open letter in the same newspaper, saying that he opposed the involuntary expulsion of the Israeli or Palestinian Arabs. Morris was very pessimistic about Israel's predicament, foreseeing a terrible catastrophe for Israel if it did not achieve a peace treaty with the Palestinian Arabs soon, which he thought was well-nigh impossible (Morris 2004b).

Four years earlier, another New Israeli Historian, Avi Shlaim, who lives and works in England, had a much rosier view of what was to come. This scholar, who thought that the previous prime minister, Benjamin Netanyhau, had been a disaster for Israel, was euphoric about the election of Ehud Barak as the new Israeli prime minister, and expected Barak to make peace with the Arabs very quickly:

> The election of May 1999 was a major landmark in the history of the Jewish state. Its most far-reaching implication was for the relations between Israel and the Palestinians. *Peace between Israel and the Palestinians was not just a pious hope or a distant dream* [italics added]. Israelis had actually touched it. Yitzhak Rabin laid the foundations for this peace with the Oslo accord of 1993 and the Oslo II agreement of 1995. His successor lost the election of 1996 not because the peace project had lost its appeal but largely due to the intervention of the *Hamas* suicide bombers. As prime minister Netanyahu employed all his destructive powers to freeze and undermine the Oslo agreements, only to discover how irreversible the Oslo process had become. In 1999 the Israeli electorate passed a severe judgment on Netanyahu and gave a clear mandate to Barak to follow in the footsteps of his slain mentor [Yitzhak Rabin] down the potholed path to peace. Barak won by a landslide. His victory entailed the biggest political change since the upheaval of 1977, when the *Likud* swept to power under the leadership of Menachem Begin. Not surprisingly, the result of the 1999 election was compared to a political earthquake. But it was more than an earthquake. It was the sunrise after the three dark and terrible years during which Israel had been led by the unreconstructed proponents of the iron wall. (Shlaim 2000, p. 609)

Unfortunately, the ardent hopes for peace of this New Israeli Historian were dashed shortly after his book was published. In July 2000, at the U.S. presidential retreat of Camp David, Israeli prime minister Ehud Barak failed to achieve a peace treaty with Palestinian leader Yassir Arafat. Despite the able mediation and pressure of U.S. President Bill Clinton, the Palestinian president rejected the Israeli prime minister's fargoing concessions, and the second Camp David peace talks collapsed. One of its fascinating moments was the dance-on-the-doorstep scene described in Chapter 4. The world observed two narcissistic and stubborn leaders, each refusing to let the other push him around.

At the end of his recent essay on the Middle East conflict, Bernard Lewis imagined two opposing scenarios for the future of the Middle East—one dark, the other hopeful:

> If the peoples of the Middle East continue on their present path, *the suicide bomber may become a metaphor for the whole region,* and there will be no escape from a downward spiral of hate and spite, rage and self-pity, poverty and oppression, culminating sooner or later in yet another alien domination— perhaps from a new Europe reverting to old ways, perhaps from a resurgent Russia, perhaps from some expanding super-power in the East. But if they can abandon grievance and vic-timhood, settle their differences, and join their talents, ener-gies, and resources in a common creative endeavor, they can once again make the Middle East, in modern times as it was in antiquity and in the Middle Ages, a major center of civiliza-tion. For the time being, the choice is theirs. (Lewis 2002, p. 45)

It is horrifying to contemplate the first scenario. As we have seen, the Is-raeli Jews have been truly living in constant fear of annihilation ever since the *Shoah,* and after Israel became an independent state. In fact, Israel has never really been independent: it has always depended on the United States and other countries for military, economic, and dip-lomatic support. Although Israel will not admit to it officially, it has stockpiled weapons of mass destruction in order to deter the Arab countries from attempting or even contemplating its destruction. If Iran and other Middle Eastern countries also pursue the acquisition of weapons of mass destruction, the whole Middle East may suicide-bomb itself, and many millions of people will be killed. Will the peoples of the Middle East, as Bernard Lewis put it, be able to "abandon griev-ance and victimhood, settle their differences, and join their talents, energies, and resources in a common creative endeavor"? This chapter considers the tragically dimming prospects for a rational resolution of the Arab-Israeli conflict, this most intractable of interethnic and politi-cal conflicts in our modern world.

By the summer of 2003 the Arab-Israeli conflict was worsening, and the prospects for its resolution were rather gloomy. Palestinian Arab sui-cide bombings inside Israel were multiplying, Israel was in ever deeper occupation of Palestinian lands, most of the Israeli Jews were living in fear and anguish, most of the Palestinian Arabs in misery and despair. Rising to the occasion, Avraham Burg, a prominent Israeli Jewish Labor member of the Knesset, published a prophetic article in a major Hebrew newspaper that some of his countrymen saw as heresy and even trea-son. This article was adapted by its author to an English-speaking audi-ence and published in the American Jewish weekly *Forward.* Sounding like a latter-day Isaiah, the former speaker of the Israeli Knesset chastised his countrymen for bringing about "the end of Zionism":

> The Zionist revolution has always rested on two pillars: a just path and an ethical leadership. Neither of these is operative any longer. The Israeli nation today rests on a scaffolding of corruption, and on foundations of oppression and injustice. As such, the end of the Zionist enterprise is already on our doorstep. There is a real chance that ours will be the last Zionist generation. There may yet be a Jewish state here, but it will be a different sort, strange and ugly. There is time to change course, but not much. What is needed is a new vision of a just society and the political will to implement it. Nor is this merely an internal Israeli affair. Diaspora Jews for whom Israel is a central pillar of their identity must pay heed and speak out. If the pillar collapses, the upper floors will come crashing down. The opposition does not exist, and the coalition, with Arik Sharon at its head, claims the right to remain silent. In a nation of chatterboxes, everyone has suddenly fallen dumb, because there's nothing left to say. (Burg 2003, pp. 1, 7)

Burg was referring, among other things, to the ongoing investigations of Ariel Sharon, his sons, and his business associates, on suspicion of graft, in which the suspects exercised their legal right to remain silent.

> We live in a thunderously failed reality. Yes, we have revived the Hebrew language, created a marvelous theater and a strong national currency. Our Jewish minds are as sharp as ever. We are traded on the Nasdaq. But is this why we created a state? The Jewish people did not survive for two millennia in order to pioneer new weaponry, computer security programs or anti-missile missiles. We were supposed to be a light unto the nations. In this we have failed. It turns out that the 2,000-year struggle for Jewish survival comes down to a state of settlements, run by an amoral clique of corrupt lawbreakers who are deaf both to their citizens and to their enemies. A state lacking justice cannot survive. More and more Israelis are coming to understand this as they ask their children where they expect to live in 25 years. Children who are honest admit, to their parents' shock, that they do not know. The countdown to the end of Israeli society has begun. (Burg 2003, p. 7)

Burg's prophetic outburst had personal as well as political motives, both conscious and unconscious. This 48-year-old rising star of Israeli politics, son of the popular Israeli Interior Minister Joseph Burg (1909–1995), had become a falling star. Burg had suffered several humiliating defeats after Ariel Sharon came to power in 2001. He lost his political positions of Speaker of the Knesset and Chairman of the Jewish Agency, and also lost the race for the leadership of the Israeli Labor Party to his much older rival Shimon Peres, who was being feted by the world's leaders on his eightieth birthday. Burg may have felt a deep sense of failure, and may have needed to repair his damaged self-esteem by externalizing his feelings of failure onto his countrymen and seeing himself as their prophet and savior.

In September 2003 Burg's "End of Zionism" article was reprinted in *The Guardian* and other English-language newspapers (Burg 2003b). It was also translated into French by Burg's father-in-law, the French-born Israeli Jewish historian Lucien Lazare, an expert on the Jewish resistance to the German Nazis in occupied France during World War II, and published in the French newspaper *Le Monde* under the title "La révolution sioniste est morte" (The Zionist Revolution Is Dead). Some rightwing members of Lazare's Orthodox Jewish synagogue in Jerusalem were so incensed by his collaboration with his son-in-law on what they saw as an anti-Israeli article that they called him a traitor and sought to have him excommunicated. This was a devastating blow to the well-meaning Lazare, who had emigrated from France after the Six-Day War of 1967 and founded the religious community together with some of his fellow French Jewish Israelis.

Along with Burg's "Death of Zionism" article, *Le Monde* published a Zionist piece by Alain Ilan Greilsammer, a left-wing French-born Israeli Jewish political scientist. Greilsammer said he wished to sound the alarm about a perverse new trend among left-wing European intellectuals, a racist, anti-Semitic, anti-Zionist, and anti-Israeli trend, that of stating that the creation of Israel as a Jewish state in 1948 was an error, and that the only solution to the Arab-Israeli conflict was a binational Arab-Jewish state of Palestine with an Arab majority and a Jewish minority. He charged the French intellectual elite with having developed a sudden passion for extreme anti-Zionist Israeli leftists and ignoring the reasonable Zionist ones. "Yes, give us people who will tell us that the Israeli soldiers act like Nazis and that Jenin is like Oradour-sur-Glane!" Greilsammer quoted the French leftists as saying (Greilsammer 2003, p. 20, author's translation from the French). Oradour-sur-Glane was the French village where the German Nazis massacred the entire population in 1944.

In October 2003 a European Commission public-opinion poll conducted among 7,500 European subjects found that 59% of Europeans regard Israel as a major threat to world peace—ahead of North Korea and Iran. American Jewish groups denounced the poll as anti-Semitic and demanded that the European Union leave the "quartet" (the United States, Russia, the United Nations, and European Union) trying to mediate peace between Israel and the Palestinians. At the same time, a month after the publication of his "End of Zionism" article, Avraham Burg and his Israeli colleagues, mostly leftists but also some right-wingers, met in Jordan with liberal Palestinian Arab leaders to hammer out a new Israeli-Palestinian peace accord, which they hailed as a breakthrough in the stalled Israeli-Arab peace process. The accord made very specific territorial arrangements for both parties and included detailed maps with the new borders between the two states clearly delineated.

The Israeli Jewish and Palestinian Arab politicians who met in Jordan had been negotiating their accord in secret ever since Ariel Sharon won the Israeli national election in 2001. They planned to sign it in the Swiss city of Geneva, symbol of peace and home of the United Nations, on the symbolic date of November 4, 2003—the eighth anniversary of the assassination of Israeli Prime Minister and Nobel Peace Prize winner, Yitzhak Rabin. The signing was postponed, however, and the Geneva Accord was eventually signed by the left-wing Israeli leader Yossi Beilin and the liberal Palestinian leader Yassir Abd-Rabbo, on December 1, 2003. Beilin, a relatively young former Israeli justice minister, may have hoped to use the emotional appeal of the Accord to wrest control of the Israeli Labor Party and win the Israeli government from Ariel Sharon; Abd-Rabbo may have had similar ideas with regard to Yassir Arafat. At the time of the signing, the Geneva Accord had no binding legal or political force, as neither the Israeli nor the Palestinian government had been party to it. It did, however, have significant psychological power over the minds of both Israelis and Palestinians, and that was no small feat in this tragic conflict (Lerner 2004).

Large-Group Psychology

The bitterness, intractability, and hopelessness of the Arab-Israeli conflict have few parallels anywhere. Many attempts have been made to resolve this conflict—and other inter-ethnic conflicts—through official diplomacy and through unofficial track-two diplomacy (McDonald & Bendahmane 1987; Volkan, Julius, & Montville 1990). Large-group psychology is an essential aspect of such attempts. In addition to the psychological processes discussed in this book, we have learned many things about large-group psychology since the French social psychologist Gustave Le Bon published his *Psychologie des foules* (Psychology of Crowds) in 1895. The first big breakthrough came in 1921, when Sigmund Freud published his *Massenpsychologie und Ich-Analyse* (Group Psychology and the Analysis of the Ego).

We now know that large groups may act in more primitive and archaic ways than individuals, that they often need dangerous, charismatic, and narcissistic leaders to follow and identify with, that they need to preserve a "group self" that defines them as separate from neighboring groups, that they need to maintain psychological borders between themselves and neighboring groups consisting of language, culture, and other hallmarks of their ethnic group identity (Volkan 2003, 2004). Despite all this knowledge, all attempts to end war during the past century have largely failed. There does not seem to be any kind of psychotherapy for large groups, such as nations, that can help end these tragic conflicts. One must wonder whether humankind is condemned to a never-ending cycle of bloodshed and war that today, with the proliferation of weapons of mass destruction, threatens the very existence of life on our planet.

Having read my ideas about the unconscious aspects of the Israeli-Palestinian conflict, some skeptical readers may still argue, as did at least one Israeli scholar, that the Israeli-Palestinian conflict has clear, rational causes and roots in reality, that there is no need to look for unconscious motives (Harkabi 1972). Aren't things in reality much simpler? Isn't this simply a dispute over territory? Were not hundreds of thousands of Palestinian Arabs driven from their homes to become refugees between 1947 and 1949? Did not the Arabs of Hebron massacre the Jews in 1929? Did not the Palestinian Jewish *Irgun* terrorists massacre the Palestinian Arab villagers of Deir-Yassin outside Jerusalem (now the state psychiatric hospital of Kfar Shaul) in 1948? Do not the Palestinian Arabs wish to throw us Israeli Jews into the sea?

Fortunately, such simplistic views of the conflict are no longer entertained by serious Israeli scholars (Rejwan 2000). Indeed, if we examine the violent feelings, thoughts, and fantasies of both sides in this conflict, we shall find that they are often irrational. We Israeli Jews have been taught that the Palestinian Arab refugee problem did not result from our own actions in the war of 1948, but from the concerted attack of several Arab armies upon Israel and from the call issued by the attacking countries to the Palestinian Arabs to leave their villages and towns to make it possible for the Arab armies to liquidate Israel. To the chagrin of self-righteous Israeli Jews, the New Israeli Historians have found that there were hardly any cases of Palestinian Arabs abandoning their villages as a result of an order from some Arab authority, and that most of them fled out of fear for their lives or were driven out by our own military forces (Morris 1987, 1999, 2004; Pappé 1988, 1992, 2004; Shlaim 1988, 1999).

Historical scholarship, however, is one thing, while memory and beliefs are another. It will be a long time before our collective Israeli Jewish views change on this matter. The massacre of the Hebron Jews by the town's Arabs in 1929 was horrible, but it did not involve all the Arabs of that town, nor all the Jews of Palestine. There were even some cases of Hebron Arabs who saved Jews, risking their own lives. The Deir-Yassin massacre of 1948 was carried out by an extreme right-wing Jewish terrorist group. It was indeed terrible, yet the massacres of 20,000 Lebanese Christian Arabs by Lebanese Druze or Shiite Muslim Arabs during the Lebanese civil war of 1975–1976, and the massacre of up to 1,000 Muslim Palestinian-Arab refugees by Christian Lebanese Arabs at the Sabra and Shatila refugee camps in Lebanon in 1982—to avenge the earlier assassination of their leader Bashir Gemayel—were still worse.

Similarly, whether all Palestinian Arabs do in fact wish to throw us Israeli Jews into the sea is not certain. Many scholars have pointed out the Arab tendency to exaggerate, both emotionally and in their perception of reality. Nonetheless, the Israeli Jewish *fear* of being thrown into the sea is a palpable psychological reality—despite Israel's superior military might, which greatly surpasses that of any of its neighbors. Neither are Israel's peace treaties with Egypt and with Jordan pieces of paper only. They have deep psychological significance, even if it is a distant, cold peace for the time being, and despite the widespread hostility among Egyptian and Jordanian Arabs toward Israeli Jews.

The Resistance of Rationalistic Scholars to Psychoanalytic Views

It might be appropriate to end this book with a brief discussion of the ambivalent attitude of political scientists and historians toward psychoanalysis. A typical example was the Israeli scholar General Yehoshafat Harkabi (1921–1994), a former head of Israeli military intelligence who became an Arabist and a military historian. In one of his early books, Harkabi warned his readers against the "limitations of psychological explanation": Arab hostility to Israel, said Harkabi was "not a response to any psychological need to relieve tension or aggressive impulses. In the beginning this hostility was the outcome of [Arab] opposition to Jewish settlement [in Palestine], and it reached its peak as a reaction to the establishment of the Jewish state of Israel, which the Arabs regarded as the usurpation of a homeland. The main cause of the conflict, wrote Harkabi, was not psychological but political: a conflict over territory and a clash over real interests" (Harkabi 1972, p. 413).

As John Mack (2003, p.174) has put it in the case of the political scientist Michael Walzer, seeing the psychological and the political as two separate and distinct entities is a defect of reality testing, a symptom of black-and-white thinking or unconscious splitting. The psychological is an integral part of the political, and both are equally real. Viewing the psychological causes of war—or any other human phenomenon—as unreal is a fundamental error. Violent unconscious feelings are just as real as conscious conflict over territory and, in fact, may even cause it. The very need for a national territory is in itself a powerful large-group psychological motive. So are the need for self-definition, national identity, and political recognition. Unconscious emotional motives are in themselves real causes of intergroup strife.

In fact, the rationalistic Israeli scholar himself cited many psychological theories about the Arab-Israeli conflict (Harkabi, 1972, pp. 113-170). Some of these touched upon the question of each party's self-image and its view of the other. Others dealt with the processes of projection and externalization in each party, the selective perception of reality, repression, denial, filtering, and other unconscious processes. Harkabi himself also noted the pervasive Arab tendency to externalize blame and assign it to others. He also pointed out that the Arabic language contains many expressions of hostility, contempt, derision, defamation, loathing, and hatred. Nevertheless, Harkabi was threatened by psychological insight.

Understanding the unconscious Muslim Arab splitting that leads to the dualistic belief in *Dar al-Islam* and *Dar al-Harb* is most important psychologically. To extreme Muslim believers, the House of Islam is all-good while the rest of the world is all-bad. Islam is not only a religion of peace, it is also a conquering, warlike religion. The *jihad* reminds Muslims of the glorious days of the caliphate. Harkabi (1972, pp. 139-142) quoted psychologists who explained Arab behavior by using the model of the authoritarian personality, as well as others who disputed this theory. He even quoted from the Arabic literature to show that important Arab writers had criticized the Arab tendency to externalize guilt, and that the Arab attitude to Israel is highly ambivalent (Harkabi 1972, pp. 151–153). All of this seems to indicate that Harkabi had some knowledge of psychoanalytic theory, yet the Israeli scholar rejected what he called the psychologistic explanations of the conflict.

Harkabi was also aware of the fact that the Arabs have a problem with their self-image and self-esteem. He understood that the negative self-image of the Arabs causes them to rewrite their history in a distorted fashion. Yet, despite this psychological insight, Harkabi came out strongly against psychological theories of the Arab-Israeli conflict. However, this attitude to psychoanalysis is deeply ambivalent. In contrast, while the Norwegian scholar Daniel Heradstveit mainly cited cognitive psychological theories about the conscious causes of the Arab-Israeli conflict, he did not rule out the psychoanalytic ones (Heradstveit 1979).

How can one explain the ambivalent attitude of Israeli scholars such as Harkabi and their American colleagues, such as Walzer, to psychoanalysis—in particular, the psychoanalytic approach to the Israeli-Palestinian conflict and to their own history? I believe that a discussion of unconscious motives and emotions threatens such scholars emotionally. It exposes the complexity and the ambivalence behind national feelings, the fact that every feeling may conceal its opposite, and that our image of our enemy derives from our own self-image. This is a profound threat to the rationalistic viewpoint of historians, political scientists, international relations scholars, and even psychologists, which protects them against the anxiety provoked by an examination of the irrational in human affairs—and in their own.

In other words, rationalistic scholars fear their own unconscious feelings. The rationalistic scholarship is in itself an unconscious defense against the emotional difficulty of understanding this conflict—and oneself. Israeli Jewish scholars in particular, who are part of a culture that refuses to mourn its losses, are resistant to psychoanalytic explanations. On the whole, American scholars seem much more open to psychoanalytic theories in history and politics than their Israeli colleagues, as the readers of American journals like *Political Psychology, Clio's Psyche,* and the now-defunct *Psychohistory Review* can attest. They are less threatened by such theories than their Israeli colleagues because they do not need to maintain a rigidly ideological Zionist posture in this conflict. The relatively more flexible attitude of some Israeli politicians may yet facilitate the resolution of the conflict. It is my hope that the insights I have offered in this book into the unconscious aspects of this tragic conflict will help open their eyes, if ever so slightly, and make a modest contribution to its resolution.

Bibliography

Index

Bibliography

Abbas, Mahmoud. (2000, July 29). *No Peace Agreement with Israel without Jerusa-lem.* Interview with Palestine Television.

Abdullah, King of Jordan. (1950). *Memoirs of King Abdullah of Transjordan.* Ed. Philip P. Graves. Intro. R. J. C. Broadhurst. London: Jonathan Cape. New York: Philosophical Library. New edition (1954) *My Memoirs Completed (al-Takmilah).* Trans. Harold Walker Glidden. Foreword Hussein Ibn Talal. Washington, DC: American Council of Learned Societies. New edition (1978) London and New York: Longman.

Abdullah, Sharif. (2002). The Soul of a Terrorist: Reflections on Our War with the "Other." In Chris E. Stout (Ed.), *The Psychology of Terrorism: Clinical Aspects and Response* (Vol. 2). 129–141. Westport, CT: Praeger.

Abramov, Sheneur Zalman. (1976). *Perpetual Dilemma: Jewish Religion in the Jewish State.* Cranbury, NJ: Associated Universities Presses.

Abrams, Irwin (Ed.). (1997). *Nobel Lectures in Peace, 1991–1995.* Singapore and River Edge, NJ: World Scientific Publishing Co.

Abu El-Assal, Riah. (1999). *Caught in Between: The Story of an Arab Palestinian Christian Israeli.* London: Society for Promoting Christian Knowledge.

Abu-Lughod, Ibrahim A. (1971). *The Transformation of Palestine: Essays on the Origin and Development of the Arab-Israeli Conflict.* Evanston, IL: Northwestern University Press.

Abu-Lughod, Ibrahim A. (Ed.). (1970). *The Arab-Israeli Confrontation of June 1967: An Arab Perspective.* Evanston, IL: Northwestern University Press.

Abu-Lughod, Ibrahim A. & Abu-Laban, Baha. (Eds.). (1974). *Settler Regimes in Africa and the Arab World: The Illusion of Endurance.* Wilmette, IL: Medina University Press International.

Abu-Nimer, Mohammed. (1999). *Dialogue, Conflict Resolution, and Change: Arab-Jewish Encounters in Israel.* Albany: State University of New York Press.

Abu-Sharif, Bassam & Mahnaimi, Uzi. (1995). *The Best of Enemies: The Memoirs of Bassam Abu-Sharif & Uzi Mahnaimi.* Boston: Little, Brown.

Aburish, Saïd K. (1989). *Children of Bethany: The Story of a Palestinian Family.* Bloomington: Indiana University Press. New edition (1999) London: Bloomsbury Publishing.

Aburish, Saïd K. (1994). Consorting with the Enemy: A Palestinian Describes His Many Friendships with Jews throughout His Life and Asks His Jewish Friends to Encourage Generosity in Applying the Peace Process. *Palestine-Israel Journal of Politics, Economics and Culture,* 1 (4), 62–68.

Aburish, Saïd K. (1996). *The Rise, Corruption and Coming Fall of the House of Saud.* New York: St. Martin's Press.

Aburish, Saïd K. (1997). *A Brutal Friendship: The West and the Arab Elite.* London: Victor Gollancz. Reprinted (1998) New York: St. Martin's Press.

Aburish, Saïd K. (1998). *Arafat: From Defender to Dictator.* London: Bloomsbury Publishing.

Adelson, Dorothy. (1982). *Operation Susannah.* New York: Pemberley Press.

Adler, Renata. (1986). *Reckless Disregard: Westmoreland v. CBS et al., Sharon v. Time.* New York: Alfred A. Knopf. Reprinted (1988) New York: Vintage Books.

Ahad Ha'am [Asher Ginsberg]. (1912). *Selected Essays.* Ed. Leon Simon. Philadelphia: Jewish Publication Society of America. New edition (1962) *Selected Essays of Ahad Ha'Am.* New York: Atheneum.

Aharoni, Dov. (1985). *General Sharon's War against Time Magazine: His Trial and Vindication.* New York: Ian Shapolsky. Tel Aviv: Steimatzky.

Ahmad, Aijaz. (1991). *"Orientalism" and After: Ambivalence and Cosmopolitan Location in the Work of Edward Said.* New Delhi: Centre for Contemporary Studies, Nehru Memorial Museum and Library. New version (1992) in Ahmad Aijaz, *In Theory: Classes, Nations, Literatures.* London: Verso. Reprinted (1993) in Patrick Williams & Laura Chrisman, *Colonial Discourse and Post-Colonial Theory: A Reader.* London: Harvester Wheatsheaf. Reprinted (1994) New York: Columbia University Press.

Ahmad, Eqbal. (1998, September 6). Islam as Refuge from Failure. *Dawn* (Pakistan).

Ahmad, Eqbal. (1999, January 24). Roots of the Religious Right. *Dawn* (Pakistan). (1999, March 7). Profile of the Religious Right. *Dawn* (Pakistan).

Ahmad, Eqbal. (1999a). *Living with Eqbal Ahmad, 1932–1999: A Homage to Academician, Intellectual & Revolutionary.* Lahore: Democratic Commission for Human Development.

Ahmad, Eqbal. (2000). *Eqbal Ahmad, Confronting Empire: Interviews with David Barsamian.* Foreword Edward W. Said. Cambridge, MA: South End Press.

Ahmed, Akbar S. (1988). *Discovering Islam: Making Sense of Muslim History and Society.* London and New York: Routledge and Kegan Paul. Revised edition (2002) Intro. Lawrence Rosen. New York: Routledge.

Ahmed, Akbar S. (1992). *Postmodernism and Islam: Predicament and Promise.* London and New York: Routledge.

Ahmed, Akbar S. (2003). *Islam under Siege: Living Dangerously in a Post-Honour World*. Cambridge: Polity Press.

Ahmed, Akbar S. & Donnan, Hastings. (Eds.). (1994). *Islam, Globalization, and Postmodernity*. London and New York: Routledge.

Ajami, Fouad. (1981). *The Arab Predicament: Arab Political Thought and Practice since 1967*. Cambridge and New York: Cambridge University Press. New edition (1992) Cambridge and New York: Cambridge University Press. New edition (2001) Cambridge and New York: Cambridge University Press.

Ajami, Fouad. (1999). *The Dream Palace of the Arabs: A Generation's Odyssey*. New York: Vintage Books.

Al-Maqrizi, Taqi al-Din Ahmad ibn-Ali. (1895-1900). *Description topographique et historique de l'Egypte* (17 vols.). Paris: Editions Leroux.

Al-Maqrizi, Taqi al-Din Ahmad ibn-Ali. (1980). *A History of the Ayyubid Sultans of Egypt*. Trans. and Intro. Ronald J. C. Broadhurst. Boston: Twayne Publishers.

Al-Maqrizi, Taqi al-Din Ahmad ibn-Ali. (1983). *Al-Maqrizi's Book of Contention and Strife Concerning the Relations between the Banu-Umayya and the Banu-Hashim*. Trans. and Intro. Clifford Edmund Bosworth. *Journal of Semitic Studies. Monograph 3*. Manchester: Manchester University Press.

Albright, William Foxwell. (1940). *From the Stone Age to Christianity: Monotheism and the Historical Process*. Baltimore: Johns Hopkins University Press.

Albright, William Foxwell. (1949). *The Archeology of Palestine*. Harmondsworth: Penguin Books.

Albright, William Foxwell. (1953). *Archeology and the Religion of Israel*. Baltimore: Johns Hopkins University Press.

Alcalay, Ammiel. (1993). *After Jews and Arabs: Remaking Levantine Culture*. Minneapolis: University of Minnesota Press.

Alcalay, Ammiel. (Ed.). (1996). *Keys to the Garden: New Israeli Writing*. San Francisco: City Light Books.

Ali, Tariq. (2002). *The Clash of Fundamentalisms: Crusades, Jihads and Modernity*. London: Verso.

Alland, Alexander. (1972). *The Human Imperative*. New York: Columbia University Press.

Allon, Yigal. (1970). *Shield of David: The Story of Israel's Armed Forces*. London: Weidenfeld and Nicolson. Reprinted (1970) as *The Making of Israel's Army*. New York: Universe Books. Reprinted (1971) London: Sphere Books.

Allon, Yigal. (1976). *My Father's House*. New York: Norton.

Alpher, Joseph & Feldman, Shai. (Eds.). (1989). *The West Bank and Gaza: Israel's Options for Peace*. Jerusalem: The Jerusalem Post Press. Tel Aviv: Jaffe Center for Strategic Studies, Tel Aviv University.

AlRoy, Gil Carl. (1975). *The Kissinger Experience: American Policy in the Middle East*. New York: Horizon Press.

AlRoy, Gil Carl. (1975a). *Behind the Middle East Conflict: The Real Impasse between Arab and Jew*. New York: Putnam.

AlRoy, Gil Carl. (Ed.). (1971). *Attitudes toward Jewish Statehood in the Arab World*. New York: American Academic Association for Peace in the Middle East.

American Psychiatric Association. (1995). *Diagnostic and Statistical Manual of Mental Disorders: DSM-IV. International Version with ICD-10 Codes*. Washington, DC: American Psychiatric Association.

Ammar, Hamid. (1954). *Growing up in an Egyptian Village: Silwa, Province of Aswan*. London: Routledge and Kegan Paul. New edition (1966) New York: Octagon Books.

Anderson, Benedict. (1983). *Imagined Communities: Reflections on the Origin and Spread of Nationalism*. London and New York: Verso.

Anderson, Benedict. (1991). *Imagined Communities: Reflections on the Origin and Spread of Nationalism* (Rev. and ext. ed.). London and New York: Verso.

Andrae, Tor. (2000). *Mohammed: The Man and His Faith*. Trans. Theophil Menzel. Mineola, NY: Dover.

Antonius, George. (1938). *The Arab Awakening: The Story of the Arab National Movement*. London: Hamish Hamilton. Reprinted (1939) Philadelphia: Lippincott. Second edition (1945) London: Hamish Hamilton. Reprinted (1946) New York: G. P. Putnam's Sons.

Antonius, George. (1965). *The Arab Awakening: The Story of the Arab National Movement* (New ed.). London: Capricorn. Reprinted (1969) Beirut: Librairie du Liban. Reprinted (1981) New York: Gordon Press. Third edition (2000) London: Kegan Paul.

Archer, Jules. (1976). *Legacy of the Desert: Understanding the Arabs*. Boston: Little, Brown.

Ardrey, Robert. (1966). *The Territorial Imperative: A Personal Inquiry into the Animal Origins of Property and Nations*. Drawings by Berdine Ardrey. New York: Atheneum. New edition (1997) Intro. Irven DeVore. New York: Kodansha International.

Arian, Asher Alan. (1985). *Politics in Israel: The Second Generation*. Chatham, NJ: Chatham House. Revised edition (1989) Chatham, NJ: Chatham House.

Armstrong, Karen. (1997). *Jerusalem: One City, Three Faiths*. New York: Ballantine Books.

Aronson, Geoffrey. (1987). *Creating Facts: Israel, Palestinians and the West Bank*. Washington, DC: Institute for Palestine Studies. New edition (1990) *Israel, Palestinians, and the Intifada: Creating Facts on the West Bank*. London and New York: Kegan Paul. Washington, DC: Institute for Palestine Studies.

Aruri, Naseer Hasan. (1995). *The Obstruction of Peace: The United States, Israel, and the Palestinians*. Monroe, ME: Common Courage Press.

Aruri, Naseer Hasan. (Ed.). (1983). *Occupation: Israel over Palestine*. Belmont, MA: Association of Arab-American University Graduates.

Ashrawi, Hanan. (1995). *This Side of Peace*. New York: Simon and Schuster.

Ateek, Naim S. (1989). *Justice and Only Justice: A Palestinian Theology of Liberation*. Maryknoll, NY: Orbis Books.

Ateek, Naim S. & Prior, Michael. (Eds.). (1999). *Holy Land, Hollow Jubilee: God, Justice, and the Palestinians.* London: Melisende.

Atran, Scott. (2002). *In Gods We Trust: The Evolutionary Landscape of Religion.* Oxford: Oxford University Press.

Atran, Scott. (2003). The Genesis of Suicide Terrorism. *Science,* 299, 1534–1539.

Auerbach, Elias. (1910). *Die Welt* (Vienna), 1101.

Auerbach, Elias. (1912). *Palästina als Judenland.* Berlin and Leipzig: Jüdischer Verlag.

Auerbach, Elias. (1932). *Wüste und Gelobtes Land: Geschichte Israels von den Anfängen bis zum Tode Salomos.* Berlin: K. Wolff Verlag. New edition (1936–1938) Two volumes. Berlin: K. Wolff Verlag and Schocken Verlag.

Auerbach, Elias. (1953). *Moses.* Amsterdam: Ruys. Heidelberg: L. Schneider.

Auerbach, Elias. (1969). *Pionier der Verwirklichung: Ein Arzt aus Deutschland erzählt vom Beginn der zionistischen Bewegung und seiner Niederlassung in Palästina kurz nach der Jahrhundertwende.* Stuttgart: Deutsche Verlagsanstalt.

Auerbach, Elias. (1975). *Moses.* Trans. and Ed. Robert A. Barclay and Israel O. Lehman. Detroit, MI: Wayne State University Press.

Aumann, Moshe. (1976). *Land Ownership in Palestine, 1880–1948.* Jerusalem: Academic Committee on the Middle East.

Avi-Yonah, Michael. (1976). *The Jews of Palestine: A Political History from Bar-Kochba War to the Arab Conquest.* Oxford: Basil Blackwell.

Avi-Yonah, Michael. (1984). *The Jews under Roman and Byzantine Rule: A Political History of Palestine from the Bar Kokhba War to the Arab Conquest.* New York: Schocken Books.

Avineri, Shlomo. (1981). *The Making of Modern Zionism: The Intellectual Origins of the Jewish State.* New York: Basic Books.

Avineri, Shlomo. (Ed.). (1971). *Israel and the Palestinians.* New York: St. Martin's Press.

Avishai, Bernard. (1985). *The Tragedy of Zionism: Revolution and Democracy in the Land of Israel.* New York: Farrar, Straus and Giroux.

Avneri, Aryeh Leib. (1982). *The Claim of Dispossession: Jewish Land-Settlement and the Arabs, 1878–1948.* Efal, Israel: Yad Tabenkin. New edition (1984) New Brunswick, NJ: Transaction Books.

Avneri, Aryeh Leib. (1970). *The War of Attrition.* Tel Aviv: Olive Books of Israel. Second edition (1972) Tel Aviv: Olive Books of Israel.

Avnery, Uri. (1985). *My Friend, The Enemy.* London: Zed Books. Reprinted (1986) Westport, CT: Lawrence Hill.

Avnery, Uri, et al. (1975). *Israel and the Palestinians: A Different Israeli View.* Preface Arthur H. Samuelson. New York: Breira.

Awwad, Elia. (1994). From Enmity toward Peaceful Coexistence: The Search for Meaning. Israelis and Palestinians Must Find a "Why" for Tolerance, Understanding, Forgiveness and Empathy for the Construction of a New Cognitive System. *Palestine-Israel Journal of Politics, Economics and Culture,* 1 (4), 34–37.

Ayubi, Nazih. (1991). *Political Islam: Religion and Politics in the Arab World*. London: Routledge.

Bacher, John. (2002). Palestinian Pacifism. *Peace Magazine*, 18 (4): 16–20.

Balch, Robert W. & Taylor, David. (2002). Making Sense of the Heaven's Gate Suicides. In David G. Bromley & J. Gordon Melton (Eds.), *Cults, Religion, and Violence*. Cambridge and New York: Cambridge University Press.

Barakat, Ahmad. (1979). *Muhammad and the Jews: A Re-Examination*. New Delhi: Vikas Publishing House.

Barakat, Halim. (1993). *The Arab World: Society, Culture, and State*. Berkeley: University of California Press.

Bard, Mitchell G. (1999). *The Complete Idiot's Guide to Middle East Conflict*. New York: Macmillan. Indianapolis: Alpha Books. Second edition (2003) Indianapolis: Alpha Books.

Bard, Mitchell G. (Ed.). (2001). *Myths and Facts: A Guide to the Arab-Israeli Conflict*. Foreword Eli E. Hertz. Chevy Chase, MD: American-Israeli Cooperative Enterprise.

Barker, Eileen. (2002). Watching for Violence: A Comparative Analysis of the Roles of Five Types of Cult-Watching Groups. In David G. Bromley & J. Gordon Melton (Eds.), *Cults, Religion, and Violence*. Cambridge and New York: Cambridge University Press.

Bartov, Omar. (1997, October 31). Review of *Fabricating Israeli History: The "New Historians"* by Efraim Karsh. *The Times Literary Supplement*.

Basetti-Sani, Giulio. (1974). *Louis Massignon (1883–1962): Christian Ecumenist Prophet of Inter-Religious Reconciliation*. Ed. & Trans. Allan Harris Cutler. Chicago: Franciscan Herald Press.

Bat Ye'or. (1985). *The Dhimmi: Jews and Christians under Islam*. Preface Jacques Ellul. Trans. David Maisel, Paul Fenton & David Littman. Madison, NJ: Fairleigh Dickinson University Press.

Bat Ye'or. (1996). *The Decline of Eastern Christianity under Islam: From Jihad to Dhimmitude, Seventh to Twentieth Century*. Foreword Jacques Ellul. Trans. Miriam Kochan & David Littman. Madison, NJ: Fairleigh Dickinson University Press.

Bat Ye'or. (2002). *Islam and Dhimmitude: Where Civilizations Collide*. Trans. Miriam Kochan & David Littman. Madison, NJ: Fairleigh Dickinson University Press.

Bauer, Yehuda. (1973). *From Diplomacy to Resistance: A History of Jewish Palestine, 1939–1945*. New York: Atheneum.

Baumgarten, Helga. (2002). *Arafat: zwischen Kampf und Diplomatie*. Munich: Ullstein Verlag.

Bavly, Dan & Farhi, David. (1971). *Israel and the Palestinians*. London: Anglo-Israel Association.

Becker, Ernest. (1973). *The Denial of Death*. New York: Free Press.

Becker, Ernest. (1975). *Escape from Evil.* New York: Free Press.

Begin, Menachem. (1951). *The Revolt: Story of the Irgun.* Jerusalem: Steimatsky. Revised edition (1977) New York: E. P. Dutton.

Beilin, Yossi. (2000). *His Brother's Keeper: Israel and Diaspora Jewry in the Twenty-First Century.* New York: Schocken Books.

Bein, Alex. (1941). *Theodore Herzl: A Biography.* Philadelphia: Jewish Publication Society of America. Reprinted (1962) Cleveland, OH: World.

Beinin, Joel. (1990). *Was the Red Flag Flying There? Marxist Politics and the Arab-Israeli Conflict in Egypt and Israel, 1948–1965.* Berkeley: University of California Press.

Beit-Hallahmi, Benjamin. (1978). *Psychoanalysis and Religion: A Bibliography.* Norwood, PA: Norwood Editions.

Beit-Hallahmi, Benjamin. (1972). National Character and National Behavior in the Middle East Conflict: The Case of "The Arab Personality." *International Journal of Group Tensions,* 2, 19–28.

Beit-Hallahmi, Benjamin. (1972a). Some Psychosocial and Cultural Factors in the Arab-Israeli Conflict: A Review of the Literature. *Journal of Conflict Resolution,* 16 (2), 269–280.

Beit-Hallahmi, Benjamin. (1973). Religion and Nationalism in the Arab-Israeli Conflict. *Il Politico,* 38, 232–243.

Beit-Hallahmi, Benjamin. (1976). The "Arab National Character" and the Middle East Conflict. *Mental Health and Society,* 1, 320–327.

Beit-Hallahmi, Benjamin. (1977). Overcoming the "Objective" Language of Violence. *Aggressive Behavior,* 3, 251–259.

Beit-Hallahmi, Benjamin. (1979). Review of *Terrorism and Criminal Justice* by R. D. Crelinsen et al. *Aggressive Behavior,* 5, 437–439.

Beit-Hallahmi, Benjamin. (1980). Review of *Orientalism* by Edward W. Said. *Journal for the Scientific Study of Religion,* 19, 69–70.

Beit-Hallahmi, Benjamin. (1980). Review of *The Arab-Israeli Conflict: Psychological Obstacles to Peace* by Daniel Heradstveit. *Middle East Studies Association Bulletin,* 14, 41–43.

Beit-Hallahmi, Benjamin. (1980). Review of *Tin Soldiers on Jerusalem Beach* by Amia Lieblich. *The Middle East Journal,* 34, 68–69.

Beit-Hallahmi, Benjamin. (1987). *The Israeli Connection: Who Israel Arms and Why.* New York: Pantheon Books.

Beit-Hallahmi, Benjamin. (1989). Review of *For the Land and the Lord* by Ian S. Lustick. *Journal for the Scientific Study of Religion,* 28, 382.

Beit-Hallahmi, Benjamin. (1992). *Despair and Deliverance: Private Salvation in Contemporary Israel.* Albany: State University of New York Press.

Beit-Hallahmi, Benjamin. (1992a). *Original Sins: Reflections on the History of Zionism and Israel.* London: Pluto Press. Reprinted (1993) New York: Olive Branch Press.

Beit-Hallahmi, Benjamin. (2001). Fundamentalism. In Joel Krieger (Ed.), *The Oxford Companion to Politics of the World* (2nd ed.). Oxford and New York: Oxford University Press.

Beit-Hallahmi, Benjamin. (2002). Rebirth and Death: The Violent Potential of Apocalyptic Dreams. In Chris E. Stout (Ed.), *The Psychology of Terrorism: Theoretical Understandings and Perspectives* (Vol. 3). 163–189. Westport, CT: Praeger.

Beit-Hallahmi, Benjamin & Argyle, Michael. (1997). *The Psychology of Religious Behaviour, Belief and Experience.* London: Routledge.

Bell, J. Bowyer. (1977). *Terror out of Zion: Irgun Zvai Leumi, LEHI, and the Palestine Underground, 1929–1949.* New York: St. Martin's Press. New edition (1996) *Terror out of Zion: The Fight for Israeli Independence.* Piscataway, NJ: Transaction Books.

Ben-Ami, Yitshaq. (1996). *Years of Wrath, Days of Glory: Memoirs from the Irgun.* New York: Shengold Publishers.

Ben-Gurion, David. (1949–1973). Unpublished diaries. Ben-Gurion Archives, Ben-Gurion University, Sdeh Bokker, Israel.

Ben-Gurion, David. (1954). *Rebirth and Destiny of Israel.* New York: Philosophical Library.

Ben-Yehuda, Hemda & Sandler, Shmuel. (2002). *The Arab-Israeli Conflict Transformed: Fifty Years of Interstate and Ethnic Crises.* Albany: State University of New York Press.

Ben-Yehuda, Nachman. (1995). *The Masada Myth: Collective Memory and Mythmaking in Israel.* Madison: University of Wisconsin Press.

Bentwich, Norman. (1954). *For Zion's Sake: A Biography of Judah L. Magnes.* Philadelphia: Jewish Publication Society of America.

Benvenisti, Meron. (1976). *Jerusalem: The Torn City.* Minneapolis: University of Minnesota Press.

Benvenisti, Meron. (1986). *Conflicts and Contradictions.* New York: Random House. New York: Villard Books.

Benvenisti, Meron. (1995). *Intimate Enemies: Jews and Arabs in a Shared Land.* Berkeley: University of California Press.

Benvenisti, Meron. (1996). *City of Stone: The Hidden History of Jerusalem.* Berkeley: University of California Press.

Benvenisti, Meron. (2000). *Sacred Landscape: The Buried History of the Holy Land since 1948.* Berkeley: University of California Press.

Benziman, Uzi. (1985). *Sharon: An Israeli Caesar.* Trans. Louis Rousso. New York: Adama Books. Reprinted (1987) London: Robson Books.

Berg, Nancy E. (1996). *Exile from Exile: Israeli Writers from Iraq.* Albany: State University of New York Press.

Berger, Morroe. (1962). *The Arab World Today.* Garden City, NY: Doubleday. London: Weidenfeld and Nicolson.

Berger, Morroe. (1970). *The Arabs in a Changing World.* Cairo: Society of the Intellectuals of the Orient.

Berlin, Isaiah. (1979). Nationalism: Past Neglect and Present Power. *Partisan Review*, 46, 337–358.

Bernadotte, Folke. (1951). *To Jerusalem*. Trans. Joan Bulman. London: Hodder and Stoughton. Reprinted (1976) Westport, CT: Hyperion Press.

Berry, Donald L. (2003). *Islam and Modernity Through the Writings of Islamic Modernist Fazlur Rahman*. Lewiston, NY: Edwin Mellen Press.

Biale, David. (1986). *Power and Powerlessness in Jewish History*. New York: Schocken Books. New edition (1990) *Power in Jewish History*. New York: Alfred A. Knopf.

Biale, David. (Ed.). (2002). *Cultures of the Jews: A New History*. New York: Schocken Books.

Bickerton, Ian J. & Klausner, Carla L. (1991). *A Concise History of the Arab-Israeli Conflict*. Englewood Cliffs, NJ: Prentice Hall. Second edition (1995) Englewood Cliffs, NJ: Prentice Hall. Third edition (1998) Upper Saddle River, NJ: Prentice Hall. Fourth edition (2002) Upper Saddle River, NJ: Prentice Hall.

Bickerton, Ian J. & Pearson, Michael Naylor. (1986). *The Arab-Israeli Conflict: A History*. London: Longman. Second edition (1991) Melbourne, Australia: Longman Cheshire.

Bilu, Yoram. (1994). The Image of the Enemy: Cracks in the Wall of Hatred. The Inner and Outer Reality of the Conflict and Empathy in Light of Jewish and Palestinian Children's Dreams. *Palestine-Israel Journal of Politics, Economics and Culture*, 1 (4), 24–28.

Biran, Hanna. (1994). Fear of the Other: In View of the Rejection by Ashkenazi Jews of Everything with an Oriental Flavor, Is Israeli Society Mature Enough to Respect the Identity of a Different People? *Palestine-Israel Journal of Politics, Economics and Culture*, 1 (4), 44–51.

Black, Ian & Morris, Benny. (1992). *Israel's Secret Wars: A History of Israel's Intelligence Services*. New York: Grove Press.

Black, Lionel [Dudley Barker]. (1975). *Arafat Is Next!* New York: Stein and Day.

Bleaney, C. Heather & Lawless, Richard. (1990). *The Arab-Israeli Conflict, 1947–67*. London: B.T. Batsford.

Bober, Arie. (Ed.). (1972). *The Other Israel: The Radical Case against Zionism*. Garden City, NY: Doubleday Anchor.

Boltanski, Christophe & El-Tahri, Jihan. (1997). *Les sept vies de Yasser Arafat*. Paris: Editions Bernard Grasset.

Bookbinder, Hyman & Abourezk, James G. (1987). *Through Different Eyes: Two Leading Americans, a Jew and an Arab, Debate U.S. Policy in the Middle East*. Bethesda, MD: Adler and Adler.

Bouhdiba, Abdelwahab. (1985). *Sexuality in Islam*. Trans. Alan Sheridan. London and Boston: Routledge and Kegan Paul. New edition (1998) London: Saqi Books.

Boutros-Ghali, Boutros. (1997). *Egypt's Road to Jerusalem: A Diplomat's Story of the Struggle for Peace in the Middle East*. New York: Random House.

Brackett, D. W. (1996). *Holy Terror: Armageddon in Tokyo*. New York: Weatherhill.

Brandeis, Louis D. (1942). *Brandeis on Zionism: A Collection of Addresses and State-ments*. Washington, DC: Zionist Organization of America. New edition (1976) Westport, CT: Hyperion Press. Reprinted (1999) Union, NJ: Lawbook Exchange.

Bregman, Ahron. (2000). *Israel's Wars, 1947–93*. London: Routledge.

Bregman, Ahron. (2002). *Israel's Wars: From the 1947 Palestine War to the Al-Aqsa Intifada*. London: Routledge.

Bregman, Ahron. (2002a). *Israel's Wars: A History since 1947*. London: Routledge.

Bregman, Ahron. (2002b). *A History of Israel*. Basingstoke and New York: Pal-grave Macmillan. New edition (2003) Basingstoke and New York: Palgrave Macmillan.

Bregman, Ahron & El-Tahri, Jihan. (1998). *The Fifty-Years' War: Israel and the Arabs*. London: Penguin Books. Reprinted (1999) New York: TV Books.

Brenner, Lenni. (1983). *Zionism in the Age of the Dictators*. London: Croom Helm. Westport, CT: Lawrence Hill.

Brenner, Lenni. (1984). *The Iron Wall: Zionist Revisionism from Jabotinsky to Sha-mir*. London: Zed Books.

Brexel, Bernadette. (2003). *Yasser Arafat*. New York: Rosen Publishing.

Brezniak, H. (1972). *The Israeli-Arab Conflict and the Left*. Darlinghurst, New South Wales, Australia: Bridge Publishers.

Breznitz, Shlomo. (Ed.). (1983). *Stress in Israel*. New York: Van Nostrand Reinhold.

Bromley, David G. & Melton, J. Gordon. (Eds.). (2002). *Cults, Religion, and Vio-lence*. Cambridge and New York: Cambridge University Press.

Brooman, Josh. (1989). *The Arab-Israeli Conflict: Arabs, Jews, and the Middle East since 1900*. New York: Longman.

Buber, Martin. (1952). *Israel and Palestine: The History of an Idea*. Trans. Stanley Godman. London: East and West Library.

Buber, Martin. (1973). *On Zion: The History of an Idea*. Trans. Stanley Godman. Foreword Nahum N. Glatzer. New York: Schocken Books. New edition (1986) New York: Schocken Books. New edition (1997) Syracuse: Syracuse University Press.

Buehrig, Edward H. (1971). *The U.N. and the Palestinian Refugees: A Study in Non-territorial Administration*. Bloomington: Indiana University Press.

Bullock, John & Darwish, Adel. (1999). *Water Wars: Coming Conflicts in the Mid-dle East*. London: Victor Gollancz.

Bunzl, John & Beit-Hallahmi, Benjamin. (Eds.). (2002). *Psychoanalysis, Identity, and Ideology: Critical Essays on the Israel/Palestine Case*. Boston, MA: Kluwer Academic Publishers.

Burg, Avraham. (2003, August 29). A Failed Israeli Society Collapses while Its Leaders Remain Silent. Trans. J. J. Goldberg. *The Forward*, 106 (31,460), 1, 7.

Burg, Avraham. (2003a, September 10). La révolution sioniste est morte. Trans. Lucien Lazare. *Le Monde*.

Burg, Avraham. (2003b, September 15). The End of Zionism: Israel Must Shed its Illusions and Choose between Racist Oppression and Democracy. *The Guardian*.

Burge, Gary M. (2003). *Whose Land? Whose Promise? What Christians Are Not Being Told about Israel and the Palestinians*. Cleveland, OH: Pilgrim Press.

Burrell, David & Landau, Yehezkel. (1992). *Voices from Jerusalem: Jews and Christians Reflect on the Holy Land*. New York: Paulist Press.

Bychowski, Gustav. (1948). *Dictators and Disciples, from Caesar to Stalin: A Psychoanalytic Interpretation of History*. New York: International Universities Press.

Bychowski, Gustav. (1950). On Neurotic Obesity. *The Psychoanalytic Review*, 37, 301–319.

Canellas López, Ángel. (Ed.). (1981). *Diplomatario / Francisco de Goya*. Zaragoza: Institución Fernando el Católico.

Canellas López, Ángel. (Ed.). (1991). *Diplomatario: Addenda / Francisco de Goya*. Zaragoza: Institución Fernando el Católico.

Capanna, Mario. (1989). *Arafat: intervista al presidente dello Stato palestinese*. Milan: Rizzoli.

Caplan, Neil. (1978). *Palestine Jewry and the Arab Question, 1917–1925*. London: Frank Cass.

Caplan, Neil. (1983–1997). *Futile Diplomacy: A Multi-Volume Documentary History of the Arab-Israeli Conflict*. (4 vols.). London: Frank Cass.

Caplan, Neil. (1993). *The Lausanne Conference, 1949: A Case Study in Middle East Peacemaking*. Tel Aviv: The Moshe Dayan Center for Middle Eastern and African Studies, Tel Aviv University.

Carey, Roane, et al. (2001). *The New Intifada: Resisting Israel's Apartheid*. London: Verso.

Carlebach, Elisheva, et al. (Eds.). (1998). *Jewish History and Jewish Memory: Essays in Honor of Yosef Hayim Yerushalmi*. Hanover, NH: University Press of New England.

Carroll, James. (2001, October 9). Religion: Problem or Solution? *The Boston Globe*, p. A11.

Casoni, Dianne & Brunet, Louis. (2002). The Psychodynamics of Terrorism. *Canadian Journal of Psychoanalysis*, 10 (1), 5–24.

Caspary, William R. (1993). New Psychoanalytic Perspectives on the Causes of War. *Political Psychology*, 14 (3), 417–446.

Caspit, Ben & Kfir, Ilan. (1998). *Netanyahu: The Road to Power*. London: Vision.

Chacour, Elias. (1984). *Blood Brothers*. Grand Rapids, MI: Chosen. Reprinted (1985) Eastbourne: Kingsway.

Chacour, Elias, with David Hazard. (1990). *We Belong to the Land*. New York: HarperCollins.

Chejne, Anwar George. (1974). *Muslim Spain: Its History and Culture.* Minneapolis: University of Minnesota Press.

Chejne, Anwar George. (1983). *Islam and the West: The Moriscos. A Cultural and Social History.* Albany: State University of New York Press.

Chertok, Haim. (1988). *Stealing Home: Israel Bound and Rebound.* New York: Fordham University Press.

Cheshin, Amir S., et al. (2000). *Separate and Unequal: The Inside Story of Israeli Rule in East Jerusalem.* Cambridge, MA: Harvard University Press.

Chidester, David. (1988). *Salvation and Suicide: An Interpretation of Jim Jones, the Peoples Temple, and Jonestown.* Bloomington: Indiana University Press.

Chill, Dan S. (1976). *The Arab Boycott of Israel: Economic Aggression and World Reaction.* New York: Praeger.

Chomsky, Noam. (1974). *Peace in the Middle East? Reflections on Justice and Nationhood.* New York: Pantheon Books.

Chomsky, Noam. (1983). *The Fateful Triangle: The United States, Israel and the Palestinians.* Boston: South End Press. New edition (1999) Cambridge, MA: South End Press.

Church, Frank. (1972). *Prospects for Peace in the Middle East: The View from Israel.* Washington, DC: U.S. Government Printing Office.

Churchill, Randolph S. & Churchill, Winston S. (1967). *The Six Day War.* London: Heinemann. Boston: Houghton Mifflin.

Clarke, Richard A. (2004). *Against All Enemies: Inside America's War on Terror.* New York: Free Press.

Clinton, Bill. (1996). *Between Hope and History: Meeting America's Challenges for the 21st Century.* New York: Times Books.

Clinton, Bill. (2004). *My Life.* New York: Alfred A. Knopf.

Cohen, Aharon. (1970). *Israel and the Arab World.* London: W. H. Allen. New York: Funk and Wagnalls. Abridged edition (1976) Boston: Beacon Press.

Cohen, Eliezer 'Cheetah.' (1993). *Israel's Best Defense: The First Full Story of the Israeli Air Force.* Trans. Jonathan Cordis. London and New York: Orion Books. Reprinted (1994) Shrewsbury: Airlife.

Cohen, Mark, R. (1994). *Under Crescent and Cross: The Jews in the Middle Ages.* Princeton: Princeton University Press.

Cohen, Michael Joseph. (1982). *Palestine and the Great Powers, 1945–1948.* Princeton: Princeton University Press .

Cohen, Michael Joseph. (1987). *The Origins and Evolution of the Arab-Zionist Conflict.* Berkeley: University of California Press.

Cohen, Michael Joseph & Kolinsky, Martin. (1992). *Britain and the Middle East in the 1930s: Security Problems, 1935–39.* Basingstoke and New York: Macmillan.

Cohen, Michael Joseph & Kolinsky, Martin. (Eds.). (1998). *Demise of the British Empire in the Middle East: Britain's Responses to Nationalist Movements, 1943–55.* London: Frank Cass.

Cohen, Mitchell. (1987). *Zion and State: Nation, Class and the Shaping of Modern Israel*. Oxford: Basil Blackwell. New edition (1992) New York: Columbia University Press.

Cohen, Naomi Wiener. (1975). *American Jews and the Zionist Idea*. New York: Ktav Publishing House.

Cohen, Warren I. (Ed.). (1983). *Reflections on Orientalism: Edward Said, Roger Besnahan, Surjit Dulai, Edward Graham, and Donald Lammers*. East Lansing: Asian Studies Center, Michigan State University.

Cohen-Sherbok, Daniel & El-Alami, Dawoud Sudqi. (2001). *The Palestine-Israel Conflict*. London: Oneworld Publications.

Colbin, Marie. (1994). *Yasser Arafat*. London: Hamish Hamilton.

Collins, Larry & Lapierre, Dominique. (1972). *O Jerusalem!* London: Weidenfeld and Nicolson. New York: Simon and Schuster.

Comay, Michael. (1981). *Zionism, Israel and the Palestinian Arabs*. Jerusalem: Keter.

Conrad, Joseph. (1902). The Heart of Darkness. In Joseph Conrad *Youth, a Narrative, and Two Other Stories*. Edinburgh and London: William Blackwood and Sons.

Conrad, Joseph. (1907). *The Secret Agent: A Simple Tale*. New York and London: Harper & Brothers.

Coombs, James H., et al. (Eds.). (1986). *A Pre-Raphaelite Friendship: The Correspondence of William Holman Hunt and John Lucas Tupper*. Ann Arbor, MI: UMI Research Press.

Cooper, John, et al. (Eds.). (1998). *Islam and Modernity: Muslim Intellectuals Respond*. London: I. B. Tauris. New edition (2000) London: I. B. Tauris.

Cordesman, Anthony H. (1993). *After the Storm: The Changing Military Balance in the Middle East*. London: Mansell Publishers. Boulder, CO: Westview Press.

Courbage, Youssef & Fargues, Philippe. (1997). *Christians and Jews Under Islam*. London: I. B. Tauris.

Cragg, Kenneth. (1991). *The Arab Christian: A History in the Middle East*. Louisville, KY: Westminster and John Knox Press. Reprinted (1992) London: Mowbray.

Cragg, Kenneth & Speight, Marston. (Eds.). (1980). *Islam from Within: Anthology of a Religion*. Belmont, CA: Wadsworth Publishing Co.

Crenshaw, Martha. (1998). The Logic of Terrorism. In Walter Reich (Ed.), *Origins of Terrorism: Psychologies, Ideologies, Theologies, States of Mind* (New ed.). Washington: Woodrow Wilson Center. Baltimore: Johns Hopkins University Press.

Crenshaw, Martha. (Ed.). (1995). *Terrorism in Context*. University Park: Pennsylvania State University Press.

Crenshaw, Martha & Pimlock, John. (Eds.). (1997). *Encyclopedia of World Terrorism*. Armonk, NY: Sharpe Reference.

Cross, Frank Moore. (1973). *Canaanite Myth and Hebrew Epic: Essays in the History of the Religion of Israel*. Cambridge, MA: Harvard University Press.

Cuomo, Mario Matthew. (2001, Oct. 21). *Me and Mario* [Radio Broadcast]. Albany, NY: WAMC.

Curtis, Michael. (Ed.). (1971). *People and Politics in the Middle East.* New Brunswick, NJ: Transaction Books.

Curtis, Michael, et al. (1975). *The Palestinians: People, History, Politics.* Piscataway, NJ: Transaction Books.

Daftary, Farhad. (1994). *The Assassin Legends: Myths of the Isma'ilis.* London: I. B. Tauris. Reprinted (1995) New York: I. B. Tauris.

Dajani, Mohammed. (2003). Press Reporting during the Intifada: Palestinian Coverage of Jenin. *Palestine-Israel Journal of Politics, Economics and Culture,* 10 (2), 39–46.

Dan, Uri. (1987). *Blood Libel: The Inside Story of General Ariel Sharon's History-Making Suit against Time Magazine.* New York: Simon and Schuster.

Dan, Uri. (1988). *To the Promised Land: The Birth of Israel.* Garden City, NY: Doubleday.

Darwish, Adel & Alexander, Gregory. (1991). *Unholy Babylon: The Secret History of Saddam's War.* London: Victor Gollancz.

David, Ron. (1993). *Arabs and Israel for Beginners.* New York: Writers and Readers.

Davis, Leonard J. (1981). *Myths and Facts: A Concise Record of the Arab-Israeli Conflict.* Washington, DC: Near East Report. New edition (1982) *Myths and Facts 1982: A Concise Record of the Arab-Israeli Conflict.* Eds. Leonard J. Davis & Moshe Decter. Washington, DC: Near East Report. New edition (1985) *Myths and Facts 1985: A Concise Record of the Arab-Israeli Conflict.* Washington, DC: Near East Report. New edition (1988) *Myths and Facts 1988: A Concise Record of the Arab-Israeli Conflict.* Eds. Eric Rozenman & Jeff Rubin. Washington, DC: Near East Report.

Davis, Uri. (1987). *Israel: An Apartheid State.* London: Zed Books. Reprinted (2003) as *Apartheid Israel: The Struggle Within.* London: Zed Books.

Davis, Uri, et al. (Eds.). (1975). *Israel and the Palestinians.* London: Ithaca Press.

Dawson, Lorne, L. (2002). Crises of Charismatic Legitimacy and Violent Behavior in New Religious Movements. In David G. Bromley & J. Gordon Melton (Eds.), *Cults, Religion, and Violence.* Cambridge and New York: Cambridge University Press.

Dayan, Moshe. (1976). *Moshe Dayan: Story of My Life.* New York: William Morrow. Reprinted (1977) New York: Warner Books. Reprinted (1992) New York: Da Capo Press.

Dayan, Moshe. (1981). *Breakthrough: A Personal Account of the Egypt-Israel Peace Negotiations.* New York: Alfred A. Knopf.

Dayan, Moshe. (1991). *Diary of the Sinai Campaign.* New York: Da Capo Press.

Deegan, Paul J. (1991). *The Arab-Israeli Conflict.* Edina, MN: Abdo and Daughters.

Destremau, Christian & Moncelon, Jean. (1994). *Louis Massignon.* Paris: Plon.

DeVore, Ronald M. (1976). *The Arab-Israeli Conflict: A Historical, Political, Social and Military Bibliography.* Santa Barbara, CA: Clio Books.

Dietrich, David R. & Shabad, Peter. (Eds.). (1989). *The Problem of Loss and Mourning: Psychoanalytic Perspectives.* Madison, CT: International Universities Press.

Dixon, Norman F. (1976). *On the Psychology of Military Incompetence.* Foreword Brigadier Shelford Bidwell. London: Jonathan Cape. New York: Basic Books. Reprinted (1979) London: Futura.

Dodd, Clement Henry. (Ed.). (1970). *Israel and the Arab World.* London: Routledge.

Dothan, Shmuel. (1996). *A Land in the Balance: The Struggle for Palestine, 1919–1948.* Jerusalem and New York: Gefen Publishing House.

Downing, David. (2002). *Yasser Arafat.* Chicago: Heinemann Library.

Duijker, Hubertus Carl Johannes & Frijda, Nico H. (Eds.). (1960). *National Character and National Stereotypes: A Trend Report Prepared for the International Union of Scientific Psychology.* Amsterdam: North-Holland Publishing Co.

Dunstan, William E. (1997). *The Ancient Near East.* Belmont, CA: Wadsworth. Reprinted (1998) Fort Worth, TX: Harcourt Brace College Publishers.

Dupuy, Trevor. (1992). *Elusive Victory: The Arab-Israeli Wars, 1947–1974.* Dubuque, IA: Kendall/Hunt Publishing Co.

EAFORD [Elimination of All Forms of Racial Discrimination] & AJAZ [American Jewish Alternatives to Zionism]. (Eds.). (1986). *Judaism or Zionism? What Difference for the Middle East?* London: EAFORD and Zed Books.

Eban, Abba Solomon. (1972). *My Country: The Story of Modern Israel.* New York: Random House.

Eban, Abba Solomon. (1984). *Heritage: Civilization and the Jews.* New York: Summit Books.

Eban, Abba Solomon. (1988). *Prospects for Peace in the Middle East.* London: David Davis Memorial Institute of International Studies.

Edelheit, Hershel & Edelheit, Abraham J. (2000). *History of Zionism: A Handbook and Dictionary.* Boulder, CO: Westview Press.

Edelstein, E. L., et al. (Eds.). (1989). *Denial: A Clarification of Concepts and Research.* New York: Plenum Press.

Edlinger, Fritz. (Ed.). (2001). *Befreiungskampf in Palästina: von der Madrid-Konferenz zur Al Aqsa-Intifada.* Vienna: Promedia.

Eidelberg, Ludwig. (Ed.). (1968). *Encyclopedia of Psychoanalysis.* New York: Free Press. London: Collier-Macmillan.

Eisenberg, Dennis, et al. (1978). *The Mossad–Israel's Secret Intelligence Service: Inside Stories.* New York and London: Paddington Press. New edition (1988) New York: New American Library.

Eisenberg, Laura Zittrain & Caplan, Neil. (1998). *Negotiating Arab-Israeli Peace: Patterns, Problems, Possibilities.* Bloomington: Indiana University Press.

El-Deek, Jamal. (1994). The Image of the Israeli: Its Evolution in the Palestinian Mind. A Palestinian Freedom-Fighter Defines through His Life Experience How He Sees the Changing Image of the Israeli. *Palestine-Israel Journal of Politics, Economics and Culture,* 1 (4), 53–56.

Eliachar, Elie. (1983). *Living with Jews.* London: Weidenfeld and Nicolson.

Elkaim, Mony. (1994). The Israeli-Palestinian Couple: From Confrontation to Joint Construction. A Psychiatrist and Family Therapist Interpret the Evolution of the Conflict Based on a Model Developed for Couple Psychotherapy. *Palestine-Israel Journal of Politics, Economics and Culture,* 1 (4), 29–33.

Elon, Amos. (1967). *Journey through a Haunted Land.* New York: Holt, Rinehart and Winston.

Elon, Amos. (1971). *The Israelis: Founders and Sons.* London: Weidenfeld and Nicolson. Reprinted (1981) Jerusalem: Adam Publishers and Steimatzky. New edition (1983) New York: Viking Penguin.

Elon, Amos. (1975). *Herzl.* New York: Holt, Rinehart and Winston.

Elon, Amos. (1976). *Understanding Israel: A Social Studies Approach.* New York: Behrman House.

Elon, Amos. (1997). *A Blood-Dimmed Tide: Dispatches from the Middle East.* New York: Columbia University Press. Reprinted (1998) New York: Columbia University Press.

Elon, Amos & Hassan, Sana. (1974). *Between Enemies: A Compassionate Dialogue between an Israeli and an Arab.* New York: Random House. Reprinted (1974) as *between Enemies: An Arab-Israeli Dialogue.* London: Andre Deutsch.

Elpeleg, Zvi. (1993). *The Grand Mufti: Haj Amin al-Hussaini, Founder of the Palestinian National Movement.* Trans. David Harvey. Ed. Shmuel Himelstein. London: Frank Cass.

Elsarraj, Eyad. (1994). Shaping a Culture of Peace: The Palestinians Must Address Taboos and Grave Internal Weaknesses, While Israel Must Tackle Its Arrogant Colonial Stance if the Promise of Peace Is to Become a Reality. *Palestine-Israel Journal of Politics, Economics and Culture,* 1 (4), 57–61.

Enderlin, Charles. (2002). *Le rêve brisé: histoire de l'échec du processus de paix au Proche-Orient, 1995–2002.* Paris: Fayard.

Enderlin, Charles. (2003). *Shattered Dreams: The Failure of the Peace Process in the Middle East, 1995–2002.* Trans. Susan Fairfield. New York: Other Press.

Epp, Frank H. (1970). *Whose Land is Palestine? The Middle East Problem in Historical Perspective.* Grand Rapids, MI: William B. Eerdman's Publishing Co.

Erikson, Erik H. (1966). Ontogeny of Ritualization in Man. In Julian Huxley (Ed.), A Discussion of Ritualization of Behavior in Animals and Man. *Philosophical Transactions of the Royal Society of London,* Series B, Biographical Sciences, 251 (772), 523–524, 601–621. Reprinted (1966) in Rudolph M. Loewenstein et al. (Eds.), *Psychoanalysis: A General Psychology.* New York: International Universities Press.

Erikson, Erik H. (1968). *Insight and Freedom: The 9th T. B. Davie Memorial Lecture.* Cape Town: University of Cape Town Press.

Erikson, Erik H. (1969). *Gandhi's Truth: On the Origins of Militant Nonviolence.* New York: Norton.

Erlanger, Steven & Hedges, Chris. (2001, December 28). Missed Signals: Terror Cells Slip through Europe's Grasp. *The New York Times.*

Erlich, Avi & Erlich, Victor. (1994). *Ancient Zionism: The Biblical Origins of the National Idea.* New York: Free Press.

Erlich, Shmuel. (1994). On Discourse with the Enemy: A Psychoanalytical Perspective. Can Psychoanalysis Contribute to an Understanding of the Enemy? The Enemy as Part of Ourselves as well as Distinct from Us. *Palestine-Israel Journal of Politics, Economics and Culture,* 1 (4), 8–16.

Ewing, Katherine Pratt. (1997). *Arguing Sainthood: Modernity, Psychoanalysis, and Islam.* Durham, NC: Duke University Press.

Executive Intelligence Review Counterintelligence Staff. (1986). *Moscow's Secret Weapon: Ariel Sharon and the Israeli Mafia.* Washington, DC: Executive Intelligence Review.

Ezrahi, Yaron. (1997). *Rubber Bullets: Power and Conscience in Modern Israel.* New York: Farrar, Straus and Giroux. Reprinted (1998) Berkeley: University of California Press.

Faber, Mel D. (1981). *Culture and Consciousness: The Social Meaning of Altered Awareness.* New York: Human Sciences Press.

Faber, Mel D. (2002). *The Magic of Prayer: An Introduction to the Psychology of Faith.* Westport, CT: Praeger.

Falk, Avner. (1974). Border Symbolism. *The Psychoanalytic Quarterly,* 43, 650–660. Reprinted (1989) in Howard F. Stein & William G. Niederland (Eds.), *Maps from the Mind: Readings in Psychogeography,* 141–150. Norman: University of Oklahoma Press.

Falk, Avner. (1975–1976). Identity and Name Changes. *The Psychoanalytic Review,* 62, 647–657.

Falk, Avner. (1983). Border Symbolism Revisited. *International Review of Psycho-Analysis,* 10, 215–220. Reprinted (1989) in Howard F. Stein & William G. Niederland (Eds.), *Maps from the Mind: Readings in Psychogeography,* 151–160. Norman: University of Oklahoma Press.

Falk, Avner. (1983). Moshe Dayan: The Infantile Roots of Political Action. *The Journal of Psychohistory,* 11, 271–288.

Falk, Avner. (1984). Moshe Dayan: Narcissism in Politics. *The Jerusalem Quarterly,* 30, 113–124.

Falk, Avner. (1985). *Moshe Dayan, haIsh vehaAgadah: Biographia Psychoanalytit* [Moshe Dayan, the Man and the Myth: A Psychoanalytic Biography]. Jerusalem: Cana. Tel Aviv: Maariv Library.

Falk, Avner. (1987). The Meaning of Jerusalem. *The Psychohistory Review,* 16, 99–113. Expanded version (1989) The Meaning of Jerusalem: A Psychohistorical

Viewpoint. In Howard F. Stein & William G. Niederland (Eds.), *Maps from the Mind: Readings in Psychogeography*, 161–178. Norman: University of Oklahoma Press.

Falk, Avner. (1987a). Ben-Gurion: Immigration as Rebirth. *Midstream*, 33 (5), 32–34.

Falk, Avner. (1987b). *David Melech Yisrael: Biographia Psychoanalytit shel David Ben-Gurion* [David King of Israel: A Psychoanalytic Biography of David Ben-Gurion]. Tel-Aviv: Tammuz.

Falk, Avner. (1992). Unconscious Aspects of the Arab-Israeli Conflict. *The Psychoanalytic Study of Society*, 17, 213–247.

Falk, Avner. (1993). *Herzl, King of the Jews: A Psychoanalytic Biography of Theodor Herzl*. Lanham, MD: University Press of America.

Falk, Avner. (1996). *A Psychoanalytic History of the Jews*. Madison, NJ: Fairleigh Dickinson University Press.

Falk, Avner. (2001). Political Assassination and Personality Disorder: The Cases of Lee Harvey Oswald and Yigal Amir. *Mind and Human Interaction*, 12 (1), 2–34

Falk, Avner. (2001a). Osama bin Laden and America: A Psychobiographical Study. *Mind and Human Interaction*, 12 (3), 161–172.

Farrell, Em. (1995). *Lost for Words: The Psychoanalysis of Anorexia and Bulimia.* London: Process Press. Reprinted (2000) New York: Other Press.

Farsoun, Samih K. & Zacharia, Christina. (1998). *Palestine and the Palestinians.* Boulder, CO: Westview Press.

Favret, Rémi. (1990). *Arafat: un destin pour la Palestine*. Paris: Renaudot.

Feldman, Harold. (1958). Children of the Desert: Notes on Arab National Character. *Psychoanalysis and the Psychoanalytic Review*, 45, 41–50.

Feldman, Shai & Shapir, Yiftah. (Eds.). (2001). *The Middle East Military Balance.* Cambridge, MA: MIT Press.

Fields, Rona M., et al. (2002). The Palestinian Suicide Bomber. In Chris E. Stout (Ed.), *The Psychology of Terrorism: Clinical Aspects and Response* (Vol. 2). 193–223. Westport, CT: Praeger.

Fields, Rona M., et al. (2004). *Martyrdom: The Psychology, Theology, and Politics of Self-Sacrifice*. Westport, CT: Praeger.

Fineman, Howard, et al. (2003, March 10). Bush and God. *Newsweek*, pp. 22–30.

Finkelstein, Norman. (1995). *Image and Reality of the Israel-Palestine Conflict*. London: Verso.

Fisk, Robert. (1990). *Pity the Nation: Lebanon at War*. London: Andre Deutsch. Reprinted (1990) as *Pity the Nation: The Abduction of Lebanon*. New York: Athenuem. Second edition (1991) New York: Simon and Schuster. Third edition (2001) Oxford and New York: Oxford University Press. Fourth edition (2002) New York: Thunder Mouth Press.

Flapan, Simha. (1979). *Zionism and the Palestinians, 1917–1947*. New York: Barnes and Noble.

Flapan, Simha. (1987). *The Birth of Israel: Myths and Realities*. London: Croom Helm. New York: Pantheon Books.

Flint, Robert. (1893). *Historical Philosophy in France and French Belgium and Switzerland*. Edinburgh and London: William Blackwood and Sons. Reprinted (1894) New York: Charles Scribner's Sons.

Fornari, Franco. (1974). *The Psychoanalysis of War*. Trans. Alenka Pfeiffer. Garden City, NY: Doubleday Anchor. Reprinted (1975) Bloomington: Indiana University Press.

Frangi, Abdallah. (1983). *The PLO and Palestine*. London: Zed Books.

Frank, Justin A. (2004). *Bush on the Couch: Inside the Mind of the President*. New York: Regan Books.

Fraser, Thomas G. (1995). *The Arab-Israeli Conflict*. New York: St. Martin's Press.

Fraser, Thomas G. (Ed.). (1980). *The Middle East, 1914–1979*. New York: St. Martin's Press.

Freud, Sigmund. (1927). *Die Zukunft einer Illusion*. Leipzig, Vienna and Zurich: Internationaler Psychoanalytischer Verlag. Reprinted (1948) in Sigmund Freud, *Gesammelte Werke*, 14, 323–380. London: Imago Publishing Co.

Freud, Sigmund. (1933). *Warum Krieg?* Letter to Albert Einstein, September 1932. Paris: Internationales Institut für Zusammenarbeit (Völkerbund), 62–76. Reprinted (1950) in Sigmund Freud, *Gesammelte Werke*, 16, 13–27. London: Imago Publishing Co.

Freud, Sigmund. (1955–1974). *The Standard Edition of the Complete Psychological Works of Sigmund Freud* (24 vols.). Ed. James Strachey et al. London: Hogarth Press and the Institute of Psycho-Analysis.

Friedlander, Melvin A. (1983). *Sadat and Begin: The Domestic Politics of Peacemaking*. Boulder, CO: Westview Press.

Friedman, Robert I. (1990). *The False Prophet: Rabbi Meir Kahane, from FBI Informant to Knesset Member*. London: Faber and Faber. Brooklyn, NY: Lawrence Hill. Newport Beach, CA: Noontide Press.

Friedman, Robert I. (1992). *Zealots for Zion: Inside Israel's West Bank Settlement Movement*. New York: Random House. Reprinted (1994) New Brunswick, NJ: Rutgers University Press.

Friedman, S. (1972). Oral Drive Cycles in Obesity: Bulimia. *The Psychoanalytic Quarterly*, 41, 364–383.

Friedman, Thomas L. (1989). *From Beirut to Jerusalem*. New York: Farrar, Straus and Giroux. New edition (1990) New York: Farrar, Straus and Giroux. New York: Doubleday Anchor. New edition (1995) Updated with a new chapter. New York: Doubleday Anchor.

Friedman, Thomas L. (1995). Foreword. In Meron Benvenisti, *Intimate Enemies: Jews and Arabs in a Shared Land*. Berkeley: University of California Press.

Friedman, Thomas L. (1998). Essay. In Micha Bar-Am, *Israel, a Photobiography: The First Fifty Years*. New York: Simon and Schuster.

Friedman, Thomas L. (1999). *The Lexus and the Olive Tree*. New York: Farrar,

Straus and Giroux. Thorndike, ME: Thorndike Press. Revised edition (2000) New York: Farrar, Straus and Giroux.

Fromkin, David. (1989). *A Peace to End All Peace: Creating the Modern Middle East, 1914–1922.* London: Andre Deutsch. New York: Henry Holt. New edition (1990) *A Peace to End All Peace: The Fall of the Ottoman Empire and the Creation of the Modern Middle East.* New York: Avon Books. New edition (2001) New York: Owl Books.

Fromm, Erich. (1950). *Psychoanalysis and Religion.* New Haven, CT: Yale University Press. Reprinted (1951) London: Victor Gollancz.

Furlonge, Geoffrey W. (1969). *Palestine is My Country: The Story of Musa Alami.* London: John Murray. New York: Praeger.

Gainsborough, J. Russell. (1986). *The Arab-Israeli Conflict: A Politico-Legal Analysis.* Aldershot, Hampshire, England and Brookfield, VT: Gower Publishing.

Gal, Allon. (1991). *David Ben Gurion and the American Alignment for a Jewish State.* Bloomington: Indiana University Press. Jerusalem: Magnes Press.

Gaughen, Shasta & Rackers, Mark. (Eds.). (2003). *The Arab-Israeli Conflict: Contemporary Issues Companion.* San Diego, CA: Greenhaven Press.

Gear, María Carmen, et al. (1981). *Working through Narcissism: Treating Its Sadomasochistic Structure.* New York: Jason Aronson.

Gefen, Aba. (2001). *Israel at a Crossroads.* Jerusalem and Hewlett, NY: Gefen Publishing Co.

Gerner, Deborah J. (1991). *One Land, Two Peoples: The Conflict over Palestine.* Boulder, CO: Westview Press. Second edition (1994) Boulder, CO: Westview Press.

Gerner, Deborah J. (1994). *Understanding the Contemporary Middle East.* Boulder, CO: Lynne Rienner.

Gerson, Allan. (1978). *Israel, the West Bank, and International Law.* London: Frank Cass.

Gil, Moshe. (1992). *A History of Palestine, 634–1099.* Cambridge and New York: Cambridge University Press.

Gilbert, Martin. (1974). *The Dent Atlas of the Arab-Israeli Conflict.* London: J. M. Dent. London: Weidenfeld and Nicolson. Second edition (1976) *Atlas of the Arab-Israeli Conflict.* New York: Macmillan. Third edition (1979) *The Arab-Israeli Conflict: Its History in Maps.* London: Weidenfeld and Nicolson. Fourth edition (1984) London: Weidenfeld and Nicolson. Fifth edition (1992) London: Weidenfeld and Nicolson. Sixth edition (1993) *Atlas of the Arab-Israeli Conflict.* Oxford and New York: Oxford University Press. Reprinted (1996) *The Routledge Atlas of the Arab-Israeli Conflict.* London: Routledge. Seventh edition (2002) London and New York: Routledge.

Gilbert, Martin. (1978). *Exile and Return: The Struggle for a Jewish Homeland.* Philadelphia: Lippincott.

Gilbert, Martin. (1998). *Israel: A History.* New York: William Morrow.

Gilboa, Eytan. (Ed.). (1993). *The Arab-Israeli Conflict: Sources, Evolution and Prospects for Resolution.* Jerusalem: Academon.

Gilman, Sander L. (1986). *Jewish Self-Hatred: Anti-Semitism and the Hidden Language of the Jews.* Baltimore: Johns Hopkins University Press.

Gilman, Sander L. (1991). *The Jew's Body.* London and New York: Routledge.

Gilman, Sander L. (1996). *Smart Jews: The Construction of the Image of Jewish Superior Intelligence.* Lincoln: University of Nebraska Press.

Gilman, Sander L. (2003). *Jewish Frontiers: Essays on Bodies, Histories, and Identities.* New York: Palgrave Macmillan.

Gilman, Sander L. & Zipes, Jack. (Eds.). (1997). *Yale Companion to Jewish Writing and Thought in German Culture, 1096–1996.* New Haven, CT: Yale University Press.

Gilmour, David. (1980). *Dispossessed: The Ordeal of the Palestinians, 1917–1980.* London: Sidgwick and Jackson.

Ginzburg, Louis. (1909–1938). *The Legends of the Jews* (7 vols.). Trans. Henrietta Szold. Philadelphia: Jewish Publication Society of America. Second edition (1942) Philadelphia: Jewish Publication Society of America. Third edition (1967–1968) Philadelphia: Jewish Publication Society of America. New edition (1998) Baltimore: Johns Hopkins University Press.

Glad, Betty. (Ed.). (1990). *Psychological Dimensions of War.* Newbury Park, London and New Delhi: Sage Publications. Reprinted (1994) Newbury Park, London and New Delhi: Sage Publications.

Glidden, Harold Walker. (1972). The Arab World. *American Journal of Psychiatry,* 128, 984–988.

Glover, Edward. (1933). *War, Sadism & Pacifism. Three Essays.* London: George Allen & Unwin. New edition (1947) London: George Allen & Unwin.

Glubb, John Bagot. (1948). *The Story of the Arab Legion.* London: Hodder & Stoughton. New edition (1976) New York: Da Capo Press.

Glubb, John Bagot. (1957). *A Soldier with the Arabs.* London: Hodder & Stoughton. New York: Harper and Row.

Glubb, John Bagot. (1959). *Britain and the Arabs: A Study of Fifty Years, 1908 to 1958.* London: Hodder & Stoughton.

Glucksman, Myron L. & Rand, C. S. (1978). Psychodynamics of Obesity. *Journal of the American Academy of Psychoanalysis,* 6, 103–116.

Glucksman, Myron L. (1989). Obesity: A Psychoanalytic Challenge. *Journal of the American Academy of Psychoanalysis,* 17, 151–172.

Glueck, Nelson. (1965). *Deities and Dolphins: The Story of the Nabataeans.* New York: Farrar, Straus and Giroux. Reprinted (1966) London: Cassell.

Goertzel, Ted G. (2002). Terrorist Beliefs and Terrorist Lives. In Chris E. Stout (Ed.), *The Psychology of Terrorism: A Public Understanding* (Vol. 1). 97–112. Westport, CT: Praeger.

Goffman, Daniel. (2002). *The Ottoman Empire and Early Modern Europe.* Cambridge and New York: Cambridge University Press.

Golan, Aviezer. (1978). *Operation Susannah, as Told to Aviezer Golan by Marcelle Ninio, Victor Levy, Robert Dassa, and Philip Nathanson.* Trans. Peretz Kidron. New York: Harper and Row.

Golan, Matti. (1976). *The Secret Conversations of Henry Kissinger: Step-by-step Diplomacy in the Middle-East.* Trans. Ruth Gieyna Stern & Sol Stern. New York: New York Times Book Co. Chicago: Quadrangle.

Golan, Matti. (1982). *Shimon Peres: A Biography.* London: Weidenfeld and Nicolson.

Golani, Motti. (1998). *Israel in Search of a War: The Sinai Campaign, 1955–1956.* Brighton: Sussex Academy Press.

Gold, Dore. (2003). *Hatred's Kingdom: How Saudi Arabia Supports the New Global Terrorism.* Washington, DC: Regnery Publishing.

Goldberg, David J. (1996). *To the Promised Land: A History of Zionist Thought from Its Origins to the Modern State of Israel.* Harmondsworth and New York: Penguin Books.

Goldfield, Steve. (1985). *Garrison State: Israel's Role in U. S. Global Strategy.* San Francisco: Palestine Focus Publications. London and New York: EAFORD.

Goldschmidt, Arthur, Jr. (1979). *A Concise History of the Middle East.* Boulder, CO: Westview Press. Folkestone: Dawson. Second edition (1983) Boulder, CO: Westview Press. Reprinted (1985) Cairo, Egypt: American University in Cairo Press. Third edition (1988) Boulder, CO: Westview Press. Fourth edition (1991) Boulder, CO: Westview Press. Fifth edition (1996) Boulder, CO: Westview Press. Reprinted (1997) Cairo, Egypt: American University in Cairo Press. Sixth edition (1998) Boulder, CO: Westview Press. Seventh edition (2002) Boulder, CO: Westview Press.

Gonen, Jay Y. (1975). *A Psychohistory of Zionism.* New York: Mason/Charter.

Gonen, Jay Y. (1978). The Israeli Illusion of Omnipotence Following the Six-Day War. *The Journal of Psychohistory,* 6, 241–271.

Gonen, Jay Y. (2000). *The Roots of Nazi Psychology: Hitler's Utopian Barbarism.* Lexington: University Press of Kentucky.

Gonen, Jay Y. (2002). The Impossible Palestinians and Israelis. *Clio's Psyche,* 9 (3), 125–127.

Gonen, Jay Y. (2004). *Yahweh versus Yahweh: The Enigma of Jewish History.* Madison: University of Wisconsin Press.

Goodman, Martin D. (1983). *State and Society in Roman Galilee, AD 132–212.* Totowa, NJ: Rowman and Allanheld. Second edition (2000) London: Vallentine Mitchell.

Goodman, Martin D. (1987). *The Ruling Class of Judaea: The Origins of the Jewish Revolt against Rome, AD 66–70.* Cambridge: Cambridge University Press.

Gopin, Marc. (2002). *Holy War, Holy Peace: How Religion Can Bring Peace to the Middle East.* Oxford and New York: Oxford University Press.

Gordon, Michael R. & Trainor, Bernard E. (1995). *The Generals' War: The Inside Story of the Conflict in the Gulf.* Boston: Little, Brown.

Gorenberg, Gershom. (2000). *The End of Days: Fundamentalism and the Struggle for the Temple Mount.* New York: Free Press.

Gorkin, Michael. (1991). *Days of Honey, Days of Onion: The Story of a Palestinian Family in Israel.* Boston: Beacon. New edition (1993) Berkeley: University of California Press.

Gorkin, Michael & Othman, Rafiqa. (1996). *Three Mothers, Three Daughters: Palestinian Women's Stories.* Berkeley: University of California Press.

Gowers, Andrew & Walker, Tony. (1990). *Behind the Myth: Yasser Arafat and the Palestinian Revolution.* London: W. H. Allen. Reprinted (1992) New York: Olive Branch Press. New edition (1994) *Arafat: The Biography.* London: Virgin Books.

Goya y Lucientes, Francisco José de. (1967). *The Disasters of War.* Ed. Philip Hofer. New York: Dover Publications.

Goya y Lucientes, Franciscode José de. (1982). *Cartas a Martín Zapater.* Edición de Mercedes Agueda y Xavier de Salas. Madrid: Turner.

Granott [Granovsky], Abraham. (1952). *The Land System in Palestine: History and Structure.* London: Eyre and Spottiswoode.

Greenspahn, Frederick E. (Ed.). (1991). *Essential Papers on Israel and the Ancient Near East.* New York: New York University Press.

Greilsammer, Alain Ilan. (1991). *Israël, les hommes en noir: essai sur les partis ultra-orthodoxes.* Paris: Presses de la Fondation nationale des sciences politiques.

Greilsammer, Alain Ilan. (1998). *La Nouvelle Histoire d'Israël: essai sur une identité nationale.* Paris: Gallimard.

Greilsammer, Alain Ilan. (2003, September 11). Tous les périls, plus la trahison perverse. *Le Monde,* p. 20.

Greilsammer, Ilan. (2003a, September 24). La pente savonneuse de l'antisémitisme. *Libération.*

Grosbard, Ofer. (2003). *Israel on the Couch: The Psychology of the Peace Process.* Foreword Vamık D. Volkan. Albany: State University of New York Press.

Grossman, David. (1993). *Sleeping on a Wire: Conversations with Palestinians in Israel.* London: Jonathan Cape. New York: Farrar, Straus and Giroux. New edition (1994) London: Picador Books.

Grotstein, James S. (1981). *Splitting and Projective Identification.* New York: Jason Aronson. New edition (1985) New York: Jason Aronson.

Group for the Advancement of Psychiatry. (1978). *Self-Involvement in the Middle East Conflict.* GAP Report 103. Formulated by the Committee on International Relations. New York: Group for the Advancement of Psychiatry.

Group for the Advancement of Psychiatry. (1987). *Us and Them: The Psychology of Ethnonationalism.* GAP Report 123. Formulated by the Committee on International Relations. New York: Brunner/Mazel.

Gruber, Ruth. (1948). *Destination Palestine: The Story of the Haganah Ship Exodus 1947.* New York: Current Books. New edition (1999) *Exodus 1947: The Ship That Launched a Nation.* New York: Times Books.

Gubbay, Lucien. (2000). *Sunlight and Shadow: The Jewish Experience of Islam.* New York: Other Press.

Gude, Mary Louise. (1996). *Louis Massignon: The Crucible of Compassion*. Notre Dame: University of Notre Dame Press.

Guillaume, Alfred. (1924). *The Traditions of Islam: An Introduction to the Study of the Hadith Literature*. Oxford: Clarendon Press. New edition (1966) Beirut: Khayats. Reprinted (1980) New York: Books for Libraries.

Guillaume, Alfred. (1954). *Islam*. Harmondsworth, Middlesex: Penguin Books. New edition (1963) London: Cassell.

Gunaratna, Rohan. (2002). *Inside Al-Qaeda: Global Network of Terror*. New York: Columbia University Press. Reprinted (2003) New York: Berkley Books.

Gurevitch, Zali. (1994). The Dialectics of a Handshake: The Rabin-Arafat Handshake Symbolized Recognition, but the Harsh Terrain of Dialogue Is Still Ahead. *Palestine-Israel Journal of Politics, Economics and Culture*, 1 (4), 38–43.

Guyatt, Nicholas. (1998). *The Absence of Peace: Understanding the Israeli-Palestinian Conflict*. Basingstoke and New York: Palgrave Macmillan. London: Zed Books.

Habiby, Emile. (1985). *The Secret Life of Saeed the Pessoptimist*. London: Zed Books.

Hadawi, Sami. (1967). *The Arab-Israeli Conflict: Cause and Effect*. Beirut: Institute for Palestine Studies.

Hadawi, Sami. (1967a). *Bitter Harvest: Palestine between 1914–1967*. New York: New World Press. Reprinted (1979) Delmar, NY: Caravan Books. Second edition (1989) *Bitter Harvest: A Modern History of Palestine*. Ithaca, NY: Olive Branch Press. Third edition (1990) Ithaca, NY: Olive Branch Press. New edition (1991) Ithaca, NY: Olive Branch Press. New edition (1998) Northampton, MA: Interlink Publishing.

Hadawi, Sami. (1988). *Palestinian Rights and Losses in 1948: A Comprehensive Study*. London: Saqi Books.

Haim, Sylvia G. (Ed.). (1962). *Arab Nationalism: An Anthology*. Berkeley: University of California Press. New edition (1976) Berkeley: University of California Press.

Haim, Sylvia G. (Ed.). (1971). *Arab Nationalism and a Wider World*. New York: American Academic Association for Peace in the Middle East.

Haj-Yahya, Yusuf Mahmud, et al. (1999). *Alleged Palestinian Collaborators with Israel and Their families: A Study of Victims of Internal Political Violence*. Jerusalem: The Harry S. Truman Research Institute for the Advancement of Peace, The Hebrew University of Jerusalem.

Haj-Yahia, Muhammad M. (1999). Wife Abuse and Its Psychological Consequences as Revealed by the First Palestinian National Survey on Violence against Women. *Journal of Family Psychology*, 13 (4), 642–662.

Haj-Yahia, Muhammad M. (1999a). *Wife-Abuse and Battering in the West Bank and Gaza: Results of Two National Surveys*. Ramallah: Bisan Center for Research and Development.

Haj-Yahia, Muhammad M. (2000). Wife Abuse and Battering in the Sociocultural Context of Arab Society. *Family Process*, 39 (2), 237–255.

Halamish, Aviva. (1998). *The Exodus Affair: Holocaust Survivors and the Struggle for Palestine.* Syracuse: Syracuse University Press.

Halevi, Yossi Klein. (1995). *Memoirs of a Jewish Extremist: An American Story.* Boston: Little, Brown.

Halkin, Hillel. (1977). *Letters to an American Jewish Friend: A Zionist's Polemic.* Philadelphia: Jewish Publication Society of America.

Hall, John R. (2002). Mass Suicide and the Branch Davidians. In David G. Bromley & J. Gordon Melton (Eds.), *Cults, Religion, and Violence.* Cambridge and New York: Cambridge University Press.

Hall, John R. & Schuyler, Phillip. (1997). The Mystical Apocalypse of the Solar Temple. In Thomas Robbins & Susan J. Palmer (Eds.), *Millennium, Messiahs, and Mayhem: Contemporary Apocalyptic Movements,* 285–311. London and New York: Routledge.

Hallo, William W. & Simpson, William Kelley. (1971). *The Ancient Near East: A History.* New York: Harcourt Brace Jovanovich. Second edition (1997) Washington, DC: International Thomson Publishing.

Halpern, Ben. (1961). *The Idea of the Jewish State.* Cambridge, MA: Harvard University Press. Second edition (1969) Cambridge, MA: Harvard University Press. Third edition (1976) Cambridge, MA: Harvard University Press.

Halpern, Ben & Reinharz, Jehuda. (1998). *Zionism and the Creation of a New Society.* New York: Oxford University Press. New edition (2000) Waltham, MA: Brandeis University Press. Hanover, NH: University Press of New England.

Halsell, Grace. (1981). *Journey to Jerusalem.* London and New York: Macmillan.

Hamady, Sania. (1960). *Temperament and Character of the Arabs.* New York: Twayne Publishers. New York: Irvington Publishers.

Hanif, N. (1997). *Islam and Modernity.* New Delhi: Sarup & Sons.

Haque, Abdul & Lawson, E. (1980). The Mirror-Image Hypothesis in the Context of the Arab-Israeli Conflict. *International Journal of International Relations,* 4, 107–112.

Harkabi, Yehoshafat. (1972). *Arab Attitudes to Israel.* London: Vallentine Mitchell. New York: Hart Publishing Co. New edition (1974) Piscataway, NJ: Transaction Books. Jerusalem: Israel Universities Press.

Harkabi, Yehoshafat. (1975). *Palestinians and Israel.* New York: Wiley. Reprinted (1981) as *The Palestinians and Israel.* London: Valentine Mitchell.

Harkabi, Yehoshafat. (1983). *The Bar Kokhba Syndrome: Risk and Realism in International Politics.* Trans. Max D. Ticktin. Ed. David Altshuler. Chappaqua, NY: Rossel Books.

Harkabi, Yehoshafat. (1988). *Israel's Fateful Hour.* New York: Harper and Row.

Harkabi, Yehoshafat. (1992). *The Arab-Israeli Conflict on the Threshold of Negotiations.* Princeton: Princeton University Press.

Harper, Paul. (1990). *The Arab-Israeli Conflict.* New York: Bookwright Press.

Harsgor, Michaël & Stroun, Maurice. (1996). *Israël/Palestine: l'histoire au-delà des mythes.* Geneva: Editions Metropolis.

Hart, Alan. (1984). *Arafat: Terrorist or Peacemaker?* London: Sidgwick and Jackson. Third edition (1987) London: Sidgwick and Jackson. American edition (1989) *Arafat: A Political Biography.* Bloomington: Indiana University Press.

Hart, Alan. (1994). *Arafat: A Political Biography* (2nd ed.). London: Sidgwick and Jackson.

Hartman, David. (2000). *Israelis and the Jewish Tradition: An Ancient People Debating Its Future.* New Haven, CT: Yale University Press.

Hary, Benjamin H., et al. (Eds.). (2000). *Judaism and Islam: Boundaries, Communication, and Interaction.* Essays in honor of William M. Brinner. Leiden and Boston: E. J. Brill.

Hass, Amira. (2000). *Drinking the Sea at Gaza: Days and Nights in a Land Under Siege.* New York: Owl Books.

Hassassian, Manuel Sarkis. (1990). *Palestine: Factionalisms in the National Movement, 1919–1939.* Jerusalem: Palestinian Academic Society for the Study of International Affairs.

Havel, Václav. (1997). *The Art of the Impossible: Politics as Morality in Practice. Speeches and Writings, 1990–1996.* Trans. Paul Wilson et al. New York: Alfred A. Knopf. New edition (1998) New York: Fromm International.

Hay, Peter. (1986). *Ordinary Heroes: Chana Szenes and the Dream of Zion.* New York: Putnam. New edition (1989) *The Life and Death of Chana Szenes, Israel's National Heroine.* New York: Paragon House.

Hazony, Yoram. (2000). *The Jewish State: The Struggle for Israel's Soul.* New York: Basic Books.

Headlam, George. (2004). *Yasser Arafat.* Minneapolis: Lerner Publications.

Hedges, Chris. (2001, October 28). French Police Glimpse Terror Cell Operations: News Leaks Foil More Surveillance, Several Arrests. *New York Times.*

Heggy, Tarek. (2003). *Culture, Civilization, and Humanity: Selections.* London: Frank Cass.

Heilman, Sam. (1992). *Defenders of the Faith: Inside Ultra-Orthodox Jewry.* New York: Schocken Books.

Heller, Joseph. (1995). *The Stern Gang: Ideology, Politics, and Terror, 1940–1949.* London: Frank Cass.

Heller, Joseph. (2000). *The Birth of Israel, 1945–1949: Ben-Gurion and His Critics.* Gainesville: University Press of Florida.

Heller, Mark A. & Nusseibeh, Sari. (1991). *No Trumpets, No Drums: A Two-State Settlement of the Israeli-Palestinian Conflict.* New York: Hill and Wang.

Heradstveit, Daniel. (1979). *The Arab-Israeli Conflict: Psychological Obstacles to Peace.* Oslo: Universitetsforlaget. New York: Columbia University Press.

Hersh, Seymour. (1983). *The Price of Power: Kissinger in the Nixon White House.* New York: Summit Books.

Hersh, Seymour. (1991). *The Samson Option: Israel, America and the Bomb.* London and Boston: Faber and Faber.

Hertzberg, Arthur. (1959). *The Zionist Idea.* New York: Atheneum.

Herzl, Theodor. (1960). *The Complete Diaries of Theodor Herzl* (5 vols.). Ed. Raphael Patai. New York: Herzl and Thomas Yoseloff Press.

Herzl, Theodor. (1987). *The Diaries of Theodor Herzl.* Trans. and Ed. M. Löwenthal. New York: Dial Press. New edition (1987) New York: Peter Smith. New edition (1990) New York: Peter Smith.

Herzl, Theodor. (1989). *The Jewish State.* New York: Dover. New edition (1997) *The Jews' State: A Critical English Translation.* Trans. Henk Overberg. Northvale, NJ: Jason Aronson.

Herzog, Chaim. (1975). *The War of Atonement.* Tel Aviv: Steimatzky. New edition (1998) Mechanicsburg, PA: Stackpole Books.

Herzog, Chaim. (1978). *Who Stands Accused? Israel Answers Its Critics.* New York: Random House.

Herzog, Chaim. (1982). *The Arab-Israeli Wars: War and Peace in the Middle East.* New York: Vintage Books.

Herzog, Chaim. (1996). *Living History: A Memoir.* New York: Pantheon Books.

Hinnebusch, Raymond A. (1985). *Egyptian Politics under Sadat.* Cambridge: Cambridge University Press.

Hirst, David. (1966). *Oil and Public Opinion in the Middle East.* London: Faber and Faber. New York: Praeger.

Hirst, David. (1977). *The Gun and the Olive Branch: The Roots of Violence in the Middle East.* London: Faber and Faber. New York: Harcourt Brace Jovanovich. Reprinted (1984) London: Faber and Faber. New edition (2003) New York: Thunder's Mouth Press.

Hirst, David. (2001, April 30). Arafat So Near yet So Far in Long March to Jerusalem. *The Guardian.*

Hirst, David & Beeson, Irene. (1981). *Sadat.* London: Faber and Faber.

Hitti, Philip Khuri. (1951). *History of Syria, Including Lebanon and Palestine.* London: Macmillan.

Hoffer, Eric. (1968, May 26). Israel's Peculiar Position. *The Los Angles Times.* Reprinted (1973) in Eric Hoffer, *Reflections on the Human Condition.* New York: Harper and Row. Reprinted (1982) in Eric Hoffer, *Between the Devil and the Dragon: The Best Essays and Aphorisms of Eric Hoffer.* New York: Harper and Row.

Hoffman, Bruce. (1983). *The Failure of British Military Strategy within Palestine, 1939–1947.* Ramat Gan, Israel: Bar Ilan University Press.

Hofman, John E. & Beit-Hallahmi, Benjamin. (1977). The Palestinian Identity and Israel's Arabs. *Peace Research,* 9, 13–23. Reprinted (1978) in Gabriel Ben Dor (Ed.), *The Palestinians and the Middle East Conflict: An International Conference Held at the Institute of Middle Eastern Studies, University of Haifa, April 1976.* Ramat-Gan, Israel: Turtledove Publishing Co.

Hofman, John E., Beit-Hallahmi, Benjamin & Lazarowitz, R. (1982). Self-Description of Jewish and Arab Adolescents in Israel: A Factor Study. *Journal of Personality and Social Psychology,* 43, 786–792.

Hofman, John E., et al. (1988). *Arab-Jewish Relations in Israel: A Quest in Human Understanding.* Bristol, IN: Wyndham Hall Press.

Hohenberg, John. (1998). *Israel at 50: A Journalist's Perspective.* Syracuse: Syracuse University Press.

Holly, David C. (1969). *Exodus 1947.* Boston: Little, Brown. Revised edition (1995) Annapolis, MD: Naval Institute Press.

Holmes, John Haynes. (1929). *Palestine Today and Tomorrow: A Gentile's Survey of Zionism.* New York: Macmillan.

Homans, Peter. (1989). *The Ability to Mourn: Disillusionment and the Social Origins of Psychoanalysis.* Chicago: University of Chicago Press.

Horowitz, David. (1953). *State in the Making.* New York: Alfred A. Knopf. New edition (1981) New York: Greenwood Press.

Horowitz, David. (Ed.). (1996). *Shalom, Friend: The Life and Legacy of Yitzhak Rabin.* New York: Newmarket Press.

Hourani, Albert. (1991). *A History of the Arab Peoples.* Cambridge, MA: Harvard University Press.

Hovannisian, Richard G. & Vryonis, Speros. (Eds.). (1983). *Islam's Understanding of Itself.* Malibu, CA: Undena Publications.

Howard, Harry Nicholas. (1963). *The King-Crane Commission: An American Inquiry in the Middle-East.* Beirut: Khayats.

Hudson Michael C. (1977). *The Arab Debate.* Cambridge: Cambridge University Press.

Hudson, Michael C. (1979). *Arab Politics: The Search for Legitimacy.* New Haven, CT: Yale University Press.

Hudson, Rex A. (1999). *The Sociology and Psychology of Terrorism: Who Becomes a Terrorist and Why? A Report.* Ed. Marilyn Majeska et al. Washington, DC: Federal Research Division, Library of Congress. Reprinted (2002) as *Who Becomes a Terrorist and Why: The 1999 Government Report on Profiling Terrorists.* Guilford, CT: Lyons Press.

Hughes, Judith M. (1989). *Reshaping the Psychoanalytic Domain: The Work of Melanie Klein, W. R. D. Fairbairn, and D. W. Winnicott.* Berkeley: University of California Press.

Hughes, Matthew. (1999). *Allenby and British Strategy in the Middle East, 1917–1919.* London: Frank Cass.

Humphreys, R. Stephen. (2001). *Between Memory and Desire: The Middle East in a Troubled Age.* Berkeley: University of California Press.

Hunt, William Holman. (1905–1906). *Pre-Raphaelitism and the Pre-Raphaelite Brotherhood* (2 vols.). New York: Macmillan.

Hunter, Jane. (1987). *Israeli Foreign Policy: South Africa and Central America.* Boston: South End Press.

Huntington, Samuel P. (1993). The Clash of Civilizations? *Foreign Affairs,* 72 (3), 22–28.

Huntington, Samuel P. (1996). *The Clash of Civilizations and the Remaking of World Order*. Washington: Council on Foreign Relations. New York: Simon and Schuster.

Huntington, Samuel P., et al. (1996). *The Clash of Civilizations? The Debate*. New York: Foreign Affairs. Reprinted (1997) as *Samuel P. Huntington's "The Clash of Civilizations?" The Debate*. New York: Norton.

Hurewitz, Jacob Coleman. (1950). *The Struggle for Palestine*. New York: Norton. Reprinted (1976) New York: Schocken Books.

Hurewitz, Jacob Coleman. (1956). *Diplomacy in the Near and Middle East: A Documentary Record*. New York: Van Nostrand.

Hurewitz, Jacob Coleman. (1969). *Middle East Politics: The Military Dimension*. New York: Praeger.

Hurwitz, Deena. (Ed.). (1992). *Walking the Red Line: Israelis in Search of Justice for Palestine*. Philadelphia: New Society Publishers.

Hurwitz, Harry Zvi & Denker, Patrick R. (Eds.). (1994). *Begin: A Portrait*. Washington, DC: B'nai B'rith Books.

Ibn Khaldun. (1958). *The Muqaddimah: An Introduction to History* (3 vols.). Trans. Franz Rosenthal. London: Routledge and Kegan Paul. New York: Pantheon. Second edition (1967) Princeton: Princeton University Press.

Indian Society of International Law. (1967). *The Arab-Israeli Conflict: Documents and Comments*. New Delhi: Indian Society of International Law.

Indyk, Martin S. (2002, March 17). The Three Faces of Sharon, a Man Alone. *The Washington Post*.

Inkeles, Alex. (1990–1991). National Character Revisited. *The Tocqueville Review*, 12, 83–117.

Introvigne, Massimo & Mayer, Jean-François. (2002). Occult Masters and the Temple of Doom: The Fiery End of the Solar Temple. In David G. Bromley & J. Gordon Melton (Eds.), *Cults, Religion, and Violence*. Cambridge and New York: Cambridge University Press.

Isaacs, Michal. (2002). Psychological Reflections on the Palestinian Mindset. *Clio's Psyche*, 9 (3), 127–129.

Iskandar, Marwan. (1966). *The Arab Boycott of Israel*. Beirut: Palestine Liberation Organization.

Israeli, Raphael. (1985). *Peace Is in the Eye of the Beholder: Images of Israel in the Arab Media*. Berlin, New York and Amsterdam: Mouton Press.

Israeli, Raphael. (1993). *Fundamentalist Islam and Israel: Essays in Interpretation*. Lanham, MD: University Press of America. Jerusalem: Jerusalem Center for Public Affairs.

Israeli, Raphael. (1993a). *Muslim Fundamentalism in Israel*. London and Washington: Brassey's.

Israeli, Raphael. (1997). Islamikaze and Their Significance. *Terrorism and Political Violence*, 9 (3), 96–121.

Israeli, Raphael. (2002). *Palestinian Women and Children in the Throes of Islamikaze Terrorism.* Shaarei Tikva, Israel: Ariel Center for Policy Research (ACPR).

Israeli, Raphael. (2002a). *Green Crescent over Nazareth: The Displacement of Christians by Muslims in the Holy Land.* London: Frank Cass.

Israeli, Raphael. (2003). *Islamikaze: Manifestations of Islamic Martyrology.* London: Frank Cass.

Israeli, Raphael. (Ed.). (2002). *Dangers of a Palestinian State.* Jerusalem and New York: Gefen Publishing House.

Issar, Arie. (1990). *Water Shall Flow from the Rock: Hydrogeology and Climate in the Lands of the Bible.* New York: Springer.

Jabotinsky, Vladimir Ze'ev. (1987). *The War and the Jew.* New York: Altalena Press.

Jabotinsky, Vladimir Ze'ev. (1998). *The Political and Social Philosophy of Ze'ev Jabotinsky: Selected Writings.* Ed. Mordechai Sarig. New York: Valentine Mitchell.

Jaffe Center for Strategic Studies of Tel Aviv University. (1989). *The West Bank and Gaza: Toward a Solution.* Tel Aviv: Tel Aviv University Press.

John, Robert & Hadawi, Sami. (1970). *The Palestine Diary, 1914–1948* (2 vols.). New York: New World Press.

Jones, Arnold Hugh Martin. (1938). *The Herods of Judaea.* Oxford: Clarendon Press. Revised edition (1967) Oxford: Clarendon Press.

Jones, Clive & Pedahzur, Ami. (2004). *Between Terrorism and Civil War: The Al-Aqsa Intifada.* London: Routledge.

Josephus, Flavius. (1959). *The Jewish War.* Harmondsworth: Penguin Books.

Journalists of Reuters. (2002). *The Israeli-Palestinian Conflict: Crisis in the Middle East.* London: Reuters. Reprinted (2003) Upper Saddle River, NJ: Prentice Hall.

Kadi, Leila S. (1973). *The Arab-Israeli Conflict: The Peaceful Proposals, 1948–1972.* Beirut: Palestine Research Center.

Kadi, Leila S. (Ed.). (1969). *Basic Political Documents of the Armed Palestinian Resistance Movement.* Beirut: Palestine Research Center.

Kahan, Yitzhak, et al. (1983). *Final Report.* Jerusalem: The Israel Commission of Inquiry into the Events at the Refugee Camps in Beirut. Reprinted (1983) as *The Beirut Massacre: The Complete Kahan Commission Report.* Intro. Abba Eban. Princeton, NJ: Karz-Cohl Publishing.

Kakar, M. Hassan. (1997). *The Soviet Invasion and the Afghan Response, 1979–1982.* Berkeley: University of California Press.

Kapeliouk, Amnon. (1984). *Sabra and Shatila: Inquiry into a Massacre.* Belmont, MA: Arab-American University Graduates Press.

Kaplan, Robert D. (1993). *The Arabists: The Romance of an American Elite.* New York: Free Press. New edition (1995) New York: Free Press.

Karsh, Efraim. (1997). *Fabricating Israeli History: The "New Historians."* London: Frank Cass. Second edition (2000) London: Frank Cass.

Karsh, Efraim. (2003). *Arafat's War: The Man and His Battle for Israeli Conquest.* New York: Grove Press.

Karsh, Efraim & Karsh, Inari. (1999). *Empires of the Sand: The Struggle for Mastery in the Middle East, 1789–1923.* Cambridge, MA: Harvard University Press.

Kaspit, Ben & Kfir, Ilan. (1998). *Netanyahu: The Road to Power.* London: Vision. Secaucus, NJ: Birch Lane Press.

Katz, Amnon. (1999). *Israel: The Two Halves of the Nation.* Northport, AL: Inverted-A.

Katz, David. (1998). *50 Faces of Israel.* Jerusalem: Gefen Publishing House.

Katz, Doris. (1953). *The Lady Was a Terrorist: During Israel's War of Liberation.* New York: Shiloni Publishers.

Katz, Shmuel. (1973). *Battleground: Fact and Fantasy in Palestine.* New York and Toronto: Bantam Books. London and New York: W. H. Allen. New edition (1985) New York: Steimatzky / Shapolsky.

Katz, Shmuel. (1996). *Lone Wolf: A Biography of Vladimir (Ze'ev) Jabotinsky.* New York: Barricade Books.

Kaufman, Gershen. (1989). *The Psychology of Shame: Theory and Treatment of Shame-Based Syndromes.* New York: Springer. Second edition (1996) New York: Springer. Reprinted (2002) New York: Springer.

Kayyali, Abd al-Wahhab. (1978). *Palestine: A Modern History.* London: Croom Helm.

Kedar, Benjamin Z. (1999). *The Changing Land between the Jordan and the Sea: Aerial Photographs from 1917 to the Present.* Jerusalem: Yad Ben-Zvi Press.

Kedourie, Elie. (1976). *In the Anglo-Arab Labyrinth: The MacMahon / Hussein Correspondence and Its Interpretations, 1914–1921.* Cambridge and New York: Cambridge University Press.

Kedourie, Elie. (1992). *Politics in the Middle East.* Oxford and New York: Oxford University Press.

Kedourie, Elie & Haim, Sylvia G. (Eds.). (1982). *Zionism and Arabism in Palestine and Israel.* London: Frank Cass.

Keesing's Publications. (1968). *The Arab-Israeli Conflict: The 1967 Campaign.* Bristol: Keesing's Publications. New York: Charles Scribner's Sons.

Kelly, Walt. (1972). *Pogo: We Have Met the Enemy and He Is Us.* New York: Simon and Schuster.

Kenyon, Kathleen M. (1974). *Digging Up Jerusalem.* London: Ernest Benn.

Kernberg, Otto F. (1980). *Internal World and External Reality: Object-Relations Theory Applied.* New York: Jason Aronson.

Kfir, Nira. (2002). Understanding Suicidal Terror through Humanistic and Existential Psychology. In Chris E. Stout (Ed.), *The Psychology of Terrorism: A Public Understanding* (Vol. 1). 143–157. Westport, CT: Praeger.

Khalidi, Rashid. (1997). *Palestinian Identity: The Construction of Modern National Consciousness.* New York: Columbia University Press.

Khalidi, Walid. (1984). *Before their Diaspora: A Photographic History of the*

Palestinians, 1876–1948. Washington, DC: Institute for Palestine Studies. New edition (1991) Washington, DC: Institute for Palestine Studies.

Khalidi, Walid. (1991). *The Gulf Crisis: Origins and Consequences.* Washington, DC: Institute for Palestine Studies.

Khalidi, Walid. (1992). *All That Remains: The Palestinian Villages Occupied and Depopulated by Israel in 1948.* Washington, DC: Institute for Palestine Studies.

Khalidi, Walid. (1992). *Palestine Reborn.* London: I. B. Tauris.

Khalidi, Walid. (Ed.). (1971). *From Haven to Conquest: Readings in Zionism and the Palestine Problem until 1948.* Beirut: Institute for Palestine Studies. New edition (1987) Washington, DC: Institute for Palestine Studies.

Khalidi, Walid & Khadduri, Jill. (Eds.). (1974). *Palestine and the Arab-Israeli Conflict: An Annotated Bibliography.* Washington, DC: Institute for Palestine Studies.

Khashan, Hilal. (1996). *Partner or Pariah? Attitudes toward Israel in Syria, Lebanon, and Jordan.* Washington, DC: Washington Institute for Near East Policy.

Khashan, Hilal. (2000). *Arabs at the Crossroads: Political Identity and Nationalism.* Gainesville: University Press of Florida.

Khouri, Fred J. (1968). *The Arab Israeli Dilemma.* Syracuse: Syracuse University Press. New edition (1985) Syracuse: Syracuse University Press.

Khourry, Philip Shukry. (1987). *Syria and the French Mandate: The Politics of Arab Nationalism, 1920–1945.* Princeton: Princeton University Press.

Khundmiri, Alam. (2001). *Secularism, Islam and Modernity: Selected Essays of Alam Khundmiri.* Ed. and Intro. M. T. Ansari. New Delhi and London: Sage Publications.

Khuri, Richard K. (1998). *Freedom, Modernity, and Islam: Toward a Creative Synthesis.* London. Athlone Press.

Kiernan, Thomas. (1976). *Arafat: The Man and the Myth.* New York: Norton.

Kimche, Jon. (1970). *The Second Arab Awakening.* London: Thames and Hudson. Reprinted (1973) New York: Henry Holt.

Kimche, Jon. (1973). *Palestine or Israel: The Untold Story of Why We Failed, 1917–1923, 1967–1973.* London: Secker and Warburg. U.S. edition (1973) *There Could Have Been Peace: The Untold Story of Why We Failed with Palestine and Again with Israel.* New York: Dial Press.

Kimche, Jon. (1976). *The Secret Roads: The "Illegal" Migration of a People, 1938–1948.* New York: Hyperion Press.

Kimche, Jon. (1991). *The Last Option: After Nasser, Arafat and Saddam Hussein, the Quest for Peace in the Middle East.* New York: Charles Scribner's Sons.

Kimche, Jon & Kimche, David. (1960). *A Clash of Destinies: The Arab-Jewish War and the Founding of the State of Israel.* New York: Praeger.

Kimche, Jon & Kimche, David. (1960a). *Both Sides of the Hill: Britain and the Palestine War.* London: Secker and Warburg.

Kimhi, Shaul & Even, Shmuel. (2003). Yassir Arafat: Behavioral and Strategic Analysis. *Social Behavior and Personality,* 31 (4), 363–374.

Kimmerling, Baruch. (1983). *Zionism and Economy.* Cambridge, MA: Schenkman.

Kimmerling, Baruch. (1983). *Zionism and Territory: The Socioterritorial Dimensions of Zionist Politics.* Berkeley: University of California, Institute of International Studies.

Kimmerling, Baruch. (1985). *The Interrupted System: Israeli Civilians in War and Routine Times.* New Brunswick, NJ: Transaction Books.

Kimmerling, Baruch. (1989). *The Israeli State and Society: Boundaries and Frontiers.* Albany: State University of New York Press.

Kimmerling, Baruch. (2001). *The Invention and Decline of Israeliness: Society, Culture and Military.* Berkeley: University of California Press.

Kimmerling, Baruch & Migdal, Joel S. (1993). *Palestinians: The Making of a People.* New York: Free Press. Reprinted (1994) Cambridge, MA: Harvard University Press.

Kinglake, Alexander William. (1844). *Eothen: Traces of Travel Brought Home from the East.* London: J. Ollivier. Reprinted (1845) New York: Wiley and Putnam. New York: W. H. Colyer. New edition (1849) New York: G. P. Putnam. Reprinted (1879) New York: Harper & Brothers. New edition (1898) With a critical and biographical introduction. Aldine edition. New York: D. Appleton. Reprinted (1906) Oxford: Oxford University Press. New edition (1970) *Eothen: A Classic of Travel in the Middle East.* Intro. V. S. Pritchett. Lincoln: University of Nebraska Press. New edition (1992) Intro. Barbara Krieger. Marlboro, VT: Marlboro. Reprinted (1996) Evanston, IL: Northwestern University Press.

Kirk, George. (1948). *A Short History of the Middle East from the Rise of Islam to Modern Times.* London: Methuen. Seventh revised edition (1964) New York: Frederick Praeger.

Kissinger, Henry Alfred. (1969). Domestic Structure and Foreign Policy. In James N. Rosenau (Ed.), *International Politics and Foreign Policy: A Reader in Research and Theory* (Rev. ed.). New York: Free Press.

Kissinger, Henry Alfred. (1997). *United States and Middle Eastern Policy in a Changing Global Arena.* Tel-Aviv: Yitzhak Rabin Center for Israel Studies.

Klein, Melanie. (1946). Notes on Some Schizoid Mechanisms. *International Journal of Psycho-Analysis, 27,* 99–110. Reprinted (1952) in Joan Riviere (Ed.), *Developments in Psycho-Analysis.* London: Hogarth Press and the Institute of Psycho-Analysis.

Klein, Melanie. (1950). *Contributions to Psychoanalysis, 1921–1945.* Intro. Ernest Jones. London: Hogarth Press and the Institute of Psycho-Analysis. Reprinted (1975) in *The Writings of Melanie Klein,* Ed. Roger Ernle Money-Kyrle, Vol. 1. London: Hogarth Press and the Institute of Psycho-Analysis.

Klein, Melanie. (1957). *Envy and Gratitude: A Study of Unconscious Sources.* London: Tavistock Publications. New York: Basic Books. Reprinted (1975) in *The Writings of Melanie Klein,* Ed. Roger Ernle Money-Kyrle, Vol. 3. London: Hogarth Press and the Institute of Psycho-Analysis. Reprinted (1984) New York: Free Press.

Klein, Melanie. (1959). Our Adult World and Its Roots in Infancy. *Human Relations*, 12, 291–303. Reprinted as a pamphlet (1960) *Our Adult World and Its Roots in Infancy.* London: Tavistock Publications. Reprinted (1963) in Melanie Klein *Our Adult World, and Other Essays.* London: Heinemann Medical Books. New York: Basic Books.

Klein, Melanie. (1975). *The Writings of Melanie Klein* (4 vols.). Ed. Roger Ernle Money-Kyrle. London: Hogarth Press. Reprinted (1984) New York: Free Press.

Klein, Uta & Sigrist, Christian. (Eds.). *Prospects of Israeli-Palestinian Co-existence.* Münster: Lit.

Kliot, Nurit. (1994). *Water Resources and Conflict in the Middle East.* London: Routledge.

Kobrin, Nancy H. (2002). A Psychoanalytic Approach to Bin Laden, Political Violence and Islamic Suicidal Terrorism. *Clio's Psyche,* 8 (4), 181–183.

Kobrin, Nancy H. (2003). Psychoanalytic Explorations of the New Moors: Converts for Jihad. *Clio's Psyche,* 9 (4), 157, 172–187.

Koestler, Arthur. (1949). *Promise and Fulfillment in Palestine, 1917–1949.* London: Macmillan.

Kohut, Heinz. (1971). *The Analysis of the Self.* New York: International Universities Press.

Kohut, Heinz. (1972). Thoughts on Narcissism and Narcissistic Rage. *The Psychoanalytic Study of the Child,* 27, 360–400.

Kohut, Heinz. (1976). Creativeness, Charisma, Group Psychology: Reflections on the Self-Analysis of Freud. In John E. Gedo & George H. Pollock (Eds.), *Freud, the Fusion of Science and Humanism: The Intellectual History of Psychoanalysis* New York: International Universities Press.

Kohut, Heinz. (1978). *The Search for the Self.* Ed. Paul H. Ornstein. New York: International Universities Press.

Kohut, Thomas August. (1991). *Wilhelm II and the Germans: A Study in Leadership.* New York: Oxford University Press.

Kolinsky, Martin. (1999). *Britain's War in the Middle East: Strategy and Diplomacy, 1936–1942.* Basingstoke and New York: Macmillan.

Kolko, Gabriel. (1988). *Confronting the Third World: United States Foreign Policy 1945–1980.* New York: Pantheon Books.

Kornberg, Jacques. (1983). At the Crossroads: Essays on Ahad Ha'Am. Albany: State University of New York Press.

Koskas, Marco. (1994). *Yasser Arafat, ou, Le Palestinien imaginaire.* Paris: Jean-Claude Lattès.

Kramer, Martin S. (1996). *Arab Awakening and Islamic Revival. The Politics of Ideas in the Middle East.* New Brunswick, NY: Transaction Books.

Kupfer, David J., et al. (2002). *A Research Agenda for DSM-V.* Washington, DC: American Psychiatric Association.

Kurland, Gerald. (1973). *The Arab-Israeli Conflict*. Charlotteville, NY: SamHar Press.

Kurzman, Dan. (1970). *Genesis 1948: The First Arab-Israeli War*. New York: World Publishing Co.

Kurzman, Dan. (1983). *Ben-Gurion: Prophet of Fire*. New York: Simon and Schuster.

Kurzman, Dan. (1998). *Soldier of Peace: The Life of Yitzhak Rabin, 1922–1995*. New York: HarperCollins.

Kutz, Ilan & Kutz, Sue. (2002, April 8). How the Trauma Takes Its Toll on Us: Two Therapists Tell How Israelis Are Trapped between Vigilance and Numbness. *TIME Europe*, 159 (14).

Labib, Fakhry & Salem, Nehad. (Eds.). (1997–1999). *Clash of Civilizations, or Dialogue of Cultures?* Cairo: Afro-Asian Peoples' Solidarity Organization.

Laffin, John. (1975). *The Arab Mind: A Need for Understanding*. London: Cassell. Reprinted (1975) as *The Arab Mind Considered: A Need for Understanding*. New York: Taplinger Publishing.

Laffin, John & Chappell, Michael. (1994). *The Israeli Army in the Middle East Wars 1948–1973*. Botley, Oxford: Osprey Publishing.

Lamb, Franklin. (Ed.). (1984). *Israel's War in Lebanon*. Nottingham: Bertrand Russell Peace Foundation.

Lambton, Ann K. S. (1981). *State and Government in Medieval Islam*. Oxford and New York: Oxford University Press.

Langer, Felicia. (1975). *With My Own Eyes: Israel and the Occupied Territories, 1967–1973*. Foreword Israel Shahak. Reading, Berkshire: Ithaca Press.

Lapidoth, Ruth. (2003). *Israel and the Palestinians: Some Legal Issues*. Jerusalem: Jerusalem Institute for Israel Studies, Teddy Kollek Center for Jerusalem Studies.

Laqueur, Walter. (1970). *The Struggle for the Middle East: The Soviet Union in the Mediterranean*. London: Routledge and Kegan Paul.

Laqueur, Walter. (1972). *A History of Zionism*. London: Weidenfeld and Nicolson. New York: Holt, Rinehart and Winston. Reprinted (1976) New York: Schocken Books. New edition (1989) New York: Schocken Books. Reprinted (1996) New York: MJF Books. Reprinted (1997) New York: Fine Communications.

Laqueur, Walter. (1980). *The Terrible Secret: An Investigation into the Suppression of Information about Hitler's "Final Solution."* London: Weidenfeld and Nicolson. Boston: Little, Brown. Reprinted (1982) as *The Terrible Secret: Suppression of the Truth about Hitler's "Final Solution."* Harmondsworth and New York: Penguin Books.

Laqueur, Walter. (Ed.). (1969). *The Israel-Arab Reader: A Documentary History of the Middle East Conflict*. New York: Citadel Press. Second edition (1970) Harmondsworth: Penguin Books. Third edition (1976) New York: Bantam Books.

Fourth edition (1984) Eds. Walter Laqueur & Barry Rubin. Harmondsworth
and New York: Penguin Books. Reprinted (1991) New York: Penguin Books.
Fifth edition (1995) Harmondsworth and New York: Penguin Books. Sixth
edition (2001) New York: Viking Penguin.

Laroui, Abdallah. (1967). *L'Idéologie arabe contemporaine: essai critique.* Préface
de Maxime Rodinson. Paris: F. Maspéro. New edition (1982) Paris: La
Découverte.

Laroui, Abdallah. (1974). *La Crise des intellectuels arabes: traditionalisme ou histori-
cisme?* Paris: F. Maspéro. New edition (1978) Paris: La Découverte.

Laroui, Abdallah. (1976). *The Crisis of the Arab Intellectual: Traditionalism or His-
toricism?* Trans. Diarmid Cammell. Berkeley: University of California Press.

Laroui, Abdallah. (1977). *The History of the Maghrib: An Interpretive Essay.* Princeton: Princeton University Press.

Laroui, Abdallah. (1987). *Islam et modernité.* Paris: La Découverte.

Laroui, Abdallah. (1999). *Islam et histoire: essai d'épistémologie.* Paris: Albin Michel.

Lasswell, Harold Dwight. (1948). *Power and Personality.* New York: Norton.

Lasswell, Harold Dwight. (1930). *Psychopathology and Politics.* Chicago: University of Chicago Press. New edition (1960) New York: Viking Press.

Lasswell, Harold Dwight. (1977). *Psychopathology and Politics.* With a new Introduction by Fred I. Greenstein. Chicago: University of Chicago Press.

Lavie, Smadar. (1990). *The Poetics of Military Occupation: Mzeina Allegories of Bed-
ouin Identity under Israeli and Egyptian Rule.* Berkeley and Los Angeles: University of California Press.

Lawrence, Thomas Edward. (1926). *The Seven Pillars of Wisdom: A Triumph.* Lon-
don: Jonathan Cape. New York: G. H. Doran. New edition (1935) Garden
City, NY: Doubleday, Doran & Co. New edition (1973) With amendments.
London: Jonathan Cape. New edition (1991) New York: Doubleday Anchor.

Lea, Henry Charles. (1968). *The Moriscos of Spain: Their Conversion and Expulsion.*
New York: Haskell House.

Lerner, Michael. (2004). *The Geneva Accord and Other Strategies for Healing the
Israeli-Palestinian Conflict.* Berkeley: North Atlantic Books.

Lesch, Ann Mosely & Tessler, Mark A. (1989). *Israel, Egypt and the Palestinians:
From Camp David to Intifada.* Foreword Richard B. Parker. Bloomington: Indiana University Press.

Levine, Daniel. (1991). *The Birth of the Irgun Zvai Leumi: A Jewish Resistance
Movement.* Jerusalem: Gefen Publishing. Reprinted (1996) Jerusalem: Gefen
Publishing.

Levins, Hoag. (1983). *Arab Reach: The Secret War against Israel.* Garden City, NY:
Doubleday.

Lewis, Bernard. (1966). *The Arabs in History.* New York: Harper and Row. Sixth
edition (1993) Oxford and New York: Oxford University Press.

Lewis, Bernard. (1967). *The Assassins: A Radical Sect in Islam.* London: Weidenfeld and Nicolson. Reprinted (1968) New York: Basic Books. New edition

(1980) New York: Octagon Books. New edition (1987) Oxford and New York: Oxford University Press.

Lewis, Bernard. (1984). *The Jews of Islam*. Princeton: Princeton University Press.

Lewis, Bernard. (1988). *The Political Language of Islam*. Chicago: University of Chicago Press. New edition (1991) Chicago: University of Chicago Press.

Lewis, Bernard. (1990, September). The Roots of Muslim Rage. *The Atlantic Monthly*, 266 (3), 47–60.

Lewis, Bernard. (1995). *The Middle East: 2000 Years of History from the Rise of Christianity to the Present Day*. London: Weidenfeld and Nicolson. U.S. edition (1995) *The Middle East: A Brief History of the Last 2,000 Years*. New York: Charles Scribner's Sons. British edition reprinted (1997) London: Phoenix. U.S. edition reprinted (1997) New York: Touchstone Books.

Lewis, Bernard. (1998). *The Multiple Identities of the Middle East*. London: Weidenfeld and Nicolson. U.S. edition (1999) New York: Schocken Books. Reprinted (2001) New York: Schocken Books.

Lewis, Bernard. (2002, January). What Went Wrong? *The Atlantic Monthly*, 289 (1), 43–45.

Lewis, Bernard. (2002a). *What Went Wrong? The Clash between Islam and Modernity in the Middle East*. London: Weidenfeld and Nicolson. Reprinted (2002) as *What Went Wrong? Western Impact and Middle Eastern Response*. New York: Oxford University Press.

Lewis, Bernard. (2003). *The Crisis of Islam: Holy War and Unholy Terror*. London: Weidenfeld and Nicolson.

Lieblich, Amia. (1978). *Tin Soldiers on Jerusalem Beach*. New York: Pantheon Books.

Liebman, Charles S. & Don-Yehiya, Eliezer. (1983). *Civil Religion in Israel: Traditional Judaism and Political Culture in the Jewish State*. Berkeley and Los Angeles: University of California Press.

Lifton, Robert Jay. (1997). Reflections on Aum Shinrikyo. *The Psychohistory Review*, 25 (3), 221–234.

Lifton, Robert Jay. (1999). *Destroying the World to Save It: Aum Shinrikyo, Apocalyptic Violence, and the New Global Terrorism*. New York: Henry Holt.

Lilienthal, Alfred M. (1965). *The Other Side of the Coin: An American Perspective of the Arab-Israeli Conflict*. New York: Devin-Adair.

Lippman, Thomas W. (1982). *Understanding Islam: An Introduction to the Moslem World*. New York: New American Library. Second edition (1995) *Understanding Islam: An Introduction to the Muslim World*. New York: Meridian Books.

Little, Tom. (1971). *The Arab World Today*. London: Hart-Davis.

Livni, Michael & Skirball, Henry F. (1999). *Reform Zionism: Twenty Years—an Educator's Perspective*. Jerusalem: Gefen Publishing.

Lochery, Neill. (1997). *The Israeli Labour Party: In the Shadow of the Likud*. Reading, Berkshire: Ithaca Press.

Lockman, Zachary. (1996). *Comrades and Enemies: Arab and Jewish Workers in Palestine, 1906–1948*. Berkeley: University of California Press.

Lockman, Zachary & Beinin, Joel. (Eds.). (1989). *Intifada: The Palestinian Uprising against Israeli Occupation.* Boston: South End Press.

Loewenberg, Peter. (1994). The Psychological Reality of Nationalism: Between Community and Fantasy. *Mind and Human Interaction,* 5 (1), 6–18. Reprinted (1995) in Peter Loewenberg, *Fantasy and Reality in History.* Oxford: Oxford University Press.

Lorch, Netanel. (1976). *One Long War: Arab versus Jew since 1920.* New York: Herzl Press.

Lorenz, Konrad Zacharias. (1963). *Das sogenannte Böse: zur Naturgeschichte der Aggression.* Vienna: G. Borotha-Schoele.

Lorenz, Konrad Zacharias. (1966). *On Aggression.* Trans. Marjorie Latzke [Marjorie Kerr Wilson]. Foreword Julian Huxley. London: Methuen. New York: Harcourt Brace Jovanovich. Reprinted (1974) New York: Harcourt Brace Jovanovich.

Lowdermilk, Walter. (1944). *Palestine: Land of Promise.* New York: Harper & Brothers.

Luel, Steven A. & Marcus, Paul. (Eds.). (1984). *Psychoanalytic Reflections on the Holocaust: Selected Essays.* Denver: Holocaust Awareness Institute, Center for Judaic Studies, University of Denver. New York: Ktav Publishing House.

Lukacs, Yehuda. (1992). *The Israeli-Palestinian Conflict: A Documentary Record.* Cambridge and New York: Cambridge University Press.

Lukacs, Yehuda. (1997). *Israel, Jordan, and the Peace Process.* Syracuse: Syracuse University Press.

Lukacs, Yehuda & Battah, Abdallah M. (Eds.). (1988). *The Arab-Israeli Conflict: Two Decades of Change.* Boulder, CO: Westview Press.

Lustick, Ian S. (1980). *Arabs in the Jewish State: Israel's Control of a National Minority.* Austin: University of Texas Press.

Lustick, Ian S. (1980a). Israel and the West Bank after Elon Moreh: The Mechanics of De Facto Annexation. *The Middle East Journal,* 35 (4), 557–577.

Lustick, Ian S. (1988). *For the Land and the Lord: Jewish Fundamentalism in Israel.* New York: Council on Foreign Relations.

Lustick, Ian S. (1997). Israeli History: Who Is Fabricating What? Review of *Fabricating Israeli History: The "New Historians"* by Efraim Karsh. *Survival,* 39 (3), 156–166.

Lustick, Ian S. (Ed.). (1994). *Arab-Israeli Relations: A Collection of Contending Perspectives and Recent Research* (10 vols.). New York and Hamden, CT: Garland Publishing Co.

Luttwak, Edward N. & Horowitz, Daniel. (1975). *The Israeli Army, 1948–1973.* London: Allen Lane. New edition (1983) Lanham, MD: University Press of America.

Luz, Ehud. (1988). *Parallels Meet: Religion and Nationalism in the Early Zionist Movement, 1882–1904.* Philadelphia: Jewish Publication Society.

MacBride, Sean. (Ed.). (1983). *Israel in Lebanon: Report of the International*

Commission to Enquire into Reported Violations of International Law by Israel during Its Invasion of Lebanon. London: Ithaca Press.

Maccoby, Hyam. (1996). *A Pariah People: The Anthropology of Antisemitism.* London: Constable.

Maccoby, Hyam. (1998, April). Pernicious Revisionism Exposed. Review of *Fabricating Israeli History: The "New Historians"* by Efraim Karsh. *Midstream,* 44 (3), 40–41.

Mack, John E. (1976). *A Prince of Our Disorder: The Life of T. E. Lawrence.* Boston: Little, Brown.

Mack, John E. (1979). Foreword to Vamık D. Volkan *Cyprus-War and Adaptation: A Psychoanalytic History of Two Ethnic Groups in Conflict.* Charlottesville: University Press of Virginia.

Mack, John E. (1983). Nationalism and the Self. *The Psychohistory Review,* 11 (2–3), 47–69.

Mack, John E. (2002). Looking beyond Terrorism: Transcending the Mind of Enmity. In Chris E. Stout (Ed.), *The Psychology of Terrorism: A Public Understanding* (Vol. 1). 173–184. Westport, CT: Praeger.

Magnus, Ralph H. & Naby, Eden. (1998). *Afghanistan: Mullah, Marx, and Mujahid.* Boulder, CO: Westview Press.

Makovsky, David. (1996). *Making Peace with the PLO: The Rabin Government's Road to the Oslo Accords.* Boulder, CO: Westview Press.

Mahler, Margaret S., et al. (1975). *The Psychological Birth of the Human Infant: Symbiosis and Individuation.* New York: Basic Books. London: Hutchinson.

Malik, Iftikhar Haider. (2003). *Islam and Modernity: Muslims in Europe and the United States.* Sterling, VA: Pluto Press.

Mandel, Neville Julian. (1976). *The Arabs and Zionism Before World War I.* Berkeley: University of California Press.

Mansfield, Peter. (1976). *The Arab World: A Comprehensive History.* New York: Crowell.

Mansfield, Susan. (1982). *The Gestalts of War: An Inquiry into Its Origin and Meaning as a Social Institution.* New York: Dial Press.

Maqsood, Ruqaiyyah Waris. (2001). *A Basic Dictionary of Islam.* New Dehli: Goodword Books.

Margalit, Avishai. (1990, April 26). High Noon at the Likud Corral. *The New York Times Review of Books.*

Margalit, Avishai. (1998). *Views in Review: Politics and Culture in the State of the Jews.* New York: Farrar Straus and Giroux.

Marr, Wilhelm. (1879). *Der Sieg des Judenthums über das Germanenthum, vom nicht-confessionellen Standpunkt aus betrachtet.* Bern: Rudolph Costenoble.

Marr, Wilhelm. (1880). *Der Judenkrieg, seine Fehler und wie er zu organisieren ist.* Chemnitz, Germany: E. Schmeitzner.

Marty, Martin E. & Appleby, R. Scott. (1992). *The Glory and the Power: The Fundamentalist Challenge to the Modern World.* Boston: Beacon Press.

Marty, Martin E. & Appleby, R. Scott. (Eds.). (1995). *Fundamentalism Compre-hended.* Chicago: University of Chicago Press.

Masalha, Nur. (1992). *The Expulsion of the Palestinians: The Concept of "Transfer" in Zionist Political Thought, 1882–1948.* Washington, DC: Institute for Pales-tine Studies.

Masalha, Nur. (1997). *A Land without People: Israel, Transfer and the Palestinians, 1949–1996.* London: Faber and Faber.

Masalha, Nur. (2000). *Imperial Israel and the Palestinians: The Politics of Expansion, 1967–2000.* Sterling, VA: Pluto Press. Reprinted (2001) London: Pluto Press.

Mason, Herbert Molloy. (Ed.). (1970). *Reflections on the Middle East Crisis.* The Hague: Mouton.

Massignon, Louis. (1982). *The Passion of al-Hallaj: Mystic and Martyr of Islam* (4 vols.). Trans. & Intro. Herbert Masson. Princeton: Princeton University Press. One-volume abridgement (1994) Princeton: Princeton University Press.

Massignon, Louis. (1997). *Les Trois Prières d'Abraham.* Ed. Daniel Massignon. Paris: Institut international de recherches sur Louis Massignon. Paris: Edi-tions du Cerf.

Mattar, Philip. (1988). *The Mufti of Jerusalem: Al-Hajj Amin al-Husayni and the Pal-estinian National Movement.* New York: Columbia University Press. Revised edition (1992) New York: Columbia University Press.

McDonald, John W., Jr. & Bendahmane, Diane B. (Eds.). (1987). *Conflict Resolu-tion: Track Two Diplomacy.* Washington, DC: Center for the Study of Foreign Affairs, Foreign Service Institute, U.S. Dept. of State. Revised edition (1995) Washington, DC: Institute for Multi-Track Diplomacy.

McDowall, David. (1989). *Palestine and Israel: The Uprising and Beyond.* Berkeley: University of California Press. New edition (1991) Berkeley: University of California Press.

McGowan, Daniel A. & Ellis, Marc H. (Eds.). (1998). *Remembering Deir Yassin: The Future of Israel and Palestine.* Ithaca, NY: Olive Branch Press.

Medoff, Rafael, et al. (Eds.). (2000). *Historical Dictionary of Zionism.* Lanham, MD: Scarecrow Press.

Meinertzhagen, Richard. (1959). *Middle East Diary, 1917–1956.* London: Cresset Press.

Meir, Golda. (1975). *My Life.* New York: Dell.

Melman, Yossi. (1992). *The New Israelis: An Intimate View of a Changing People.* New York: Birch Lane Press.

Melman, Yossi & Raviv, Dan. (1988, February 7). Expelling Palestinians. *The Washington Post.*

Melton, J. Gordon & Baumann, Martin. (Eds.). (2002). *Religions of the World: A Comprehensive Encyclopedia of Beliefs and Practices.* Intro. Donald Wiebe. Santa Barbara, CA: ABC-CLIO.

Millar, Fergus. (1993). *The Roman Near East, 31 BC–AD 337.* Cambridge, MA: Harvard University Press.

Miller, Aaron. (1986). *The Arab States and the Palestine Question.* Westport, CT: Praeger.

Miller, Anita, Miller, Jordan & Zetouni, Sigalit. (2002). *Sharon: Israel's Warrior-Politician.* Chicago: Academy Chicago Publishers and Olive Publishing.

Miller, Judith. (1997). *God Has Ninety-Nine Names: Reporting from a Militant Middle East.* New York: Touchstone Books.

Miller, R. (1988). The Literature of Terrorism. *Terrorism,* 11, 63–87.

Milstein, Uri. (1996–1999). *History of Israel's War of Independence* (4 vols.). Trans. and Ed. Alan Sacks. Lanham, MD: University Press of America.

Minnis, Ivan. (2003). *The Arab-Israeli Conflict.* Austin, TX: Raintree Steck-Vaughn.

Mitchell, Richard P. (1969). *The Society of the Muslim Brothers.* Oxford and New York: Oxford University Press.

Mitscherlich, Alexander & Mitscherlich, Margarete. (1975). *The Inability to Mourn: Principles of Collective Behavior.* Pref. Robert Jay Lifton. Trans. Beverley R. Placzek. New York: Grove Press. Reprinted (1978) Ann Arbor, MI: University Microfilms International.

Moghaddam, Fathali M. (2003). *Understanding Terrorism: Psychosocial Roots, Consequences, and Interventions.* Washington, DC: American Psychological Association.

Moktefi, Mokhtar, et al. (1992). *The Arabs in the Golden Age.* Brookfield, CT: Millbrook Press.

Money-Kyrle, Roger Ernle. (1951). *Psychoanalysis and Politics: A Contribution to the Psychology of Politics and Morals.* London: Duckworth. New York: Norton. Reprinted (1963) Englewood Cliffs, NJ: Prentice-Hall.

Money-Kyrle, Roger Ernle. (1961). *Man's Picture of His World: A Psycho-Analytic Study.* New York: International Universities Press.

Moore, John Norton. (Ed.). (1992). *The Arab-Israeli Conflict: The Difficult Search for Peace (1975–1988)* (3 vols.). Princeton: Princeton University Press.

Moore, John Norton. (Ed.). (1974). *The Arab-Israeli Conflict: Readings and Documents* (4 vols.). Princeton: Princeton University Press. Abridged and revised edition (1977) Princeton: Princeton University Press.

Moorey, Peter Roger Stuart. (1991). *A Century of Biblical Archaeology.* Louisville, KY: Westminster and John Knox Press.

Morgan, Jay Scott. (2001). The Mystery of Goya's *Saturn. New England Review,* Summer issue.

Morris, Benny. (1987). *The Birth of the Palestinian Refugee Problem, 1947–1949.* Cambridge and New York: Cambridge University Press. New edition (1988) Cambridge and New York: Cambridge University Press.

Morris, Benny. (1990). *1948 and After: Israel and the Palestinians.* Oxford and New York: Oxford University Press.

Morris, Benny. (1993). *Israel's Border Wars, 1949–1956: Arab Infiltration, Israeli Retaliation, and the Countdown to the Suez War.* Oxford and New York: Oxford University Press.

Morris, Benny. (1999). *Righteous Victims: A History of the Zionist-Arab Conflict 1881–1999.* New York: Alfred A. Knopf.

Morris, Benny. (2001). *Righteous Victims: A History of the Zionist-Arab Conflict, 1881–2001.* New York: Vintage Books.

Morris, Benny. (2002). *The Road to Jerusalem: Glubb Pasha, Palestine and the Jews.* London and New York: I. B. Tauris.

Morris, Benny. (2004). *The Birth of the Palestinian Refugee Problem Revisited.* Cambridge and New York: Cambridge University Press.

Morris, Benny. (2004a, January 9). [Interview with Ari Shavit]. *Ha'aretz Magazine.*

Morris, Benny. (2004b, January 23). Open letter. *Ha'aretz Magazine.*

Moses, Rafael. (1980). Psychoanalytic Perspectives on the Middle East Peace Process: Obstacles to Peace, with Special Reference to Narcissism. *Samiksa, Journal of the Indian Psychoanalytical Society,* 34, 117–129.

Moses, Rafael. (1982). The Group Self and the Arab-Israeli Conflict. *International Review of Psycho-Analysis,* 9, 55–65.

Moses, Rafael. (1985). Empathy and Dis-Empathy in Political Conflict. *Political Psychology,* 6 (1), 135–139.

Moses, Rafael. (1990). On Dehumanizing the Enemy. In Vamık D. Volkan, Demetrios A. Julius & Joseph V. Montville (Eds.), *The Psychodynamics of International Relationships,* 1, 111–118. Lexington, MA: Lexington Books.

Moughrabi, Fouad M. (1978). The Arab Basic Personality: A Critical Survey of the Literature. *International Journal of Middle Eastern Studies,* 9, 99–112.

Moughrabi, Fouad M. & Aruri, Naseer. (Eds.). (1977). *Lebanon: Crisis and Challenge in the Arab World.* Detroit, MI: Association of Arab-American University Graduates.

Mullins, Mark R. (1997). Aum Shinrikyo as an Apocalyptic Movement. In Thomas Robbins & Susan J. Palmer (Eds.), *Millennium, Messiahs, and Mayhem: Contemporary Apocalyptic Movements.* London and New York: Routledge.

Murphy, Emma C. (1995). *Israel and the Palestinians: The Economic Rewards of Peace?* Durham, England: University of Durham, Centre for Middle Eastern and Islamic Studies.

Muslih, Muhammad Y. (1988). *The Origins of Palestinian Nationalism.* New York: Columbia University Press.

Naff, Thomas & Matson Ruth C. (Eds.). (1984). *Water in the Middle East: Conflict or Cooperation?* Boulder, CO: Westview Press.

Naipaul, Vidiadhar Surajprasad. (1998). *Beyond Belief: Islamic Excursions among the Converted Peoples.* New York: Random House.

Nassar, Jamal R. & Heacock, Roger. (Eds.). (1990). *Intifada: Palestine at the Crossroads.* New York: Praeger.

Nazzal, Nafez Y. (1978). *The Exodus from Galilee, 1948.* Washington, DC: Institute for Palestine Studies.

Nazzal, Nafez Y. & Nazzal, Laila A. (1978). *Historical Dictionary of Palestine*. Lanham, MD: Scarecrow Press.

Neff, Donald. (1984). *Warriors for Jerusalem: The Six Days That Changed the Middle East*. New York: Simon and Schuster.

Netanyahu, Benjamin. (1983). *A Place among Nations: Israel and the World*. London: Bantam Books. New edition (1993) New York: Bantam Books.

Netanyahu, Benzion. (1966). *The Marranos of Spain: From the Late XIVth to the Early XVIth Century, according to Contemporary Hebrew Sources*. New York: American Academy for Jewish Research. Second edition (1972) New York: American Academy for Jewish Research. Reprinted (1973) Millwood, NY: Kraus Reprint Co. Third edition (1999) Ithaca, NY: Cornell University Press.

Nevo, Joseph & Pappé, Ilan. (Eds.). (1994). *Jordan in the Middle East: The Making of a Pivotal State, 1948–1988*. London: Frank Cass.

Nicosia, Francis R. (1985). *The Third Reich and the Palestine Question*. London: I. B. Tauris. Second edition (1999) New Brunswick, NJ: Transaction Books.

Niederland, William G. (1971). The Naming of America. In Mark Kanzer (Ed.), *The Unconscious Today: Essays in Honor of Mas Schur*, New York: International Universities Press. 459–472. Reprinted (1989) in Howard F. Stein & William G. Niederland (Eds.), *Maps from the Mind: Readings in Psychogeography*, 82–96. Norman: University of Oklahoma Press.

Nisan, Mordechai. (1977). *The Arab-Israeli Conflict: A Political Guide for the Perplexed*. Jerusalem: HaMakor and The Joshua Group.

Nisan, Mordechai. (1978). *Israel and the Territories: a Study in Control, 1967–1977*. Ramat Gan, Israel: Turtledove Publications.

Nisan, Mordechai. (1991). *Minorities in the Middle East: A History of Struggle and Self-Expression*. Jefferson, NC: McFarland.

Nisan, Mordechai. (1992). *Toward a New Israel: The Jewish State and the Arab Question*. New York: AMS Press.

Nisan, Mordechai. (1999). *Identity and Civilization: Essays on Judaism, Christianity, and Islam*. Lanham, MD: University Press of America.

Norton, Augustus Richard. (1987). *Amal and the Shi'a: Struggle for the Soul of Lebanon*. Foreword, Leonard Binder. Austin: University of Texas Press.

Nusseibeh, Sari. (1994). The Peace Process and the Palestinian Interest: An Interview. A Palestinian Leader's View on Israeli-Palestinian Separation, the Poisoned Atmosphere, Hamas, Palestinian Priorities and Solutions. *Palestine-Israel Journal of Politics, Economics and Culture*, 1 (4), 69–73.

Nye, Naomi Shihab. (1997). *Habibi*. New York: Simon and Schuster.

O'Ballance, Edgar. (1998). *Civil War in Lebanon, 1975–92*. New York: St. Martin's Press. Reprinted (1999) Basingstoke and New York: Macmillan.

O'Brien, Conor Cruise. (1986). *The Siege: The Story of Israel and Zionism*. New York: Simon and Schuster.

O'Mahony, Anthony. (Ed.). (1999). *Palestinian Christians: Religion, Politics, and Society in the Holy Land*. London: Melisende.

Oman, Douglas & Myers, Dennis. (2002). Ghaffar Khan: A Muslim Advocate of Nonviolence. *Clio's Psyche,* 9 (3), 138–140.

Oren, Michael B. (2002). *Six Days of War: June 1967 and the Making of the Modern Middle East.* Oxford and New York: Oxford University Press.

Ostow, Mortimer. (1995). *Myth and Madness: The Psychodynamics of Antisemitism.* New Brunswick, NJ: Transaction Books.

Ostow, Mortimer. (Ed.). (1982). *Judaism and Psychoanalysis.* New York: Ktav Publishing House.

Oz, Amos. (1983). *In the Land of Israel.* New York: Harcourt Brace Jovanovich. Reprinted (1985) London: Fontana.

Oz, Amos. (1994). *Israel, Palestine and Peace.* New York: Harcourt Brace.

Pacepa, Ion Mihai. (1987). *Red Horizons: Chronicles of a Communist Spy Chief.* Washington, DC: Regnery Gateway.

Palumbo, Michael. (1987). *The Palestinian Catastrophe: The 1948 Expulsion of a People from Their Homeland.* London: Faber and Faber. Reprinted (1991) Ithaca, NY: Olive Branch Press.

Palumbo, Michael. (1990). *Imperial Israel: The History of the Occupation of the West Bank and Gaza.* London: Bloomsbury Publishing. Revised edition (1992) London: Bloomsbury Publishing.

Pape, Robert A. (2003). The Strategic Logic of Suicide Terrorism. *American Political Science Review,* 97 (3), 343–361.

Pappas, Theodore, et al. (Eds.). (2004). *Encyclopaedia Britannica 2004 DVD.* Chicago: Encyclopaedia Britannica.

Pappé, Ilan. (1988). *Britain and the Arab-Israeli Conflict, 1948–1951.* London: Macmillan.

Pappé, Ilan. (1992). *The Making of the Arab-Israeli Conflict, 1947–1951.* New York: St. Martin's Press. London: I. B. Tauris. Reprinted (1994) New York: I. B. Tauris.

Pappé, Ilan. (2004). *A History of Modern Palestine: One Land, Two Peoples.* Cambridge and New York: Cambridge University Press.

Pappé, Ilan. (Ed.). (1999). *The Israel/Palestine Question: Rewriting Histories.* London: Routledge.

Pappé, Ilan & Ma'oz, Moshe. (Eds.). (1997). *Middle Eastern Politics and Ideas: A History from Within.* London: I. B. Tauris.

Parker, Richard B. (Eds.). (1996). *The Six-Day War: A Retrospective.* Gainesville: University Press of Florida.

Parkes, James William. (1949). *A History of Palestine from 135 A.D. to Modern Times.* London: Victor Gollancz.

Parkes, James William. (1970). *Whose Land? A History of the Peoples of Palestine.* Harmondsworth: Penguin Books.

Parkes, James William. (1972). *Israel in the Middle-Eastern Complex.* London: The Anglo-Israel Association.

Patai, Raphael. (1973). *The Arab Mind.* New York: Charles Scribner's Sons. Reprinted (1976) New York: Charles Scribner's Sons. Revised edition (1983)

New York: Charles Scribner's Sons. Reprinted (2002) New York: Hatherleigh Press.

Patai, Raphael. (1976). Ethnohistory and Inner History. *The Jewish Quarterly Review*, 67, 1–15. Reprinted (1977) in Raphael Patai, *The Jewish Mind*, 28–37. New York: Charles Scribner's Sons.

Patai, Raphael. (1977). *The Jewish Mind*. New York: Charles Scribner's Sons.

Patai, Raphael. (Ed.). (1971). *Encyclopedia of Zionism and Israel*. New York: Herzl Press.

Patai, Raphael & Wing, Jennifer Patai. (1975). *The Myth of the Jewish Race*. New York: Charles Scribner's Sons. Revised edition (1989) Detroit, MI: Wayne State University Press.

Peace Committee for International Co-operation and Disarmament. (1970). *The Arab-Israeli Conflict: Comments and Criticisms*. Brisbane, Queensland, Australia: Peace Committee for International Co-operation and Disarmament.

Peled, Alisa Rubin. (2001). *Debating Islam in the Jewish State: The Development of Policy toward Islamic Institutions in Israel*. Albany: State University of New York Press.

Peleg, Ilan. (Ed.). (1998). *The Middle East Peace Process: Interdisciplinary Perspectives*. Albany: State University of New York Press.

Penkower, Monty Noam. (1991). *The Emergence of Zionist Thought*. New York: Peter Lang.

Penkower, Monty Noam. (1994). *The Holocaust and Israel Reborn: From Catastrophe to Sovereignty*. Champaign: University of Illinois Press.

Perednik, Gustavo Daniel. (2001). *La Judeofobia: Cómo y Cuándo Nace, Dónde y por qué Pervive*. Barcelona: Flor del Viento Ediciones.

Peres, Shimon. (1970). *David's Sling*. London: Weidenfeld and Nicolson. Reprinted (1971) New York: Random House. New edition (1995) New York: Random House.

Peres, Shimon & Littell, Robert. (1998). *For the Future of Israel*. Baltimore: Johns Hopkins University Press.

Peres, Shimon, with Arye Naor. (1993). *The New Middle East*. New York: Henry Holt.

Peretz, Don. (1990). *Intifada: The Palestinian Uprising*. Boulder, CO: Westview Press.

Peretz, Don. (1993). *Palestinians, Refugees, and the Middle East Peace Process*. Washington, DC: United States Institute of Peace Press.

Peri, Yoram. (2002). *The Israeli Military and Israel's Palestinian Policy: From Oslo to the Al Aqsa Intifada*. Washington, DC: United States Institute of Peace.

Perlmutter, Amos. (1969). *Military and Politics in Israel*. London: Frank Cass.

Perlmutter, Amos. (1982). Begin's Rhetoric and Sharon's Tactics. *Foreign Affairs*, 61 (1), 66–83.

Perlmutter, Amos. (1987). *The Life and Times of Menachem Begin*. Garden City, NY: Doubleday.

Perry, Mark. (1994). *A Fire in Zion: The Israeli-Palestinian Search for Peace*. New York: William Morrow.

Peters, Joan. (1984). *From Time Immemorial: The Origins of the Arab-Jewish Conflict over Palestine*. New York: Harper and Row.

Piven, Jerry S. (2002). On the Psychosis (Religion) of Terrorists. In Chris E. Stout (Ed.), *The Psychology of Terrorism: Theoretical Understandings and Perspectives* (Vol. 3). 119–148. Westport, CT: Praeger.

Piven, Jerry S. (Ed.). (2004). *The Psychology of Death in Fantasy and History*. Westport CT: Praeger.

Plaut, Steven. (2004, March 26). Pacifism: A Recipe for Suicide. *Front Page Magazine*.

Podeh, Elie. (2002). *The Arab-Israeli Conflict in Israeli History Textbooks, 1948–2000*. Westport, CT: Bergin and Garvey.

Polito, Ennio. (1992). *Arafat*. Rome: Datanews. New edition (2002) *Arafat e gli altri*. Rome: Datanews.

Polk, William Roe. (1991). *The Arab World Today*. Cambridge, MA: Harvard University Press.

Pollock, George H. (1989). *The Mourning-Liberation Process* (2 vols.). Madison, CT: International Universities Press.

Polo, Marco. (1928). *Il Milione*. Prima edizione integrale, a cura di Luigi Foscolo Benedetto, sotto il patronato della città di Venezia. Florence: Leo Samuel Olschki.

Porath, Yehoshua. (1974). *The Emergence of the Palestinian-Arab National Movement, 1918–1929*. London: Frank Cass.

Porath Yehoshua. (1977). *The Palestinian-Arab National Movement, 1929–1939: From Riots to Rebellion*. London: Frank Cass.

Porath, Yehoshua. (1986). *In Search of Arab Unity, 1930–1945*. London: Frank Cass.

Post, Jerrold M. (1998). Terrorist Psycho-Logic: Terrorist Behavior as a Product of Psychological Forces. In Walter Reich (Ed.), *Origins of Terrorism: Psychologies, Ideologies, Theologies, States of Mind* (New ed.). Washington: Woodrow Wilson Center Press. Baltimore: Johns Hopkins University Press.

Quandt, William B. (1986). *Camp David: Peacemaking and Politics*. Washington, DC: Brookings Institution.

Quandt, William B. (1993). *The Peace Process: American Diplomacy and the Arab-Israeli Conflict since 1967*. Washington, DC: Brookings Institution.

Quandt, William B. (Ed.). (1988). *The Middle East: Ten Years after Camp David*. Washington, DC: Brookings Institution.

Rabin, Yitzhak. (1979). *The Rabin Memoirs*. Boston: Little, Brown. Expanded edition (1996) Boston: Little, Brown.

Rabinovich, Itamar. (1998). *The Brink of Peace: The Israeli-Syrian Negotiations*. Princeton: Princeton University Press.

Rabinovich, Itamar. (1999). *Waging Peace: Israel and the Arabs at the End of the Century*. New York: Farrar Straus and Giroux.

Rafael, Gideon. (1981). *Destination Peace.* New York: Stein and Day.

Raheb, Mitri. (1995). *I Am a Palestinian Christian.* Trans. Ruth C. L. Gritsch. Foreword Rosemary Radford Ruether. Minneapolis: Fortress Press.

Rahman, Fazlur. (1982). *Islam and Modernity: Transformation of an Intellectual Tradition.* Chicago and London: University of Chicago Press.

Rand, Colleen S. W. & Stunkard, Albert J. (1977). Psychoanalysis and Obesity. *Journal of the American Academy of Psychoanalysis, 5,* 459–498.

Randal, Jonathan C. (1983). *Going All the Way: Christian Warlords, Israeli Adventurers, and the War in Lebanon.* New York: Viking Press. New edition (1984) New York: Vintage Books.

Rao, Sudha V. (1972). *The Arab-Israeli Conflict: The Indian View.* New Delhi: Orient Longman.

Rashid, Salim. (Ed.). (1997). *The Clash of Civilizations? Asian Responses.* Karachi, New York and Oxford: Oxford University Press. Dhaka: Dhaka University Press.

Ratzabi, Shalom. (2002). *Between Zionism and Judaism: The Radical Circle in Brith Shalom, 1925–1933.* Leiden and Boston: Brill Academic Publishers.

Ratzer, Beryl. (1966). *A Historical Tour of the Holy Land: A Concise History of the Land of Israel with Photographs and Illustrations.* Jerusalem: Gefen Publishing House. New edition (2000) Jerusalem and New York: Gefen Publishing House.

Ravitzky, Aviezer. (1996). *Messianism, Zionism, and Jewish Religious Radicalism.* Chicago: University of Chicago Press.

Reader, Ian. (2002). Dramatic Confrontations: Aum Shinrikyo against the World. In David G. Bromley & J. Gordon Melton (Eds.), *Cults, Religion, and Violence.* Cambridge and New York: Cambridge University Press.

Reich, Bernard. (Ed.). (1995). *Arab-Israeli Conflict and Conciliation: A Documentary History.* Westport, CT: Greenwood Press.

Reich, Walter. (1984). *A Stranger in My House: Jews and Arabs in the West Bank.* New York: Holt, Rinehart and Winston.

Reich, Walter. (Ed.). (1990). *Origins of Terrorism: Psychologies, Ideologies, Theologies, States of Mind.* Washington: Woodrow Wilson Center for Scholars. Cambridge and New York: Cambridge University Press. New edition (1998) Washington: Woodrow Wilson Center Press. Baltimore: Johns Hopkins University Press.

Reich, Walter. (1991, March 25). *Burying Old Bones: Overcoming Tragedy and Risking Compromise in the Arab-Israeli Conflict.* Albert S. Kahn Memorial Lecture, Boston University.

Reik, Theodor. (1951). *Dogma and Compulsion: Psychoanalytic Studies of Religion and Myths.* Trans. Bernard Miall. New York: International Universities Press. Reprinted (1973) Westport, CT: Greenwood Press.

Reische, Diana L. (1991). *Arafat and the Palestine Liberation Organization.* New York: F. Watts.

Reiser, Lynn Whisnant. (1988). Panel: Compulsive Eating: Obesity and Related Phenomena. *Journal of the American Psychoanalytic Association*, 36, 163–172.

Rejwan, Nissim. (1998). *Arabs Face the Modern World: Religious, Cultural, and Political Responses to the West*. Gainesville: University Press of Florida.

Rejwan, Nissim. (1998a). *Israel's Place in the Middle East: A Pluralist Perspective*. Gainesville: University Press of Florida.

Rejwan, Nissim. (1999). *Israel in Search of Identity: Reading the Formative Years*. Gainseville: University Press of Florida.

Rejwan, Nissim. (2000). *Arab Aims and Israeli Attitudes: A Critique of Yehoshafat Harkabi's Prognosis of the Arab-Israeli Conflict*. Jerusalem: Leonard Davis Institute for International Relations, Hebrew University of Jerusalem.

Rejwan, Nissim. (Ed.). (2000). *The Many Faces of Islam: Perspectives on a Resurgent Civilization*. Gainseville: University Press of Florida.

Renshon, Stanley Allen. (2004). *In His Father's Shadow: The Transformations of George W. Bush*. New York: Palgrave Macmillan.

Richards, Alan & Waterbury, John. (1990). *A Political Economy of the Middle East: State, Class and Economic Development*. Boulder, CO: Westview Press.

Richards, Alan & Waterbury, John. (1990). *A Political Economy of the Middle East: State, Class and Economic Development*. Boulder, CO: Westview Press.

Ripley, Amanda. (2004, April 5). Chief Accuser: How Credible is Clarke? *TIME Europe*, 163 (4), 20–21.

Robben, Antonius C. G. M. & Suárez-Orozco, Marcelo M. (Eds.). (2000). *Cultures under Siege: Collective Violence and Trauma*. Cambridge and New York: Cambridge University Press.

Robbins, Thomas. (2002). Sources of Volatility in Religious Movements. In David G. Bromley & J. Gordon Melton (Eds.), *Cults, Religion, and Violence*. Cambridge and New York: Cambridge University Press.

Robbins, Thomas & Palmer, Susan J. (Eds.) (1997). *Millennium, Messiahs, and Mayhem: Contemporary Apocalyptic Movements*. London and New York: Routledge.

Robertson, Ritchie & Timms, Edward. (Eds.). (1997). *Theodor Herzl and the Origins of Zionism*. Edinburgh: Edinburgh University Press.

Robins, Robert S. (Ed.). (1977). *Psychopathology and Political Leadership*. New Orleans, LA: Tulane University.

Robins, Robert S. & Post, Jerrold M. (1997). *Political Paranoia: The Psychopolitics of Hatred*. New Haven, CT: Yale University Press. New edition (1998) New Haven, CT: Yale University Press.

Robinson, Francis. (Ed.). (1999). *The Cambridge Illustrated History of the Islamic World*. Cambridge and New York: Cambridge University Press.

Rochlin, Gregory. (1973). *Man's Aggression: The Defense of the Self*. Boston: Gambit.

Rodinson, Maxime. (1968). *Israel and the Arabs*. New York: Pantheon. Reprinted (1969) Harmondsworth: Penguin Books.

Rodinson, Maxime. (1973). *Israel: A Colonial Settler State?* New York: Monad Press.

Rogan, Eugene L. & Shlaim, Avi. (Eds.). (2001). *The War for Palestine: Rewriting the History of 1948.* Cambridge and New York: Cambridge University Press.

Rogers, H. John. (2002). The Myth of Return. *Clio's Psyche,* 9 (3), 133–134.

Rokach, Livia. (1986). *Israel's Sacred Terrorism: A Study Based on Moshe Sharett's Personal Diary and Other Documents.* Belmont, MA: Association of Arab-American University Graduates.

Rolef, Susan Hattis. (Ed.). (1993). *Political Dictionary of the State of Israel* (2nd ed.). New York: Macmillan.

Rosenberg, Jerry Martin. (1999). *Arafat's Palestinian State and JIPTA: The Best Hope for Lasting Peace in the Middle East.* Stamford, CT: JAI Press.

Ross, Stewart. (1996). *Causes and Consequences of the Arab-Israeli Conflict.* Austin, TX: Raintree Steck-Vaughn.

Rothstein, Arnold. (1980). *The Narcissistic Pursuit of Perfection.* New York: International Universities Press.

Rothstein, Robert L., et al. (Eds.). (2002). *The Israeli-Palestinian Peace Process: Oslo and the Lessons of Failure: Perspectives, Predicaments and Prospects.* Brighton: Academic Press.

Roy, Arundhati. (2001, September 29). The Algebra of Infinite Justice: As the US Prepares to Wage a New Kind of War, Arundhati Roy Challenges the Instinct for Vengeance. *The Guardian Saturday Review,* pp. 1–2.

Rubenberg, Cheryl A. (2003). *The Palestinians: In Search of a Just Peace.* Boulder, CO: Lynne Rienner.

Rubin, Barry M. (1997). *Revolution Until Victory? The Politics and History of the PLO.* Cambridge, MA: Harvard University Press.

Rubin, Barry M. (1999). *The Transformation of Palestinian Politics: From Revolution to State-Building.* Cambridge, MA: Harvard University Press.

Rubin, Barry M. (2002). *The Modern Middle East.* Cambridge and New York: Cambridge University Press.

Rubin, Barry M. (2002a). *The Tragedy of the Middle East.* Cambridge and New York: Cambridge University Press.

Rubin, Barry M. & Rubin, Judith Colp. (2002). *Anti-American Terrorism and the Middle East: Understanding the Violence.* Oxford and New York: Oxford University Press.

Rubin, Barry M. & Rubin, Judith Colp. (2003). *Yasir Arafat: A Political Biography.* New York: Oxford University Press.

Rubinstein, Alvin Zachary. (Ed.). (1984). *The Arab-Israeli Conflict: Perspectives.* New York: Praeger. Second edition (1991) New York: HarperCollins.

Rubinstein, Amnon. (1984). *The Zionist Dream Revisited.* New York: Schocken Books.

Rubinstein, Amnon. (2000). *From Herzl to Rabin: The Changing Image of Zionism.* New York: Holmes and Meier.

Rubinstein, Danny. (1991). *The People of Nowhere: The Palestinian Vision of Home*. New York: Times Books.

Rubinstein, Danny. (1995) *The Mystery of Arafat*. Trans. Dan Leon. Royalton, VT: Steerforth Press.

Ruskay, John S. & Szonyi, David M. (Eds.). (1990). *Deepening a Commitment: Zionism and the Conservative/Masorti Movement*. New York: Jewish Theological Seminary of America.

Ruthven, Malise. (1984). *Islam in the World*. New York: Oxford University Press.

Ruthven, Malise. (1997). *Islam: A Very Short Introduction*. New York: Oxford University Press. New edition (2000) New York: Oxford University Press.

Sabella, Bernard. (1994). Palestinian-Israeli Enmity: The Process of Transformation. The Peace Process, against the Background of the Historical Israeli-Palestinian Enmity, Is Not yet Reconciliation. This Must Await a Process of Transformation Which Will Take Time. *Palestine-Israel Journal of Politics, Economics and Culture*, 1 (4), 17–23.

Sachar, Howard M. (1944). *The Emergence of the Middle East, 1914–1924*. New York: Alfred A. Knopf.

Sachar, Howard M. (1998). *A History of Israel from the Rise of Zionism to Our Time*. New York: Alfred A. Knopf.

Safrai, Zeev. (1994). *The Economy of Roman Palestine*. London: Routledge.

Safran, Nadav. (1963). *The United States and Israel*. Cambridge, MA: Harvard University Press.

Safran, Nadav. (1968). *From War to War: The Arab-Israeli Confrontation, 1948–1967. A Study of the Conflict from the Perspective of Coercion in the Context of Inter-Arab and Big Power Relations*. New York: Pegasus.

Safran, Nadav. (1978). *Israel: The Embattled Ally*. Cambridge, MA: Harvard University Press.

Sahliyeh, Emile F. (1988). *In Search of Leadership: West Bank Politics since 1967*. Washington, DC: Brookings Institution.

Said, Edward W. (1978). *Orientalism*. New York: Pantheon Books. Reprinted (1979) New York: Vintage Books.

Said, Edward W. (1979). *The Question of Palestine*. New York: Times Books. New edition (1980) Vintage Books. New edition (1992) New York: Vintage Books.

Said, Edward W. (1986). *After the Last Sky: Palestinian Lives*. London: Faber and Faber. New York: Pantheon Books. New edition (1999) New York: Columbia University Press.

Said, Edward W. (1993). *Culture and Imperialism*. London: Verso.

Said, Edward W. (1994). *The Politics of Dispossession*. New York: Random House.

Said, Edward W. (1995). *Peace and Its Discontents: Essays on Palestine in the Middle East Peace Process*. New York: Vintage Books.

Said, Edward W. (1997). *Covering Islam: How the Media and the Experts Determine How We See the Rest of the World*. New York: Vintage Books.

Said, Edward W. (1999). *Out of Place: A Memoir*. New York: Alfred A. Knopf.

Said, Edward W. (2001, October 22). The Clash of Ignorance. *The Nation*, 273 (12), pp. 11–14.

Said, Edward W. & Hitchens, Christopher. (Eds.). (1988). *Blaming the Victims: Spurious Scholarship and the Palestinian Question*. London: Verso.

Saint-Prot, Charles. (1990). *Yasser Arafat: biographie et entretiens*. Paris: Jean Picollec.

Salibi, Kamal Suleiman. (1988). *A House of Many Mansions: The History of Lebanon Reconsidered*. Berkeley: University of California Press. London: I. B. Tauris.

Samuel, Herbert Louis. (1945). *Memoirs by the Rt. Hon. Viscount Samuel* . . . London: Cresset Press. New edition (1946) *Grooves of Change: A Book of Memoirs by the Rt. Hon. Viscount Samuel* . . . Indianapolis and New York: Bobbs-Merrill.

Sanua, Victor D. (1971). Is Peace in the Middle East Possible? A Study of Psychological Factors. *The International Psychologist*, 12 (2), 14–29.

Sanua, Victor D. (Ed.). (1983). *Fields of Offerings: Studies in Honor of Raphael Patai*. Rutherford, NJ: Fairleigh Dickinson University Press.

Sarfati, Georges-Elia. (1999). *Discours ordinaires et identités juives: la représentation des juifs et du judaïsme dans les dictionnaires et les encyclopédies de langue française: du Moyen âge au XXe siècle*. Paris: Berg international.

Sarfati, Georges-Elia. (2002). *L'Antisionisme: Israël-Palestine aux miroirs d'Occident*. Paris: Berg international.

Sarsar, Saliba. (2002). Jerusalem and Peacemaking in Palestinian Arab and Israeli Jewish Relations. *Clio's Psyche*, 9 (3), 136–138.

Saunders, Harold H. (1985). *The Other Walls: The Politics of the Arab-Israeli Peace Process*. Washington, DC: American Enterprise Institute for Public Policy Research.

Savir, Uri. (1998). *The Process: 1,100 Days That Changed the Middle East*. New York: Random House.

Sayegh, Fayez, Abdullah. (1956). *The Arab-Israeli Conflict*. New York: Arab Information Center. Condensed version (1967) *The Arab-Israeli Conflict, up to July 1964*. Cairo, Egypt: Permanent Secretariat of the Organization for Afro-Asian Peoples Solidarity.

Sayigh, Rosemary. (1979). *Palestinians: From Peasants to Revolutionaries*. London: Zed Books.

Sayigh, Rosemary. (1994). *Too Many Enemies: The Palestinian Experience in Lebanon*. London: Zed Books.

Sayigh, Yezid. (1997). *Armed Struggle and the Search for State: The Palestinian National Movement, 1949–1993*. Oxford: Clarendon Press. New York: Oxford University Press.

Sayigh, Yezid & Shlaim, Avi. (Eds.). (1997). *The Cold War and the Middle East*. Oxford: Clarendon Press. New York: Oxford University Press.

Schäfer, Peter. (1997). *Judeophobia: Attitudes toward the Jews in the Ancient World*. Cambridge, MA: Harvard University Press.

Schechter, Erik. (2003, April 20). Psychohistorians Put Bush on the Couch. *The Jerusalem Post*, p. 1.

Schechtman, Joseph Borisovich. (1956–1961). *The Vladimir Jabotinsky Story* (2 vols.). New York: Thomas Yoseloff. New edition (1986) *The Life and Times of Vladimir Jabotinsky*. Silver Spring, MD: Eshel Books.

Schemla, Elisabeth. (2001). *"Ton rêve est mon cauchemar": les six mois qui ont tué la paix*. Paris: Flammarion.

Schick, Alfred. (1947). Psychosomatic Aspects of Obesity. *The Psychoanalytic Review*, 34, 173–183.

Schiff, Ze'ev. (1985). The Spectre of Civil War in Israel. *The Middle East Journal*, 39 (2), 231–245.

Schiff, Ze'ev. (1997). *Israel-Syria Negotiations: Lessons Learned, 1993–1996*. Washington, DC: Washington Institute For Near East Policy.

Schiff, Ze'ev & Ya'ari, Ehud. (1984). *Israel's Lebanon War*. New York: Simon and Schuster.

Schiff, Ze'ev & Ya'ari, Ehud. (1990). *Intifada, the Palestinian Uprising: Israel's Third Front*. Trans. & Ed. Ina Friedman. New York: Simon and Schuster. Touchstone edition (1991) New York: Simon and Schuster.

Schiffer, Irvine. (1973). *Charisma: A Psychoanalytic Look at Mass Society*. Toronto: University of Toronto Press.

Schoepflin, Julia. (1994). *The Arab Boycott of Israel: Can it Withstand the Peace Process?* London: Institute of Jewish Affairs.

Schulze, Kirsten E. (1999). *The Arab-Israeli Conflict*. New York: Longman.

Schürer, Emil. (1973–1987). *The History of the Jewish People in the Age of Jesus Christ: 175 B.C. – A.D. 13* (3 vols.). Edinburgh: T. & T. Clark.

Seale, Patrick. (1988). *Asad of Syria: The Struggle for the Middle East*. With the assistance of Maureen McConville. London: I. B. Tauris. Reprinted (1989) Berkeley: University of California Press.

Segel, Benjamin W. (1934). *The Protocols of the Elders of Zion: The Greatest Lie in History*. Trans. Sascha Czazckes-Charles. New York: Bloch Publishing Co.

Segev, Tom. (1986). *1949: The First Israelis*. New York: Free Press.

Segev, Tom. (1993). *The Seventh Million: The Israelis and the Holocaust*. Trans. Haim Watzman. New York: Hill and Wang.

Segev, Tom. (2000). *One Palestine, Complete: Jews and Arabs under the Mandate*. New York: Metropolitan Books.

Segev, Tom. (2002). *Elvis in Jerusalem: Post-Zionism and the Americanization of Israel*. New York: Henry Holt.

Seidman, Hillel & Schreiber, Mordecai. (1990). *Menachem Begin: His Life and Legacy*. New York: Shengold.

Sela, Avraham. (Ed.). (1999). *Political Encyclopedia of the Middle East*. New York: Continuum. Jerusalem: Jerusalem Publishing House.

Selfktar, Ofira. (1986). *New Zionism and the Foreign Policy System of Israel*. London: Croom Helm.

Senghor, Léopold Sédar. (1967). *Négritude, arabisme et francité: réflexions sur le problème de la culture.* Pref. Jean Rous. Beirut: Éditions Dar al-Kitab Allubnani.

Shafir, Gershon & Peled, Yoav. (2002). *Being Israeli: The Dynamics of Multiple Citizenship.* Cambridge and New York: Cambridge University Press.

Shahak, Israel. (1982). *Israel's Global Role: Weapons for Repression.* Belmont, MA: Association of Arab-American University Graduates.

Shahak, Israel. (1982a). *The Zionist Plan for the Middle East.* Belmont, MA: Association of Arab-American University Graduates.

Shahak, Israel & Mezvinsky, Norton. (1999). *Jewish Fundamentalism in Israel.* London: Pluto Press.

Shalit, Erel [Harald Fürst]. (1994). The Relationship Between Aggression and Fear of Annihilation in Israel. *Political Psychology, 15* (3), 415–434.

Shalit, Erel [Harald Fürst]. (1999). *The Hero and His Shadow: Psychopolitical Aspects of Myth and Reality in Israel.* Lanham, MD: University Press of America. Revised edition (2004) Lanham, MD: University Press of America.

Shami, Yitzhaq. (2000). *Hebron Stories.* Lancaster, CA: Labyrinthos.

Shammas, Anton. (1988). *Arabesques.* New York: Harper and Row. Reprinted (2001) Berkeley: University of California Press.

Shapira, Avraham. (Ed.). (1970). *The Seventh Day: Soldiers' Talk about the Six-Day War, Recorded and Edited by a Group of Young Kibbutz Members.* Trans. & Ed. Henry Near. London: Andre Deutsch. New edition (1971) Harmondsworth and Baltimore: Penguin Books. New York: Charles Scribner's Sons.

Sharif, Regina. (1983). *Non-Jewish Zionism: Its Roots in Western History.* London: Zed Books.

Sharma, Jagadish Prasad. (1990). *The Arab Mind: A Study of Egypt, Arab Unity, and the World.* New Delhi: H. K. Publishers.

Sharon, Ariel, with Chanoff, David. (1989). *Warrior: An Autobiography.* New York: Simon and Schuster. Edinburgh: Macdonald Publishers.

Sharon, Ariel, with Chanoff, David. (2001). *Warrior: The Autobiography of Ariel Sharon* (2nd Touchstone ed.). New Foreword by Uri Dan. New York: Simon and Schuster.

Shavit, Yaacov. (1987). *The New Hebrew Nation: A Study of Israeli Heresy and Fantasy.* London: Frank Cass.

Shavit, Yaacov. (1988). *Jabotinsky and the Revisionist Movement, 1925–1948.* London: Frank Cass.

Shavitt, Matti. (1972). *On the Wings of Eagles: The Story of Arik Sharon, Commander of the Israeli Paratroopers.* Tel-Aviv: Pondview Books.

Shehadeh, Raja. (1984). *Samed: A Journal of a West Bank Palestinian.* New York: Adama Books.

Shehadeh, Raja. (1993). *The Law of the Land: Settlements and Land Issues under Israeli Military Occupation.* Jerusalem: Passia Publications.

Shehadeh, Raja. (2002). *Strangers in the House: Coming of Age in Occupied Palestine.* South Royalton, VT: Steerforth Press.

Sherman, John. (Ed.). (1978). *The Arab-Israeli Conflict, 1945–1971: A Bibliography.* New York: Garland Publishing.

Shiblak, Abbas F. (1986). *The Lure of Zion: The Case of the Iraqi Jews.* London: Saqi Books.

Shimoni, Gideon. (1995). *The Zionist Ideology.* Hanover, NH: University Press of New England for Brandeis University Press.

Shindler, Colin. (1995). *Israel, Likud and the Zionist Dream: Power, Politics, and Ideology from Begin to Netanyahu.* London: I. B. Tauris. New York: St. Martin's Press.

Shipler, David K. (1986). *Arab and Jew: Wounded Spirits in a Promised Land.* New York: Random House. Reprinted (1987) Harmondsworth and New York: Penguin Books.

Shlaim, Avi. (1988). *Collusion across the Jordan: King Abdullah, the Zionist Movement, and the Partition of Palestine.* Oxford and New York: Oxford University Press.

Shlaim, Avi. (1994). *War and Peace in the Middle East: A Critique of American Policy.* New York: Whittle Books and Viking Press. New edition (1995) *War and Peace in the Middle East: A Concise History.* New York : Penguin Books.

Shlaim, Avi. (1999). *The Iron Wall: Israel and the Arab World.* New York: Norton. Reprinted (2000) London: Allen Lane.

Shohat, Ella. (1989). *Israeli Cinema: East/West and the Politics of Representation.* Austin: University of Texas Press.

Sibony, Daniel. (1983). *La Juive: une transmission d'inconscient.* Paris: B. Grasset.

Sibony, Daniel. (1988). *Ecrits sur le racisme.* Paris: C. Bourgois.

Sibony, Daniel. (1992). *Le peuple "psy."* Paris: Balland.

Sibony, Daniel. (1997). *Le "racisme," ou, La haine identitaire.* Paris: C. Bourgois.

Sibony, Daniel. (2002). *Nom de Dieu: par-delà les trois monothéismes.* Paris: Editions du Seuil.

Sibony, Daniel. (2003). *Proche-orient: psychanalyse d'un conflit.* Paris: Editions du Seuil.

Sicker, Martin. (1989). *Between Hashemites and Zionists: The Struggle for Palestine, 1908–1988.* New York: Holmes and Meier.

Silberstein, Laurence Jay. (1999). *The Postzionism Debates: Knowledge and Power in Israeli Culture.* London and New York: Routledge.

Silver, Eric. (1984). *Begin: The Haunted Prophet.* New York: Random House.

Simpson, John Hope. (1930). *Palestine: Report on Immigration, Land Settlement and Development, Presented by the Secretary of State for the Colonies to Parliament by Command of His Majesty* (2 vols.). London: His Majesty's Stationery Office.

Sisco, Joseph, et al. (1977). *Prospects for Peace in the Middle East.* Washington, DC: American Enterprise Institute for Policy Research.

Slochower, Joyce Anne. (1987). The Psychodynamics of Obesity: A Review. *Psychoanalytic Psychology, 4,* 145–160.

Smallwood, E. Mary. (1981). *The Jews under Roman Rule from Pompey to Diocletian: A Study in Political Relations.* Leiden: E. J. Brill.

Smith, Anthony David. (1979). *Nationalism in the Twentieth Century.* New York: New York University Press.

Smith, Charles D. (1988). *Palestine and the Arab-Israeli Conflict: A History with Documents.* New York: St. Martin's Press. Basingstoke: Macmillan. Second edition (1992) New York: St. Martin's Press. Basingstoke: Macmillan. Third edition (1996) New York: St. Martin's Press. Basingstoke: Macmillan. Fourth Edition (2001) New York: St. Martin's Press. Basingstoke: Macmillan.

Smith, Gary V. (1974). *Zionism: The Dream and the Reality. A Jewish Critique.* Newton Abbott, Devon, UK: David and Charles.

Smith, Joseph H. & Handelman, Susan A. (Eds.). (1990). *Psychoanalysis and Religion.* Baltimore: Johns Hopkins University Press.

Smith, Wilbur M. (1967). *The Israeli/Arab Conflict and the Bible.* Glendale, CA: Regal Books.

Sobel, Zvi & Beit-Hallahmi, Benjamin. (Eds.). (1991). *Tradition, Innovation, Conflict: Jewishness and Judaism in Contemporary Israel.* Albany: State University of New York Press.

Sofer, Arnon. (1999). *Rivers of Fire: The Conflict over Water in the Middle East.* Trans. Murray Rosovsky and Nina Copaken. Lanham, MD: Rowman & Littlefield.

Sofer, Sasson. (1988). *Begin: An Anatomy of Leadership.* Oxford: Basil Blackwell.

Sokolow, Nahum. (1919). *History of Zionism, 1600–1918.* London and New York: Longmans, Green.

Solarz, Stephen J. (1977). *The Prospects for Peace in the Middle East.* Washington, DC: U.S. Government Printing Office.

Sprinzak, Ehud. (1991). *The Ascendance of Israel's Radical Right.* Oxford and New York: Oxford University Press.

St. John, Robert. (1959). *Ben-Gurion: The Biography of an Extraordinary Man.* Garden City, NY: Doubleday. Reprinted (1971) as *Ben-Gurion: A Biography.* New edition (1986) *Ben-Gurion: Builder of Israel.* Washington, DC: B'nai B'rith Books. Reprinted (1998) Washington, DC: London Publication Company.

Stav, Arieh. (Ed.). (2001). *Israel and a Palestinian State: Zero Sum Game?* Tel Aviv: Zmora-Bitan. Shaarei Tikva, Israel: Ariel Center for Policy Research (ACPR).

Stebbing, John. (1993). *A Structure of Peace: The Arab-Israeli Conflict.* Oxford: New Cherwell Press.

Stein, Howard F. (1987). *Developmental Time, Cultural Space: Studies in Psychogeography.* Norman: University of Oklahoma Press.

Stein, Howard F. (1994). *The Dream of Culture: Essays on Culture's Elusiveness.* New York: Psyche Press.

Stein, Howard F. & Apprey, Maurice. (1987). *From Metaphor to Meaning: Papers in Psychoanalytic Anthropology.* Charlottesville: University Press of Virginia.

Stein, Howard F. & Niederland, William G. (Eds.). (1989). *Maps from the Mind: Readings in Psychogeography.* Norman: University of Oklahoma Press.

Stein, Janice Gross. (1999). *The Widening Gyre of Negotiation: From Management to Resolution in the Arab-Israeli Conflict.* Jerusalem: Leonard Davis Institute for International Relations, Hebrew University of Jerusalem.

Stein, Kenneth W. (1984). *The Land Question in Palestine, 1917–1936.* Chapel Hill: University of North Carolina Press.

Stein, Kenneth W. (1999). *Heroic Diplomacy: Sadat, Kissinger, Carter, Begin and the Quest for Arab-Israeli Peace.* New York: Routledge.

Stein, Leonard. (1961). *The Balfour Declaration.* London: Valentine Mitchell.

Steinberg, Blema S. (1996). *Shame and Humiliation: Presidential Decision Making on Vietnam.* Pittsburgh: University of Pittsburgh Press.

Stern, Jessica. (2003). *Terror in the Name of God: Why Religious Militants Kill.* New York: Ecco.

Sternhell, Ze'ev. (1997). *The Founding Myths of Israel.* Princeton: Princeton University Press.

Stevens, Richard Paul. (1960). *The Political and Diplomatical Role of American Zionists as a Factor in the Creation of the State of Israel, 1942–1947.* Washington, DC: Institute of Palestine Studies. New edition (1962) *American Zionism and U. S. Foreign Policy, 1942–47.* New York: Pageant Press.

Stewart, Alva. (1989). *The Israeli-Palestinian Conflict: A Brief Checklist of Sources.* Monticello, IL: Vance Bibliographies.

Stock, Ernest. (1967). *Israel on the Road to Sinai, 1949–1956.* Ithaca, NY: Cornell University Press.

Stock, Ernest. (1968). *From Conflict to Understanding: Relations between Jews and Arabs in Israel since 1948.* New York: Institute of Human Relations.

Stone, Hal & Stone, Sidra L. Winkelman. (2003). *An Open Letter to President George W. Bush,* Retrieved February 18 2003, from http://www.delos-inc.com/cgi-bin/webbbs/news_config.pl?read=26

Storrs, Ronald. (1937). *Orientations: Memoirs of Sir Ronald Storrs.* London: Ivor Nicholson and Watson.

Stout, Chris E. (Ed.). (2002). *The Psychology of Terrorism* (4 vols.). Westport, CT: Praeger.

Strachey, Alix. (1957). *The Unconscious Motives of War: A Psycho-Analytical Contribution.* London: George Allen & Unwin. New York: International Universities Press.

Strozier, Charles B. (1994). *Apocalypse: On the Psychology of Fundamentalism in America.* Boston: Beacon Press.

Stunkard, Albert J. (1967). Obesity. In Alfred M. Freedman & Harold I. Kaplan (Eds.), *Comprehensive Textbook of Psychiatry.* Baltimore: Williams & Wilkins.

Suleiman, Ramzi & Beit-Hallahmi, Benjamin. (1997). National and Civic Identities of Palestinians in Israel. *Journal of Social Psychology,* 137 (2), 219–228.

Swamy, M. R. Narayan. (1994). *Tigers of Lanka: From Boys to Guerillas*. Delhi: Konark Publishers.

Swirski, Shlomo. (1989). *Israel: The Oriental Majority*. London: Zed Books.

Sykes, Christopher. (1965). *Crossroads to Israel*. Cleveland, OH: World Publishing Co. Reprinted (1973) Bloomington: Indiana University Press.

Symington, Neville. (1994). *Psychoanalysis and Religion*. London and New York: Cassell.

Tabor, James D. & Gallagher, Eugene V. (1995). *Why Waco? Cults and the Battle for Religious Freedom in America*. Berkeley: University of California Press.

Tames, Richard. (1980). *The Arab World Today*. London: Kaye and Ward.

Tawil, Raymonda Hawa. (1979). *My Home, My Prison*. New York: Holt, Rinehart and Winston.

Taylor, Alan R. (1959). *Prelude to Israel: An Analysis of Zionist Diplomacy, 1897–1947*. New York: Philosophical Library.

Taylor, Alan R. (1988). *The Islamic Question in Middle East Politics*. Boulder, CO: Westview Press.

Taylor, Alan R. & Tetlie, Richard N. (Eds.). (1970). *Palestine: A Search for Truth. Approaches to the Arab-Israeli Conflict*. Washington, DC: Public Affairs Press.

Taylor, Joan E. (1993). *Christians and the Holy Places: The Myth of Jewish-Christian Origins*. Oxford and New York: Oxford University Press.

Tel, Jonathan. (2002). *Arafat's Elephant*. Washington, DC: Counterpoint.

Telhami, Shibley. (1990). *Power and Leadership in International Bargaining: The Path to the Camp David Accords*. New York: Columbia University Press.

Temko, Ned. (1987) *To Win or To Die: A Personal Portrait of Menachem Begin*. New York: William Morrow.

Tessler, Mark A. (1994) *A History of the Israeli-Palestinian Conflict*. Bloomington: Indiana University Press.

Teveth, Shabtai. (1973). *Moshe Dayan: The Soldier, the Man, the Legend*. Boston: Houghton Mifflin.

Teveth, Shabtai. (1985). *Ben Gurion and the Palestinian Arabs: From Peace to War*. Oxford and New York: Oxford University Press.

Teveth, Shabtai. (1987). *Ben Gurion: The Burning Ground, 1886–1948*. Boston: Houghton Mifflin.

Teveth, Shabtai. (1996). *Ben-Gurion and the Holocaust*. New York: Harcourt Brace.

Teveth, Shabtai. (1996). *Ben-Gurion's Spy: The Story of the Political Scandal That Shaped Modern Israel*. New York: Columbia University Press.

Thomas, Gordon. (1999). *Gideon's Spies: The Secret History of the Mossad*. New York: St. Martin's Press.

Tibi, Bassam. (1988). *The Crisis of Modern Islam: A Preindustrial Culture in the Scientific-Technological Age*. Trans. Judith von Sivers. Foreword Peter von Sivers. Salt Lake City: University of Utah Press.

Timerman, Jacobo. (1982) *The Longest War: Israel in Lebanon*. New York: Alfred A. Knopf.

Tinbergen, Nikolaas. (1972). *The Animal in its World: Explorations of an Ethologist, 1932–1972* (2 vols.). London: Allen & Unwin. Cambridge, MA: Harvard University Press.

Tinbergen, Nikolaas, et al. (1965). *Animal Behavior.* New York: Time Books. New edition (1968) New York: Time-Life Books. Second edition (1978) Alexandria, VA: Time-Life Books.

Tisdall, W. St. Claur. (1905). *The Original Sources of the Qur'an.* London: Society for Promoting Christian Knowledge. New York: E. S. Gorham.

Toufée, Farah. (1998). *The Arab-Israeli Conflict.* Woodbridge, NJ: Ken and Scatter.

Toynbee, Arnold Joseph. (1962). *A Study of History: The Growth of Civilizations* (10 vols.). London and New York: Oxford University Press.

Toynbee, Arnold Joseph. (1970). Reflections on the Crisis. In Herbert Molloy Mason (Ed.), *Reflections on the Middle East Crisis*, 193–204. The Hague: Mouton.

Tschirgi, Dan. (1994). *The Arab World Today.* Boulder, CO: Lynne Rienner.

Tubb, Jonathan N. (1998). *Canaanites.* Norman: University of Oklahoma Press.

Tuchman, Barbara Wertheim. (1956). *Bible and Sword: England and Palestine from the Bronze Age to Balfour.* New York: New York University Press.

Turki, Fawaz. (1972). *The Disinherited: Journal of a Palestinian Exile.* New York: Monthly Review Press.

Turki, Fawaz. (1975). *Poems from Exile.* Washington: Free Palestine Press.

Turki, Fawaz. (1988). *Soul in Exile: Lives of a Palestinian Revolutionary.* New York: Monthly Review Press.

Turki, Fawaz. (1994). *Exile's Return: The Making of a Palestinian-American.* New York: Free Press.

Ulman, Richard Barrett & Abse, David Wilfred. (1983). The Group Psychology of Mass Madness: Jonestown. *Political Psychology,* 4 (4), 637–661.

United Nations. (1992). *Prospects for Peace in the Middle East: An Israeli-Palestinian Dialogue.* New York: United Nations.

United Nations. (1993). *Building for Peace in the Middle East: A European Perspective.* New York: United Nations.

Urofsky, Melvin I. (1995). *American Zionism from Herzl to the Holocaust.* Lincoln: University of Nebraska Press.

Van Assche, Tobias. (2002). Yasser Arafat's Personality and Leadership Style. *Clio's Psyche,* 9 (3), 131–133.

Van Creveld, Martin. (1998). *The Sword and the Olive: A Critical History of the Israeli Defense Force.* New York: Public Affairs.

Vanaert, Philippe. (1992). *Yasser Arafat: président sans frontières.* Brussels: Editions du Souverain.

Varvin, Sverre & Volkan, Vamık D. (Eds.). (2004). *Violence or Dialogue: Psychoanalytic Insights on Terrorism.* London: International Psychoanalytic Association.

Vico, Giambattista. (1725). *La Nuova Scienza.* Naples. Reprinted (1730) in *Cinque libri di Giambattista Vico de' Principj d'una scienza nuova d'intorno alla comune natura delle nazioni... in questa seconda impressione con più propia maniera condotti, e di molto accresciuti. Principi di una scienza nuova.* Naples: A spese di Felice Mosca.

Victor, Barbara. (2003). *Army of Roses: Inside the World of Palestinian Women Suicide Bombers.* Emmaus, PA: Rodale.

Viorst, Milton. (1994). *Sandcastles: The Arabs in Search of the Modern World.* New York: Alfred A. Knopf. Reprinted (1995) Syracuse, NY: Syracuse University Press.

Viorst, Milton. (2001). *In the Shadow of the Prophet: The Struggle for the Soul of Islam.* New York and Boulder, CO: Westview Press.

Vital, David. (1982). *Zionism: The Formative Years.* Oxford: Clarendon Press. New York: Oxford University Press.

Volkan, Vamık D. (1979). *Cyprus—War and Adaptation: A Psychoanalytic History of Two Ethnic Groups in Conflict.* Charlottesville: University Press of Virginia.

Volkan, Vamık D. (1981). *Linking Objects and Linking Phenomena: A Study of the Forms, Symptoms, Metapsychology and Therapy of Complicated Mourning.* New York: International Universities Press.

Volkan, Vamık D. (1988). *The Need to Have Enemies and Allies: From Clinical Practice to International Relationships.* Northvale, NJ: Jason Aronson.

Volkan, Vamık D. (1997). *Bloodlines: From Ethnic Pride to Ethnic Terrorism.* New York: Farrar, Straus and Giroux.

Volkan, Vamık D. (1999). Psychoanalysis and Diplomacy Part I: Individual and Large Group Identity. *Journal of Applied Psychoanalytic Studies,* 1 (1), 29–55.

Volkan, Vamık D. (1999a). Psychoanalysis and Diplomacy Part II: Large-Group Rituals. *Journal of Applied Psychoanalytic Studies,* 1 (3), 223–247.

Volkan, Vamık D. (2001). Observations on Religious Fundamentalism and the Taliban. *Mind and Human Interaction,* 12 (3), 156–160.

Volkan, Vamık D. (2001a). September 11 and Societal Regression. *Mind and Human Interaction,* 12 (3), 196–216.

Volkan, Vamık D. (2003). Large-Group Identity: Border Psychology and Related Processes. *Mind and Human Interaction,* 13 (2), 49–76.

Volkan, Vamık D. (2004). *Blind Trust: Large Groups and Their Leaders in Times of Crisis and Terror.* Charlottesville, VA: Pitchstone Publishing.

Volkan, Vamık D. & Itzkowitz, Norman. (1984). *The Immortal Atatürk: A Psychobiography.* Chicago: University of Chicago Press.

Volkan, Vamık D., et al. (Eds.). (1990). *The Psychodynamics of International Relationships* (2 vols.). Lexington, MA: Lexington Books.

Vryonis, Speros. (Ed.). (1975). *Islam and Cultural Change in the Middle Ages.* Wiesbaden: Harrassowitz.

Wallach, Janet & Wallach, John Paul. (1990). *Arafat: In the Eyes of the Beholder.* Secaucus, NJ: Carol Publishing. Reprinted (1991) London: Heinemann. Reprinted (1992) London: Mandarin. Revised and updated edition (1997) Secaucus, NJ: Carol Publishing.

Wallach, John Paul & Wallach, Janet. (1989). *Still Small Voices.* Intro. Teddy Kollek. New York: Harcourt Brace Jovanovich. New edition (1990) Secaucus, NJ: Carol Publishing.

Walzer, Michael. (2001, October 22). Excusing Terror: The Politics of Ideological Apology. *The American Prospect*, 12 (18), 16–17.

Ward, Richard J., et al. (1977). *The Palestine State: A Rational Approach.* Port Washington, NY: Kennikat Press.

Warschawski, Michel. (2001). *Israël-Palestine: le défi binational.* Afterword Elias Sanbar. Paris: Editions Textuel.

Warschawski, Michel. (2003). *A tombeau ouvert: la crise de la société israélienne.* Paris: La Fabrique.

Wasserstein, Bernard. (1978). *The British in Palestine: The Mandatory Government and The Arab-Jewish Conflict, 1917–1929.* London: Royal Historical Society. Second edition (1991) Oxford: Basil Blackwell.

Wasserstein, Bernard. (1979). *Britain and the Jews of Europe, 1939–1945.* London: Institute of Jewish Affairs.

Wasserstein, Bernard. (2001). *Divided Jerusalem: The Struggle for the Holy City.* New Haven, CT: Yale University Press.

Waterbury, John. (1983). *The Egypt of Nasser and Sadat: The Political Economy of Two Regimes.* Princeton: Princeton University Press.

Watt, William Montgomery. (1953). *Muhammad at Mecca.* Oxford: Clarendon Press.

Watt, William Montgomery. (1956). *Muhammad at Medina.* Oxford: Clarendon Press. New edition (1981) Karachi and New York: Oxford University Press.

Watt, William Montgomery. (1961). *Muhammad: Prophet and Statesman.* London: Oxford University Press.

Watzal, Ludwig. (1999). *Peace Enemies: The Past and Present Conflict between Israel and Palestine.* Jerusalem: PASSIA [Palestinian Academic Society for the Study of International Affairs].

Webb, Liliane. (1980). *The Marranos.* Kansas City, MO: Andrews and McMeel.

Weiner, Justus Reid. (1999, September). "My Beautiful Old House" and Other Fabrications by Edward Said. *Commentary*, 108 (2), 23–31.

Weisfeld, Abraham Harvey [Eibie Weizfeld]. (1984). *Sabra and Shatila: A New Auschwitz.* Ottawa: Jerusalem International Publishing House.

Weisfeld, Abraham Harvey [Eibie Weizfeld]. (Ed.). (1989). *The End of Zionism and the Liberation of the Jewish People.* Atlanta: Clarity Press.

Weizmann, Chaim. (1949). *Trial and Error: The Autobiography of Chaim Weizmann.* London: Hamish Hamilton. Reprinted (1966) New York: Schocken Books.

Wensinck, Arent Jan. (1975). *Muhammad and the Jews of Medina, with an Excursus Muhammad's Constitution of Medina by Julius Wellhausen.* Trans. & Ed. Wolfgang Behn. Freiburg im Breisgau: K. Schwarz.

Whitaker, Brian. (2004, May 24). "Its Best Use Is as a Doorstop." Brian Whitaker Explains Why a Book Packed with Sweeping Generalisations about Arabs Carries So Much Weight with Both Neocons and Military in the US. *The Guardian.* www.guardian.co.uk/elsewhere/journalist/story/0,7792,122352 5,00.html.

Wigoder, Geoffrey. (Ed.). (1994). *New Encyclopedia of Zionism and Israel.* New York: Herzl Press.

Winnik, Heinrich Z., et al. (Eds.). (1973). *The Psychological Bases of War.* New York: Quadrangle Books. Jerusalem: Academic Press.

Wolf, Aaron T. (1995). *Hydropolitics along the Jordan River: Scarce Water and Its Impact on the Arab-Israeli Conflict.* New York, Paris and Tokyo: United Nations University Press.

Wolfenstein, Martha. (1966). Goya's Dining Room. *The Psychoanalytic Quarterly,* 35 (1), 47–83.

Wordsworth, William. (1802). *Lyrical Ballads, with Other Poems.* Philadelphia: James Humphreys.

Wright, Marvin. (Ed.). (1989). *Israel and the Palestinians.* Harlow, Essex, UK: Longman. Chicago: St. James Press.

Wright, Stuart A. (Ed.). (1995). *Armageddon in Waco: Critical Perspectives on the Branch Davidian Conflict.* Chicago: University of Chicago Press.

Yehoshua, A. B. (1992). *Mr. Mani.* New York: Doubleday.

Yermiya, Dov. (1983). *My War Diary: Lebanon, June 5–July 1, 1982.* Boston: South End Press.

Yerushalmi, Yosef Hayim. (1982). *Zakhor: Jewish History and Jewish Memory.* Seattle: University of Washington Press. Reprinted (1996) Seattle: University of Washington Press.

Zadka, Saul. (1995). *Blood in Zion: How the Jewish Guerrillas Drove the British out of Palestine.* London: Brassey's.

Zaitoun, Safa. (1983). *Sabra & Shatila: The Massacre.* Trans. Maysoon Shaath and Mona Taji. Cairo, Egypt: Dar al-Fata al-Arabi.

Zangwill, Israel. (1901). The Return to Palestine. *The New Liberal Review,* vol. 2, December.

Zertal, Idith. (1998). *From Catastrophe to Power: Holocaust Survivors and the Emergence of Israel.* Berkeley: University of California Press.

Zilboorg, Gregory. (1962). *Psychoanalysis and Religion.* Ed. & Intro. Margaret Stone Zilboorg. New York: Farrar, Straus and Cudahy. Reprinted (1967) London: George Allen & Unwin.

Zipperstein, Steven J. (1993). *Elusive Prophet: Ahad Ha'Am and the Origins of Zionism.* Berkeley: University of California Press.

Zipperstein, Steven J. & Frerichs, Ernest S. (Eds.). (2000). *Zionism, Liberalism and the Future of the Jewish State: Centennial Reflections on Zionist Scholarship and Controversy.* Providence, RI: The Dorot Foundation.

Zonis, Marvin. (1991). *Majestic Failure: The Fall of the Shah.* Chicago: University of Chicago Press.

Zonis, Marvin & Offer, Daniel. (1985). Leaders and the Arab-Israeli Conflict: A Psychodynamic Interpretation. In Charles B. Strozier & Daniel Offer (Eds.), *The Leader: Psychohistorical Essays.* New York: Plenum.

Zurayk, Elia T. (1979). *The Palestinians in Israel: A Study in Internal Colonialism.* London: Routledge and Kegan Paul.

Zwingmann, Charles & Pfister-Ammende, Maria. (Eds.). (1973). *Uprooting and after. . .* New York, Heidelberg and Berlin: Springer-Verlag.

Index